Praise for *Fintech Explained*

"*Fintech Explained* brilliantly deciphers the complex fintech landscape, making it accessible to everyone. King's astute observations and innovative thinking make this book a beacon for anyone looking to understand and leverage the disruptive power of fintech. It's an unparalleled guide in an era of rapid change, and essential reading for anyone interested in the future of finance."

Craig Asano, Founder and CEO, National Crowdfunding & Fintech Association of Canada

"An ambitious and timely project that combines insights from rigorous research and deep understanding of the practice. A really informative book for everyone interested in fintech."

Will Cong, Rudd Family Professor of Management and Professor of Finance, Cornell SC Johnson College of Business, Cornell University

"Fintech companies are transforming the financial industry by offering a diverse range of financial services and products, including payment solutions, financial advice, loans, and digital currencies, using cutting-edge technologies such as blockchain and artificial intelligence. *Fintech Explained* serves as an invaluable resource to understand this evolution, presenting a clear, pedagogical, and systematic account of this process, drawing upon the latest academic research. I highly recommend this textbook to instructors seeking to develop a course on Fintech 3.0, students eager to enhance their knowledge of the fintech industry, and professionals aiming to stay abreast of the fintech revolution."

Thierry Foucault, HEC Foundation Chaired Professor, HEC Paris

"Few people know fintech as well as Michael King. *Fintech Explained* provides a comprehensive overview, complete with many colorful examples, of the fintech trends that are driving disruptive change today."

Andrew Graham, Co-Founder and CEO, Borrowell

"The most impressive feature of Michael King's *Fintech Explained* is its breadth of scope. While so many others focus – often exclusively – on digital assets, blockchain technology, dominant players in the cryptocurrency realm, and DeFi, this book goes well beyond. Fintech, we learn, is just as much about robo-advising, online lending and crowdfunding platforms, insurtech, and bigtech financial services. Michael's analytical strengths shine through as he deconstructs the business models and economic foundations underlying the value propositions in fintech world. And all of it is done in an accessible, everyday language that ensures it is worthy for all eager to build up their fintech bona fides."

Andrew Karolyi, Charles Field Knight Dean and Professor of Finance, Cornell SC Johnson College of Business, Cornell University

"*Fintech Explained* provides an incisive peek into the technological forces and dynamic innovators currently reshaping every corner of the financial system. From brokerage to bitcoin, the text provides a comprehensive and easy-to-understand view of the problems fintech innovators (whether incumbent or entrepreneur) are seeking to fix and the hurdles they must overcome to achieve those goals."

R. Jesse McWaters, Senior Vice President, Global Head of Regulatory Advocacy, Mastercard

"Michael King is a leading academic expert in the exciting field of technology in the world of finance. In his book *Fintech Explained*, the reader will learn about the current and future trends that these forces will bring to industry, profound change which will largely benefit customers. However, change is always difficult and some may get left behind unless we take steps to avoid this. King provides insights on how the entire society can benefit."

Richard Nesbitt, Adjunct Professor and Executive-in-Residence, Rotman School of Management, University of Toronto

"This is exactly the book I've been seeking for my students! *Fintech Explained* fills an important gap in financial education by unravelling the complexities of fintech. Drawing on extensive interactions with key stakeholders, including founders, VCs, angel investors, and influencers, the book offers a rigorous and meticulously crafted analysis supported by Michael King's deep experience in the financial services industry and solid academic research. I appreciate how the author captures the multidisciplinary nature of fintech, providing a holistic view of the field. The text not only offers a clear and expert explanation of various fintech verticals, complemented by a multitude of case studies, but also delves into fundamental aspects such as monetization strategies, funding, and valuation of fintech companies. This book has the potential to establish itself as the go-to textbook and become an indispensable resource for students, professors, and practitioners alike."

Maria Pacurar, Associate Professor of Finance, Dalhousie University

"Michael R. King's book offers a comprehensive and insightful exploration of how financial technology companies are revolutionizing the customer experience in the financial services industry. Through real-world case studies, clear descriptions, and the latest academic research, King highlights the transformative power of fintech, showcasing how it provides cheaper, faster, and more convenient financial products and services. This pedagogical guide is a must-read for anyone interested in understanding the dynamic and evolving world of fintech."

Raghavendra Rau, Sir Evelyn de Rothschild Professor of Finance, University of Cambridge

"Michael King leverages his deep experience in investment and central banking, as well as his international academic background as a finance professor, to offer a masterful handbook on fintech. Using the dual lens of disruptive innovation and financial intermediation theory, King unpacks 30+ real cases of fintech businesses, ranging from crypto protocols to niche lending startups and from globally established unicorns to bigtech's attempts at competing with traditional banks. It's concise and crystal-clear, and yet somehow manages to be exhaustive."

Jean-Philippe Vergne, Associate Professor of Strategy, UCL School of Management

"*Fintech Explained* is the ideal introductory companion for all things fintech. It provides a solid educational resource for students and educators as well as a point of entry to professionals who are keen to understand further the applications and strategic impact of technology in financial services."

Markos Zachariadis, Chair in Financial Technology & Information Systems, University of Manchester; Member of the World Economic Forum's Council on the Future of Resilient Financial Systems

Fintech Explained

How Technology Is Transforming
Financial Services

MICHAEL R. KING

UNIVERSITY OF TORONTO PRESS
Toronto Buffalo London

Rotman-UTP Publishing
An imprint of University of Toronto Press
Toronto Buffalo London
utorontopress.com

ISBN 978-1-4875-4408-9 (cloth)   ISBN 978-1-4875-4410-2 (EPUB)
ISBN 978-1-4875-4409-6 (paper)   ISBN 978-1-4875-4411-9 (PDF)

We welcome comments and suggestions regarding any aspect of our publications – please feel free to contact us at news@utorontopress.com or visit us at utorontopress.com.

Library and Archives Canada Cataloguing in Publication

Title: Fintech explained : how technology is transforming financial services / Michael R. King.
Names: King, Michael R. (Michael Robert), 1967– author.
Description: Includes bibliographical references and index.
Identifiers: Canadiana (print) 20230458467 | Canadiana (ebook) 20230458505 | ISBN 9781487544089 (cloth) | ISBN 9781487544096 (paper) | ISBN 9781487544119 (PDF) | ISBN 9781487544102 (EPUB)
Subjects: LCSH: Financial services industry – Information technology. | LCSH: Financial services industry – Information technology – Case studies. | LCGFT: Case studies.
Classification: LCC HG173 .K56 2023 | DDC 332.0285–dc23

Cover design: Heng Wee Tan

We wish to acknowledge the land on which the University of Toronto Press operates. This land is the traditional territory of the Wendat, the Anishnaabeg, the Haudenosaunee, the Métis, and the Mississaugas of the Credit First Nation.

University of Toronto Press acknowledges the financial support of the Government of Canada and the Ontario Arts Council, an agency of the Government of Ontario, for its publishing activities.

Printed and bound by CPI Group (UK) Ltd, Croydon, CR0 4YY

ONTARIO ARTS COUNCIL
CONSEIL DES ARTS DE L'ONTARIO
an Ontario government agency
un organisme du gouvernement de l'Ontario

Funded by the   Financé par le
Government   gouvernement
of Canada   du Canada

Canadä

To my wife, Yanna, and our sons, Robert and Peter.

Contents

Contents

Figures

Preface

WHAT IS *FINTECH EXPLAINED?*

This book provides the foundations for understanding financial technologies, or fintech. Fintech is the digital delivery of financial products and services via the internet or a device such as a mobile phone. We explore how entrepreneurial start-ups, mature businesses, digital-only banks, and global technology companies are transforming the customer experience in financial services. Fintechs are leveraging technologies to solve customer pain points and provide financial products and services that are cheaper, easier to use, faster, and more convenient than traditional methods.

Fintech Explained evaluates this paradigm shift and provides a roadmap to understand how fintech is reshaping the competitive landscape of financial services. We evaluate the business models, monetization strategies, funding, and valuation of fintechs. We examine the disruptive strategies of new entrants and the response of incumbents across a range of lines of business. We take a deeper dive into the world of Bitcoin, Ethereum, and decentralized finance (DeFi) to see how cryptoassets are radically transforming financial intermediation.

Fintech Explained focuses on fintech applications developed since the mid-2000s that primarily target individuals (retail) and small business customers. This latest wave of innovation has seen the growth of multi-sided portals providing peer-to-peer (P2P) capital raising and payments, challenger banks and apps for managing personal finances, robo-advisors and digital wealth management, insurtechs, and the entry of techfins and bigtech into financial services. Below, we outline the content chapter by chapter, summarizing the key learning outcomes.

WHO SHOULD READ THIS BOOK?

Like the successful fintechs profiled in this book, *Fintech Explained* solves a pain point for an underserved target customer by providing a compelling value proposition. This course book fills a gap for instructors (the customer) looking for a comprehensive educational resource on fintech (the pain point) that will delight undergraduates, graduate students, and interested professionals alike (the value proposition).

What sets this book apart? *Fintech Explained* provides a structured, pedagogical introduction to the fintech landscape. It combines clear descriptions and real-world case studies with the findings from the latest academic research. It summarizes insights from founders, early-stage investors, incumbents, and other stakeholders in this vibrant ecosystem. The chapters share a common theme but are standalone and can be read in any order. Each chapter ends with key terms, questions for discussion, and suggestions for additional reading.

This book is for anyone who wants to understand this transformational paradigm. Maybe you are interested in a career in financial services and need a roadmap to this field. Or perhaps you are a professional working in financial services wondering where your industry is headed. You might be contemplating launching an entrepreneurial start-up and want to identify the profit pools and develop your business plan. Or you may be an angel, venture capitalist, or institutional investor looking to identify the most innovative fintechs. *Fintech Explained* is your guide to this dynamic, evolving space.

The book provides a comprehensive introduction to a growing, complex topic. Learning about fintech on your own is not easy. If you go onto the internet, you will be overwhelmed by the thousands of blogs, articles, reports, videos, and other resources available. While some are excellent, others are dubious or questionable. Many are thinly veiled self-promotion or sponsored advertising. It is hard to sort the good from the bad. *Fintech Explained* is your curated guide to this field.

ROADMAP OF *FINTECH EXPLAINED*

Figure P.1 provides an overview of the book. *Fintech Explained* has two sections. **Section 1: The Fintech Toolbox** provides the tools needed to evaluate and understand this disruptive industry. It describes the foundations, economic theories, business models, funding, and valuation of fintech companies. **Section 2: Fintech Products and Services** explores the main lines of business and players in fintech. We examine the world of cryptocurrencies and DeFi, capital raising using online lending and crowdfunding, robo-advisors and digital wealth management, payments and insurtech, digital

Figure P.1. Overview of *Fintech Explained*

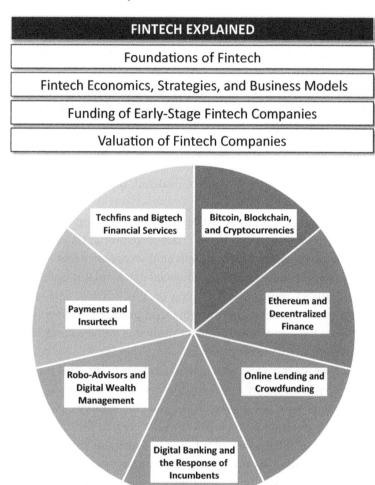

banking and the response of incumbents, and the entry of techfins and bigtech into financial services. These chapters profile successful fintechs to illustrate how they are leveraging technology to solve customer pain points in financial services.

SECTION 1: THE FINTECH TOOLBOX

The four chapters in Section 1 provide a toolbox for understanding and evaluating a fintech business.

Chapter 1: Foundations of Fintech

The first chapter defines fintech and describes its growth before presenting two paradigms of fintech: the traditional (evolutionary) paradigm and the transformational (revolutionary) paradigm.

The traditional paradigm is held by many professionals working in financial services today. They see fintech as an evolutionary process where new technologies create digital distribution channels, increasing the profitability of existing businesses. Examples of fintech businesses that fit under this paradigm are balance sheet lending, digital wallets, and automated investing using robo-advisors. These fintechs are product-centric and employ the same centralized, one-sided business models as incumbents.

The transformational paradigm sees fintech as a revolution disrupting financial services by disintermediating incumbents. Transformational fintechs leverage technology to solve customer pain points and deliver an experience that is cheaper, easier, faster, and more convenient. Examples are financial marketplaces built on multi-sided platforms, decentralized applications running on blockchains, and techfin/bigtech ecosystems that bundle financial and non-financial products and services. These innovations reimagine the customer experience, how it is delivered, and how financial products and services are monetized.

In this first chapter we introduce *The Fintech Explained Lens*. This framework helps you see clearly why fintechs are successful by asking four questions: Who is the customer, what is their pain point, why is the fintech's solution valuable to the customer, and how does the fintech share in the value created for the customer? These four questions make up the essence of a founder's elevator pitch to a venture capitalist. This lens highlights that fintechs are customer-centric, not product-centric. It illustrates how technology is only valuable if it solves a customer pain point and provides a compelling value proposition. Finally, successful fintechs adopt a business model that allows them to monetize (or capture) some of the value created for the customer.

This opening chapter concludes by reviewing the main fintech lines of business, describing the types of fintech companies, and highlighting the importance of the fintech ecosystem. We consider how fintechs are promoting financial inclusion. The chapter concludes with an overview of 10 key technologies underpinning fintech.

Chapter 2: Fintech Economics, Strategies, and Business Models

The study of fintech requires a multidisciplinary lens covering financial intermediation, disruptive innovation theory, digital strategy, and business models. Financial intermediation theory examines how intermediaries address five dimensions: information asymmetry, transaction costs, liquidity creation, risk sharing, and trust. The theory of disruptive innovation recommends that new entrants build a foothold by targeting underserved customers with a cheaper product or service, before moving into the mainstream. Digital innovations may be classified by whether they involve a new technology, a new business model, or both. Many companies fail at innovation because they do not align their business strategy with their digital strategy.

We will see that business models in financial services may be one-sided, such as a bank selling to its customers, or multi-sided, with some groups treated as a loss leader (subsidy-side) while others are the profit center (money-side). In general, one-sided financial businesses make money by acting as agents who collect fees and commissions or by acting as principals who profit from risk taking. Many fintechs belong to the traditional paradigm and have created digital versions of their bricks-and-mortar counterparts. These traditional paradigm fintechs have replaced banking with digital banking, lending with online lending, asset managers with robo-advisors, and insurance with insurtech.

Transformational fintechs have adopted multi-sided business models that generate revenues from multiple sides of their digital platforms. We see them in all lines of business: crowdfunding, online lending, banking and personal finance, wealth management, and insurance. The key to success is to generate network effects, where adding some customers attracts others to join.

While the primary fintech narrative used to be one of disruption by start-ups who were targeting underserved end-customers through business-to-consumer (B2C) business models, it is now one of partnership as more and more fintechs pivot to sell innovative products and services through business-to-business (B2B) business models.

Chapter 3: Funding of Early-Stage Fintech Companies

This chapter examines the funding of fintech start-ups. We discuss the founder's elevator pitch to an investor, review the different funding rounds, look at a capitalization table, and examine the types of securities issued to raise capital. A founder's elevator pitch identifies the customer segment, their pain point, the fintech start-up's value proposition, and their monetization strategy.

Before deciding to invest, a venture capitalist will want to know the size of the market opportunity (or total addressable market) and the background of the founding team. Fintechs raise capital in funding rounds starting with early stage (pre-seed, seed), advancing to growth stage (Series A through F), and exit via an initial public offering (IPO) or acquisition. A capitalization table shows the pre-money and post-money ownership stakes at each funding round, reflecting dilution from broadening the shareholder base. Start-up funding takes the form of equity (common, preferred, Simple Agreement for Future Equity) and debt (convertible note, venture debt) with the rights and seniority of different securities set out in a contract.

Chapter 4: Valuation of Fintech Companies

This chapter examines the valuation of fintech companies at different stages in their lifecycle. We describe the methods used by angel investors and venture capitalists for early-stage companies and investors in mature companies. Valuation of a pre-revenue company is an art, not a science. The buyer and seller negotiate the value, relying on experience and qualitative judgments. Angel investors use scorecards and risk factors; they may delay putting a value on the start-up until it has gained traction with customers.

Venture capitalists (VCs) look for a minimum viable product and growth in monthly recurring revenues. VCs work backward based on a targeted internal rate of return, adjusted for the risk of default and equity dilution. Valuation of mature companies for IPOs or strategic acquisition is based on the market multiples of comparable companies, precedent transactions, or a discounted cash flow (DCF) model. Some financial intermediaries such as banks cannot be valued using the DCF model, so relative valuation using market multiples is used.

SECTION 2: FINTECH PRODUCTS AND SERVICES

The second section dives into the fintech lines of business, evaluating them using the tools from the first section.

CASE STUDIES OF LEADING GLOBAL FINTECHS
Fintech Explained illustrates the transformational paradigm of fintech and the tools in the fintech toolbox using more than 30 case studies of leading global fintechs and incumbents:

- The robo-advisor Wealthsimple's seed-stage pitch to angel investors
- Wise Financial's pain point and market opportunity in payments
- JPMorgan's value drivers and valuation in traditional banking
- Funding Circle's financial ratios and performance in online lending
- Adyen's market multiples vs. comparable companies

- Bitcoin's solution to the double-spend problem
- Ripple XRP's search for a use-case
- The rise and fall of the FTX cryptoexchange
- Ethereum's vision and dominance of DeFi
- The DAO Hack and the immutability of blockchains
- LUNA's unstable stablecoin TerraUSD
- MakerDAO and Curve Finance's use-cases
- R3 Corda's DLT for regulated financial services
- Lendified's use of artificial intelligence
- Kickstarter's mission to bring creative projects to life
- LendingClub's marketplace lending platform
- SoFi's evolution from P2P lender to full-service bank
- Vanguard's move into robo-advice
- Wealthfront's sophisticated, low-cost financial advice
- Robinhood's commission-free trading for retail
- Paytm's business model and monetization strategy
- Innovations by Alipay, M-PESA, WorldRemit, and Octopus in payments
- ZhongAn, China's online-only insurance company
- Sensibill and Moven's personal finance apps
- Credit Karma's $7 billion multi-sided platform
- Nubank building Latin America's sixth largest bank
- Goldman Sachs' entry into consumer banking with Marcus
- Ant Group and Tencent's multi-sided platforms
- Amazon's path into financial services
- Apple's partnering with incumbents
- Facebook's troubles with regulators
- Google's struggle to find product-market fit

Chapter 5: Bitcoin, Blockchain, and Cryptocurrencies

In this chapter, we dive into the world of Bitcoin, cryptocurrencies, and other digital tokens. Ownership of these cryptoassets is recorded on an electronic ledger called a blockchain and secured using cryptography. The emergence of blockchain technology is driving innovations in how companies are organized, contracts are set up, and incentives are established, known as the field of cryptoeconomics.

In 2009 Bitcoin was the first cryptocurrency to be launched, providing an innovative solution to the double-spend problem using hashing. Ownership of bitcoins is recorded in an electronic distributed ledger called the blockchain, so named because transactions are batch processed in blocks and secured using cryptography in an immutable, append-only public ledger. Other developers soon launched alternative cryptocurrencies to Bitcoin ("altcoins") and, later, digital tokens. The common feature of these cryptoassets is they are all recorded on separate blockchains.

Many cryptoassets were pre-mined and sold to the public through initial coin offerings (ICOs), before this market was shut down by regulators in mid-2018 due to the large number of scams. As the cryptocurrency market has grown, innovations such as cryptowallets for storage and cryptoexchanges for trading have emerged to address user pain points. Academic researchers have studied the economics of Bitcoin as a means of payment, the ability to conduct arbitrage across cryptocurrency exchanges, and the returns from investing in cryptocurrencies versus traditional assets.

Chapter 6: Ethereum and Decentralized Finance

This chapter takes us into the world of Ethereum, smart contracts, and decentralized applications. *Decentralized* is a magic word in the crypto world. It means no single entity has control; decision making is distributed across a network of computers.

The Ethereum network has built a foundation for an internet of value where P2P transactions take place securely without a trusted intermediary. Smart contracts are coded on the Ethereum blockchain, automating execution. Developers combine them like LEGO blocks to create decentralized applications (dapps) and decentralized autonomous organizations (DAOs). To run smart contracts and dapps, users buy "gas" using the cryptocurrency ether (ETH), one of many tokens that can be exchanged on Ethereum. Stablecoins are a cryptocurrency with a value kept stable by pegging it to another asset, with the token backed by fiat currency, commodities, cryptocurrencies, or nothing at all.

Decentralized finance, or DeFi, is a new financial system and "internet of money" built on blockchain that allows P2P trading that is faster, cheaper, more personalized, and secure. An estimated 10% of cryptocurrencies are locked into DeFi smart contracts used for decentralized exchanges, borrowing or lending, liquidity staking, yield farming, stablecoins, service tokens, and derivatives.

Chapter 7: Alternative Finance, Online Lending, and Crowdfunding

This chapter looks at how individuals, small businesses, and social causes can raise capital through centralized portals that connect them to the crowd. Crowdfunding platforms allow individuals, businesses, and social causes to raise capital directly from individuals and institutional investors. As of 2021, activity is concentrated in the US and Europe. Crowdfunding portals are categorized as investment and non-investment. Investment portals issue debt (loans) and equity. Non-investment portals are donation-based and rewards-based. P2P/marketplace lending and balance sheet lending represent 90% of all money raised. Equity crowdfunding represents only 3%, with donation-based and rewards-based crowdfunding at 7%.

Online portals charge a variety of fees but feature high operating expenses. Losses have forced some of the biggest pioneers to pivot their business away from retail, move into financial services, or allow themselves to be acquired. The main benefit of digital capital raising for borrowers is ease of application, speed, and access to capital, but costs are high and success is uncertain. The main risks for investors are illiquidity, principal-agent problems, and the potential for fraud. In theory alternative finance may be able to increase financial inclusion, but for now most capital is raised by borrowers and issuers who have access to traditional sources but prefer to use fintechs.

Chapter 8: Robo-advisors and Digital Wealth Management

This chapter examines the rise and stumble of robo-advisors, the online investment portals that automate retail investment in a portfolio of exchange traded funds (ETFs). It also looks more broadly at how technology is transforming the wealth management industry, increasing transparency, and reducing fees, while also making financial advisors more efficient.

Robo-advisors are the most visible fintechs driving innovation and disruption in investing and financial planning. These new entrants have faced an uphill battle to acquire customers, with many start-ups pivoting to serve incumbents or being acquired. Incumbent financial institutions have been fast-followers, launching successful robo-advisor services that have captured most of the assets under management (AUM) in the robo segment.

The wealth management industry manages $100 trillion in investments with three distinct activities: financial planning, investing, and operations. Digital wealth management uses technology to automate and improve the customer experience, while generating fees and commissions from asset acquisition, portfolio management, and automation of back-office operations. Many successful fintechs in wealth management are working behind the scenes to partner with incumbents and provide B2B products and services. The future of digital wealth management is a hybrid model of a human advisor supported by computer algorithms that automate routine tasks and improve the customer experience.

Chapter 9: Payments and Insurtech

This chapter shows how fintechs have successfully attacked the profit pools of the payments and insurance industries, both of which are complex, regulated, and fragmented. The secret is to develop apps that solve customer pain points and automate processing.

Payments is a $2 trillion industry that generates close to 40% of bank revenues. It is complex, with many players collaborating and competing in overlapping networks. The large profit pools and many pain points in payments have attracted many successful fintechs, with more fintech unicorns born in payments than any other area of financial services. These fintechs started with a single use-case (such as a new form of mobile money or fair currency exchange) and have expanded their product offerings over time. Successful payment fintechs have solved pain points around e-commerce, money transfers, foreign exchange, international remittances, and cashless means of payment.

Insurance is a $6 trillion industry broken down into life insurance, property and casualty insurance, and health insurance. Insurtechs are exploiting mobile apps, cloud computing, biometrics, sensors, data science, and artificial intelligence (AI) to disrupt this industry. Insurtechs leverage technology and big data to develop customized insurance products that meet the needs of underserved and niche customers. Digital-only insurance companies are using AI and machine learning to develop and price innovative products that formerly were not possible given the underwriting history required and the high distribution costs.

Chapter 10: Digital Banking and the Response of Incumbents

This chapter examines the strategies of three categories of fintechs in banking and personal finance: fintech app developers, challenger banks, and financial marketplaces. It then looks at the various strategies used by incumbents to respond to this disruptive threat. Fintechs are targeting customer pain points in managing their day-to-day banking and personal finances, delivering a superior customer experience that is easier, cheaper, faster, and more convenient. This disruption has been enabled by technological advancements and the loss of trust post-Global Financial Crisis, propelled by open banking legislation around the globe.

Fintech app developers are unbundling financial services and solving specific use-cases, selling directly to end-customers (B2C), or partnering with incumbents (B2B). Challenger banks began by unbundling but are now rebundling financial products and services with transparent fees, faster service, and more personalized products. Financial marketplaces use application programming interfaces (APIs) to build an online platform offering third-party financial products and services to consumers.

Financial incumbents have responded with a range of strategies based on their own capabilities and scale, including building in-house, setting up innovation labs, forming strategic partnerships, licensing software, buying equity, or acquiring and targeting fintechs as customers.

Chapter 11: Techfins and Bigtech in Financial Services

This chapter reveals that the biggest threat to incumbents is coming from outside the financial service industry. Global technology platforms from China and North America are bundling financial and non-financial products and services on their platform ecosystems, creating network effects that attract billions of customers.

While fintech startups were initially seen as disrupting financial services, the consensus is that the greatest threat comes from Chinese techfins and North American bigtech companies. Alibaba and Tencent have built platform ecosystems that addressed institutional voids in China's economy by providing financial services to underserved or unbanked consumers. From a foundation in payments, Alibaba's Ant Group and Tencent WePay expanded to offer money market funds, loans, wealth management, insurance, and banking to their large user bases.

The North American bigtech companies are following the techfin playbook by moving into select financial services. Amazon's payments, cash products, and merchant loans support its e-commerce business. It has built internally, learning through trial and error, rather than relying on external partnerships. Apple has partnered with incumbents to protect its share of the smartphone market by providing increased functionality on the iPhone and Apple ecosystem. Facebook and Google have struggled to move beyond payments; Facebook's cryptocurrency project was canceled, while Google's launch of bank accounts was scrapped.

WHAT IS NOT COVERED IN THIS BOOK?

This book does not examine Fintech 2.0, the wave of IT investment from the late 1960s to mid-2000s. These investments focused on wholesale markets, improving the speed, communications, and efficiency of trading in financial markets. Fintech 2.0 targeted the experience of financial intermediaries, corporations, and institutional investors. It saw the computerization of financial services, the creation of electronic communication networks (ECNs) and alternative trading systems (ATS), the founding of Nasdaq, the growth of electronic brokers and Bloomberg terminals, and the creation of ETFs.

Fintech 2.0 gave us algorithmic trading, which began in the 1990s and grew exponentially in early 2000s. With algorithmic trading, a computer algorithm determines an order-submission strategy and executes trades without human intervention. Some algorithms simply automate existing strategies – for example, they break up large trades to minimize transaction costs – while others take advantage of superior execution speeds, known as high frequency trading. Algorithmic trading, earlier known as program trading, is behind many successful quantitative investment strategies.

Similarly, this book does not focus on the many B2B innovations developed for banks, other financial intermediaries, and institutional investors. Examples are applications for commercial lending, equity and debt underwriting, institutional sales and trading, and the asset management industry. To find excellent research and policy papers on these topics, visit the Centre for Economic Policy Research's site on "Finance & Fintech" at https://cepr.org/themes/finance-and-fintech.

A WORD ON JARGON

Jargon is a common problem in finance. Financial insiders and specialists use language that is unfamiliar or complex to demonstrate their expertise and exclude outsiders. Fintech is no exception. Fintech insiders use unfamiliar expressions (digitization, decentralization, disintermediation), acronyms and abbreviations (P2P, SHA-256, DAO), and computer-speak (algorithms, protocols, hashing).

An insider might describe the blockchain as *a cryptographically secured distributed ledger that is immutable, append-only, and the common source of truth.* But they could just as easily say a blockchain is *a secure electronic database recording ownership of an asset that is shared among different people.*

Fintech Explained demystifies fintech, translating jargon into everyday language. Like fintech itself, the goal is to provide a delightful experience for the reader built on easy-to-understand descriptions, accessible summaries of academic findings, and real-world case studies. Some fintech terminology and concepts are going to be new or unfamiliar. *Fintech Explained* addresses this pain point by defining and explaining new concepts and highlighting key terms at the end of each chapter.

A NOTE ON ACADEMIC RESEARCH

Academic research on fintech has grown rapidly over the past decade, mirroring the growth of the industry. A naïve search of the three words *fintech bitcoin crypto** using

EBSCOhost's Business Source Complete generates over 114,000 hits, of which around 13,000 are classified as "peer-reviewed" publications. This wave of academic research began post-2008 but kicked into high gear a decade later, spurred by specialized conferences and special issues from the *Journal of Economics and Business* (2018), the *Review of Financial Studies* (2019), and *Financial Management* (2019). Leading researchers and newly minted PhDs alike jumped on the topic. Some of the 5,000+ working papers on fintech posted on the Social Science Research Network (SSRN) have been published or were forthcoming by year-end 2022. This book only references articles published in the finance and economics journals in the FT 50 journals list used by the *Financial Times* to rank business schools.[1]

ACKNOWLEDGMENTS

This book is the culmination of six years of research and engagement with the fintech ecosystem in Canada and abroad. On this journey I have learned from many fintech founders, investors, academics, financial professionals, and other fintech stakeholders whom I met and interviewed along the way. These individuals have been very welcoming and generous with their time and insights.

I thank Scotiabank for the vision, funding, and support of Ivey Business School's Scotiabank Digital Banking Lab. Professor Jean-Philippe (JP) Vergne and I founded the Lab in April 2016, supported by a $3 million gift from Scotiabank. As the first Canadian research center focused on fintech, the Lab's mandate is to study and understand the implications of digital disruption for banking and financial services, and to prepare students to operate in an environment of changing technology and innovation. *Fintech Explained* continues this aspirational goal. At the Lab I learned a tremendous amount from JP Vergne, Chuck Grace, Amy Young, Murray Bryant, and Andrew Sarta; Ivey alumni working in fintech; the students in my fintech elective and the Ivey FinTech Club; and participants in Ivey's executive education courses.

I thank Richard Nesbitt, with whom I collaborated to write *The Technological Revolution in Financial Services: How Banks and Fintech Customers Win Together* (Toronto: Rotman-UTP). Published in 2020, this edited volume introduced me to many thought leaders in fintech and financial services who shaped my ideas: Jesse McWaters, Jon Frost, Tiff Macklem, Brian O'Donnell, Markos Zachariadis, Greg Wilson, Jay D. Wilson, Andrew Graham, Satwik Sharma, Peter Levitt, Tom McGuire, Evan Siddall, Vicki Martin, and Brenda Trenowden, CBE.

I am grateful for the insights from many fintech entrepreneurs and founders, including Tim Nixon (Trolley); Andrew Graham (Borrowell); Randy Cass (Nest Wealth); Peter-Paul Van Hoeken (FrontFundr); Kevin Clark and Troy Wright (Lendified);

Cato Pastoll and Brandon Vlaar (Lending Loop); David Rutter, Kevin Rutter, and Grant McDaniel (R3); Alan Wunsche (TokenFunder); Rubson Ho (CrowdMatrix); Dan Rosen (d1g1t); Pauline Shum Nolan (Wealthfront); Matthew Spoke (Nuco); and Andre Boysen (SecureKey).

To scale their business, a founder needs to raise funding from angels, venture capitalists, or incumbents. I listened carefully to the insights from Dubie Cunningham (Zafin), Peter Misek (Framework Venture Partners), Ray Sharma (Extreme Venture Partners), Matt Roberts (ScaleUP Ventures), Jonathan Shepherd (RBC Ventures), Alan Lysne (Fastbreak), Neil Peet (Greensky), David Unsworth and Robert Antoniades (Information VP), and Philippe Daoust (National Bank NAventures). I thank Sonya Ferhava and colleagues from the Scotiabank Digital Factory in Toronto who hosted my visits.

I interacted with more fintech stakeholders over the years than I can remember. Chief among them is Craig Asano, who has worked tirelessly to promote fintech in Canada as founder and CEO of the National Crowdfunding & Fintech Association of Canada (NCFA). I also thank Jan Christopher Arp, Michelle Beyo, Ghela Boskovich, Julien Brazeau, Sue Britton, Pat Chaukos, Kristy Duncan, Robin Ford, Robin Hibberd, Roy Kao, Bilal Khan, Alan Kotai, James Leong, Yoni Levy, Dinaro Ly, Zach Masum, Thayde Olarte, Martin Pasek, Erik Rasmussen, Gary Schwartz, Tal Schwartz, Dan Sinai, Peter Tilton, Peggy Van de Plassche, Joseph Villamizar, Elvis Wong, and Michael Young.

I am indebted to fellow finance academics whose research and interest in fintech provided so many insights, including Bill Cong, Darrell Duffie, Cam Harvey, Katya Malinova, Pinar Ozcan, Andreas Park, Raghu Rau, Ryan Riordan, Fahad Saleh, and Bob Wardrop. A special thanks to Andrew Karolyi for sowing the seed of this book and pointing a spotlight on this topic while executive editor at the *Review of Financial Studies*. Many more researchers have presented working papers and published articles cited in this book. On the practitioner side, I highlight the great reports and market commentary by CB Insights and 11:FS (host of the *Fintech Insider* podcast).

This research was made possible by the Tangerine Chair in Finance at Western's Ivey Business School and the Lansdowne Chair in Finance at University of Victoria's Gustavson School of Business.

Finally, I wish to thank Jennifer DiDomenico, Megan Hunt, Lisa Jemison, Stephanie Mazza, and the team at Rotman-UTP for supporting this work. A book does not get published without your tireless work behind the scenes.

1

Foundations of Fintech

SUMMARY

- Fintech is the digital delivery of financial products and services through the internet, a mobile phone, or other electronic device.
- While holders of the traditional paradigm see fintech as a natural evolution, believers in the transformational paradigm see it as a revolution transforming financial services.
- The fintech label describes companies with vastly different capabilities, scale, and funding: from entrepreneurial start-ups to mature global players to technology companies (techfins, bigtech).
- Fintechs operate in different lines of business, leveraging technology to solve customer pain points in managing their finances.
- The current fintech wave has been made possible due to a combination of existing technologies (computers, smartphones, peer-to-peer networks, application programming interfaces) with newer ones (big data, blockchain, cloud computing, machine learning).

This chapter defines fintech, describes its growth and evolution, outlines the traditional and transformational paradigms, provides a lens for evaluating successful fintechs, and presents other building blocks that make up the foundational knowledge in this field.

FINTECH DEFINED

Fintech is shorthand for *financial tech*nology. The "fin" refers to financial products and services, such as taking out a loan, making an investment, or sending a payment. The "tech" describes the technologies used to deliver financial products and services over the internet or a device like your mobile phone. Fintech is defined as *the digital delivery of financial products and services through the internet, a mobile phone, or other electronic device.* There is no accepted spelling, so you may see it styled as FinTech, Fintech, or fintech.

Starting around 2006, a growing number of innovative digital-only companies began disrupting and transforming the financial services industry globally. These fintech companies, or simply fintechs, target customers who are underserved by the traditional financial services industry, typically individuals and small businesses. These entrepreneurial start-ups focus initially on a problem, or pain point, related to financial services. Fintechs then leverage technology to offer a solution to this problem electronically that is less expensive, easier to use, faster, and more convenient than traditional methods. That is the fintech value proposition: cheaper, easier, faster, and more convenient.

Growth of Fintech

The growth of fintech can be measured in many ways. We can count the number of fintech companies, the number of fintech apps, or the number of Google searches for the term. The consultancy KPMG measures fintech by collecting data on global investment over time. KPMG began publishing "The Pulse of Fintech" in 2016 and has collected data back to 2008.[1] KPMG defines *fintech* as "businesses who are using technology to operate outside of traditional financial services business models to change how financial services are offered."[2] KPMG adds up dollars invested in equity by angel investors, venture capitalists, and private equity firms, and through mergers and acquisitions (M&A) by banks and non-financial businesses. The data does not include the value of initial public offerings (IPOs), where a fintech goes public and lists on a stock exchange.

Figure 1.1 shows the dollars invested in US billions on the left axis and the number of deals on the right axis. Fintech has seen waves of activity. Investment falls around the Global Financial Crisis of 2008–2009, hitting a low in 2012 before rising to a peak in 2016, then falling again in 2017. A third wave begins in 2018 and tops $200 billion in 2019, before dropping with the COVID-19 pandemic in 2020. It then rebounds to close to $240 billion in 2021, with around 7,300 transactions. There is a pull-back in 2022 reflecting the rise in global interest rates, causing a broad fall in the valuation of high-growth companies and an increase in the cost of capital.

Figure 1.1. Global Investment in Fintech Companies

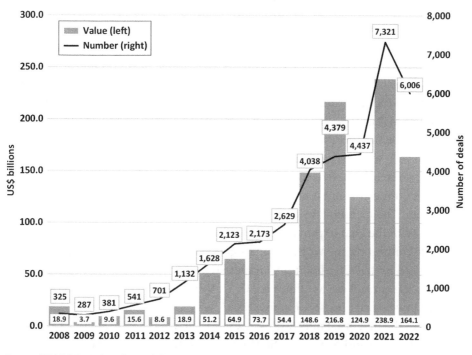

Source: KPMG, "The Pulse of Fintech," various years.

KPMG estimates that more than $1.2 trillion has been invested in close to 38,000 transactions over this 15-year period. Schumpeter's theory of creative destruction suggests much of this equity investment will be lost as many start-ups inevitably fail. Consistent with this view, research by the consultancy CB Insights suggests much of the investment in recent years has been follow-on equity investments in the most successful fintechs.

Revolution or Evolution?

Does fintech represent a natural evolution of the financial system or a revolution? Let's consider both perspectives.

Fintech believers describe it as a revolution transforming financial services. The goal is to overturn the existing financial order, empowering consumers by disrupting the gatekeepers who dominate the financial system – banks, lenders, brokerages, asset managers, financial advisors, insurance companies, money transfer companies, foreign exchange dealers, and other financial intermediaries (collectively called "incumbents"). These incumbents control access to capital and serve large corporations and institutional investors. The incumbents charge high fees and commissions that are not transparent, estimated at 2% of all financial transactions,[3] and provide mediocre service to retail customers and small businesses.

Fintechs are disrupting the incumbents using technology. They are armed with big data, blockchain, peer-to-peer (P2P) networks, cloud computing, artificial intelligence (AI), and other technologies. Using these tools, agile new entrants are bypassing traditional bricks-and-mortar branches and offices, unbundling expensive and complicated product offerings, and democratizing finance by increasing access to capital. Seen from this perspective, fintech is part of what the World Economic Forum calls the *Fourth Industrial Revolution*, a technological revolution that will fundamentally alter the way we live, work, and relate to one another.[4] This fusion of technologies is blurring the lines between the physical, digital, and biological spheres.

For skeptics, fintech is not a revolution; it is a natural evolution of the current financial system. The incumbents have been investing in information technology (IT) for centuries with the goal of providing all customers with better products and faster service while connecting the world's banking systems and financial markets. A 2017 study published by the CFA Institute, an industry association of finance professionals, describes the current era as "Fintech 3.0" – a third wave of digital transformation that followed two earlier bursts of innovation.[5]

In this view, the first era, Fintech 1.0, began in 1858 when a transatlantic cable was laid between London and New York. Starting in 1867, the electronic ticker tape made possible rapid transmission of information about the prices of stocks, bonds, and foreign exchange in the financial centers in North America and Europe. Fintech 1.0 lasted for a century, characterized by analog technology where data was transmitted using continuous electrical pulses of varying amplitude.

The second era, Fintech 2.0, started with the computer revolution in the late 1960s. These machines allowed the rapid transmission of discrete binary data over local and wide area networks. Examples were the facsimile (fax) machine invented in 1966, the automated teller machine (ATM) launched in 1967, and the fully electronic Nasdaq stock exchange that opened in 1971. The first portable cell phone was developed by Motorola in 1973, weighing over a kilogram and known affectionately as "the brick."[6]

By the 1980s, the global financial system was running on networks powered by mainframe computers and personal computers (PCs). The invention of the first web browser in 1989 (called the World Wide Web) made it possible for users to access pages of information located on different computers via the internet.[7] This paved the way for the arrival in the 1990s of e-commerce websites such as Amazon and eBay, electronic payments such as PayPal, personal financial software such as Intuit and Mint, and online banking and investing. The number of mobile phones grew exponentially, receiving a boost from the launch of second-generation (2G) mobile networks in 1991 that enabled data encryption, text messages, and multimedia messages. The launch of third generation (3G) mobile networks in 1998 made possible mobile internet access and voice over internet (VOIP).

Figure 1.2. Count of Fintech in Digital and Print Media, 2000 to 2018

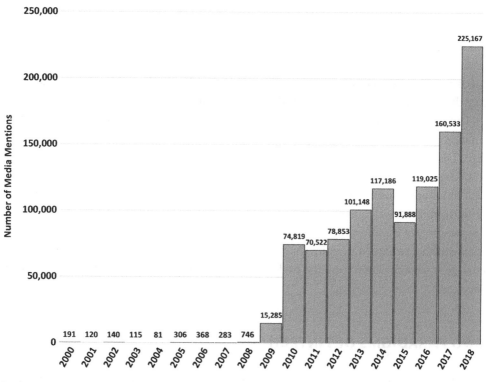

Source: Factiva.

The first two fintech waves, Fintech 1.0 and 2.0, used technology to improve wholesale financial markets. Incumbents developed digital financial products and services that targeted their largest clients, namely publicly listed corporations and institutional investors.

Our current era, Fintech 3.0, has used technology to broaden and deepen the financial system. The third wave of innovation focuses on underserved retail and small business customers. The year 2006 saw the launch of the P2P lending platforms LendingClub and Zopa, followed by the crowdfunding platform Kickstarter in 2008 and the cryptocurrency Bitcoin in 2009. Figure 1.2 shows that mentions of the term *fintech* increased exponentially in digital and print media from 2008 onwards.

The latest wave of fintech innovation has been made possible by a perfect storm of innovative technologies. The launch of Amazon Web Services (AWS) in 2006 provided massive, scalable computing power and data storage at a relatively low cost. Fintech start-ups could get to market quickly, without having to purchase and maintain expensive servers and infrastructure. The arrival of the Apple iPhone in 2007 and Google Android devices in 2008 put a powerful computer in the pocket of consumers. Smartphones made possible the rapid transmission of financial data through mobile networks.

There has been a downside to this technological change. Technology contributed to the Global Financial Crisis of 2007–2008 where excessive risk taking by banks in mortgage-backed securities, credit default swaps, and other derivatives led to the collapse of Lehman Brothers and the near-failure and government bailouts of banks and insurance companies in the US and Europe. These speculative activities were made possible by computers and trading algorithms, with the contagion spread globally through interbank networks and financial markets.

The Global Financial Crisis had an unexpected side effect. Many experienced finance professionals lost their jobs or became motivated to reform the financial system. Disgruntled, knowledgeable insiders launched innovative fintech businesses that targeted the profit pools of their former employers. These entrepreneurial start-ups developed innovative websites and mobile apps that found a ready audience with digital-native millennials who joined the workforce over this period. Millennials put greater trust in consumer brands, such as Apple, Google, and Facebook, than in traditional banks. Millennials had heightened expectations for user experience and customer service. They were the early adopters who provided a foothold in financial services for fintech start-ups.

TWO PARADIGMS OF FINTECH

Whether you subscribe to the revolution or evolution perspective, a main conclusion of this book is that *fintech is causing a paradigm shift in financial services.*

A paradigm is a way of looking at the world – a shared point of view or understanding about how things work.[8] The theory of paradigm shift was popularized by Thomas Kuhn in his 1962 book *The Structure of Scientific Revolutions.* Kuhn argued that some event causes the dominant paradigm to be updated or overturned, causing people to see the world in a new way. The catalyst may be a discovery, an invention, or a crisis.

Technology is causing such a paradigm shift in the global economy, of which financial services is one part. The arrival of the desktop computer, the internet, and web browsers has ushered in a paradigm shift known as e-commerce, creating a new way for consumers to shop. Similarly, the arrival of smartphones, digital apps, and cloud computing has caused a similar paradigm shift in how we manage our personal finances.

With every paradigm shift, some people hold on to the status quo. These people are heavily invested in the old way of doings things and cling to the existing paradigm. In the sixteenth century, the Catholic Church maintained the belief that the sun revolved around the Earth despite the scientific findings of Copernicus and Galileo.

Table 1.1. Two Paradigms of Fintech

The Traditional Paradigm	The Transformational Paradigm
• Fintech is an evolution, not a revolution, of the financial system. • Incumbents are product-centric, with business units organized around the products they sell. • Incumbents use technology to improve efficiency of back-office tasks and increase the profitability of their one-sided business models. • The goal: to capture more rents for bank insiders and shareholders.	• Fintech is a revolution disrupting an oligopolistic, rent-extracting industry. • Fintechs are customer-centric, focused on providing a delightful experience to consumers. • Fintechs are leveraging technology to solve customer pain points in financial services. • The goal: to deliver a customer experience that is cheaper, easier, faster, and more convenient.

The Church's paradigm reinforced their authority over society. Today's incumbents are clinging to the belief that the financial system revolves around them. It is a source of rents that benefits their employees and shareholders, not customers or broader society. In both periods, a new paradigm transformed how we view the economy, markets, and society.

Kuhn observed that the old and new paradigms may coexist for some time, which can make it difficult to see the bigger picture. This observation is true about fintech. We see two competing views of fintech that coexist, which I call the traditional paradigm and the transformational paradigm. Table 1.1 compares these two paradigms of fintech. This description is intentionally stark, provocative, and controversial. It illustrates the extreme position on each side, highlighting their main differences.

The Traditional Paradigm

Incumbents holding the traditional paradigm see fintech as an evolution of the current financial system, not a revolution. They see the financial system as a global marketplace where banks, asset managers, and insurance companies earn high profits from selling products and services to customers. Insiders pay themselves high salaries, extracting rents from this oligopolistic industry. Incumbents benefit disproportionately by capturing most of the value added from their activities.

This product-centric view is reflected in how incumbents organize their businesses. A typical bank is organized into divisions: retail banking, commercial banking, investment banking, asset management, and so on. Each division is organized into sub-units that sell a homogeneous product: deposits, loans, mortgages, credit cards, payments, mutual funds, equities, fixed income, currencies, and so on. Employee job titles reflect this product-centric orientation: manager of corporate lending, vice-president of payments, global head of securities. The list goes on. This structure is designed to maximize profitability through specialization, not to deliver the best possible experience to the customer.

Incumbents holding the traditional paradigm do not have a holistic view of the customer and their needs. Different parts of the same organization sell products to the same customer without even knowing it. These large, diversified businesses have deep pockets and talented employees who have a narrow focus. They pay lip service to the customer lifecycle, where individuals naturally require different financial products and services as they move through life. Each division and product team sees only their part of the puzzle, not the bigger picture.

From the perspective of the traditional paradigm, the current wave of investment in technology is designed to reduce costs and increase profitability of their traditional business models. The goal is to upgrade legacy computer systems and automate back-office processes to capture more rents. The incumbents have always invested in technology, with the latest wave (Fintech 2.0) designed to upgrade their wholesale and institutional businesses.

Now these incumbents are investing in Fintech 3.0 to increase the profitability of their retail and small business franchises. But rather than trying to solve customer pain points, the aim is to create a digital distribution channel for existing products that is more efficient. Fintech 3.0 is an expansion of the incumbent's omnichannel, adding to the existing physical (bank branches, ATMs) and electronic (telephone banking, online banking) distribution channels. The mobile channel may be new, but the underlying products (deposits, loans, payments) have not changed. Fintech investments are doing little to improve the customer experience or reduce the price charged to the consumer.

The Transformational Paradigm

Believers in the transformational paradigm see fintech as a revolution disrupting an oligopolistic, rent-seeking industry. In this view, the financial system exists to serve customers, not insiders. The incumbents are powerful and have built moats around their businesses to overcharge customers. Under the transformational paradigm, incumbents are oligopolies who cannot be trusted and should be turned into utilities, their profitability regulated. In this paradigm, financial products are commodities and should be priced accordingly, eliminating monopoly rents made possible by a lack of true competition in the financial system.

Transformational fintechs are customer-centric, not product-centric. They focus on the customer experience – how customers perceive and consume financial services, both now and in the future. Managing finance is a major source of stress and anxiety for customers. Fintechs are leveraging technology to eliminate customer pain points and provide a delightful customer experience. Using design thinking, fintechs are developing apps and online dashboards that are uncluttered and easy to read, making them simpler to use. Technologies such as the internet, mobile phones, the cloud, and P2P networks make it possible to provide faster service at a lower cost. Digital access to financial services can be convenient, available 24/7 online.

We are seeing some technology companies unbundling financial products and services, then rebundling them with non-financial activities. From a customer's point of view, many financial and non-financial activities are part of the same experience or transaction. Buying a house and financing the purchase are part of home ownership. Earning a living and investing savings for future expenses or retirement are part of a career. Going out with friends and making a digital payment are part of entertainment. Fintech is erasing the artificial boundaries between financial services and non-financial day-to-day activities.

This bundling of financial and non-financial products and services has opened the door to non-traditional players in financial services. We see the entry into payments, lending, investing, and insurance by technology companies such as Apple, Amazon, Google, Facebook, Shopify, Alibaba, and Tencent. These bigtech and techfin companies are building platforms that offer end-to-end experiences where non-financial and financial products and services are consumed together. China's Ant Group, which was spun out of the e-commerce company Alibaba, describes it this way: Financial services should be like water – you just turn on the tap and it comes out. Consumers do not need to ask which utility or what plumbing makes this possible; it just happens.

We will talk about bigtech and techfins in Chapter 11. We will also look at how the leading incumbents are responding to the threat of disruption by partnering, acquiring, or launching fintech businesses of their own. The most successful incumbents recognize that the key to success is maintaining the customer relationship and controlling the user experience. They are embracing the transformational paradigm and seeking to be part of the customer journey from end to end. They see the risk of being relegated to a drop-down list for financial products sold on a multi-sided platform run by one of these technology companies.

THE FINTECH EXPLAINED LENS

Having introduced the two paradigms of fintech, we now lay out a framework for evaluating fintechs that we use in the rest of the book. I call this framework *The Fintech Explained Lens*. It is a series of questions about a fintech's strategy and business that will allow you to see more clearly what makes a fintech successful. *The Fintech Explained Lens* is shown in Figure 1.3.

Figure 1.3. The Fintech Explained Lens

The four questions of *The Fintech Explained Lens* are

1 Who is the fintech's customer?
2 What customer pain point is the fintech solving?
3 Why is the fintech's solution valuable to the customer?
4 How does the fintech share in the value created for the customer?

These four questions – who, what, why, and how – provide a successful fintech with a roadmap to product-market fit and customer adoption. A successful fintech must have clear, succinct answers to these questions to acquire customers, to raise capital, and to scale their business. These questions form the basis of a standard elevator pitch to a venture capitalist (VC), a customer sales pitch, or a presentation to a bank partner. Let's take a closer look at each question.

Customer (Who?)

The first question in *The Fintech Explained Lens* is "Who is the customer?" Every business exists to serve customers who pay for the company's product or service. The customers may be individuals or small businesses, few or many, near or far away. A founder may call them early adopters. A marketer may call them the target market or customer segment. A VC may call them the serviceable available market. (We will have more to say about VCs later.)

The first step to building a successful fintech is to identify the targeted customers and their unmet need. Then the fintech creates a product that fits this customer, leading them to pay for it and hopefully tell others about it. Founders and VCs call this product-market fit. Without product-market fit, any venture will fail.

Too often, aspiring fintech entrepreneurs create a product where there is no customer demand. These fintechs develop a solution for a problem that does not exist. They focus on a cool technology and build something without asking the customer whether they need it. As a result, the fintech fails to get traction and is forced to pivot their business to survive. In the early years of fintech, for example, many developers coded digital wallets to replace physical wallets. What a cool idea! But retail customers didn't want or need a digital wallet. They liked their physical wallets. So most digital wallet start-ups failed. Eventually bigtech companies like Apple and Google developed mobile wallets that combined payments (a financial product) with their expanding lifestyle ecosystems (non-financial products and services). These mobile wallets now dominate this space, but they were not built by the fintech start-ups or incumbents.

Successful fintechs identify their target customer. They segment these customers based on demographics, location, or some other feature. The crowdfunding portal Kickstarter targets *creators of artistic projects who have something to share with others*. The payments fintech Wise targets *professional millennials who travel frequently with a need for cash in many countries*. The online lender SoFi targets *young urban professionals who are high earners but not rich yet (HENRYs)*. The mobile money transfer service M-PESA targets *underbanked households in Africa without a bank account*. These successful fintechs developed a product that fit their target customer; they did not simply build a product that was cool but no one needed.

Successful fintechs may describe their business with reference to their customer segment using the acronyms B2C, B2B, B2B2C, and C2C. Let's look at each one in turn.

Business-to-consumer (B2C) fintechs sell financial products and services directly to end-customers, such as individuals or small businesses. B2C fintechs are the developers of mobile apps and online websites that allow you to manage your financial life electronically, when and where you want to. Challenger banks, payment companies, robo-advisors, and insurtechs are examples of B2C fintechs.

Business-to-business (B2B) fintechs sell their products or services to an incumbent, such as a bank, an asset manager, or an insurance company. The fintech's software, app, or other technology is used by the incumbent to improve their digital offering to their end-customers. The incumbent may integrate the fintech's product into a mobile app developed in-house. This relationship may be white-labeled, which means the identity of the fintech is not disclosed to the end-customer. Or the fintech's brand may be disclosed using phrases such as "Powered by PayPal." The distinguishing feature of a B2B fintech is that the end-customer relationship remains with the incumbent, not the fintech.

Some fintechs describe themselves as business-to-business-to-consumer (B2B2C). In this case, they sell a product or service through a financial intermediary to the intermediary's end-customer. The fintech's brand is visible to the end-customer, and the fintech may develop a relationship with and collect data from the customer. An example might be a financial marketplace such as Borrowell or Credit Karma. Both marketplaces sell financial products from bank and non-bank financial partners to individuals. Similar platforms exist for crowdfunding, online lending, banking, personal finance, wealth management, and insurance. The platform collects a fee or commission and may sell the customer data to third parties if it operates a multi-sided business model.

Finally, a customer-to-customer (C2C) fintech is more commonly known as P2P. This fintech provides a technology platform that allows end-customers to deal directly with each other, bypassing traditional financial intermediaries. Most cryptocurrency exchanges are P2P, as they allow individuals to buy and sell cryptocurrencies and digital tokens directly with each other. The exchange runs the network, maintains the software, and collects a fee for these services.

But beware, many businesses may describe themselves as P2P when they involve a financial intermediary. An example is P2P lending platforms, where a fintech operates the online space where savers and borrowers transact. From the perspective of the customer, it may appear to be a P2P relationship. But from the point of view of the fintech, an online lender is a B2C business model. True P2P businesses are hard to find as there is often an intermediary who is making money in between somehow.

Pain Point (What?)

Once they identify the target customer, a successful fintech must create something the customer will pay for. The best approach is to solve a customer pain point.

A pain point is a negative experience that a customer would be willing to pay to have fixed. If you have a painful tooth, chances are you will pay a dentist to make it go away. The same goes for banking. People view managing their finances as a pain point and are willing to pay a financial intermediary to look after them, even when they do not enjoy the experience. Most people are as excited about visiting their bank as they are to see their dentist!

Financial services are full of pain points. You may feel anxious asking for a loan. You may hate paying a fee to withdraw your money. You may struggle to manage your personal finances. You may waste time driving to a bank to deposit a check. You may be overcharged when you send money abroad. You may be overwhelmed when looking to invest. In surveys of consumers, individuals list concern with their personal finances as a leading cause of stress.

These customer pain points create a market opportunity for fintechs. A fintech can leverage technology to provide an innovative solution to a specific pain point for a target customer. The fintech may develop a website or mobile app that allows a customer to apply for a loan, deposit a check, manage day-to-day banking, make fast and cheap payments, or invest their savings online. It goes without saying that the solution needs to be cheaper, easier, faster, and more convenient than the incumbent's product or service.

Instead of solving an existing pain point, a fintech may find success by addressing an unmet customer need or filling a gap in the market. Customers may not realize they want something because they are unaware of what is possible. For example, Credit Karma provided customers with their credit score, when many did not realize this score existed or understand its importance. Credit Karma then built a multi-sided platform that allows consumers to find the financial products they need easily and conveniently, saving time and money.

B2B fintechs develop products that address pain points facing incumbents. Yes, banks have pain points. They may be held back by a legacy (or old) IT system programmed in Fortran, Cobalt, or C that must be run on a mainframe computer. Or a bank may have undergone several mergers, leaving them with siloed IT systems that are not integrated. An incumbent may not have the design talent or research and development capacity in-house. Or they may lack the budget of larger rivals. By working with a B2B fintech, an incumbent can gain access to innovative, specialized software without the need to develop or maintain it in-house.

B2B fintechs such as Finastra, Moven, Plaid, and Zafin have developed innovative software solutions that allow banks to onboard customers, aggregate data, generate customer insights, and track customer relationships. An incumbent may license software from these B2B fintechs to automate the incumbent's sales and trading, product distribution, or back-office processes such as record keeping, reporting, compliance, security, and risk management. By working together, fintechs and incumbents can deliver the superior user experience that end-customers are seeking.

Value Proposition (Why?)

A successful fintech must offer a clear value proposition to their customer. We call it a "value" proposition because the customer must be willing to pay for it. It is not enough to develop a product that addresses a customer pain point. The customer must be willing to exchange something of value (i.e., money) to have it. If no one will pay for a product or service, it has no value. It is easy to grow a customer base by giving something away for free; it is harder to stay in business over the long run if you do.

Successful fintechs highlight their value proposition on their app or website:

- Wealthsimple (robo-advisor): "Grow your money. Invest on autopilot. Send cash in seconds. Commission-free stock trading. The simplest way to invest in crypto. File your tax return online. Powerful technology + human help."[9]
- Funding Circle (online lender): "Fast, affordable loan programs with a simple online process and funding in as little as 48 hours. See what's possible for your business when you have it all."[10]

- Revolut (challenger bank): "One app, all things money. From easy money management, to travel perks and investments. Open your account in a flash. Send, spend, and save smarter. All your accounts, all in one place."[11]
- Wise (foreign exchange and transfer provider): "Send money cheaper and easier than old-school banks at the real exchange rate with no hidden fees. Spend abroad in 175 countries and withdraw anywhere. Receive payments like a local in 10 currencies. Holding multiple currencies is completely free, and we use the real exchange rate to convert."[12]

Notice these value propositions promise cheaper (commission-free, affordable, free), easier and faster (send cash in seconds, simple online process, send money cheaper and easier, open your account in a flash), and convenient (auto-pilot, online process, like a local, one app, all in one place). Because people have short attention spans, the value proposition must be short and easy to understand. The customer must immediately be hooked.

Monetization (How?)

Once the fintech has created a valuable product that addresses a customer pain point, the next question is how to profit from it. Monetization means to make money. A fintech needs to capture some of the value created for its customers in order to earn a profit. A business is not viable if it cannot pay its bills and reward its employees and investors. The million-dollar question: What fintech product or service will be profitable, and how can a fintech grow and scale this business over time?

Fintechs use many different strategies to generate revenues and monetize their businesses: charging a fee or commission, selling advertising or data, profiting from risk taking, and more. A common technology business model is software-as-a-service (SaaS). SaaS is a subscription strategy where the customer pays a regular fee to license software, much like Netflix charging a monthly fee for movie streaming. A SaaS product is delivered using cloud computing and computer networks. For this reason, SaaS may be called web-based software, on-demand software, or hosted software. There are a variety of related SaaS business models known by different acronyms, including platform-as-a-service (PaaS), infrastructure-as-a-service (IaaS), and banking-as-a-service (BaaS). We will discuss these more later.

We will use *The Fintech Explained Lens* to evaluate different fintechs in the coming chapters. Each time you read about a fintech business, ask yourself: who (customer), what (pain point), why (value proposition), and how (monetization). The answers to these questions will help you to see clearly.

FINTECH BUILDING BLOCKS

Now that we have a lens for understanding what makes a fintech successful, let's review the main fintech lines of business, the types of fintechs, and the fintech ecosystem. We also highlight how fintechs are promoting financial inclusion.

Fintech Lines of Business

It is human nature to want to organize things into groups because our brains are wired to remember information in chunks.[13] Not surprisingly, fintech devotees have proposed many ways to classify fintechs, from simple tree diagrams to kaleidoscopic collections of logos. Most schemes classify fintechs based on their main product or service. *Fintech Explained* focuses on eight categories:

- **Cryptocurrencies**: electronic money and tokens whose ownership is recorded on a distributed electronic ledger called a blockchain secured using cryptography.
- **Decentralized Finance (DeFi)**: an "internet of money" built on blockchain using smart contracts and distributed applications (dapps) that allow secure P2P transactions without human intervention.
- **Online Lending**: digital platforms that allow individuals and businesses to borrow directly from other individuals, banks, and institutional investors. Also called debt crowdfunding.
- **Crowdfunding**: digital platforms that allow individuals, businesses, and social causes to raise capital directly in the form of equity, donations, and rewards.
- **Digital Banking**: fintechs that provide solutions for day-to-day banking and the management of personal finances.
- **Digital Wealth Management**: fintechs that use technology to automate investing, portfolio management, and back-office operations, as well as provide analytics.
- **Payments**: fintechs that provide digital means of payment, money transfers, and international remittances, as well as software for payments processing and analytics.
- **Insurtech**: fintechs that distribute insurance digitally or provide data analytics and software for the insurance industry.

This classification system is useful, but it is getting harder to use. Why? Many fintechs that built an initial foothold around a single product or service have since diversified and now offer a portfolio of products that defy easy classification.

Take SoFi, for example. From its roots as a P2P platform specializing in student loans, SoFi's goal today is to offer a one-stop shop for financial services where members can borrow, save, spend, invest, and protect their money.[14] In other words, SoFi wants to become a full-service bank like JPMorgan, HSBC, Deutsche Bank, or BNP Paribas.

Fintech has many more lines of businesses that are not covered in this book. We do not examine earlier innovations from Fintech 2.0 such as algorithmic and high frequency trading, which are the topic of many excellent books. We also do not cover the many B2B technologies developed for banks, institutional investors, regulators, and supervisors. Examples of such technologies are applications for commercial lending, underwriting, sales and trading, regtech, and suptech. Readers interested in these topics may look at the 2022 e-book *Technology and Finance*, written by four leading academics.[15] It provides an excellent summary on the impact of technology on trading costs and financial markets, highlighting the benefits and risks of the use of massive data for the provision of financial services.

Types of Fintech Companies

The fintech label is used to describe businesses with vastly different capabilities, scale, and funding. We see at least four different types:

- An **entrepreneurial start-up** with low revenues, fewer than 10 employees, and owned by its founders and early-stage investors.
- A **mature company** with thousands of employees, high revenues, and a stock exchange listing (such as PayPal or Square).
- A **digital-only bank** or an incumbent that has launched a digital business (such as Chime or Nubank).
- A **global technology platform** bundling financial and non-financial products and services (such as Apple or Ant Group). May be called a bigtech or techfin.

Each of these four types has different strengths, highlighted in Table 1.2.

THE ENTREPRENEURIAL START-UP

If you are asked to describe a fintech company, you will likely think of an entrepreneurial start-up. You probably picture a couple of twenty-somethings leaning over their laptops in a garage, coding their idea into the night. KPMG's data shows that thousands of such fintech start-ups have been launched globally over the past decade.

Take the example of Funding Circle, a UK online lending platform. It was founded in 2010 by three university friends who hatched the idea in a pub.[16] So far, this start-up fits our preconceptions. But if we dig a little deeper, we find that most fintech

Table 1.2. Strengths of Different Types of Fintechs

Type of fintech	Entrepreneurial start-up	Mature company	Digital-only bank	Global technology platform
Description	New ventures founded and run by entrepreneurs	Former ventures that have scaled and gone public	Banks, insurance companies, asset managers, and other financial intermediaries	E-commerce, gaming, social media, telecommunication, and consumer product companies
Innovation culture	√	√		√
Technical expertise	√	√	√	√
Financial expertise		√	√	
Regulatory expertise			√	
Risk management expertise			√	
IT systems	√	√	√	√
Economies of scale		√		√
Access to customers		√		√
Access to funding		√	√	√
Access to talent	√	√		√

start-ups have one or more middle-aged founders with significant financial sector or management experience. Two of Funding Circle's founders had worked as management consultants, while the other had worked in risk management for a bank.

We find many examples of fintechs created by experienced professionals. The blockchain company R3 was founded in 2014 by the former head of foreign exchange and fixed income for the global brokerage firm ICAP Plc. The UK challenger bank Revolut was founded by a trader and a programmer from London's financial district. The US robo-advisor Wealthfront was started by a former VC and a trader. Kenya's money transfer service M-PESA was created by an e-commerce expert and a telecommunication executive. The list goes on.

While they may not have the same origin story, fintech start-ups do share one thing in common: They are born digital. The customer experience is electronic from start to finish, replacing bricks-and-mortar with clicks-and-servers. Software, big data, and cloud computing allow fintechs to ramp up and launch a minimum viable product into the marketplace quickly to see how it is received. Often the first few tries are unsuccessful, leading the start-up to evolve or "pivot" their business model to survive. If they find product-market fit, the start-up thrives. If not, it dies. While there are no conclusive statistics for fintechs, the broader evidence suggests that 90% of start-ups fail.[17]

Entrepreneurial start-ups are viewed as the most innovative, employing small, agile teams to rapidly prototype products at a low cost with little bureaucracy or constraints from existing regulations. They employ the latest technologies and can motivate staff due to the perceived financial upside of their equity ownership. They are willing to experiment and fail, prototyping products to test in the marketplace.

But start-ups are disadvantaged by their small scale and relative inexperience. They lack customers, and the cost of acquiring customers is very high. Start-ups lack funding, often devoting precious management time to pitching investors and keeping the business afloat. They face difficulty in attracting qualified staff, whether it is hiring for business development or acquiring the necessary financial expertise in risk management and compliance.

THE MATURE COMPANY

A second category of fintechs is mature companies. While smaller in number, mature fintech companies have been around for decades or have grown rapidly and gone public. A high-profile example is PayPal, the global payments company founded in 1998. PayPal went public in 2002 as the US dot-com bubble was bursting, was acquired by eBay soon after, then was spun out in 2015. By year-end 2022, PayPal had 30,000+ employees serving 420 million active customers with annual revenues of US$27.5 billion and a stock market capitalization of around $80 billion.

As of year-end 2022, the venture consultancy CB Insights was tracking more than 300 fintech "unicorns" globally. A unicorn is a privately held company with a valuation over $1 billion based on its latest funding round. The number of fintech unicorns tripled from 2020 to 2022. The list includes a handful of fintech decacorns – unicorns with market valuations of $10 billion or more – including Stripe (US, payments), Checkout.com (UK, payments), Revolut (UK, banking), Chime (US, banking), and Plaid (US, data aggregator).

Mature fintechs have passed the start-up phase and succeeded in attracting customers and finding product-market fit. They have the innovation culture of a start-up but with less agility and more bureaucracy. They have both technical and financial expertise, and they employ the newest technologies and systems. Unlike start-ups, they have significant revenues, funding, talent, and scale. They are typically less regulated than incumbents or unregulated, although this arbitrage becomes harder to maintain as they grow. They may lack the risk management and regulatory expertise of incumbents.

THE DIGITAL-ONLY BANK

A third category of fintechs is digital-only banks. They may be challenger banks that were born digital, also called a neo-bank. Or they may be traditional banks that have re-positioned themselves as primarily digital or have launched a digital-only division.

Challenger banks such as the UK's Revolut, Germany's N26, Brazil's Nubank, and the US's Chime offer the same products and services as bricks-and-mortar banks but do it electronically. They offer bank accounts, debit and credit cards, personal and business loans, mortgages, investments, and other banking products to individuals and small businesses. The end-to-end digital experience is what sets a challenger bank apart. We will profile Nubank in Chapter 10.

A high-profile digital-only fintech division of an incumbent was Marcus by Goldman Sachs, a consumer bank launched in 2016 and named after the investment bank's founder, Marcus Goldman.[18] Marcus offered savings accounts and personal loans to retail clients, combining the new technology of a fintech with the risk management and banking expertise of an incumbent. What made Marcus unique was that it was launched by an investment bank to target a new customer segment, namely retail banking.

The future initially seemed bright for Goldman's fintech offering. Marcus attracted four million customers through a combination of advertising and acquisitions. It partnered with Apple to launch a digital-only credit card. It attracted more than $50 billion in deposits without having any bricks-and-mortar presence. But Marcus also lost lots of money – $3 billion dollars over 2020 to 2022.[19] In late 2022 Goldman announced it was pulling back from consumer banking, no longer originating loans to retail, and restricting Marcus to its existing wealth management clients. Marcus is an example of a high-profile fintech failure by an incumbent. We will revisit Marcus later in the book.

Digital-only banks and the fintech divisions of incumbents share features of both a start-up and an incumbent. They have deep pockets and the expertise of an incumbent in finance, regulation, and risk management. They employ newer technologies but not likely the cutting edge. Like a start-up, they lack scale and need to invest to acquire customers. They may struggle to attract talent due to a different culture and greater bureaucracy, being influenced by their parent company if they are a division.

THE GLOBAL TECHNOLOGY PLATFORM

The fourth category of fintech companies is new entrants from outside the financial sector. The most visible are global technology companies called techfins and bigtech. The term *techfin* was coined by Alibaba's Jack Ma in 2016 to describe Ant Financial (now Ant Group), but it also applies to rival Tencent's WePay. These two Chinese techfins dominate their home market but have faced obstacles expanding abroad.

North America features a handful of global technology companies known collectively as *bigtech* due to their size and market capitalizations. Think of Google, Apple, Facebook (now called Meta), Amazon, and Shopify. Bigtech companies have been moving relentlessly into financial services since 2010 or even earlier.

Both techfins and bigtech have built online marketplaces and mobile apps that combine e-commerce, social networking, and gaming with financial products, including payments, deposits, loans, investments, bank accounts, and insurance. Their platform ecosystems connect billions of users with a wide variety of financial services manufactured in-house or sold by third parties. They are mining their customer data for insights and identifying needs before users even know they have them. The consensus among bank insiders and industry commentators is that techfins and bigtech, not fintech start-ups, represent the greatest threat to incumbents.

How real is the threat? It is very serious. Techfins and bigtech combine the innovation culture and technical expertise of start-ups with the access to customers and scale of incumbents. They have data from billions of customer transactions that they can mine to identify customer needs. They are bundling financial products and services with non-financial offerings on their platform ecosystems. They do not face the regulatory burden of incumbents, although scrutiny of their business practices has been increasing. A key shortcoming is the lack of financial expertise, although this can be addressed by hiring talent from incumbents. We will explore the techfins and bigtech in the final chapter of *Fintech Explained*.

The Fintech Ecosystem

If you spend enough time around fintech, you will hear someone talking about the importance of the "fintech ecosystem." What do they mean exactly?

In biology, an ecosystem is a community of living organisms and the non-living components that support them. Think of a rainforest or underwater reef. In nature, greater diversity is an indication of a healthy ecosystem.

Similarly, new businesses do not emerge and grow in isolation. They depend on a diverse ecosystem that incubates new ideas, supports innovation, and nurtures talent. The fintech ecosystem consists of the actors, institutions, and infrastructure that support this growing sector. Each of the following stakeholders serves an important function in the fintech ecosystem:

- Fintech *companies* include entrepreneurial start-ups, mature players, digital-only businesses, and other new entrants. Fintechs are the source of innovative financial products and services.

- *Innovation labs* are specialized workplaces designed to promote research and development (R&D) and beta testing of new products. A bank, asset manager, insurance company, local government, or community may set up an innovation lab.
- *Incubators* and *accelerators* are shared workplaces set up to help entrepreneurs prototype and commercialize their ideas. Incubators work with entrepreneurs at the seed stage of development, providing office space, education, and mentoring for a limited period. Start-ups that are more financially viable may graduate to an accelerator where they receive more mentoring, business development, commercial contacts, and potentially equity capital. Level39 and Y Combinator are leading technology accelerators in the UK and US, respectively.
- *Technology hubs* are collections of more advanced entrepreneurial businesses in the same building or district that promote interactions among stakeholders. Every major city likely has one, with consultancies such as KPMG providing rankings.[20] For example, Toronto's innovation hub is the MaRS Discovery District at University Avenue and College Street, which has relationships with 60 fintech start-ups.[21]
- *Investors and capital providers* include founders, family, and friends (FFFs); angel investors; VCs; private equity; institutional investors; and strategic investors such as incumbents. They provide capital, mentoring, and connections for fintech start-ups.
- *Regulators and policymakers* include supervisors, government officials, and other public-sector bodies. They establish and enforce the rules governing the offering of fintech products and services to the public. In the fintech space, regulators may also host a regulatory sandbox to assist start-ups, as well as an innovation hub.
- *Other stakeholders* include universities and colleges, trade and business associations, research organizations, consultancies, shared workspaces, and technology partners. These organizations support the fintech ecosystem by providing talent, marketing opportunities, R&D, strategic and financial advice, and other capabilities needed for a fintech company to succeed.

Various fintech commentators rank the fintech ecosystems in different cities and countries. These consultants, accountants, and industry associations evaluate the ecosystem based on the ease of doing business, political stability, government and regulatory policies, legal institutions, financial sector development and infrastructure, availability of talent, and innovation and research culture. Table 1.3 provides examples of the 2020 rankings by country and by city. The top of the list usually includes the United States (Silicon Valley, New York), the United Kingdom (London), Singapore, and Hong Kong. Europe, Australia, Canada, China, and the UAE also receive mentions.

Table 1.3. 2020 Rankings of Fintech Ecosystems

Rank	Country	Rank	City
1	United States	1	Silicon Valley (US)
2	United Kingdom	2	New York (US)
3	Singapore	3	London (UK)
4	Lithuania	4	Hong Kong
5	Switzerland	5	Boston (US)
6	The Netherlands	6	Singapore
7	Sweden	7	Berlin
8	Australia	8	Dubai
9	Canada	9	Toronto
10	Estonia	10	Shanghai

Source: Findexable Ltd., Accenture.

PROMOTING FINANCIAL INCLUSION

Fintech has the potential to democratize access to finance and increase financial inclusion for unbanked or underbanked populations. The World Bank defines *financial inclusion* as individuals and businesses having access to useful and affordable financial products and services that meet their needs – transactions, payments, savings, credit, and insurance – delivered in a responsible and sustainable way.[22]

The World Bank estimates that more than 1.7 billion adults around the world were unbanked at last count, defined as individuals without a bank account or access to basic financial services. Typically, unbanked individuals are poor, dispossessed, and living in countries with underdeveloped, costly financial systems.

Of course, unbanked people can also be found in the richest countries of the world. The US central bank estimates that 6% of adults were unbanked, without a checking, savings, or money market account.[23] Living without access to basic financial services removes opportunities to increase basic incomes and standard of living. It is associated with poor physical and mental health, low education, and poverty.

The good news is that the World Bank estimates that two-thirds of unbanked adults own a mobile phone. And a mobile phone can provide access to financial services. Governments, non-governmental organizations (NGOs), and the private sector are looking to fintech to help these individuals. And we are seeing results. Over the last decade, 1.2 billion previously unbanked adults gained access to financial services, and the unbanked population fell by 35%, primarily boosted by the increase in mobile money accounts.[24]

Many fintechs have an explicit societal agenda that can be found in their mission statement or "About Us" section on their company website. Fintechs looking to democratize access to financial services fall under the label *social finance* – a term that refers to a style of investing or banking that seeks to earn a social return along with an economic return. A social return is an investment that benefits society, such as reducing poverty, advancing challenged segments of the population, or supporting the environment.

Social finance covers a variety of organizations, including charities, NGOs, and impact-focused organizations, as well as a variety of activities, including microfinance, socially responsible investment, impact investment, and sustainable finance. A key area of impact for social finance is to promote financial inclusion through the delivery of financial services at an affordable cost to poor and unbanked customers.

The number of fintech start-ups in the social finance space has grown rapidly, though the reality of the "social" in these approaches has varied. Broadly speaking, social finance fintechs fall into two groups: those who use technology to make a profit while providing a service to an underserved customer segment, and those who use technology to disrupt the power of traditional incumbents.

The first category of social finance fintechs includes success stories such as M-PESA in Kenya and SoFi in the United States. Launched in 2007, M-PESA provides cheap and accessible banking using widely available mobile phone, text messages, and a network of local representatives from the telecom company Safaricom (owned by Vodafone). Founded in 2011, SoFi is an online finance company that initially provided loans on favorable terms to students attending the most reputable US universities and colleges, using funding from alumni who screened applicants. By 2016, SoFi had provided more than US$12 billion in student loans to 175,000 members. For both M-PESA and SoFi, technology provided a means to an end: namely, creating shareholder value by providing a superior customer experience at a lower cost to an unbanked segment of the population.

The second group of social finance fintechs had a more ambitious goal: to democratize finance by disintermediating the incumbents and disrupting their monopoly rents. This goal was behind the creation of cryptocurrencies such as Bitcoin, the first digital currency that is not controlled by a central bank or government authority.

A similar goal motivated Wise (formerly TransferWise) in 2010 to provide a cheaper and faster alternative for cross-border currency transfers by eliminating the hidden costs charged by banks. It motivates P2P lending platforms such as Zopa, founded in 2005, that provide loans on ethical terms to individuals to help them grow, not hold them back. And it is part of the philosophy of robo-advisors such as Wealthsimple, founded in 2014, whose stated mission is to bring smarter financial services to everybody, regardless of age or net worth.

Ten Technologies behind Fintech

The current wave of fintech, Fintech 3.0, has been made possible by a combination of existing and emerging technologies. While we tend to focus on the newest developments, most technologies underpinning fintech have been around for decades. Computers, P2P networks, and distributed databases became widely available starting in the 1970s. The internet and World Wide Web (WWW) arrived in the 1990s. The number of mobile phones in circulation increased exponentially at this time, from around 11 million in 1990 to 2.5 billion by 2020, supported by improvements in mobile networks, which advanced from analog (1G) to digital (2G, 3G) over the course of the 1990s. This infrastructure, developed during Fintech 1.0 and 2.0, allowed fintechs to reach consumers directly using electronic means during Fintech 3.0.

Let's look at 10 technologies used by fintechs, presented in alphabetical order.

APPLICATION PROGRAMMING INTERFACE (API)

An application programming interface, or API, is a computer program and set of rules that allows computers to exchange data over a network. The API is the messenger that delivers a request from one computer to a connected computer, then returns with the requested information. APIs were first developed in the 1960s and became widespread in the 1970s and 1980s. APIs rely on rules known as communication protocols that define what information can be accessed and how it is transmitted. An API may connect with a database, a library of code, an operating system, or other parts of a network. An API connection over the internet is called a web API.

APIs can be closed or open. A closed API is internal to an organization and not accessible to outsiders. Banks, for example, employ closed APIs to manage movement of data across branches and offices over internal networks. An open API is public and allows third-party computers to connect to a company's internal network safely and securely. In between closed and open we have a partner API that establishes a secure connection with approved third parties subject to a contract.

APIs are central to open banking. Open banking (or open data) is the label for regulations that allow consumers to control electronic access to their financial data. Open banking regulations were legislated by the European Union in 2016 under its Payments Service Directive II (PSD2). PSD2 was designed to promote the development and use of innovative online and mobile payments. The United Kingdom passed its Open Banking Act in 2016 to allow licensed fintech start-ups direct access to customer data when requested by the customer. Both the EU and UK legislation require banks to build open APIs to allow third parties to access customer data safely and securely. Similar legislation is being reviewed or introduced in many countries around the world.

ARTIFICIAL INTELLIGENCE AND MACHINE LEARNING

Artificial intelligence (AI) is the field of computer science where machines are taught to perform tasks that mimic human intelligence. AI research began in the late 1950s and 1960s, but fell quiet for many decades before making a comeback in the 2000s. AI is not a single technology, but rather a collection of technologies that tackle various use-cases: reasoning, problem solving, knowledge representation, planning, learning, perception, motion and manipulation, and general knowledge. AI fields include expert systems, machine learning, neural networks, natural language processing, planning, robotics, speech processing, and vision.

The sub-field of machine learning teaches computers to learn and act by themselves without being explicitly programmed by a person. Machine learning is the technology behind self-driving cars, genome mapping, speech recognition, web search, spam filters, and recommender systems. Machine learning uses three approaches to teach a computer to program itself:

- **Supervised learning** is where the computer is trained by asking questions and then being fed the correct answers using a specific training dataset. The algorithm can then teach itself to replicate the correct answers using logistic regression.
- **Unsupervised learning** is where the computer learns on its own. It is given data to analyze, but the relationship between the variables is not known. The computer algorithm identifies relationships among variables using cluster analysis.
- **Reinforcement learning** is where the computer takes actions to maximize some reward, almost like playing a video game. The computer is given a specific dataset and searches for patterns. It receives a reward when it does well and is punished when it does badly. The computer learns what steps to follow to maximize the reward.

BIG DATA

Big data, or data analytics, is the science of examining large datasets to uncover relationships and inform decisions for businesses, researchers, and other audiences. Professionals specializing in this field are called data scientists or data engineers.

In 2006, the British mathematician and data scientist Clive Humby famously stated that "Data is the new oil."[25] How right he was! In 2018, *Forbes* reported that 90% of the data in the world was generated in the previous two years.[26] This incredible figure reflects the reality that more than 3.7 billion humans are using the internet with more than 5 billion searches daily.

The field of data science has advanced dramatically over the past decade due to increases in computing power, the decline in the cost of storage, the greater availability of real-time data (both structured and unstructured), the widespread adoption of open-source software for storage and processing (such as Apache Hadoop), and the development of better data querying and visualization tools. Big data is a critical input to AI and machine learning methods. And big data has many applications to fintech, primarily to understand customer behavior and needs.

BLOCKCHAIN AND DISTRIBUTED LEDGER TECHNOLOGY

Blockchain originally referred to the electronic distributed ledger that recorded ownership of the cryptocurrency Bitcoin, developed by founder Satoshi Nakamoto in 2008. The ledger was called blockchain because the transactions were collected in batches and processed into 1-megabyte blocks of data before they were added to the ledger. The chain refers to the process of adding and protecting the blocks using a secure hash algorithm, in this case the SHA-256 algorithm. The process of securing blocks is called hashing. The process of verifying transactions in blocks is called mining. Over time, the word *blockchain* has become a generic term that refers to all varieties of encrypted, distributed ledgers. Bitcoin and blockchain are discussed in Chapter 5.

While it might sound complicated, a ledger is just a record of information, such as a database. Ledgers used to be physical, written in a book, but became electronic with the widespread availability of computers. You can create a ledger using Microsoft Excel, for example.

An electronic distributed ledger has multiple identical copies of the ledger held on different computers (called nodes) connected over a network. This duplication of the ledger avoids a single point of failure but creates a problem as the distributed databases must be synchronized to ensure their accuracy and alignment. If entries are different across copies of the distributed ledger, the truth can be verified by comparing the values recorded by the majority of copies. While synchronizing distributed databases used to be complex and time-consuming, software programs called distributed ledger technology (DLT) synchronize electronic ledgers instantaneously, cheaply, and securely.

CLOUD COMPUTING

Cloud computing refers to the ability to store data, host websites, and run applications over the internet using computer servers owned and operated by a third party. This business model was created by Amazon when it launched Amazon Web Services (AWS) in 2006. AWS provides subscribers with access to a virtual cluster of computers available 24/7 over the internet. Subscribers access AWS using a web browser and log in to their virtual systems just as they would with a desktop computer. Amazon was quickly followed by competing cloud computing services from Google, IBM, Microsoft, and Oracle.

The emergence of cloud computing has driven innovative business models such as software-as-a-service (SaaS), platform-as-a-service (PaaS), infrastructure-as-a-service (IaaS), and banking-as-a-service (BaaS). These business models are all variations on a monthly subscription service like Netflix, where users pay to gain access to computer software or hardware. Recall that SaaS is a subscription strategy where the customer pays a regular fee to license software.

PaaS provides a technology platform where customers can develop, run, and deploy applications by renting software and hardware. The customer controls software deployment and configuration options. The PaaS supplier provides the networks, servers, storage, operating system, middleware, database, and other services to host the customer's app.

IaaS provides access to network infrastructure such as physical computing resources, storage, data partitioning, scaling, security, and backup using APIs. A customer does not manage or control the underlying cloud infrastructure, but instead has control over operating systems, storage, the network, and distributed applications.

BaaS allows fintechs to add banking services into apps and websites using APIs, enabling any start-up to offer banking solutions to its customers. A fintech connects securely into a bank's core digital platform, where they can access APIs to transfer money, verify customer identity, open and maintain bank accounts, issue debit and credit cards, and more. The bank providing the BaaS is responsible for complying with regulatory requirements, including capital and liquidity requirements, know your customer (KYC), and anti-money laundering (AML) requirements.

CRYPTOGRAPHY

Cryptography secures private data using techniques from mathematics, computer science, engineering, and physics. Cryptography has existed since the great empires of Egypt and Ancient Rome using ciphers and invisible ink. In the era of computers, the ability to secure messages through encryption has become inexpensive and widely available. These mathematical techniques ensure private data transmitted over the airwaves or a public computer network cannot be read by third parties.

Cryptography secures data by encrypting it at the source, then decrypting it when received using a specified cipher. But not all forms of cryptography follow this encryption-decryption format. Cryptography for digital currencies – also called cryptocurrencies – involves securing transactions using a hash algorithm that cannot be inverted. In other words, any user who puts the identical text, numbers, and punctuation into a standard encryption algorithm will receive the same hash. A hash is a hexadecimal representation of the binary data. This hash cannot be decrypted (or reversed) using conventional computing power.

The best way to understand hashing is to try it out yourself! Try inputting the word *fintech* (all lower case) into a SHA-256 algorithm online, and you will get:[27]

110599ccb008c6746985524be4ba99ff588fed6bc5c4d65d2a15b6a92eda16a7

Next, try entering *Fintech* (with a capital F) and it will return a different hash:

2dd47261bf9305896542a63678477884cba21c4b70fab4b8fafb69be2672608d

ETHEREUM

The Ethereum Network, or simply Ethereum, is the name of a decentralized, open-source, programmable blockchain and software development network run by the Ethereum Foundation. It was conceived in late 2013 by 19-year-old Vitalik Buterin, a Russian-Canadian programmer. Buterin was an early enthusiast in Bitcoin but saw limitations in its design, particularly its simplistic scripting language and limited block size. Following circulation of his whitepaper, Buterin launched this community-run technology in mid-2014, funded through the crowdsale of the cryptocurrency ether (ETH).[28]

Ethereum provided an open and secure platform for developers to build decentralized applications (or "dapps") and smart contracts that run over the internet without human interference.[29] While coding and hosting a dapp on Ethereum is free, running a dapp requires "gas," which must be purchased using ETH, with the amount of gas related to the computational power required on Ethereum's servers. We will discuss Ethereum and dapps in Chapters 5 and 6.

MULTI-SIDED PLATFORM

A computing platform, or digital platform, is a combination of hardware and software built to facilitate interactions over a P2P network between different users or groups. The platform features a server, an operating system, a web browser, and software tools to manage network connections (such as APIs). The platform may be decentralized and may feature distributed decision making based on its governance. Digital platforms typically rely on big data stored in the cloud to perform algorithmic computations that facilitate user interactions.

A multi-sided platform (sometimes called a two-sided platform) is a digital business that makes money by bringing together two or more groups of users to transact with each other online. The different groups are called the "sides" of the platform. A multi-sided platform may also be called a marketplace or platform ecosystem. Some of the most successful companies use this business model, including Google, Amazon, and Tencent. Multi-sided platforms are discussed in greater detail in Chapter 2.

PEER-TO-PEER (P2P) NETWORK

A peer-to-peer (P2P) network describes a network of computers that allow two parties to interact with each other to complete some task. To understand how this works over the internet, we need to distinguish between two types of network connections: client-server and P2P.

A client-server connection allows computers to access data stored on a central server. With a client-server connection, the content only flows in one direction. A client-server network is centralized and run by a single supernode that coordinates connections and stores the network data in one place. A client computer requests and receives data from a server, and then the server ends the connection. The server does not query the client, although it may keep a record of the transaction using a cookie.

With a P2P connection, the computers on the network have equal access to each other, with content flowing in both directions. These connected computers are called nodes. A server (or supernode) manages and monitors the flows among nodes, recording the locations of the computers using domain names, maintaining security, and optimizing traffic on the network.

A P2P network is decentralized and relies on multiple servers to coordinate different parts of the network, with each server storing data and user information relevant to their local nodes. No single supernode controls the system. Software applications run on several computers, which use protocols to connect to each other to complete a shared function or a task. Online lending and crowdfunding platforms run on P2P networks. We discuss these businesses in Chapter 7.

In fintech, cryptocurrencies and DeFi run on distributed networks, as we will see in Chapters 5 and 6. A distributed network treats all nodes as equal with no supernode. Software applications and data are spread across nodes that relay messages and communicate with each other using agreed rules called protocols. A distributed network is not designed to complete a shared function or task. A distributed network may feature both client-server and P2P connections.

The internet is an example of a distributed network. Different computers (nodes) host pages of information written in a common scripting language (such as HTML) that are accessed using web browsers running internet protocols (called TCP/IP).

SMART CONTRACT

A smart contract is a computer program that executes automatically when a designated event occurs. Smart contracts were developed by Vitalik Buterin, the founder and creator of Ethereum, to allow the processing of transactions without human intervention. A smart contract is coded to take the form: if A happens, then B follows. For example, a smart contract to transfer ownership of a house would say: if payment of $X is received, then change the record of ownership to name Y. To prevent the code from being altered or manipulated, smart contracts are encrypted on a blockchain, typically the Ethereum blockchain. Smart contracts are discussed in Chapters 5 and 6.

That's it – one chapter finished, and you have started your journey to becoming a fintech expert. Well done!

Key Terms

accelerator	business-to-consumer (B2C)
application programming interface (API)	cloud computing
artificial intelligence (AI)	cryptography
banking-as-a-service (BaaS)	customer-to-customer (C2C)
big data	decentralized network
bigtech	digital ledger technology (DLT)
blockchain	distributed network
business-to-business (B2B)	ecosystem
business-to-business-to-consumer (B2B2C)	Ethereum

financial technologies (fintech)

incumbents

machine learning

multi-sided platform

node

open banking

pain point

paradigm shift

peer-to-peer (P2P) network

smart contract

social finance

software-as-a-service (SaaS)

techfin

unbanked

unicorn

QUESTIONS FOR DISCUSSION

1 What is fintech? What do the "fin" and the "tech" represent? Give examples of both.

2 In your opinion, does fintech represent an evolution of the financial system or a revolution? Why?

3 What is a paradigm shift, and what causes it? What are the two paradigms of fintech and what are their key differences?

4 What are the four questions of *The Fintech Explained Lens* used in this book? How does this framework help to evaluate fintechs?

5 What are the different fintech lines of business? What are their main products or services?

6 What four types of companies are engaged in fintech? What are their respective strengths?

7 What role does the fintech ecosystem play and who are the key stakeholders?

8 How is fintech promoting financial inclusion? What are the two types of social finance fintechs?

9 What is cryptography and why is it important for blockchain?

10 What is a peer-to-peer (P2P) network and how is it related to a multi-sided platform?

ADDITIONAL READING

Cambridge Centre for Alternative Finance, "CCAF Publications," University of Cambridge, accessed December 15, 2021, https://www.jbs.cam.ac.uk/faculty-research/centres/alternative-finance/publications/.

The Economist, "Slings and Arrows – Special Report," May 7, 2015, https://www.economist.com/special-report/2015/05/07/slings-and-arrows.

Ernst and Young Global, "Fintech and Ecosystems," accessed December 15, 2021, https://www.ey.com/en_gl/banking- capital-markets/fintech-ecosystems.

International Monetary Fund, "Fintech: The Experience So Far," IMF Policy Paper No. 19/024, June 27, 2019, https://www.imf.org/en/Publications/Policy-Papers/Issues/2019/06/27/Fintech-The-Experience-So-Far-47056.

King, Michael R., and Richard Nesbitt, "Introduction," in *The Technological Revolution in Financial Services* (Toronto: University of Toronto Press, 2020), accessed April 27, 2023, https://www.book2look.com/book/F3Ntf54Dnd.

Vives, Xavier, Thierry Foucault, Laura Veldkamp, and Darrell Duffie (eds.), *Barcelona 4: Technology and Finance* (London: CEPR Press, 2022), https://cepr.org/publications/books-and-reports/barcelona-4-technology-and-finance.

World Economic Forum, "The Future of Financial Services – How Disruptive Innovations Are Reshaping the Way Financial Services Are Structured, Provisioned and Consumed," June 2015, https://www3.weforum.org/docs/WEF_The_future__of_financial_services.pdf.

2

Fintech Economics, Strategies, and Business Models

SUMMARY

- The study of fintech requires a multidisciplinary approach including financial intermediation, disruptive innovation, digital strategy, and business models in financial services.
- Financial intermediation theory examines how intermediaries address five dimensions: information asymmetry, transaction costs, liquidity creation, risk sharing, and trust.
- The theory of disruptive innovation argues that new entrants first build a foothold by targeting underserved customers with a cheaper product or service, before moving into the mainstream.
- Digital innovations may be classified by whether they involve a new technology, a new business model, or both. Many companies fail at innovation because they do not align their business strategy with their digital strategy.
- Business models in financial services may be one-sided, with a bank selling to its customers, or multi-sided, with some groups treated as a loss leader (subsidy-side) while others are the profit center (money-side).
- Financial intermediaries such as fintechs make money by acting as agents who collect fees and commissions, or by acting as principals who profit from risk taking.

The previous chapter laid the foundations for understanding fintech, defined as the digital delivery of financial products and services through the internet or a mobile phone.

This chapter examines the theories underpinning fintech, focusing on financial intermediation, disruptive innovation theory, digital strategies, and business models.

A MULTIDISCIPLINARY APPROACH TO FINTECH

The study of fintech requires an understanding of a range of subjects: finance, economics, strategy, entrepreneurship, information technology, and marketing, just to name a few. These topics must be mastered for a fintech to be successful in the financial services sector, which is experiencing rapid technological change.

These changes in financial services are part of a larger change in the global economy. As we learned in Chapter 1, the World Economic Forum labels it the Fourth Industrial Revolution, a technological revolution that is disrupting value chains and business models in every part of the economy.[1] The same forces are transforming manufacturing, energy, utilities, health care, transportation, agriculture, hospitality, and more. All industries are being reconfigured and transformed. These changes are not cyclical; they are structural.

Given this breadth of change, we need to adopt a multidisciplinary lens to see the big picture. We cannot understand fintech by considering only a narrow set of finance or computer science theories. We need to bring together knowledge of economics, strategy, industrial organization, and entrepreneurship.

Our first stop is the theory of financial intermediation. A financial intermediary is a business that brings together two parties to a financial transaction and charges a fee or commission for this service. The stereotypical financial intermediary is a retail bank that collects deposits from savers and makes loans to borrowers. A large body of academic research has outlined the theory of financial intermediation, which concerns itself with five dimensions: information asymmetry, transaction costs, liquidity creation, risk sharing, and trust. We need to understand how fintech affects these five dimensions of financial intermediation to see how it is transforming financial services.

Our second stop is the theory of disruptive innovation from the field of strategy. Disruption describes a radical change to an existing industry or market due to technological innovation. Harvard professor Clayton Christensen's influential disruptive innovation theory provides a blueprint for how entrepreneurial start-ups gain a foothold in an industry. He also outlined how existing businesses that dominate the industry (i.e., the incumbents) should respond. We consider what makes a business vulnerable to disruption, then look more closely at four digital strategies across the innovation landscape.

Our third stop is the field of industrial organization to learn about the business models used by financial intermediaries and fintech companies. Industrial organization is a field of economics that examines the structure of firms and markets. A business model explains how a company makes money by selling to a targeted set of customers. The traditional one-sided business model that dominates finance is being challenged by new multi-sided businesses (or platforms) used by technology companies such as Google, Apple, Facebook, and Amazon. Fintech marketplaces are multi-sided businesses that are disrupting financial services, providing one-stop shopping for payments, credit, investments, insurance, and much more.

THE FIVE DIMENSIONS OF FINANCIAL INTERMEDIATION

Financial intermediation explains how money circulates through the economy from savers to investors, and how financial risks are managed. The term *financial intermediary* refers to any business that facilitates financial transactions between two parties. The financial system features a bewildering array of financial intermediaries fulfilling many different functions, including

- **Banks and credit unions**, which accept deposits and extend loans; some focus on commercial clients (i.e., commercial bank), some on individuals (i.e., retail bank), and some on a specific type of loan (i.e., mortgage bank).
- **Brokers and dealers**, which facilitate the buying and selling of stocks, bonds, and other financial assets.
- **Investment banks**, which help corporations to issue bonds or equity or to acquire other companies.
- **Asset (or money) managers**, which pool savings and invest in a portfolio of securities on behalf of investors. Examples of asset managers are pension funds, mutual funds, hedge funds, private equity firms, and venture capitalists (VCs).
- **Insurance companies**, which collect premiums from policy holders in exchange for covering the cost if some bad event occurs, such as destruction of property, personal injury, or death.
- **Exchanges, clearinghouses, and depositories**, which run the infrastructure of financial markets.

To keep things simple, we will refer to banks in the remainder of this chapter, although there may be various non-bank financial intermediaries that provide a product or service.

Figure 2.1. The Five Dimensions of Financial Intermediation

Financial intermediation works through two channels – the financial markets and the banking system – which together are called the financial system.

Financial markets exist to bring together savers and investors to buy and sell financial assets such as stocks, bonds, foreign exchange (fiat and crypto currencies), commodities, and their derivatives. These transactions may take place in a centralized location, called an exchange (such as a stock exchange or a commodity exchange), or through decentralized computer networks called the over-the-counter (OTC) market. Financial market trades may be completed with the assistance of a broker (or agent), via the order book of a market maker (or dealer), or directly between two counterparties.

The banking system brings together savers and borrowers, converting liquid, short-term deposits into illiquid, longer-term loans. Unlike financial markets, the banks allow this exchange to take place on their balance sheet, exposing themselves to risks from both sides. On one hand, depositors may decide to withdraw their savings at short notice, requiring the bank to provide liquidity. On the other hand, creditors may default and fail to repay their loan. A big part of what a bank does is manage these risks.

Economists explain financial intermediaries' role using five dimensions: information asymmetry, transaction costs, liquidity creation, risk sharing, and trust (Figure 2.1).

Information Asymmetry

Information asymmetry describes a setting where two individuals enter an agreement but have different amounts of information. The information is asymmetric because one party generally knows more than the other. Financial services and fintech are full of these types of situations.

Take the example of the CEO of a publicly listed company and a shareholder (or equity holder) who owns the stock. The CEO can see how the business is doing in real time, including sales, margins, and profits. The shareholder only learns how the business is doing at specific points in time, such as quarterly earnings releases. The shareholder needs to monitor information made public by the company when deciding whether to buy, sell, or hold the stock.

Information asymmetry in this example leads to a well-known principal-agent problem. In the example above, the shareholder is the principal, or owner of the business. The CEO is an agent hired to run the business by the shareholders. Of course, the CEO may hold some shares, aligning their interests more closely with shareholders. Given the information asymmetry between them, how can the shareholder ensure the CEO is running the business to maximize value for the shareholder?

Information asymmetry between principals and agents creates a problem called moral hazard. Moral hazard is where the agent (i.e., CEO) does not personally bear the costs of risky decisions that affect the claims of the principal (i.e., shareholder). For example, the CEO wants to take over another company and is willing to overpay for the transaction to be completed due to their ego and desire to run a bigger company. In fact, most mergers destroy value, rather than create it, so this is a constant concern for shareholders.[2]

The 2008–2009 Global Financial Crisis provided a dramatic example of how information asymmetry between principals and agents created a catastrophic moral hazard problem. In the years leading up to the crisis, global banks invested billions of dollars of shareholders' money in risky securities backed by US subprime mortgages, known as mortgage-backed securities (MBS). The bank employees who made these investments received large bonuses.

Many MBS defaulted between 2007 and 2008, leading to losses and write-downs that caused some banks to fail. Shareholders at these banks saw their investments wiped out. A post-mortem showed that even after the default of these MBS, the bank employees responsible collected more bonuses. In other words, the agents were rewarded for taking excessive risks while the principals bore the cost.

The field of corporate governance focuses on solutions to principal-agent problems, information asymmetry, and moral hazard. One remedy is to align the incentives of both parties by designing a compensation contract where they win or lose together. A second remedy is to ensure the bank's board of directors is rewarded for monitoring management to reduce moral hazard. A third remedy is to use regulation to increase transparency and reduce information asymmetry, while holding bank employees accountable.

The loss of trust caused by the 2008–2009 Global Financial Crisis allowed fintechs to gain a foothold in financial services. Many fintechs provide solutions that lower information asymmetry by increasing transparency around fees and compensation contracts. These fintechs may provide more education on the risks to end-customers. Nevertheless, fintechs are also plagued by principal-agent problems with mixed incentives for insiders versus outsiders. We will see many examples in the coming chapters, notably in the collapse of the FTX cryptoexchange.

Transaction Costs

Most economic transactions have costs, which may be direct or indirect. Examples of direct costs are the commission or fee when buying or selling an asset, the costs to search for information or a counterparty to a transaction, and the cost to create and sign a contract between two parties. Examples of indirect costs are the costs to enforce contracts and regulate financial entities.

The Nobel prize–winning economists Ronald Coase, Douglass North, and Oliver Williamson used transaction costs to explain the existence of companies, markets, financial intermediaries, and other parts of our modern economy. They argued that companies exist to internalize many forms of transaction costs, while markets exist to solve the search problem for buyers and sellers.

Despite tremendous advancements in the technologies supporting the financial system, the cost of financial intermediation remains stubbornly high. Research shows that the average cost of financial intermediation has not really changed over 130 years, hovering around 2% of financial transactions.[3] This transaction cost is measured as the profits of financial intermediaries as a share of credit, equity, and liquid assets in the financial system. This 2% cost has persisted since the 1880s, with any benefits from productivity-enhancing improvements being captured by financial services employees in the form of higher wages, rather than being passed on to consumers.

Many fintechs are motivated to reduce the costs of financial services and broaden financial inclusion, whether it is providing a cheaper means of payment, raising capital, simplifying investing, or buying insurance. We will see that most fintechs have gained a foothold in these businesses by providing comparable financial products and services at a lower cost by using technology to reduce or eliminate various transaction costs.

Liquidity Creation

Banks provide two vital services to the economy: liquidity creation and maturity transformation.

The term *liquidity* has several meanings. It can describe the availability of cash to pay for purchases. It may refer to the ease of buying and selling assets in financial markets. Or it may refer to the ability of the financial system to meet the needs of a growing economy.

Broadly speaking, banks create liquidity in three ways. First, banks accept deposits from households, businesses, and government and lend out this money as various forms of credit (such as loans and mortgages). The business of transforming liquid deposits into illiquid loans is risky but profitable, allowing the bank to earn a profit on average.

Second, banks create liquidity by providing checking, credit cards, lines of credit, and other payment methods that allow consumers to spend money today without being constrained by how much cash and coins are in circulation at a given point in time.

Third, investment banks and dealers create liquidity in financial markets by buying and selling financial securities using their own balance sheet. A dealer quotes prices where they will buy or sell a security (called the bid and ask), exposing themselves to the risk of market movements that may generate gains or losses. The bid-ask spread compensates the dealer for making a market and taking on this risk of price movements. Investment dealers may provide short-term liquidity by selling and repurchasing stocks or bonds through repo markets or by loaning out securities belonging to an investor, called securities lending.

Liquidity creation is often tied up with maturity transformation, where a shorter-term liability is used to finance the purchase of a longer-term asset. This maturity transformation may happen through the banking system or financial markets. For example, a typical retail bank accepts a cash deposit from an individual, who has the right to demand repayment at any point in time (hence the name demand deposit). The bank uses these deposits to extend mortgages to other customers, with final repayment contracted up to 30 years in some countries. The bank cannot simply ask for the mortgage to be paid back early when depositors need money. So a short-term deposit is funding a long-term mortgage, creating a maturity mismatch on the bank's balance sheet.

As we examine different lines of business, we will see fintechs creating liquidity and engaging in maturity transformation. In these cases, we need to be aware of the risks that need to be managed to protect the financial intermediary, which is the next topic: risk sharing.

Risk Sharing

One of the main functions of financial intermediaries is risk sharing. A financial intermediary like a bank gets paid to take on and manage a variety of risks. A risk describes an uncertain outcome, either positive or negative. The future value of any asset cannot be known with certainty, as it may be higher, lower, or unchanged from the price paid for it. We say the asset is risky because the price will vary over time.

We categorize financial risks based on their source: market risk, liquidity risk, credit risk, operational risk, settlement risk, counterparty risk … The list of risks goes on and on.

Financial intermediaries and financial markets have developed tools for managing, sharing, hedging, or insuring risks. One example is financial contracts that transfer risk using options, forwards, futures, and swaps. A second example is insurance, where a specialized company pools the risks associated with known events across many parties and sells contracts to protect against an adverse outcome.

Risks that cannot be eliminated must be borne by some party. Many financial intermediaries specialize in matching a party that wants to reduce its risk with another party willing to bear it. The difficulty is negotiating a price for this risk sharing or risk transfer. Financial markets assign a price to risk through buying and selling of financial instruments. Banks rely on their prior experience to price risk.

The main tools for evaluating, pricing, and sharing risks are data, models, computer algorithms, and procession power. As we will see, the fintech revolution has increased the availability of all these inputs. We will find many fintechs that are providing tools and analytics to manage risk based on big data, AI, and machine learning. But many financial activities create new risks that are not understood due to information asymmetry and moral hazard.

To take one example, investors in peer-to-peer (P2P) loans purchased through an online lending platform bear the risk of default by the borrower. You may think that contributing to a crowdfunded loan in this way would be a safe bet. It is not. A P2P loan is an illiquid investment that exposes the lender (i.e., you) to the risk that the creditor (i.e., the borrower) does not repay. In this case, the loan will be written down and the lender will lose money. Most online platforms do not bear any risk of loss for loans that they intermediate. The online platform does not pay back the investor or create a market for investors who may wish to sell their portion of a loan. All risk is transferred from the creditor to the lender. We will highlight more examples of risks and who really bears them as we describe different fintech businesses.

Trust

Historically, financial intermediation was a relationship business built on trust between a bank and their customers. This trust was built up through repeated interactions over time. An individual or small business would start with a few financial products or services, and the bank would cross-sell more products over time to grow its revenues. Research on banking and financial intermediation has shown that franchise value increases with the number of customers and their loyalty to the bank. Strong customer relationships lead to a higher franchise value for a bank and a higher stock price, which benefits the bank's shareholders. The key message is that repeated interactions over time can contribute to trust between two parties.

Of course, this trust in the financial system is underpinned by a number of institutions that we may take for granted until something bad happens (like a deposit run on a bank). First, there is the rule of law that governs a contract between two parties. The legal system protects the rights of one side in case the other side violates a contract. There are regulations on how much risk a financial intermediary can take and how it must be managed and disclosed. There are bank supervisors who ensure banks are obeying these regulations. There are safety nets when they do not, such as government-sponsored deposit insurance and lender-of-last-resort functions. Similar institutions support trust in asset management, insurance, and payments.

Take the example of lending. Lending is built on trust between a borrower and a creditor. Lending is a low-margin, stable business that – done right – generates a long-term, low-risk income stream for a bank. Borrowers such as retail, small businesses, and corporations that are capital constrained can get access to financing over the business cycle by developing a lending relationship with a bank. Research shows that banking relationships formed during good economic times leads to increased credit availability during economic downturns and financial crises.[4]

Researchers have found that investments in technology change the way banks interact with their customers, undermining relationships and trust. Technology promotes more transaction-based activities and greater risk taking.[5] In the decade prior to the 2008–2009 Global Financial Crisis, for example, large, global banks invested heavily in hardware, software, and electronic networks to support their asset securitization and proprietary trading businesses. The growth of these profitable transactional businesses led to a declining emphasis on relationship businesses, such as lending. In other words, banks focused less on serving their end-customers and more on making money through securitization and trading.

The collapse of many banks during the 2008–2009 Global Financial Crisis and the subsequent economic recession caused many individuals and businesses to lose trust in incumbents. This loss reduced the barrier to entry into financial services, as customers were willing to try something new and turned to fintechs.

As we examine different lines of business in the coming chapters, we will ask how successful fintechs address the five dimensions of financial intermediation. Are fintechs reducing information asymmetry and moral hazard problems between principals and agents? Are fintechs reducing transaction costs, creating liquidity, and providing risk sharing for end-customers? And are fintechs engaged in relationship businesses that build trust over time, or transactional businesses that do not?

DISRUPTIVE INNOVATION AND DIGITAL STRATEGY

With millennials as important agents of change, new business models for crowdfunding, peer-to-peer lending, socialized payments, and automated investing are rising to take market share from existing banking channels ... We see over $4.7 trillion of revenue at the traditional financial services companies at risk for disruption by the new, technology-enabled, entrants.[6]

This statement from the investment bank Goldman Sachs made for an eye-catching headline when it came out in a 2015 report titled "The Future of Finance." Everyone loves to root for the underdog. In the early days of fintech, countless articles portrayed fintechs as disruptors that would threaten or replace banks and other financial incumbents. This David-versus-Goliath narrative was repeated by the media (CNBC, *The Economist*, *Forbes*), reports from consulting firms (Accenture, Deloitte, McKinsey & Company, PwC), and policy forums (Milken Institute, World Economic Forum).

Is it true that fintechs are disrupting the financial system? To answer this question, we need to agree on the meaning of two terms: disruption and innovation.

A *disruption* is a break or interruption in the normal course of some activity. Disruptions may be caused by storms, a pandemic, political upheaval, or war. When applied to business, disruption describes a situation where the established companies (i.e., the incumbents) are facing a new competitor who is winning customers and gaining market share. This competitor may come from inside or outside the industry. Left unchecked, this trend may drive some incumbents out of business.

An *innovation* is an improvement on an existing product, service, or way of doing things. Unlike an invention, where something is created for the first time, an innovation is an improvement on something that has already been invented and exists. The telephone was an invention, but the mobile phone and smartphone were innovations.

Most fintech entrepreneurs are innovators, not inventors, and create a better experience for customers using existing financial products and services. Some fintechs are motivated by a desire to disrupt incumbent financial institutions, while others are not. If your goal is to transform the financial system, your strategy for doing this is outlined in the theory of disruptive innovation. And as you plan how to do this, you need to develop a digital innovation strategy.

Theory of Disruptive Innovation

The theory of disruptive innovation is credited to Harvard professor Clayton Christensen, who wrote the 1997 book *The Innovator's Dilemma: When New Technologies Cause Great Firms to Fail.*[7] Two decades later, Christensen updated his theory in a 2015 *Harvard Business Review* article.[8] Let's take a closer look at what he said.

Christensen defined a *disruptive innovation* as a process where a smaller company with fewer resources successfully challenges an established business. A disruptor, either an entrepreneurial start-up or other new entrant, gains a foothold in an industry by targeting overlooked or underserved customers. These customers become the early adopters of the disruptor's product.

These early adopters are dissatisfied with the status quo. They feel they are being overcharged for an existing product that contains many features they do not want. These customers want something cheaper and more customized to their needs. The disruptor offers a lower quality, cheaper product with more suitable functionality that is viewed as "good enough" by the overlooked and underserved customers.

According to Christensen's theory, the disruptor gains a foothold with this cheaper product that is initially considered inferior to existing products by mainstream customers. Mainstream customers are not willing to switch even though the new product is cheaper.

Over time, the disruptor uses their low-end foothold to improve the quality and performance of their product. As the product quality improves, the disruptor targets the mainstream and high-end customers, who are now offered a similar-quality product at a lower price. When the quality rises enough to satisfy them, mainstream and high-end customers switch to the lower-cost offering. By the time this switch happens, it is too late for the incumbent to react. Disruptive innovations typically drive down prices, reducing the profitability of the industry and benefiting consumers.

Take the example of the personal computer (PC). The first models were sold in the late 1970s, with the market dominated by International Business Machines (IBM). By the 1980s, PCs had become very expensive. Consumers who wanted a cheaper PC without all the bells and whistles were not being served. This situation led Michael Dell to create an online, direct-to-consumer business called Dell Computer in 1987. By going online, customers could customize and purchase a PC built to their own specifications: processor, hard drive, screen, and so on. Frustrated, underserved customers loved this business model, and Dell's sales took off. Dell went public in 1988 and joined *Fortune*'s list of the 500 largest companies in 1992.

Michael Dell did not invent the PC. His innovation on IBM's business model was to allow consumers to buy a customized PC online. Dell disrupted IBM's business model, building a billion-dollar business that led to the collapse of IBM's PC business, which was sold to Lenovo in 2005.

Disruptive versus Sustaining Innovations

Christensen argues that people mistakenly confuse disruptive innovations, which are rare, with sustaining innovations, which are relatively common.

A disruptive innovation describes a process by which a product or service powered by a technology targets underserved customers in the low end of an established market, allowing the disruptor to gain a foothold. In other cases, a disruptive innovation creates a market where none existed previously. Disruptive innovations don't catch on with mainstream customers until quality catches up to their standards. This is a process that takes time, with some disruptive innovations succeeding while others fail. But when they do succeed, disruptive innovations transform a market, with the new entrant winning market share at the expense of the incumbents.

Christensen states, "Disruptive innovations are not breakthrough innovations or 'ambitious upstarts' that dramatically alter how business is done but, rather, consist of products and services that are simple, accessible, and affordable. These products and services often appear modest at their outset but over time have the potential to transform an industry."[9]

Sustaining innovations are everyday, routine improvements in an existing product. Take the example of the iPhone. A new model is released every couple of years. Apple may improve the operating system and add some new features, but the product is fundamentally the same. Existing customers can easily upgrade to the latest model, and new customers may purchase it. But the new model is still targeting mainstream and high-end buyers of cell phones. A new iPhone is a sustaining innovation, not a disruptive innovation, even though it showcases a new technology.

Christensen argues that it is a mistake to label all successful new entrants as disruptive. To make this point, he argues that the ride-sharing pioneer Uber is not a disruptive innovation. Why? Uber targeted existing mainstream customers who were already served by taxis, not underserved customers looking for a cheaper alternative to taxis. True, Uber offered a service that was more convenient, but it was not necessarily cheaper. Customers did not consider Uber's service to be inferior in quality to existing alternatives when it was launched. For these reasons, Uber would be classified as a sustaining innovation that complemented the existing taxi business and grew the market, but it was not a disruptive innovation.

While you may disagree, Christensen's point is that not all innovations are alike – some are disruptive, but others are simply sustaining innovations that improve on existing ways of doing things.

Why does it matter whether we call it a disruptive innovation or a sustaining innovation?

Christensen argues that correctly distinguishing disruptive innovations is essential for knowing how to respond. Incumbents need to decide whether to ignore a new entrant or to respond. Christensen outlined a strategy for incumbents to follow when they see a disruptor entering their industry. Don't panic, monitor the situation, and – if necessary – respond with a disruptive business targeting the underserved customers, while continuing to serve their profitable mainstream and high-end customers by adding sustaining innovations to their current product.

Christensen highlighted several caveats for incumbents to consider when responding to disruption. First, disruption is a process that takes time. Disruptive innovations start as a small-scale experiment, which is why incumbents frequently overlook the threat. This was the case with Netflix, which launched a mail-order DVD business in 1997. Early adopters (like me) subscribed to Netflix and received DVDs through the mail and returned them via the post office. There was no internet streaming in those early days. A mail-order DVD business was disruptive to the video rental business, which was dominated by one incumbent, Blockbuster. Blockbuster did not react to the threat from Netflix, even turning down an offer to buy it from its founder. It took 13 years for Netflix to disrupt Blockbuster's business model. Blockbuster filed for bankruptcy in 2010.

Second, not every disruptive innovation is successful. Some succeed but most fail. New entrants often lack the funding, the customers, and the scale to be successful. When the money runs out, they fold. So a successful incumbent should not alter its strategy in response to every disruptive threat but should monitor the situation and act when necessary.

Third, when responding, incumbents should not overreact and abandon their profitable customers. They should continue to develop sustaining innovations for these customers. To respond to the disruptor, they can create a new division focused solely on the growth opportunities that arise from the disruption but keep it separate from the core business.

Take the example of the mutual fund company Vanguard. It saw its business being disrupted by robo-advisors like Betterment in 2007 and Wealthfront in 2011. In line with Christensen's recommendations, Vanguard did not panic. It responded by launching an in-house robo-advisor in 2015. Within two years, Vanguard dominated the automated investing business with more than 50% of the assets under management of the entire robo-advisory industry.

Christensen's theory of disruptive innovation has been extremely successful, but, like all theories, it has its shortcomings.

First, it only addresses two types of innovations – disruptive and sustaining – but many innovations do not fit these labels. For example, Christensen focused on technological innovations (how the products and services are delivered) but ignored business model innovation (how businesses charge customers and earn revenues).

A technological innovation applies an innovative technology to an existing business, but business model innovation rethinks how the company makes money. A fintech example of a business model innovation is setting up an online platform to allow customers to take out a loan electronically, with the online platform charging a commission on each loan sold.

Second, Christensen's theory is better at explaining innovations involving physical products, such as computer chips, photocopiers, and video rentals. It does not fit as well with digital businesses built on human capital.[10] Many fintech businesses are software-based and sell services, not products.

Digital Innovation Strategy

Some of these shortcomings are addressed in Harvard professor Gary Pisano's work on the strategy of digital innovation.[11] A strategy is a commitment to a set of coherent, mutually reinforcing behaviors aimed at achieving a specific goal. Good strategies clarify objectives and promote alignment among diverse groups within an organization. They focus the efforts of distinct parts of the business and create a sustainable competitive advantage.

Pisano argued that most companies fail at innovation because they lack a digital innovation strategy. Without a clear objective, the business is not able to make trade-off decisions and establish company-wide priorities. Various parts of an organization wind up pursuing conflicting priorities and pulling against each other.

Pisano's key insight is that a digital innovation strategy must be aligned with a company's business strategy. Companies can only succeed at digital innovation if they change how they are organized and run. They need to evolve and cannot continue with business as usual.

A digital innovation strategy should answer the following questions:

- How will innovation create value for potential customers? Unless innovation induces customers to pay more, saves them money, or provides some societal benefit, it is not creating value.
- How will the company capture a share of the value its innovations generate? Companies must think through what complementary assets, capabilities, products, or services will keep customers from defecting to rivals. One strategy is to create a product where the customer experiences high switching costs to defect.
- What types of innovations will allow the company to create and capture value, and what resources should each type receive? Companies have a choice between technological innovation, business model innovation, or both at the same time.

Do you see how this prescription mirrors *The Fintech Explained Lens* outlined in the previous chapter? Pisano focuses on the same fundamental questions: who, what, why, and how.

To help business leaders visualize these ideas, Pisano developed a 2x2 matrix that classifies innovations along two dimensions – technological innovations and business model innovations. Technological innovations are ways in which a company uses technology to create value for customers. Business model innovations, however, are changes in how the company captures value from customers (i.e., monetization).

Figure 2.2. Pisano's Innovation Landscape Map

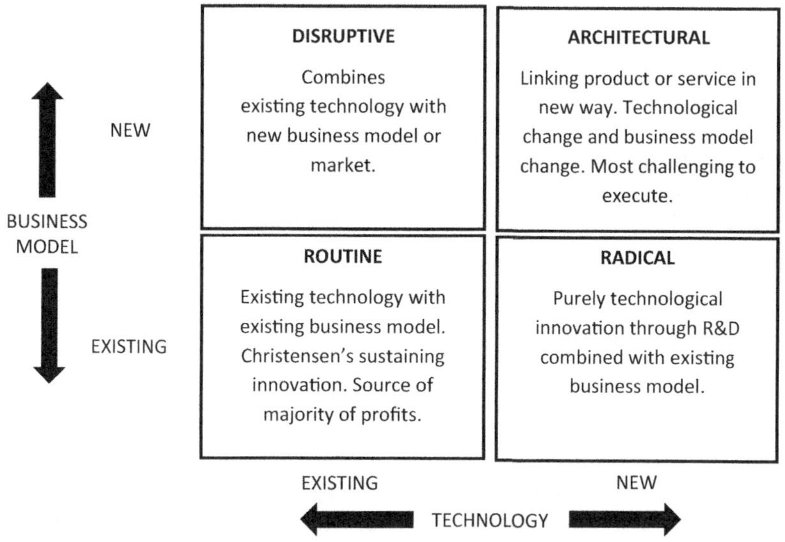

Source: Prof. Gary P. Pisano, Harvard Business School.

Pisano's Innovation Landscape Map, shown in Figure 2.2, distinguishes four types of innovations: routine, radical, disruptive, and architectural.

1 **Routine innovation** employs a company's existing technology and business model to provide an improved product or service to a company's existing customer base. Christensen calls these sustaining innovations. Routine innovations preserve the company's franchise. Examples are developing an updated version of a software program, computer chip, or mobile phone. Routine innovations are the most common and the biggest source of profitability for incumbents.

2 **Radical innovation** focuses on delivering an innovative technology using the company's existing business model. Radical innovations require investments in research and development (R&D), with the company acquiring new knowledge or capabilities. An example would be the investment by a distributor of pharmaceuticals into biotechnology or genetic engineering.

3 **Disruptive innovation**, also identified by Christensen, leverages existing technologies and competencies but requires a new business model to be successful. Innovators may develop a new way to monetize a product or service, such as giving away software, then capturing value through customer training and support.

4 **Architectural innovation** leverages a new technology and introduces a new business model. As the name suggests, this strategy involves completely rethinking a product or service. Architectural innovations are the most challenging to pursue. Pisano points to the example of digital photography that disrupted incumbents Kodak and Polaroid. To survive, both companies had to find a way to earn profits from selling cameras rather than from selling disposables (such as film, paper, and processing chemicals).

Discussions with VCs, innovation labs, and incubators suggest most fintech start-ups begin with routine or radical innovations, only to realize their business model is not viable given incumbents' customer franchise or funding advantage. To survive, these start-ups need to pivot (or evolve) their business model toward a disruptive or architectural innovation. They may also seek to partner with or be acquired by incumbents, rather than challenging them head on.

As we study different fintech companies, we will keep Pisano's Innovation Landscape Map in mind when describing their use of technology and business model. While not every fintech can be easily placed in one of these four boxes, Pisano's Innovation Landscape Map provides a useful tool that broadens Christensen's disruptive innovation theory to include business model innovations such as the multi-sided business model and SaaS businesses.

FINTECH BUSINESS MODELS

In the 1996 movie *Jerry Maguire*, the football star played by Cuba Gooding Jr. famously yells "Show me the money!" at his sports agent, played by Tom Cruise. Anyone wanting to understand fintech needs to ask the same question: How do fintechs make money?

To answer this question, we need to understand a fintech's business model. A business model describes how a business is organized to earn a profit from selling a product or service to a customer. This is also called monetization. Remember the monetization strategy is the fourth question (how?) of *The Fintech Explained Lens* introduced in Chapter 1 (Figure 2.3).

Figure 2.3. The Fintech Explained Lens

| Customer (Who?) | Pain Point (What?) | Value Proposition (Why?) | Monetization (How?) |

Figure 2.4. One-Sided Business Models in Finance

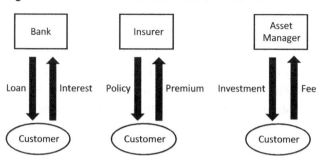

The One-Sided Business Model

A monetization strategy is tied to how the business is organized and how it charges for its products. In financial services, we distinguish two ways that incumbents and fintechs are organized: a one-sided business model and a multi-sided business model.

Traditional financial intermediaries are one-sided businesses. Banks, insurance companies, and asset managers sell products and services directly to end-customers. We call them one-sided because these businesses earn revenues from one source: the end-customer. As shown in Figure 2.4, the customer pays for a loan, an insurance policy, or investment product. The customer is charged interest on a loan, an insurance premium on a policy, or a fee as a percentage of assets under management. This is the only source of revenue from the incumbent's sale of this product.

The main products in financial services are commoditized and generic, with little to distinguish across competitors, and many close substitutes. A loan from one bank is like one offered by a rival bank. Banks, therefore, distinguish themselves from competitors based on brand and customer service, and they spend large sums on advertising. Until recently, proximity to the customer and direct contact were crucial, which explains why incumbents invested so heavily in branch networks and sales teams in the past.

Economies of scale and scope are important drivers of profitability in financial services. The largest banks, such as JPMorgan and Royal Bank of Canada, are financial conglomerates that operate like supermarkets. They combine personal and commercial banking, investment banking (also called capital markets), asset management, insurance, treasury services, and other businesses.[12] They offer the full range of financial products and services through distinct divisions, with cross-selling boosting revenues. Smaller banks tend to be more specialized, either focused on one line of business (e.g., retail or commercial banking) or focused on one jurisdiction (e.g., a country or region).

Many fintechs employ the same one-sided business models and monetization strategies as incumbents, earning agency-based and principal-based revenues. These fintechs fall under the traditional paradigm and have built digital businesses that look similar to the bricks-and-mortar incumbents. They have replaced banking with digital banking, lending with online lending, asset managers with robo-advisors, and insurance with insurtech. These fintechs may use technology to lower their costs and provide a better customer experience, but they target the same customers with the same products. In terms of Pisano's Innovation Landscape, these fintechs are engaged in routine and radical innovations, combining existing or new technologies with traditional one-sided business models. Examples are payments and billing fintechs, balance-sheet lenders, robo-advisors, digital banks, and many B2B fintechs.

The Multi-sided Business Model

Transformational fintechs are engaged in disruptive and architectural innovations, combining existing or new technologies with innovative business models. Many have adopted a multi-sided business model, which is also called a two-sided platform, a multi-sided platform, or a platform ecosystem.

A multi-sided business model brings together two or more groups to transact with each other. The business is called a platform, with the different users called the "sides" of the platform. This platform may be a physical space (such as a marketplace) or a digital one (such as a crowdfunding platform or portal). Figure 2.5 illustrates a stylized example of a multi-sided business model in fintech called the financial marketplace, which we discuss in Chapter 10.

Physical multi-sided businesses have been around for centuries. Think of a newspaper that brings together readers and advertisers, a shopping mall that brings together retail customers and stores, or a stock exchange that brings together buyers

Figure 2.5. A Multi-sided Business Model

and sellers of equities. These businesses have existed since the seventeenth century, which saw the first newspaper advertising in the UK, the covered bazaars in the Middle East, and the first stock exchange in Amsterdam.

Digital multi-sided businesses have taken off over the past two decades. This business model is employed by some of the most successful technology companies: Google, Apple, Facebook, Amazon, Alibaba, and Tencent. These companies have built multi-sided businesses around an ecosystem of products and services. The 2016 book *Matchmakers*, by David S. Evans and Richard Schmalensee, provides many case studies of multi-sided businesses that illustrate both winners and losers.[13] These authors argue that the multi-sided platform is one of the toughest business models to get right.

The growth of digital platforms since the 2000s is explained by the increased availability and low cost of computers, cloud computing and processing power, communication networks and the internet, web browsers and programming languages, and smartphones.

We find digital multi-sided businesses in crowdfunding, online lending, banking and personal finance, wealth management, and insurance. For example, the Canadian fintech Borrowell runs an online financial marketplace where traditional banks and non-bank financial companies sell credit cards, personal loans, mortgages, and other banking products to customers.[14] Borrowell subsidizes customers (subsidy-side) who get to join the platform for free and receive their free credit score. Borrowell pays for the credit score supplied by the credit bureau Equifax as part of its advertising. Borrowell earns commissions from the banks and other sellers on their platform (money-side) when customers purchase financial products.

THE IMPORTANCE OF NETWORK EFFECTS

Economists did not distinguish between the traditional one-sided business and the multi-sided business until the early 2000s. In a pioneering 2003 paper, "Platform Competition in Two-Sided Markets," the economists Jean-Charles Rochet and Nobel prize winner Jean Tirole developed an economic theory and model of multi-sided platforms.[15] They combined insights from industrial organization and network economics to describe the distinct features and business logic of this innovative business model.

Multi-sided businesses must solve a central problem: how to attract users on different sides of the platform. This is a classic chicken-and-egg problem, since users only find a multi-sided platform attractive if others are already on it. Think of a telephone network or a dating website – neither works until many users get onboard.

The key to success for a multi-sided business is to generate network effects, where adding some customers attracts others to join. We distinguish two types of network effects, called *same-side network effects* and *cross-side network effects.*

Same-side network effects, also called direct effects, occur when an increase in users on one side of the platform attracts more users on the same side. A social media platform becomes more attractive when more of your family and friends are on it; a dating app becomes more popular when more single people are on it.

Cross-side network effects, also called indirect effects, describe how attracting users on one side of the platform draws in more users on the opposite side. An increase in Facebook's monthly or daily active users makes the platform more attractive to advertisers trying to reach these users.

Increases in same-side and cross-side network effects increase the value of the multi-sided platform.

SUBSIDY-SIDE AND MONEY-SIDE

Rochet and Tirole's work generated some surprising, counterintuitive insights on the optimal pricing strategy of the multi-sided platform. They showed that a multi-sided business can maximize profits by losing money on one set of customers (called the subsidy-side) while generating revenues from another set of users (called the money-side). In other words, one set of users on the platform is a loss leader, and the other side is a profit center.

The subsidy-side customers use the platform for free or pay a small fee that does not cover the platform costs (called negative prices). These groups need to be on the platform for it to be attractive to the money-side. The money-side is charged high enough prices to cross-subsidize the losses and maximize the profit for the platform owner. Rochet and Tirole showed that it makes sense never to charge the subsidy-side, which goes against all business logic for a one-sided business model.

The reason for this subsidy business model is cross-side network effects. Think of the advertisers on Facebook's platform. If there were no users on the subsidy-side, it would not make sense to pay for advertising that no one would see. So Facebook needs to attract as many subsidy-side users as possible. And as the number of users (and their data) increases, Facebook can charge advertisers more to get in front of them with more targeted ads based on an analysis of user data.

Rochet and Tirole highlight three findings on multi-sided businesses. First, profits can be increased by heavily subsidizing marquee (or high-profile) users who make the platform more attractive to the money-side. Think of YouTube influencers who attract many subscribers to their channel.

Second, profits can be maximized by limiting access to users on the subsidy-side or the money-side to avoid competition across the platform. For example, a car company advertising on Facebook may pay more if there are fewer other auto manufacturers advertising alongside them.

Third, platform owners need to be sensitive to multihoming, where customers are active on two or more competing platforms. In these cases, the multi-sided business needs to steer users to their platform using pricing, customer experience, and other means. The profit-maximizing solution is to restore a monopoly by acquiring the competition, which explains why multi-sided platforms such as Facebook have engaged in costly acquisitions of companies like Instagram, WhatsApp, and Oculus.

Monetization Strategies in Financial Services

Let's look at how traditional financial intermediaries make money. These incumbents earn two types of revenues: agency-based revenues and principal-based revenues. These two sources are typically broken down in the financial statements but may be described using a variety of labels.

Agency-based revenues are described as fees, commissions, and insurance premiums, collectively called noninterest income. Examples of agency businesses are day-to-day banking (bank account, debit card, overdrafts), money transfer, securities settlement, and wealth management advice. Customers pay fees and commissions for these and many more agency services.

Principal-based revenues are interest income, investment income, and gains or losses on risk taking. Examples of principal businesses are lending, trading, investing, and insurance. The bank charges interest on loans or premiums on insurance policies. It invests in bonds and stocks where it receives interest and dividends. When acting as principal, a bank faces a variety of risks – credit risk on loans that default, insurance risk on policies that pay out, losses on bad investments or through trading.

Table 2.1 illustrates the revenue breakdown for four incumbents in different lines of business: a bank (JPMorgan), an asset manager (BlackRock), an insurance company (Allstate Insurance), and a payments company (Western Union). The bank earns around 65% from principal-based businesses such as lending, investing, and trading, with 35% from agency businesses. The insurance company earns most of its revenues from principal-based businesses such as insurance premiums, investment income, and gains and losses on risk taking. The asset manager and payment company earn more than 90% from agency-based businesses that generate fees and commissions.

Table 2.1 also breaks down the revenues for leading fintechs. Accurate information is available for publicly listed fintechs that disclose financial statements to their investors (LendingClub, Revolut, PayPal, SoFi, ZhongAn). For the private companies in this table (Kickstarter, Credit Karma, Wealthfront), the breakdown is based on reports by experts in this area.

Table 2.1. Revenue Breakdown for Incumbents vs. Fintechs, 2020

	Agency-Based[1] (%)	Principal-Based[2] (%)	Total Revenues (%)
INCUMBENTS:			
Bank (JPMorgan)	35	65	100
Asset manager (BlackRock)	95	5	100
Payments company (Western Union)	100	0	100
Insurance company (Allstate)	2	98	100
FINTECHS:			
Challenger bank (Revolut)	101	−1	100
Online lender (LendingClub)	116	−16	100
Online lender (SoFi)	69	31	100
Crowdfunding platform (Kickstarter)	100	0	100
Financial marketplace (Credit Karma)	100	0	100
Robo-advisor (Wealthfront)	100	0	100
Payments company (PayPal)	92	8	100
Insurtech (ZhongAn)	4	96	100

1. Fees and commissions.
2. Net interest income, investment income, net premiums earned, gains and losses on risk taking.
Source: Company annual reports.

The majority of fintechs are agency-based businesses that earn 90% or more of their revenues from fees and commissions. Agency-based revenues dominate for online lenders, challenger banks, crowdfunding platforms, financial marketplaces, payment companies, and robo-advisors. The two exceptions in this table are the on-line lender SoFi and the insurtech ZhongAn. SoFi earned 31% of revenues from lend-ing because SoFi has been transitioning from a marketplace lender to a full-service bank that holds loans on its own balance sheet. The insurtech ZhongAn looks like a traditional insurer, earning 96% of revenues from underwriting – a principal-based business.

FINANCIAL BUSINESSES AT RISK OF DISRUPTION

What makes a business vulnerable to disruption? This question has been tackled by McKinsey consultants in their article "The Economic Essentials of Digital Strategy."[16] They advise a company to "know thyself." A Goliath global bank such as JPMorgan doesn't necessarily have to fear all the entrepreneurial Davids in the fintech start-up space. But it doesn't help to be complacent and unaware of your weaknesses. The McKinsey consultants advise incumbents to check their business models for these signs of vulnerability to digital disruption:

- Some customers cross-subsidize other customers
- Customers must buy the whole product to get the part they want
- Customers cannot get what they want, where and when they want it
- The customer experience does not match global best practice

A financial intermediary is vulnerable if they offer an undifferentiated, bundled product to a large pool of customers, where the more profitable ones cross-subsidize the less profitable ones. Customers do not have choice but face an all-or-nothing proposition. And they receive poor or no service, maybe supported by one call center handling all inquiries and complaints.

This dismal image described the highly profitable credit card business in the 1990s and 2000s. Historically, credit cards have been an oligopoly controlled by MasterCard, VISA, and American Express. They operate electronic networks that connect banks and merchants globally and collect a hefty fee called interchange. In the case of MasterCard and VISA, they manage the physical infrastructure and digital network but leave the actual credit provision to banks or other card issuers, who extend loans to the holders.

The standard credit card used to offer a fixed menu of features and charged customers a high monthly interest rate. By bundling standardized features such as product insurance and rewards with all cards, card issuers kept their overhead low and spread this fixed cost over a large customer base. Pooling customers with different credit profiles allowed the card issuers to use the most creditworthy customers to cover write-offs for the least creditworthy. The customer experience may have been poor, but credit cards were accepted almost everywhere as a means of payment.

The credit card business was ripe for disruption. It was profitable and costly for the customer, with a one-sided business model built on bundling and pooling that was vulnerable to a new entrant willing to leverage technology to offer customers a cheaper, more differentiated product. Customers with lower credit risk expected to pay less. Some customers did not want to collect points and preferred to pay no fee instead. These customers were underserved by existing card issuers.

It wasn't long until fintechs like challenger bank Revolut entered the credit card business. Revolut offers a credit card under the slogan "Get the credit you deserve, and benefits you'll love."[17] Customers apply online or through Revolut's mobile app and get an answer in minutes. If approved, the credit card has no annual fee and starts with a high borrowing limit and a 14% annual percentage rate. Revolut helps customers budget by setting a spending limit and generating reports. It helps customers avoid paying interest charges by scheduling automatic payments and sending reminders. Customers can add features and customize their card, only paying for what they want.

Credit cards are just one example, but the same pooling and bundling exists in lending, capital raising, investing, payments, and insurance. We will see how fintechs in these lines of business are exploiting technology and big data to offer custom-ized, niche solutions to underserved customers at a lower cost. Remember the fintech value proposition: cheaper, easier, faster, and more convenient.

Key Terms

architectural innovation	net interest income
business model	network effects
cross-side network effects	noninterest income
digital innovation strategy	one-sided business
disruptive innovation	platform ecosystem
financial intermediary	principal-agent problem
industrial organization	radical innovation
information asymmetry	relationship banking
innovation landscape	risk sharing
liquidity creation	routine (sustaining) innovation
maturity transformation	same-side network effects
moral hazard	transaction costs
multi-sided business	transactional banking

QUESTIONS FOR DISCUSSION

1 Why does fintech require a multidisciplinary perspective to see the big picture? What disciplines are most relevant for understanding fintech?
2 What are the five dimensions of financial intermediation and how are fintechs address-ing them?
3 What is the principal-agent problem? What examples do we see in financial services?
4 What is maturity transformation and how does it relate to liquidity creation?
5 What is the meaning of disruption? What are the key features of Christensen's theory of disruptive innovation?
6 What are the four types of digital innovations from Pisano's Innovation Landscape Map?
7 What are the key differences between a one-sided business model and a multi-sided business model?
8 What are network effects, and what are the two main types?
9 What is the counterintuitive pricing structure for a multi-sided platform? What are the subsidy-side and the money-side of the platform?
10 How does the breakdown of revenues for fintechs compare to traditional financial intermediaries?

ADDITIONAL READING

Christensen, Clayton M., Michael E. Raynor, and Rory McDonald, "What Is Disruptive Innovation?" *Harvard Business Review* (December 2015): 44–53.

Dawson, Angus, Martin Hirt, and Jay Scanlan, "The Economic Essentials of Digital Strategy," *McKinsey Quarterly*, March 2016, https://www.mckinsey.com/business-functions/strategy-and-corporate-finance/our-insights/the-economic-essentials-of-digital-strategy.

Evans, David S., and Richard Schmalensee, *Matchmakers: The New Economics of Multisided Platforms* (Boston: Harvard Business Review Press, 2016).

Philippon, Thomas, "The Fintech Opportunity," NBER Working Paper 22476, August 2016, https://www.nber.org/papers/w22476.

Pisano, Gary P., "You Need an Innovation Strategy," *Harvard Business Review* (June 2015): 44–54.

Rochet, Jean-Charles, and Jean Tirole, "Platform Competition in Two-Sided Markets," *Journal of the European Economics Association* 1, no. 4 (2003): 990–1029, https://doi.org/10.1162/154247603322493212.

Rysman, Marc, "The Economics of Two-Sided Markets," *Journal of Economic Perspectives* 23, no. 3 (2009): 125–143.

3

Funding of Early-Stage Fintech Companies

SUMMARY

- Fintech founders at the pre-seed stage bootstrap their start-ups using their own savings and may raise money from family and friends.
- Once they have a minimum viable product, founders may approach angel investors for the seed funding required to survive the Valley of Death.
- Fintechs with monthly recurring revenue may pitch venture capitalists who will want to know the size of the total addressable market and the skills of the founding team.
- To scale and grow their business, fintechs raise capital through a series of funding rounds (Series A through F) until potential exit via an initial public offering or acquisition.
- Early-stage funding may take the form of a convertible note, a Simple Agreement for Future Equity (SAFE), preferred shares, common shares, or venture debt.
- A capitalization table shows the pre-money and post-money ownership at each funding round, reflecting dilution from broadening the investor base.

The previous chapter provided a theoretical framework for understanding fintech that covered different economic theories, strategies, and business models.

This chapter examines the funding of fintech start-ups. We examine the different growth stages and funding rounds, the types of securities issued to raise capital, and the capitalization table.

Figure 3.1. Growth Stages of a Fintech Start-Up

	1. EARLY STAGE		2. GROWTH STAGE	3. LATE STAGE & EXIT
FUNDING	Pre-Seed	Seed	Series A to F	IPO or Acquisition
BENCHMARKS	Idea	Minimum Viable Product	Monthly Recurring Revenue	Stable Cash Flow, Earnings
INVESTORS	Founders, Friends, & Family	Angels	Venture Capitalists	Public or Strategic (Business)
CASH FLOW ENTERPRISE VALUE				

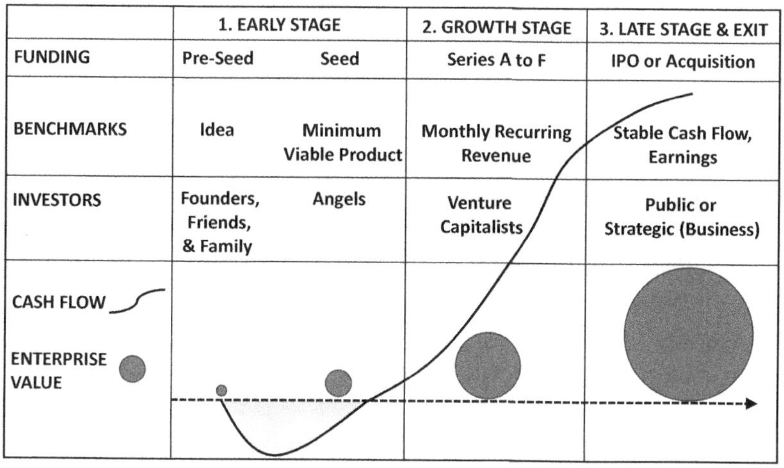

GROWTH STAGES AND FUNDING ROUNDS

Start-ups, like people, grow in stages, passing through different periods of development. Over the first 20 years of life, a human being grows from childhood through adolescence to early adulthood, with physiological changes occurring at each state. Similarly, over the first 5 to 10 years of its life, a fintech start-up may pass through three distinct stages: early stage, growth stage, and late stage and exit. Each stage has its associated challenges to overcome, particularly raising funding. Investors will monitor key benchmarks to evaluate a start-up's progress along its journey. At each stage, a fintech may raise capital by issuing different financial securities to scale the business.

Figure 3.1 illustrates the growth stages of a fintech start-up, the associated funding rounds, the benchmarks of its development, and the likely investors at each round. The solid black line shows the evolution of the start-up's cash flow. Finally, it shows the implied value of the business, called the enterprise value (EV). Despite the dilution of the founders' equity stake at each funding round, the EV of the business should grow, assuming it does not shut down or go bankrupt.

EARLY STAGE: PRE-SEED AND SEED FUNDING

Early-stage growth is divided into two funding periods called the pre-seed stage and the seed stage. This stage is when an idea for a start-up is incubated and begins to grow into a business. The founders need to fund themselves while they write a business plan, incorporate their company, prototype a product or service, and sign up their first customers.

Surviving the Pre-Seed Stage

At the pre-seed stage, the start-up's cash flow is negative. Founders typically "bootstrap" their start-up using personal savings, paying the bills out of their own pockets. They are figuratively pulling themselves up by their own shoelaces. Some founders may continue to work full-time or part-time in a salaried job. But starting a business is all-consuming and rarely leaves time for anything else. Most founders quit their jobs to work on their idea full time, in which case they lose their source of income and survive on their savings.

During these early months, many founders turn to family and friends for money when no outsiders are willing to risk their capital. Given most start-ups fail, this funding source is jokingly referred to as "Family, Friends, and Fools" (FFF).

During the pre-seed stage, founders may save money by working from home (out of the proverbial garage). Or they may use a co-working space or spend time in a business incubator.

An incubator is a specialized co-working space where entrepreneurs get free use of a desk for a limited time. Incubators are typically publicly funded and provide access to basic office services and mentoring to help founders get their idea off the ground. Incubators offer a community that allows different entrepreneurs to network with each other, cross-fertilize ideas, and potentially become business partners or customers. At last count there were 1,400+ business incubators in the US and another 3,200+ co-working spaces.[1]

Another potential source of pre-seed funding is rewards-based crowdfunding. Crowdfunding is the process of raising money through an online portal from many individuals, known as the crowd, who each contribute a small amount. The most likely source of cash for a pre-seed company is rewards-based crowdfunding. Supporters (called backers) pay upfront to finance the development of a product or service, with the expectation they will receive it when the start-up is up and running.

Founders pitch their project using a dedicated crowdfunding page on a portal like Kickstarter, where they describe their vision and their business model. Each backer contributes a small amount toward a stated funding goal, where the money may only be distributed by the platform if the targeted amount is met (called all-or-nothing crowdfunding). We will talk more about rewards-based crowdfunding in Chapter 7.

Seed Stage and Minimum Viable Product

The next stage in a fintech start-up's funding lifecycle is the seed stage. At the seed stage, the founders typically have developed a minimum viable product (MVP), which is the most basic product or service that has just enough features and functionality to attract the first paying customers. The MVP is a rough prototype, which is then improved based on feedback and discussion with these early adopters. It may be a fintech app that is in the beta phase, meaning it is the earliest working version but will undergo many more improvements.

Feedback from early adopters allows the start-up to refine their value proposition and business model as they search for product-market fit. The phrase *product-market fit* is attributed to Don Valentine, a partner at Sequoia Capital in Silicon Valley, but has since been popularized by many venture capitalists and founders.[2]

A key hurdle during the seed stage of development is surviving the "Valley of Death." The Valley of Death is the 12- to 18-month period when a new business is spending money but not earning any revenues. It is shown by the solid line in Figure 3.1, when cash flow is negative. The start-up is running out of cash and may die unless it can attract liquidity. The aspiring founders are struggling to get a new business off the ground; they have an idea but no revenues. They need to find a deeper pool of capital than can be provided by FFFs.

The length of time a start-up can survive in the Valley of Death depends on the funding raised and the cash burn rate. The burn rate measures how much cash is being spent (or burned up) each month. A start-up must "burn before you earn." Cash is spent on a long list of items: research and development (R&D), computer and other equipment, advertising, hiring, overhead, and possibly minimal salaries for the team. The rule of thumb puts the cash burn rate at $15,000 per employee per month. So, a team of four will need $1 million to survive for 18 months: $15,000 × 4 × 18.

For this reason, a seed funding round typically raises between $500,000 to $2,000,000 to finance operations for 12 to 24 months. To raise the cash required, the founders typically sell 10% to 20% of their company to outside investors.

Angel Investors

The most likely source of funding for early-stage companies is angel investors. An angel investor, also called a business angel, is a wealthy individual – typically a successful entrepreneur or business executive – who is willing to invest in high-risk, early-stage fintech companies. Angels are cautious and skeptical, particularly when approached by an early-stage company with no operating history and no profits.

They will want to conduct due diligence on the founders, their idea, the product or service, and the market opportunity before investing.

Angels have idiosyncratic motivations. They may be looking to give back by financing and mentoring young entrepreneurs. Or they may be looking to earn a high return from investing and advising a start-up. Of course, it could be both reasons.

A survey by the US Angel Capital Association found that the average US angel was 57 years old, typically male (78%), with more than half of angels having founded or been the CEO of a start-up.[3] The average angel invested in 11 start-ups (and the median angel in 7 start-ups). More experienced and, therefore, successful angels invested in more deals. The average check was $25,000, so the total portfolio was around $250,000.

Angels usually restrict their investments to 10% of their net worth and spread their bets across a portfolio of start-ups. The reason is simple: Seed stage investing is very risky. The statistics show that 9 out of 10 angel investments either return the original investment or fail completely. Given this risk, securities regulations in many countries restrict angel investing to accredited investors, who are individuals meeting minimum thresholds of net worth or income.

Discussions with angels suggest the key success factors for this risky type of investing are experience, time spent on due diligence, and coaching and mentoring founders to increase the start-up's chances of success.

Angels may screen dozens of start-ups before deciding to invest. And when they do invest at the seed stage, it is typically an unpriced round. An unpriced round means investors provide cash without putting a specific value on the start-up. It is a struggle to value an early-stage, pre-revenue business, particularly when the size of the market opportunity is unknown. For this reason, angels rely on their historical experience and rules of thumb. We will cover their valuation methodologies in the next chapter.

The Elevator Pitch

To raise early-stage funding from angels, the founder will make the rounds and give their elevator pitch. What is an elevator pitch? It is a 30-second sales pitch on a business idea that is short enough to give while riding between floors in an elevator. It must be clear, direct, and compelling. If the potential investor is not convinced by the time the elevator doors open, they will walk away and the opportunity will be lost.

Let's imagine how an elevator pitch might look.

You are a fintech founder looking to raise capital for your start-up. You have identified a local angel. They have a busy schedule and are constantly on the go between meetings and social engagements. You see they are attending a start-up conference nearby. You corner the angel at the conference (maybe during a coffee break) and make your pitch, asking them to invest. If the pitch is persuasive, they may book a time to hear more and review your business plan.

What does this angel investor need to hear? As discussed in Chapter 1, your elevator pitch needs to answer the four questions from *The Fintech Explained Lens*:

1 Who is the customer? ("customer segment")
2 What is their pain point or unmet need? ("pain point")
3 Why will customers pay for your product or service? ("value proposition")
4 How will your start-up make money? ("monetization strategy")

Let's quickly review these four questions before illustrating the elevator pitch using the case study of the robo-advisor Wealthsimple below.

First, who is the customer? Successful fintechs clearly define the targeted customer segment. Either these customers are underserved by incumbents or their needs are not being met by the market. The customers may be retail or small business customers (B2C), an incumbent (B2B), or an incumbent's customers (B2B2C). Or the fintech may be developing a multi-sided business that allows for customer-to-customer transactions (i.e., P2P).

Second, what is the customer's pain point? A successful fintech identifies a problem or unmet need experienced by their targeted customer in managing their finances. The pain point is specific and one that a customer wants to go away. The fintech leverages technology and design thinking to propose a compelling solution.

Third, what is the value proposition? The customer must be willing to pay for the solution to their pain point. If no one will pay for the fintech product or service, it obviously has no value. Because people have short attention spans, the value proposition must be short, clear, and easy to understand. If the customer does not immediately see the value in what is for sale, the start-up has not found product-market fit. The founder must change the idea in response to this feedback and pivot the business in a new direction.

Fourth, how will the fintech make money? The founder must explain how they plan to capture some of the value created for customers. This is the monetization strategy. The angel will want to see a future exit that generates a large return on their investment. The fintech may charge customers a subscription to use an app (called software-as-a-service, or SaaS) or collect a fee when a customer purchases financial products and services through the fintech's online portal. There are many creative ways to monetize a good business idea.

The Returns to Angel Investing

Angels measure their investment performance using a simple multiple called money-on-money (or cash-on-cash). They divide any money received at exit by the money invested upfront, so money out ÷ money in. If they invest $25,000 today and get back $250,000 in the future, they describe it as a 10x return ($250,000 ÷ $25,000).

The average angel targets a 9–10x return on an investment over an eight-year horizon, which equals an internal rate of return (IRR) of approximately 33%. IRR measures the compound annual rate of return (or growth rate) on the investment. While this IRR may seem great, it does not consider the probability of failure. Studies find that fewer than 10% of angel investments generate a positive return, so the angel needs to win big on one investment to cover the losses on others in their portfolio.

Surveys of angels show that bigger numbers increase the chances of a positive exit.[4] For angels making up to 10 investments, less than 8% of investments generate a positive exit, with the rest losing money or returning the original investment. For angels making more than 10 investments, the odds improve with 12% to 15% generating a positive exit. Overall, the average IRR on a diversified portfolio is estimated around 27%. But if the angel does not diversify and makes only a few investments, they can lose everything if they back losing businesses.

One way for smaller angels to diversify is to pool their capital and invest in groups. The members of an angel group combine their experience and resources to source deals, screen companies, invest, and mentor founders to a successful exit. A survey of US angels found that 66% of investors initially got involved by joining an angel group and 86% invested through an angel group at some point in time.[5]

Angels typically write only a small check initially but make follow-on investments and increase their committed capital over time as the start-up grows and passes key milestones. Around three-quarters of US angels make at least one follow-on investment, with close to half of angels making three or more follow-on investments. Angels may continue to invest all the way until exit when they sell their shares.

As angel investing becomes more popular, one criticism of angels and angel groups is they are behaving more like VCs and focusing more on financial returns and less on mentoring start-ups. Angels have become more professional, more adversarial, and more demanding, making them less attractive for founders to work with. At the same time, some VCs have moved into early-stage investing with funds dedicated to seed round investments.

Other Sources of Seed Funding

Fintech start-ups may raise cash from other sources than FFFs and angels. Three potential sources are a start-up accelerator, government grants, or equity crowdfunding.

A start-up accelerator (also called a seed accelerator) is a limited-duration program that helps cohorts of start-ups to accelerate their growth before graduating from the program. An accelerator is run by business advisors and executives-in-residence who challenge the founders, refine the customer value proposition and business model, make introductions to business contacts, and share their expertise and experiences.

Founders must apply and be accepted to the program, with the accelerator screening hundreds of applications. The cohort of start-ups then spends three to six months together in residence at the accelerator. Each day features a structured set of activities designed to accelerate the growth and success of the start-up. Participation in the accelerator usually comes with an investment of seed capital. The program concludes with a pitch day where the founders present their business to a curated group of angels or VCs in the hopes they invest down the road.

The most famous Silicon Valley accelerators are Y Combinator (founded in 2005) and Techstars (founded in 2007). Both accelerators have a 1% to 2% acceptance rate.

Since 2005, Silicon Valley's Y Combinator has invested in over 3,500 companies. Of this total, 15% were fintech and 3% were blockchain and crypto. As of 2022, Y Combinator invests $500,000 in every company that participates in its program. The estimated market valuation of its start-up alumni is nearing $1 trillion. Twice a year, Y Combinator selects a cohort of up to 400 companies to participate in their three-month curriculum. The training has 10 steps: the goal, funding, groups, office hours, networking among founders, bootcamp, talks from successful entrepreneurs, public launches, first customers, and demo day.[6]

Since 2006, Techstars has invested in 3,300 start-ups.[7] Of this total, 7% were fintech or financial services and 1.5% were blockchain and crypto. Techstars invests up to $120,000 in each of its start-ups, beginning with $20,000 upfront in equity and an optional $100,000 convertible note. Techstars then reserves the right to purchase 6% of the company's fully diluted capital stock at the time of a qualified financing, called a preemptive right. As of 2022, the combined market capitalization of Techstars graduate companies was $79 billion. Techstars has accelerators located around the world, with 38 in-person locations in 2022. Each cohort has 10 start-ups, and each month of the three-month curriculum has a different theme: grow your network, execute, and fundraising strategy and demo day.

Governments grants, programs, and tax credits are also available to help entrepreneurs get off the ground. This funding does not require giving up ownership, but it is only available once other conditions are met. For example, the Canadian government's Scientific Research and Experimental Development (SR&ED) program provides tax credits for R&D expenditures that can be used to offset taxes. But a fintech start-up will not see any benefit until they earn a profit and start to pay taxes. Government programs may provide access to business mentors, research facilities, data, or other valuable in-kind resources that help founders to succeed.

Crowdfunding is raising small amounts of capital from many individual investors. It can take the form of a pre-purchase of a product (rewards-based), a donation, a loan, or an equity investment. We talked about rewards-based crowdfunding under pre-seed funding. Equity crowdfunding is where founders sell common shares to individual investors through an online portal. For example, AngelList specializes in early-stage funding for technology start-ups. Individual investors commit between $1,000 and $10,000 to a deal. They become shareholders with a vote and a legal claim on future profits and company assets. Because of the high risk involved, regulations limit the amount a retail investor can invest in a start-up. Some crowdfunding platforms are only open to accredited investors with no restrictions on the amount invested. We will discuss equity crowdfunding in more depth in Chapter 7.

CASE STUDY: WEALTHSIMPLE'S SEED-STAGE FUNDING PITCH

Let's look at the seed-stage funding pitch for one of Canada's most successful fintechs, the robo-advisor Wealthsimple. This online investment service was founded in 2014 by 26-year-old Mike Katchen. Katchen graduated in 2009 with an undergraduate degree in business before spending three years as a business analyst with the consulting firm McKinsey & Company. Katchen left in 2011 to join the two-year-old start-up 1000memories, which was acquired by Ancestry.com in 2013. Katchen and his fellow founders found themselves with money to invest, so Katchen created an Excel spreadsheet and began investing their savings in exchange traded funds (ETFs). The positive feedback from his friends led Katchen and two of the 1000memories founders to launch Wealthsimple in 2014. By the end of the year, Wealthsimple had 1,000 investors, demonstrating they had found product-market fit.

With a minimum viable product, Katchen raised $2 million in a seed round in May 2014 from 14 angel investors. In an editorial describing his success, Katchen offered this advice to aspiring founders:[8]

> A compelling deck, aka presentation, is short, clear and well designed. If you have a solid story, then tell it in four to five pages: (1) what you do, (2) market size, (3) team, (4) growth plan, (5, optional) competition … Keep it short, pretty and exciting.

In conjunction with this article, Katchen posted his eight-page Wealthsimple pitch deck online.[9] See if you can spot the answers to the four questions from *The Fintech Explained Lens* (target customer, pain point, value proposition, monetization strategy). Here are the eight pages of his pitch deck:

1 THE INVESTMENT INDUSTRY IS TRANSFORMING

The first slide set the context for the business, using the table below to illustrate how investing was being transformed by technology.

Industry transformations by decade	
1980s	Mutual funds transform the way investors save for retirement
1990s	Discount brokerage creates an easy, low-cost solution for DIY investors
2000s	ETFs become a credible, low-cost, liquid alternative to mutual funds
2010s	Online solutions democratize access to sophisticated investment management

2 WEALTHSIMPLE – SMART INVESTING MADE SIMPLE

The second slide showed the main page from the Wealthsimple website with these words below in white against a blue background: SEE HOW WE DO IT

3 WHAT WE DO

The third slide outlined the targeted customer segment, the value proposition, and the monetization strategy.

"Wealthsimple is a technology-driven investment manager. We target young professionals that want a smarter and simpler way to invest their savings.

We invest clients' assets in a fully diversified portfolio of ETFs based on their risk profile. Clients can sign up, fund an account, and track performance via web or mobile device.

We charge 35–50 bps on assets (a lot less than everyone else). Our clients range from 19–74 years old and we currently service accounts of all sizes ($5,000, $500,000, and $5,000,000+)."

4 THE CANADIAN MARKET OPPORTUNITY

The fourth slide had a figure outlining the size of the market opportunity. To the left, a large blue circle showed that the full-service investing market generated $1 trillion in revenues. Below it read "High minimums, High fees, Service oriented." To the right, a small blue circle showed that the self-directed investing market generated $0.3 trillion in revenues, with the description "Low fees, Knowledge hurdle, No advice." In between, Wealthsimple fills a massive gap in this $1.3 trillion market with the descriptor "Low fees, Low minimums, Light advice."

5 US CASE EXAMPLE

The fifth slide showed a bar chart graphing the rise in assets under management for the US robo-advisor Wealthfront, which had grown to $1 billion in assets under management in two years from 2012 to 2014. Under the bar chart it read, "US market leader for online light advice. Added >$1B in 2014: now at almost $2B. One of several US players with >$500MM in assets."

6 OUR TEAM

The sixth slide showed the founding team and their bios, led by Mike Katchen. The other five employees included two of the founders of 1000memories, Brett Honeycutt and Rudy Adler, as Chief Operation Officer and Product Designer, respectively, plus a portfolio manager and two software engineers. It also listed two high-profile advisors, the former CEO of a leading wealth management firm and a business school professor.

7 CLIENT ACQUISITION

The seventh slide provided detail on the size of the market opportunity. The main part of the slide was blocked out with the apology "Not sharing at this time … sorry." Below, it read, "Target market: young professionals, 25–45 years old. Top income decile but don't yet have the required assets to hire traditional advisors."

8 VALUE TO CLIENTS

The final appendix slide showed key facts about the competitors, Wealthsimple's targeted client segment, and the value proposition.

	Full-Service Advisors	Wealthsimple	Self-Directed Brokerage
Minimums	$250,000+	$5,000	$1,000–5,000
Cost	145 bps	50 bps	$9–29/trade
Ease of Use	Relationship driven: relies on "expert"	Fund and go; intuitive interface	Knowledge hurdle; time and effort
Benefits	Lots of support; familiar to client	Light-support; saves time and money; accessible	Full-control; advanced features

GROWTH STAGE: SERIES A TO F FUNDING

If a start-up makes it through the Valley of Death and finds product-market fit, they enter the growth stage. The key metric to judge whether a start-up is gaining traction is monthly recurring revenue (MRR). MRR is sales income the start-up can count on receiving each month as it signs up more customers. It demonstrates the willingness of early adopters to pay repeatedly for a product or service. At this growth stage, the start-up may become cash flow positive, with inflows exceeding outflows. The founders' goal is to see exponential growth in MRR reflecting a rapid increase in number of paying customers. If MRR does not grow, the founders will be forced to pivot in a new direction or the start-up will fail.

Figure 3.2. Stripe Funding Rounds and Post-Money Valuation

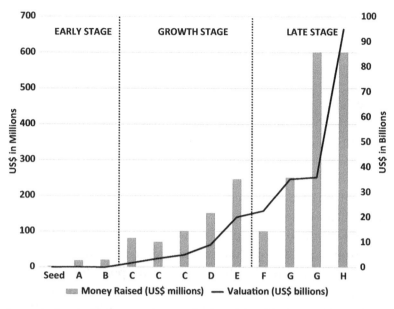

Source: Author, data from company press releases and Crunchbase.

To grow and scale the business, a fintech start-up will need to raise larger quantities of capital. The founders need to hire more employees for both product development and sales. They need to invest in R&D and spend on marketing and advertising to acquire customers. The cost of customer acquisition for a B2C fintech is very high, estimated at $500 to $1,000 in advertising per customer acquired.

The first "priced round" for a start-up is known as the Series A round. A priced round assigns an explicit valuation to the fintech start-up's business and sets a price for its common shares. The typical valuation is $2.5 million to $5.0 million. Subsequent funding rounds are referred to as Series B, Series C, and so on. Collectively they may be called growth stage or late-stage investing.

It used to be rare to see more than a handful of funding rounds for a start-up, as each one increased the shares outstanding and diluted the founders' ownership stake. But some high-profile start-ups have raised six or more rounds while remaining private.

The global payments fintech Stripe, founded in Ireland by brothers Patrick and John Collison, is building an economic infrastructure for the internet. Stripe provides software allowing businesses of all sizes to accept online payments in more than 100 countries. Figure 3.2 shows that Stripe raised a total of $2.235 billion from its seed round in August 2010 to its Series H round in March 2021. In its Series H round,

Stripe raised $600 million at a post-money valuation of $95 billion, making it the most valuable private tech company in Silicon Valley.[10] The primary investors included the venture capital firm Sequoia Capital; large financial service players (Allianz X, Axa, Baillie Gifford, Fidelity Management & Research Company); and Ireland's National Treasury Management Agency.

Venture Capitalists (VCs)

The main source of growth capital is venture capital. A VC is a professional asset manager who invests the partners' own money and the money of clients into a portfolio of growth-stage companies. A VC will target an IRR of 20% to 30% on the portfolio, reflecting the continued high risk of investing in entrepreneurial start-ups. Half the companies in a typical VC portfolio will fail, 20% will return the initial investment and break even, 20% will earn a 2–4x return, and 10% will earn a supernormal return. With an investment horizon of 5 to 10 years, this supernormal return must generate a 50x to 60x return to achieve the targeted 20% to 30% IRR for the portfolio.

A VC's clients are high net–worth individuals, family offices, and institutional investors. The VC establishes an investment fund as a limited partnership (LP) or limited liability company (LLC). The VC partners are the general partners ("GPs"), and the investors in the fund are the limited partners ("LPs"). The GPs are active and the LPs passive. VC investment funds have a limited life of up to 10 years before they must liquidate their investments and return the capital to investors. There are many famous VCs investors in the United States, with the leading technology VCs located in the San Francisco Bay Area of California, including Andreessen Horowitz, Kleiner Perkins, New Enterprise Associates, and Sequoia Capital. VCs may specialize by company lifecycle (early stage, late stage), sector, or technology. According to CB Insights, the most active VCs in fintech are reportedly Sequoia Capital, 500startups, Ribbit Capital, Accel, and Global Founders Capital (GFC).[11]

Let's take a closer look at Sequoia Capital, the VC based in Menlo Park, California. Sequoia was started in 1972 by Don Valentine, who is described as the grandfather of Silicon Valley venture capital.[12] He chose to name the firm after the Sequoia tree that lives thousands of years, symbolizing his vision to empower generations of technology entrepreneurs. Valentine's initial $3 million fund invested in both Apple Computer and the video game console Atari. He also invested in Oracle, Cisco Systems, and Electronic Arts, among many others.

By 2022, Sequoia had $85 billion of assets under management invested in a portfolio of seed stage, early-stage, and growth-stage investments in private companies across technology sectors. The LPs in Sequoia's funds have primarily been university endowments, charitable foundations, and other large institutions. Crunchbase reports that Sequoia has raised 33 funds and made 1,760 investments as of late 2022.[13] Its highest profile fintech investments are Klarna, Nubank, PayPal, Robinhood, Square, and Stripe.

Total Addressable Market

VCs, like angel investors, will also want to hear answers to the questions from *The Fintech Explained Lens*. VCs will also want to know the size of the market opportunity for a fintech's business, sometimes called the total addressable market (TAM). The TAM represents the total revenues in dollars available for a given product or service across all companies operating in this business. The TAM sets an upper bound on a fintech start-up's revenues. If a company has a 100% market share, their sales will theoretically equal the TAM, which is obviously not realistic.

Since there is no agreed definition of TAM, reasonable people disagree on how to measure it. Paul Graham from Y Combinator describes TAM this way:

> So, to prove you're worth investing in, you don't have to prove you're going to succeed, just that you're a sufficiently good bet. What makes a start-up a sufficiently good bet? In addition to formidable founders, you need a plausible path to owning a big piece of a big market. Founders think of start-ups as ideas, but investors think of them as markets. If there are x number of customers who'd pay an average of $Y per year for what you're making, then the total addressable market, or TAM, of your company is $XY. Investors don't expect you to collect all that money, but it's an upper bound on how big you can get.[14]

Some investors prefer to focus on the customer segment targeted by a business, called the serviceable available market (SAM). This is the revenues for a slice of the overall market, making the SAM a subset of the TAM.

If we take the example of at the world of investing, the TAM is the sum of all assets under management globally, which was estimated to be more than US$112 trillion in 2021.[15] If we are talking about the SAM for a robo-advisor like Wealthsimple, however, the SAM may be restricted to a subset of customers such as "high-earning not rich yet" millennials (HENRYs).

The serviceable obtainable market (SOM) is the fraction of the SAM that the fintech start-up hopes to capture. If the wealth management industry has a TAM of $112 trillion in assets under management, and the HENRYs segment represents 0.5% or $560 billion, then a robo-advisor who captures 10% of this SAM will have a SOM of $56 billion. If they charge 50 basis points on this SOM, revenues could be $280 million!

Without getting too hung up on these distinctions, how can we realistically estimate the size of the market opportunity for a fintech's products or services? There are three approaches:

1 Top-down: using industry research to identify the potential market size
2 Bottom-up: based on the number of customers times the revenue per customer
3 Theoretical: based on a best guess of what the customer is willing to pay

The top-down approach to the market opportunity may appear to be the easiest but is the least convincing. It typically relies on a third-party expert assessment, which provides the illusion of credibility, but it may not be convincing to an investor. Many firms claim to be experts and provide estimates of market size. In the technology space two examples are the global research firms Gartner Inc. and International Data Corporation (IDC). Both companies focus on the trends affecting a variety of sectors and publish research and insights on market size and growth. They are expert guessers.

A more informative approach to estimate the market opportunity is to forecast sales based on the number of customers multiplied by the price of the product or service. The starting point is to identify the number of customers in the targeted segment.

Assume you are opening a new fitness club for millennials in New York City. New York City has a population of 8.6 million, of which 1.9 million are between the ages of 18 and 34 years old. If one-quarter of this population were members of a fitness club, the targeted customer segment would be 475,000 individuals = 25% × 1.9 million. If the average fitness club membership was $50 per month, then the annual sales for this business would be $285 million = 475,000 × $50 × 12. Of course, a new fitness club might only capture a small share of this SAM. If the start-up captured a 10% market share, the expected annual revenues (or SOM) would be $28.5 million.

A bottom-up estimate of the market opportunity may be more convincing because it demonstrates the entrepreneur has thought carefully about their business. This estimate is calculated using tangible, relatable data on customers and pricing. The bottom-up approach turns the discussion from a statement of industry size into a discussion about breadth of potential product-market fit.

Top-down and bottom-up approaches to calculating the market opportunity may not work for an innovative product or service with no established market. Many high-growth technology-based companies have created new markets with their products, such as Apple with online music (iTunes), Facebook with social media, and Zopa with P2P lending. In each case, the founders could not rely on expert opinions or market statistics to generate a sales forecast. Instead, they had to rely on theory, which is a sophisticated way of saying "best guess."

CASE STUDY: WISE FINANCIAL'S PAIN POINT AND MARKET OPPORTUNITY

Wise Financial (known as TransferWise until 2021) started as an international money transfer business in 2011.[16] Wise was founded by two Estonian friends, Taavet Hinrikus and Kristo Käärmann, who were living in London, UK. Taavet was the first employee at the voice-over-internet company Skype, lived in London, and got paid in euros. Kristo worked for the consultancy Deloitte, also lived in London, and got paid in British pounds.

Here was the problem. Kristo had a mortgage back in Estonia denominated in euros. In order to make his payments, he deposited his British pounds into his bank account and had to convert it to euros to make his mortgage payments. His bank charged expensive fees and offered bad exchange rates. At the same time, Taavet was receiving euros for his salary but lived in London so needed to convert his euros to British pounds. He was also paying expensive fees and receiving a bad exchange rate.

Taavet and Kristo knew there had to be a better way, so they invented a simple workaround. Each month, Taavet deposited his euro salary into Kristo's Estonian bank account, and Kristo deposited his British pound salary into Taavet's UK account. They agreed to convert the currencies using the mid-market exchange rate from the financial website Reuters. Through this agreement, both got the currency they needed almost instantly, and neither paid fees or other charges to the banks. There was no waiting, no stress, and no extra cost.

The friends recognized that there were many other young expatriate professionals who were in the same situation as them. They therefore created a fintech start-up to address this pain point. We don't have the original pitch deck for Wise, so let's imagine how a hypothetical elevator pitch for the Wise founders might look:

1 Customer segment: young professionals living in foreign cities ("digital nomads")
2 Pain point: converting foreign exchange to home currency is expensive, slow, inconvenient, and opaque
3 Value proposition: sending money should be fast, low cost, convenient, and transparent
4 Monetization strategy: charge a transparent processing fee upfront for each transaction with no hidden fees

How big is the market opportunity for Wise's cross-border foreign exchange business for digital nomads? Let's estimate this opportunity: We start with the total dollar value of cross-border payments in 2021, which was $20 trillion (TAM). Of this total, the volume for individual transactions was $2 trillion. The digital nomad segment is estimated at 4% of individual transactions, or $80 billion in cross-border transfers (SAM).

If Wise captures 50% of this market (SOM) and charges an average processing fee of 0.5%, their revenues will be $200 million. If they capture a 35% market share and charge a 1.0% fee, their revenues will increase to $280 million.

LATE STAGE AND EXIT: IPO OR ACQUISITION

The end goal for both angels and VCs is to exit their investment within a reasonable time horizon and to earn a high return on investment. The two most desirable exits are to sell to the public via an initial public offering (IPO) or to sell to a business through an acquisition. Of course, the least desirable exit is for the start-up to go bankrupt! A close second is the start-ups that continue as "zombies" and never grow but earn enough to stay alive. They survive but never return much on the initial investment.

An IPO is when the common shares of a start-up (now a mature company) are first listed on a stock exchange. An IPO may be called going public because the shares are now available to any investor. Once the fintech is listed, it is subject to regulatory requirements from securities regulators. The fintech must make regular public disclosures of their financial statements so that retail investors are provided with the information required to make an investment decision.

The process of going public through an IPO is expensive and time consuming. The shares must be registered, and the company must file a prospectus that describes the business, its strategy, the management team, the risks of the business, and the current share structure and ownership, among many other disclosures. The company will hire an investment bank to act as lead bookrunner and organize the syndicate of underwriters and the road show, where the company's senior leadership team travels from city to city making presentations to institutional investors. IPO underwriters are paid 7% of the IPO proceeds on average, plus are reimbursed for other legal and administrative expenses. The whole process takes weeks to months and may be derailed by external events beyond the company's control, such as an economic downturn or fall in the stock market.

The existing shareholders – the founders, angels, and VCs – have the option to sell some of their shares through the IPO, called a secondary offering. But insiders may also be restricted from selling all their holdings during a lock-up period lasting six to nine months following the IPO. After the lock-up ends, these insiders may sell on the public markets or via a follow-up seasoned equity offering (SEO).

The sale of the company through an acquisition by a competitor is a faster and cleaner exit. A fintech start-up with a unique value proposition or technology may be bought by another financial intermediary. For example, JPMorgan acquired the UK wealth management start-up Nutmeg, while VISA acquired the European open banking platform Tink.[17] Following an acquisition, the founding management team may be retained and given shares and roles in the combined entity. They may be hired to run their business as a subsidiary or division of the acquirer. Or the founders may be bought out and required to sign non-compete agreements to prevent them from starting a new business that competes with their former start-up. Again, this process is not easy and ultimately requires the approval of shareholders on both sides to go ahead. But if the price is right, it can be worth it.

The Market Performance of Fintech IPOs

Many founders dream of scaling their business and listing their company on a stock exchange. This listing establishes the fintech as a high-profile success story and provides liquidity for shareholders who can buy or sell shares easily. Unfortunately, the track record of many fintech IPOs has not been a dream, but rather a nightmare for shareholders who purchased the stock after it went public.

Table 3.1 shows 13 fintech IPOs between 2014 and 2021. These fintechs are the biggest unicorns from around the world and across lines of business. The stock performance post-IPO has been disappointing. The average stock was flat after one month, down 29% after six months, and down 48% after one year. The exception was the Dutch payments fintech Adyen, which was up 55.9% over the first year.

Figure 3.3 charts the stock performance for each IPO over its first year (approximately 260 trading days). It becomes clear that the majority of fintechs saw their share prices decline soon after the IPO. Even Adyen dropped below its IPO price before rallying over the subsequent six months. It is worth noting that these sell-offs were not linked to the COVID-19 pandemic, as they occurred before or after the worst years of the pandemic.

FINANCIAL SECURITIES ACROSS FUNDING ROUNDS

We saw that a start-up will raise capital through multiple, sequential funding rounds identified by a label: seed, Series A, Series B, Series C, and so on. Over the course of these funding rounds, existing investors may either contribute more capital or sell their shares and exit. The type of investor participating varies with the age of the start-up and funding round, with angels passing to VCs and later to institutional investors and the public.

Table 3.1. Fintech Initial Public Offerings and Performance

Name	Nationality	Sector	IPO	Change in Stock Price (%)		
				First Month	First 6 Months	First Year
LendingClub	US	Lending	2014	−2.3	−18.9	−40.1
On Deck	US	Lending	2014	−33.8	−47.3	−65.1
Mogo	Canada	Banking	2015	−27.2	−75.2	−78.9
Square	US	Payments	2015	−6.1	2.5	−7.9
ZhongAn	China	Insurance	2017	23.7	7.8	−49.4
Jianpu	China	Diversified	2017	−4.8	−35.7	−32.6
Adyen	Netherlands	Payments	2018	16.4	−0.5	55.9
Funding Circle	UK	Lending	2018	−14.3	−13.4	−78.6
Wise	UK	Payments	2021	11.1	−16.4	−64.2
Robinhood	US	Trading	2021	40.7	−53.3	−74.4
Kakao Pay	Korea	Payments	2021	13.0	−33.2	−81.5
Paytm	India	Payments	2021	−11.6	−62.6	−61.5
Nubank	Brazil	Neobank	2021	−14.8	−71.6	−66.1
	Number of IPOs		13	0.4	−28.9	−48.2

Figure 3.3. Fintech IPO Performance over First Year Total Returns

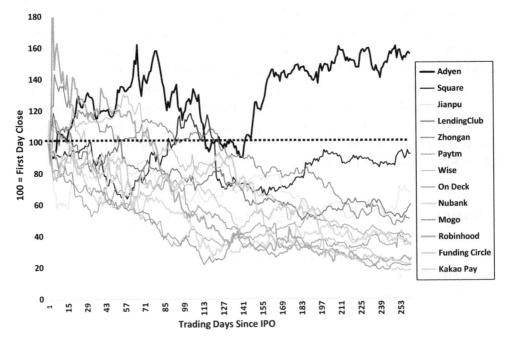

Source: Author, data from Refinitiv Eikon.

Table 3.2. Growth Stages and Financial Securities

Stage	Financial Securities	Description
Early	Convertible note	Unsecured debt that converts into equity at the option of the holder, with a higher claim than equity in bankruptcy but no voting rights.
	Simple Agreement for Future Equity (SAFE)	A non-priced form of equity that converts after a priced round into either preferred or common shares.
Growth/Late	Preferred shares	A form of equity that has a preferred claim in bankruptcy to common equity, a fixed or variable dividend, and limited voting rights.
	Common shares	A form of equity that represents proportional ownership of the firm with a residual claim in bankruptcy and voting rights.
	Venture debt	A secured loan with a maturity of 12 to 24 months, charging a high rate of interest with a higher claim than equity in bankruptcy but no voting rights.

When raising capital, founders must negotiate what financial securities are sold to investors. A financial security is a contract that has a variety of features and terms. The two main classes of financial securities are equity and debt. For early-stage companies, the most likely source of capital is some form of equity, either preferred shares or common shares. Debt may be a convertible note, secured loan, or bond. Selling equity dilutes the ownership stake of the founders, as captured in the start-up's capitalization table (or cap table). If a start-up is successful, however, the value of the founders' stake will increase through each round even when their proportional ownership is diluted.

Table 3.2 shows the financial securities that are typically issued at different growth stages. Of course, not all companies follow the same path, so this roadmap is only illustrative. Start-ups progress from unpriced funding rounds to priced rounds. An unpriced round is where funding is raised without putting an explicit value on the business. The two options are a convertible note and a Simple Agreement for Future Equity (SAFE).

As the start-up grows, the founders proceed to priced funding rounds that assign a value to the business. Equity is the dominant form of growth capital. Founders issue preferred shares or common shares, which differ in their claim on earnings and priority in case of bankruptcy. Both represent ownership in a company, but a preferred share has a higher claim in bankruptcy in exchange for limited or no voting rights. Once a start-up has sold equity and has physical assets, it may have the option to take out a secured loan called venture debt. We discuss these securities below.

When issuing a financial security, the start-up prepares a term sheet – a short, non-binding document that describes a financial security and its main features. A term sheet explains the investment in plain English and is used in negotiations between a founder and an investor. It details the investment amount, deal terms, rights of the holder, and other features. But a term sheet is not a legally binding document. Legal contracts are longer and require review by a securities lawyer. Both founders and investor need to be familiar with the various financial securities, as this knowledge is crucial in early-stage funding.

Convertible Note

It is often very difficult (if not impossible) to value a seed-stage company. There may be little to no revenues and the business is losing money. With no operating history, it is difficult to sell common or preferred shares, as both securities must be assigned a value. Issuing equity is also costly and time consuming, requiring legal documents and lawyers. For this reason, a common security used by a pre-seed or seed stage is the convertible note. A convertible note is established and well-understood, flexible, simple to execute, and founder friendly.

A convertible note (or convert) is a type of unsecured loan that converts into equity at a price determined in a future priced round (typically the Series A). Selling a convertible allows founders to raise money without having to agree to a valuation, kicking the problem down the road. Angel investors may prefer a convertible note because it is a form of debt, and so has a higher priority claim in bankruptcy than all forms of equity, reducing its risk. A convertible has features of a bond, such as a nominal interest rate, a maturity date, and protective provisions called covenants. But it retains the upside because the holder has the option to convert the note into equity at a future priced round.

Several standard features of a convertible note are

- **Standard terms**: A convertible note has a principal amount (e.g., $100,000), a nominal interest rate (e.g., 10%), and a maturity date (e.g., two years). When issued by a start-up, the interest expense is accrued but not typically paid; instead, it is taken into account when the note converts to equity. The maturity date can be extended if it takes longer for the start-up to gain traction and scale its business.
- **Conversion feature**: The principal amount and any accrued, unpaid interest is automatically converted to equity upon the closing of a qualified equity financing that raises a pre-specified amount for the company (e.g., $1 million+ of funding). The number of shares for the conversion is the total of principal plus accrued interest, divided by the price per share.

- **Conversion discount**: To compensate for uncertainty, the note may convert into equity at a price lower than the one paid by the investors in the priced round. If the note has a 15% discount and the new equity is priced at $10 per share for the new investors, the note would convert into shares based on a price of $8.50, increasing the number of shares for the convertible holder.
- **Valuation cap**: The convertible may specify a maximum pre-money valuation that is used when converting into equity. This valuation cap establishes an approximate valuation for the company. For example, if the cap is set at $5 million but the pre-money valuation implied by a Series A financing is $10 million, then the note would convert into shares at 50% of the price paid by the new investors (i.e., cap ÷ pre-money valuation = $5 million ÷ $10 million = 50%). If the Series A shares are priced at $10 per share, the note converts at a price of $5 per share.

Typically, a convertible note converts at the lower of the price implied by the conversion discount or the valuation cap.

Simple Agreement for Future Equity

The Silicon Valley accelerator Y Combinator developed the Simple Agreement for Future Equity (SAFE) in late 2013. A SAFE allows an investor to make a cash investment today but delay receipt of preferred shares until the next funding round. A SAFE looks like a convertible note but does not have a maturity date or interest rate. Like a convertible note, the SAFE receives new shares on terms more favorable than those for the new investors. But a SAFE is not considered a debt instrument for US tax purposes, although it is considered debt in Canada. A SAFE is simple, quick to execute, and founder friendly. For this reason, it has caught on as an alternative way for start-ups to raise seed capital.

A SAFE has various provisions that may be combined to create a customized agreement:

- **Valuation cap**: A maximum pre-money valuation for the start-up. The SAFE converts at the lower of (i) the price per share calculated using the valuation cap, and (ii) the actual price per share in a qualified financing. The SAFE defines what is considered a qualified financing, typically a Series A (priced) round.
- **Conversion discount**: The SAFE converts at a discount of 15% to 25% of the price per share paid in a qualified financing.
- **Liquidation preference**: A SAFE converts into preferred shares holding a higher claim in bankruptcy, where the holder is paid back their original investment and any unpaid dividends before other share classes.

- **Most favored nation (MFN)**: The SAFE investor has the right to receive the same terms as future convertible securities sold by the start-up. If the start-up issues a convertible note with a lower valuation cap or higher conversion discount, the SAFE holder gets the same preferential terms.
- **Pro-rata rights**: The SAFE holder has the right to purchase more shares in follow-on offerings, ensuring the SAFE holder can avoid dilution of their ownership if they choose.

The end of this chapter provides examples of how a convertible note or SAFE work in practice.

Common Shares

Common shares (also called common stock) are a form of equity and represent proportional ownership in a company. A sale of common equity is a priced round, so the founders and investors negotiate a value for the start-up when setting the price for each common share. Common shares are the riskiest class of financial securities with the lowest claim on the company's assets in the event of bankruptcy. We say common shareholders have a residual claim, because they are the last to be paid after all creditors and any preferred shareholders. This higher risk is compensated with a higher potential reward if the start-up is successful. The increase in value of a company is reflected in the price per common share.

Common shares typically come with the right to vote on corporate decisions, even for private companies such as a start-up, unless there are multiple share classes. With one share class, each common share has one vote. Votes are then allocated based on the percentage of shares owned relative to shares outstanding. If an investor owns 10% of the common shares, they control 10% of the votes. Founders must therefore be careful not to sell too many common shares or risk losing control of their start-up.

Voting at a large, public company takes place once per year at the annual general meeting. For a start-up, however, this voting right is more informal and happens at meetings of the founder with the other equity holders. Minority equity holders with fewer shares may not be contacted, with only the larger shareholders consulted. For this reason, angels and VCs with a significant holding of common shares may insist on having a seat on the board of directors. This position allows them to meet the founders, monitor the financial condition of the company, and voice their opinions on strategy.

Investors in early-stage common shares may negotiate the following rights:

- **Votes**: The holders of common shares have the right to vote based on their class of common. With one share class, they have one vote per share. In the case of multiple share classes, the common shares sold to investors may have fewer votes per share than the class held by founders.

- **Pro-rata rights/pre-emptive rights**: A right to participate in a subsequent sale of equity based on their pro-rata ownership. It may also be called anti-dilution rights.
- **Right of first refusal**: Before any shares are sold by an existing shareholder to a third party, those shares must first be offered on a pro-rata basis to existing shareholders.
- **Tag-along rights (or co-sale)**: If a third party offers to purchase the common shares from a shareholder, the third party must make the same offer to all shareholders.
- **Drag-along rights**: If an offer by a third party is accepted by a pre-determined percentage of shareholders, all remaining shareholders must take the same offer.
- **Price protection rights**: If the company issues new shares below the price at which existing shareholders bought in, the existing shareholders receive additional shares as if they paid the lower price.

Preferred Shares

Early-stage investors may buy preferred shares (also called preferred stock), which represent a form of equity. Preferred shares are priced based on the valuation of the company as negotiated between the founders and the investors. Preferred shares in a start-up are very different from the same securities issued by a mature company. Early-stage preferred shares have the upside of common shares but a higher claim on the company's assets in the event of bankruptcy, reducing their risk.

Investors in early-stage preferred shares may negotiate the following rights:

- **Dividends**: They may have a preferred claim on any dividends, although it is unlikely a start-up would pay a dividend. Or the preferred shares may accrue a cumulative dividend that is paid out in the form of common shares later (i.e., a stock dividend).
- **Votes**: The holders of preferred shares have the right to vote with the common shares as one class on an as-converted basis.
- **Liquidation preference**: Preferred shares have a higher priority claim in bankruptcy. They have a right to be paid back the original investment amount and any unpaid dividends before other share classes.
- **Pro-rata rights/pre-emptive rights**: A right to participate in a subsequent sale of equity based on their pro-rata ownership. It may also be called anti-dilution rights.

- **Conversion rights**: The right to be converted into common shares at the option of the holder or in the event of a later funding round.
- **Redemption rights**: The right to require the company to repay some or all of the shares if the company is not sold or listed on a stock exchange within some defined period (e.g., five years).

Venture Debt

Some VCs and specialized lenders are willing to provide debt financing to a start-up if the company has enough assets to act as collateral, or enough monthly recurring revenue to pay interest expense out of cash flow. Venture debt is a form of secured loan with a maturity of 12 to 24 months that pays a rate of interest of 15% to 25% per annum. Venture debt can be used to finance working capital or the purchase of equipment (in which case it is described as capital expenditures). The venture debt may come with warrants, which are a derivative contract that gives the lender the right (but not the obligation) to purchase equity at a specified price over a specified time horizon. The venture debt may also have a clause requiring repayment at the time of a priced round (Series A to F).

The benefit of venture debt is this form of capital does not dilute equity, although the warrants attached are dilutive. The debt has a lower implied cost than equity because it is less risky, with a higher claim in bankruptcy. The lender protects their downside, much like taking out a mortgage against a house, and has a higher claim in bankruptcy than other creditors, preferred shares, or common shares. The downside of venture debt is that the interest rate is high, and the company is legally required to make interest payments. A failure to pay principal or interest is an event of default that may lead to bankruptcy. Venture debt comes with monitoring by the lender, requiring disclosure of the start-up's finances. This financial security bears covenants, which are contract terms that restrict the founders from taking certain actions (such as taking on more debt or selling assets).

THE CAPITALIZATION TABLE

Founders, angels, and VCs are all concerned with how raising capital dilutes (or reduces) their proportional ownership of the start-up. This equity dilution is tracked using a capitalization table (or "cap table"). A cap table shows who owns what securities and how much their ownership stake is worth. There is a pre-money valuation before each funding round and a post-money valuation at the conclusion of each funding round. The pre-money valuation is the implied value of the start-up before

Table 3.3. A Hypothetical Capitalization Table

Funding Round	Seed	Series A	Series B	IPO
PANEL A: COMPANY VALUATION (in $ millions)				
Pre-money valuation	0.5	1.8	6.5	25.2
Angels invest	0.5			
VC 1 invests		2.5		
VC 2 invests			5.0	
Public invests				15.0
Post-money valuation	1.0	4.3	11.5	40.2
Money-on-money multiple	–	1.8x	1.5x	2.2x
= Pre-money current round		= $1.8	= $6.5	= $25.2
÷ Post-money previous round		÷ $1.0	÷ $4.3	÷ $11.5
PANEL B: OWNERSHIP STAKE (as % of total)				
Founders	50.0	20.9	11.8	7.4
Angels	50.0	20.9	11.8	7.4
VC1		58.2	32.8	20.5
VC2			43.7	27.4
Public				37.3
Total ownership	100.0	100.0	100.0	100.0
PANEL C: OWNERSHIP (in $ millions)				
Founders	0.5	0.9	1.3	2.9
Angels	0.5	0.9	1.3	2.9
VC1		2.5	3.8	8.2
VC2			5.0	10.9
Public				15.0
Post-money valuation	1.0	4.3	11.5	40.2

the new equity is created based on the proportional ownership of existing share-holders. The post-money valuation is the new value of the fintech start-up at the conclusion of each funding round based on the price paid by the new investors and the implied private valuation of the business. The cap table shows who owns what percentage of the business, with the total adding up to 100%.

Let's work through an example. Table 3.3 shows a hypothetical cap table for a start-up raising money through four funding rounds: seed, Series A, Series B, and IPO. The table has three panels. Panel A shows the pre-money and post-money valuation of the company through each funding round. Panel B shows the percentage ownership of the founders and investors. Panel C shows the dollar value of the shares held by the founders and investors. These numbers are fictional to illustrate a cap table.

Panel A shows the start-up's valuation at each funding round, both the pre-money and the post-money valuation. The pre-money valuation is the negotiated enterprise value (EV) prior to the funding round. The post-money valuation is the implied EV following the creation of new securities. The money-on-money multiple compares the pre-money valuation at the start of each round to the post-money valuation at the end of the previous round. During the seed round, we assume the pre-money valuation negotiated between the founders and the angels is $500,000. The angels invest an additional $500,000 leading to a post-money valuation of $1.0 million (i.e., the new EV). After this funding round, the founders and angels each own 50% of the start-up.

During the Series A round, a first VC (VC1) agrees to a pre-money valuation for the start-up of $1.8 million, or an increase of 1.8x from the $1.0 million post-money valuation following the seed round. This multiple is not fixed but is based on negotiations with the founders. In this example, VC1 invests $2.5 million and the angels do not invest. As a result, the post-money valuation is now $4.3 million, representing a money-on-money multiple of 1.5x. The start-up's valuation has increased, called an "up" round. If the valuation were to fall, it would be called a "down" round.

Panel B shows that the ownership stakes of the founders and angels are diluted during the Series A round due to the creation of new equity sold to VC1. This dilution of existing investors happens at each funding round unless they exercise their pro-rata rights and invest again. The post-money ownership stake of the founders and angels is calculated based on equation (1):

Post-money ownership % = Pre-money ownership % × (1 − New investor ownership %) (1)

At the end of the seed round, the founders own 50% of the equity and the angels own 50%. This percentage becomes the pre-money ownership in the Series A round. VC1 invests $2.5 million with an implied post-money valuation of $4.3 million. VC1's ownership stake becomes 58.2% = $2.5 million ÷ $4.3 million. The equity stakes of the founders and angels have been diluted. Using equation (1), the post-money ownership of the founders is 20.9% = 50% × (1 − 58.2%). The dilution for the angels is the same. At the end of the round, the ownership of all investors adds up to 100% = 20.9% + 20.9% + 58.2%.

Panel C shows the value of each ownership stake at the end of each round. At the end of the Series A round, the founders own 20.9% of a start-up valued at $4.3 million, or $0.9 million. Their equity has increased in value by 1.8x, which is the money-on-money multiple from the seed round to the Series A.

We repeat these calculations for the Series B round and the IPO. The increases in value compound. At the time of the IPO, the founders own 7.4% of a business valued at $40.2 million. This ownership stake is worth $3.0 million, or a money-on-money multiple of 5.94x. Figure 3.4 shows the value of the start-up through each funding round and the amount owned by the founders, the angels, and the VCs.

Notice that the money-on-money multiple for the founders at the time of the IPO is the product of the multiples through the Series A, Series B, and IPO, or

Figure 3.4. Value of Equity Stakes through Funding Rounds

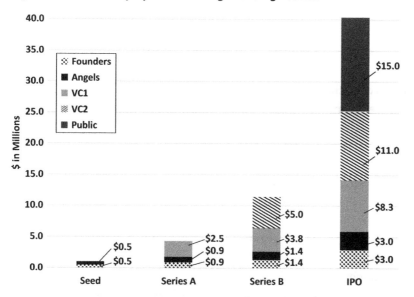

5.94x = 1.8 × 1.5 × 2.2. While a 6x multiple may not sound great, the IRR depends on how long it took to achieve it. If we assume 6 years from initial investment to IPO, the founders' IRR is 35% per annum. If we assume 10 years, the IRR is 20% per annum.

Examples: Valuation Cap, Conversion Discount, and Acquisition

Let's work through some examples of how much a SAFE holder or convertible note holder will receive based on a valuation cap, conversion discount, and acquisition.[18]

VALUATION CAP

An investor purchases a SAFE for $100,000 with a valuation cap of $5 million. The start-up raises $1 million in a Series A round at a pre-money valuation of $10 million. There are 1 million pre-money shares outstanding.

Q: What is the price per share for the Series A?
A: Price per share = Pre-money valuation ÷ Pre-money shares outstanding

$$\$10.00 = \$10 \text{ million} \div 1 \text{ million shares}$$

Q: What is the SAFE price per share given the valuation cap?
A: SAFE price per share = (Valuation cap ÷ Pre-money valuation) × Price per share

$$\$5.00 = (\$5 \text{ million} \div \$10 \text{ million}) \times \$10.00$$

Q: How many shares does the SAFE holder receive?
A: SAFE shares = Investment ÷ SAFE price per share

$$20,000 = \$100,000 \div \$5.00$$

Q: What is the post-money shares outstanding?
A: Post-money shares = Pre-money shares + Series A shares + SAFE shares

$$1,120,000 = 1 \text{ million} + (\$1,000,000 \div \$10.00) + 20,000 = 1 \text{ million} + 100,000 + 20,000$$

Q: What is the post-money valuation?
A: Post-money valuation = Post-money shares × Series A price per share

$$\$11.2 \text{ million} = 1,120,000 \times \$10.00$$

CONVERSION DISCOUNT

An investor purchases a convertible note for $20,000 with a conversion discount of 80%. The start-up raises $400,000 in a Series A round at a pre-money valuation of $2 million. There are 10 million pre-money shares outstanding.

Q: What is the price per share for the Series A?
A: Series A price per share = Pre-money valuation ÷ Pre-money shares outstanding

$$\$0.20 = \$2 \text{ million} \div 10 \text{ million shares}$$

Q: What is the convertible price per share given the conversion discount?
A: Convertible price per share = Conversion discount × Series A price per share

$$\$0.16 = 80\% \times \$0.20$$

Q: How many shares does the convertible note holder receive?
A: Convertible shares = Investment ÷ Convertible price per share

$$125,000 = \$20,000 \div \$0.16$$

Q: What is the post-money shares outstanding?
A: Post-money shares = Pre-money shares + Series A shares + Convertible shares

$$12{,}125{,}000 = 10 \text{ million} + (\$400{,}000 \div \$0.20) + 125{,}000$$
$$= 10 \text{ million} + 2 \text{ million} + 125{,}000$$

Q: What is the post-money valuation?
A: Post-money valuation = Post-money shares × Series A price per share

$$\$2.425 \text{ million} = 12{,}125{,}000 \times \$0.20$$

ACQUISITION WITH A SAFE

An investor purchases a SAFE for $100,000 with a valuation cap of $5 million. A strategic buyer makes an offer to acquire the start-up for $50 million. The start-up has 11.5 million shares outstanding.

Q: What is the price per share paid by the strategic buyer?
A: Price per share = Offer ÷ Shares outstanding

$$\$4.348 = \$50 \text{ million} \div 11.5 \text{ million shares}$$

Q: What is the SAFE price per share given the valuation cap?
A: SAFE price per share = (Valuation cap ÷ Offer) × Price per share

$$\$0.86955 = (\$5 \text{ million} \div \$50 \text{ million}) \times \$4.348$$

Q: How many shares does the SAFE holder receive?
A: SAFE shares = Investment ÷ SAFE price per share

$$115{,}008 = \$100{,}000 \div \$0.86955$$

Q: How much does the SAFE holder receive for their shares?
A: Value = SAFE shares ÷ Price per share

$$\$500{,}000 = 115{,}008 \div \$4.348$$

Q: What is the money-on-money for the SAFE holder?
A: Money-on-money = Money out ÷ Money invested

$$5.0x = \$500{,}000 \div \$100{,}000$$

Key Terms

accelerator

angel investor (business angel)

bootstrapping

capitalization table (cap table)

common shares

convertible note

crowdfunding

customer segment

elevator pitch

equity dilution

funding round

internal rate of return (IRR)

money-on-money (cash-on-cash) multiple

post-money valuation

pre-money valuation

preferred shares

seed stage

Series A, B, or C

serviceable available market (SAM)

serviceable obtainable market (SOM)

Simple Agreement for Future Equity (SAFE)

term sheet

total addressable market (TAM)

unpriced vs. priced round

valuation cap

value proposition

venture capitalist (VC)

QUESTIONS FOR DISCUSSION

1 What are the different stages of growth for a fintech? What is the "Valley of Death"?

2 What are angel investors? Why do they invest in early-stage companies?

3 What are venture capitalists? How do they manage the risk of investing in early-stage and growth-stage companies?

4 What is the total addressable market (TAM)? How is it different from the serviceable available market (SAM) and the serviceable obtainable market (SOM)?

5 What are the four types of funding rounds? What investors are most likely involved with each one?

6 What is a convertible note and what are its key features when used for early-stage investing?

7 What is a Simple Agreement for Future Equity (SAFE)? What are its main features?

8 What is the purpose of a capitalization table? What is the difference between the pre-money and post-money valuation?

9 How does an investor calculate their dilution and percentage ownership in a start-up following each funding round?

10 Assume you are an angel and purchase a convertible note for $100,000 from a fintech start-up. It pays an annual rate of interest of 12% with a 3-year maturity. You negotiate a conversion discount of 10% and a valuation cap of $5 million. What will your investment be worth if a VC invests $2 million at a pre-money valuation of $10 million? Assume there are 500,000 pre-money shares outstanding. Remember that a convertible note converts at the lower of the price implied by the conversion discount or the valuation cap.

ADDITIONAL READING

DeGennaro, Ramon P., "Angel Investors and Their Investments," SSRN, December 10, 2010, http://dx.doi.org/10.2139/ssrn.1784489.

Di Bacco, Kristine M., and Doug Sharp, "Seed Financing Overview – A Lexis Practice Advisor Practice Note," Fenwick & West, May 31, 2018, https://assets.fenwick.com/legacy/FenwickDocuments/Seed-Financing-Overview.pdf.

Fenwick & West, "Convertible Debt Terms – Survey of Market Trends 2018/2019," July 8, 2019, https://assets.fenwick.com/legacy/FenwickDocuments/Convertible-Debt-2019.pdf.

Gompers, Paul, and Josh Lerner, "The Venture Capital Revolution," *Journal of Economic Perspectives* 15, no. 2 (2001): 145–168.

Huang, Laura, Andy Wu, Min Ju Lee, Jiayi Bao, Marianne Hudson, and Elaine Bolle, "The American Angel: The First In-Depth Report on the Demographics and Investing Activity of Individual American Angel Investors," Overland Park, Wharton Entrepreneurship and Angel Capital Association, November 2017, https://www.hbs.edu/faculty/Pages/item.aspx?num=57843.

Ralston, Geoff, "A Guide to Seed Fundraising," Y Combinator, accessed December 15, 2021, https://www.ycombinator.com/library/4A-a-guide-to-seed-fundraising.

Zwilling, Martin, "10 Ways for Startups to Survive the Valley of Death," *Forbes*, February 18, 2013, https://www.forbes.com/sites/martinzwilling/2013/02/18/10-ways-for-startups-to-survive-the-valley-of-death/?sh=12bf753d69ef.

4

Valuation of Fintech Companies

SUMMARY

- Valuation of a pre-revenue company is an art, not a science. The buyer and seller negotiate the value, relying on experience and judgment.
- Angel investors use scorecards and risk factors; they may delay putting a value on the start-up until it has gained traction with customers.
- Venture capitalists work backward based on a targeted internal rate of return (IRR), adjusted for the risk of default and equity dilution.
- Valuation of mature fintech companies for initial public offerings (IPOs) or an acquisition is based on the market multiples of comparable companies, precedent transactions, or a discounted cash flow (DCF) model.
- Measures of earnings before interest, taxes, depreciation, and amortization (EBITDA) based on US Generally Accepted Accounting Principles (GAAP) for disruptive technology companies may not reflect longer-term growth and profitability potential because they penalize R&D, sales and marketing, stock-based compensation, deferred revenue, and acquisitions.
- Banks and financial intermediaries cannot be valued using a DCF model, so investors rely on relative valuation using market multiples of comparable companies.

The previous chapter examined the funding of fintech companies with a focus on early-stage start-ups. It discussed the investors and the choice of funding securities.

This chapter examines the valuation of fintech companies at various stages in their lifecycle. We describe the methods used by angel investors and venture capitalists (VCs) for valuing early-stage companies, and by shareholders for valuing mature companies. We also discuss how to value a bank.

THE ART OF VALUATION

Valuation is an art, not a science. It is subjective, not objective. Value is determined through a negotiation between a buyer and a seller. The party in the stronger bargaining position steers the value to what they are willing to pay. The value of a company is what someone will pay for it. If the buyer and seller cannot agree, there is no price and no deal.

Nowhere is this truer than with early-stage companies, where a start-up has limited operating history and negative earnings. The value at this stage depends much more on qualitative factors such as an assessment of the founding team, the business idea and value proposition, and the size of the market opportunity. With start-ups and young disruptive companies that are investing heavily to scale and acquire customers, the traditional valuation methods used for mature companies simply do not work.

We need to acknowledge that not everything is for sale. A fintech founder passionate about their business may not be willing to sell it. This passion or stubbornness could lead the venture to fail. A reasonable entrepreneur recognizes the difference between having a dream and turning it into a reality. Founders face a trade-off: They need to give up some ownership to raise the capital required to grow. But not everyone is rational.

A fintech founder looking to sell equity needs to understand the valuation methods used by angel investors and VCs. As with any negotiation, the secret to bargaining is understanding the other party's incentives and interests. Incentives motivate people and explain behavior. Incentives may be explicit or implicit, conscious or subconscious. Interests are the things that a person cares about most. Philosophers, psychologists, and economists have theories that examine the role of self-interest in motivating human action. You will find that some people are extrinsically motivated by money and wealth, while others are intrinsically motivated by a desire to change the world.

In finance and economics, our stereotype is that a buyer wants to pay the lowest price to maximize their return on investment (ROI). The seller is motivated to get the highest price. These incentives are captured in the maxim "buy low and sell high." But a large body of behavioral finance and economics suggests that humans are not rational. We respond to non-financial incentives and personal biases, both conscious and unconscious.

In a negotiation, the gap between the buyer's offer price and the seller's asking price creates the zone of possible agreement (ZOPA). This is where bargaining takes place. If the bid and ask are close to each other and the parties are motivated, the negotiation may be successful. But if the seller's price is unrealistically high or the buyer is offering too little, there will be no deal.

In this negotiation, finance professionals seek to tip the price in their favor by appealing to the concept of fundamental (or intrinsic) value. They will argue that their financial model reveals the fair value of an asset. They may appeal to a higher authority, arguing their model is supported by theories and sophisticated calculations. But a fundamental valuation model is not reality. It is just a spreadsheet filled with data and assumptions, showing forecasts of sales, margins, and earnings. Any good financial analyst can manipulate the inputs of a model to generate the valuation they are seeking.

Another approach is to compare things that are similar. We can value a target by referencing the valuation of a similar company in the same sector, line of business, or geography (if they exist). We look at standardized metrics based on earnings, cash flows, sales, or accounting values. This relative valuation approach is known as market multiples of comparable companies. But make no mistake, relative valuation is just another negotiating tactic. Change the choice of comparable companies or the ratio, and you can justify any price, either high or low.

The point to understand is that we can use fundamental or relative valuation models to arrive at any price. At the end of the day, the negotiation tools are used to justify a lower price for a buyer or a higher price for seller. That's it.

FOUR STEPS IN VALUATION

Most valuation methodologies can be boiled down to four steps: identify, forecast, discount, and divide. To identify means to figure out the value drivers of cash flows and earnings for a business. To forecast is to project what will happen in the future, such as sales and profitability. To discount means to find the present value of a future cash flow, expressing it in today's dollars by taking account of the time value of money. To divide means to allocate the present value to different capital providers, like dividing a pie. Figure 4.1 illustrates these four steps.

Let's take a closer look at each step.

Identify Value Drivers

Value drivers are economic relationships that explain the performance of a business. Both start-ups and mature companies have a handful of value drivers that explain most

Figure 4.1. The Four Steps in Valuation

of the variation in revenues and expenses. The financial analyst's job is to develop a deep understanding of the business and to identify these economic drivers that can explain and forecast future sales and profitability.

An analyst will scour company announcements, regulatory filings, industry reports, expert opinions, and other sources of information. Until the analyst identifies these value drivers, any forecast of earnings will not be credible. The "GIGO" principle applies to financial models: Put garbage in, you'll get garbage out.

Value drivers may be top-down or bottom-up. Top-down value drivers are macroeconomic and operate at the level of the country, the sector, and the industry. They include population growth and demographics, the business cycle, industry cyclicality, and the degree of competition. These macro factors play into the calculation of total addressable market (TAM) for a given product or service.

Bottom-up value drivers are microeconomic and firm-specific. These variables explain the composition of revenues, expenses, capital expenditures, working capital, and leverage. They are used to forecast sales growth, profitability, and changes in cash balances. They include the quality of leadership, the human capital, the strategy, the brand, and the sustainability of the company.

To identify top-down value drivers, the analyst may use statistical methods such as regressions of industry sales on economic conditions (interest rates, exchange rates), financial conditions (stock market or industry indices), and demographic information (population and growth).

To identify bottom-up value drivers, it helps to build a cash-flow-based valuation model and to check the sensitivity of the company's valuation to changing key assumptions. We will explain a DCF model below.

Forecast the Future

Our next step is to use our understanding of the business and the value drivers to generate a forecast. The forecast may be for the coming year, which is used to generate financial ratios and market multiples of sales, cash flow, or earnings (next 12 months or NTM). Or our forecast may be for up to 10 years when building a DCF model. Whatever the time horizon, it is important that we recognize the uncertainty of our forecast.

One way to capture uncertainty is to use scenario analysis. A scenario is a "what-if" view of the future. Financial analysts often project three scenarios: a base case, a best case (or bull case), and a worst case (or bear case). Each scenario describes a story of the future with the key assumptions adjusted to reflect the storyline. Sales growth and operating margins will be highest in the bull case and lowest in the bear case. The variation across scenarios must be plausible and tied to the narrative that goes with it.

Each scenario generates a different valuation for the company and its financial securities. It may seem difficult enough to build three plausible scenarios, but the harder part is assigning a probability to each of them, making sure they sum to 100%. If your base case valuation of a fintech's stock is $10 with a 30% probability, the bear case is $5 with a 40% probability, and the bull case is $20 with a 40% probability, then the weighted average price is $13 = ($10 × 30%) + ($5 × 40%) + ($20 × 40%). Notice this weighted average price is skewed toward the higher end of the $5 to $20 range because of the significantly higher probability and share price in the bull case.

A key problem in this process is data. Private businesses do not publish financial statements or provide investor updates. If they do publish historical data, we may find that the overall picture is changing over time with considerable variability. Company press releases may provide a point-in-time snapshot with little discussion of the growth rate ("We just passed $1 million in monthly recurring revenue"; "Assets under management are $1 billion"). In this situation, we can make reasonable assumptions by looking at comparable firms or by looking at the history of more mature firms to decide what is realistic. If a fintech start-up is creating a new market, there are no good benchmarks.

With no history of financial data to rely on, we need to use our understanding of the business and its value drivers to generate the forecast. If a customer pays a monthly subscription fee of $10 for a fintech app, for example, we can estimate how much will flow to the bottom line and how it will grow in the coming years. This process involves a lot of assumptions (or informed guesses): level and growth rate of revenues, level and growth rates of fixed and variable expenses (including taxes or tax loss carry forward), capital requirements to maintain and grow the business (investments in information technology [IT], research and development, working capital, and other assets).

While some expenses may appear idiosyncratic to a company, many start-ups face similar costs, such as

- The cost of customer acquisition (i.e., marketing and advertising expenses divided by the number of customers who sign up)
- Variable costs of goods sold (COGS) per dollar of sales for product-based businesses
- Salaries and other fixed costs (overhead) per dollar of sales or per employee
- Working capital and capital expenditures per dollar of sales or dollar of assets
- The cost of borrowing if available (i.e., lines of credit, loans, convertible notes, venture debt)

Ideally, we can pick reasonable assumptions by looking at competitors or similar businesses that are public. The profit margin and delinquency rate on a bank's credit card portfolio, for example, gives us an idea of what to forecast for a consumer credit card from fintechs like Revolut or Mogo.

Keep in mind that the fixed cost per unit of sales should decline as sales increase, known as economies of scale. We want to understand a fintech's profit margin (also called net margin), which is net income divided by total revenues. When expressed as a percentage, the net margin is a simple statistic that measures the average dollar of earnings per dollar of sales. This ratio should be positive, and ideally between 5% and 25%.

Discount to Present Value

A central principle of finance is that a dollar today is different from a dollar tomorrow. Why? If you have a dollar today and invest it, it is worth more in the future. The dollar today is the present value, or PV. The value in the future is called the future value, or FV. So, if you invest $100 today for a year and earn a rate of return of 10%, after one year it is worth $110.

Most people have no problem with a one-year calculation, but the intuition is not as easy with multiple periods. Equation (1) is the formula for calculating FV given multiple periods:

$$\text{Future value} = \text{Present value} \times (1 + \text{Periodic interest rate\%})^{\text{Periods}}$$

$$FV = PV \times (1 + r\%)^{n} \tag{1}$$

If you invest $100 today for two years at 10% per period, it grows to $121.00:

$$FV = PV \times (1 + r\%)^{n} = 100 \times (1 + 10\%)^{2} = 100 \times (1.10)^{2} = 121.00$$

Notice the total is not $120. The extra $1 value generated after the second year is due to compounding, also called interest on interest. The $10 return from year 1 is invested at 10% and becomes $11 by the end of year 2. This amount is added to the $10 return for year 2 to total $121.00.

Compounding increases the future value exponentially over time. If we invest $100 for seven years at a periodic rate of 10%, it almost doubles and grows to $194.87:

$$FV = PV \times (1 + r\%)^{n} = 100 \times (1.10)^{7} = 100 \times (1.9487) = 194.87$$

Notice we use a periodic rate of interest, r%, and the number of periods, n. It could be an annual rate that compounds each year. Or it could be a quarterly rate that compounds each quarter. Equation (1) can accommodate any frequency of compounding.

Discounting is a finance term that means calculating the present value of a future cash flow. Discounting shows you what you need to invest today to receive $1.00 in the future. The discount rate is the same rate, r%. If you receive $100 one year in the future and the discount rate is 10%, then the amount you need to invest today is $90.91. This amount can be calculated by re-arranging equation (1) to have PV on the left-hand side, as seen in equation (2):

$$PV = \frac{FV}{\left(1+r\%\right)^n} = FV \times \frac{1}{\left(1+r\%\right)^n} \tag{2}$$

$$90.91 = \frac{100}{\left(1+10\%\right)^1} = \frac{100}{\left(1.10\right)^1} = 100 \times 0.9091$$

Notice that we can express the discount factor in equation (2) as a fraction, $\frac{1}{\left(1+r\%\right)^n}$. This fraction is sometimes called the present value interest factor (PVIF). Before computers became so widely available, textbooks would include a table of PVIFs to allow for ease of computation of present value.

What is the present value of $100 received seven years in the future when the discount rate is 10%? The answer is $51.32.

$$PV = \frac{FV}{\left(1+r\%\right)^n} = \frac{100}{\left(1+10\%\right)^7} = 100 \times 0.5132 = 51.32$$

Check for yourself that FV = $100 if you plug PV = 51.32, r% = 10%, and n = 7 into equation (1).

When we make a forecast for a company over multiple periods, we view it as a series of individual cash flows that happen at distinct points in time: end of year 1, end of year 2, end of year 3, and so on. Once we know what each cash flow will be in the future, we can use what we learned about discounting to find the value today for the sum of these cash flows. To get the present value of a string of future cash flows generated by business, we discount each of the individual cash flows and sum them up. This relationship is shown using equation (3):

$$PV = \frac{FV_1}{\left(1+r\%\right)^1} + \frac{FV_2}{\left(1+r\%\right)^2} + \frac{FV_3}{\left(1+r\%\right)^3} + \ldots + \frac{FV_n}{\left(1+r\%\right)^n} \tag{3}$$

Equation (3) forms the basis for valuation models based on discounting future cash flows. Notice it assumes that each cash flow is discounted at the same periodic rate. The periodic rate that sets a string of future cash flows equal to the present value today is called the internal rate of return (IRR).

Divide the Pie

The last step in valuation is to determine who gets what. I call this "dividing the pie." Some of the present value of future cash flows generated by the business belongs to the founders and some to the different investors and creditors.

In finance, we use the term *enterprise value*, or EV, to describe the value of a company (aka the size of the pie today). Think of EV as the market value of all the assets of the business. In this case, we are not interested in the historical (or book) value of the assets, which may be shown on the company's balance sheet. Instead, we want to know what these assets could be sold for today.

When valuing a business, we assume it is a going concern and will generate cash flows into the future. Anyone who buys the company will benefit from the physical capital, the intellectual capital, and the human capital. In other words, the going-concern value is the present value of all cash flows generated by both the tangible (fixed) assets and the intangible assets.

Think of EV as the value that we would receive if we held an auction. This EV is almost always different from the historical value. The EV is also higher than the liquidation value, which assumes the company is bankrupt, broken up, and sold in pieces. EV is based on a going-concern assumption, where the business is solvent and the assets are generating cash flows each year in the future.

The assets of a business belong to two groups of capital providers (also called investors): the creditors and the shareholders. Each group of capital providers has a claim on the EV, as shown in equation (4):

$$EV = (Total\ debt - Cash) + Equity = Net\ debt + (Preferred\ shares +$$
$$Common\ shares + NCI) \qquad (4)$$

where NCI is non-controlling interest, the share of assets owned by another business on the consolidated balance sheet for a company.

Creditors have lent money to the business and expect to be repaid. The start-up might have a bank loan, a mortgage, a convertible note, or venture debt. The amount owed to all creditors is total debt. Technically, any cash on the balance sheet could be used to repay these creditors. We therefore reduce the amount owed to creditors by the amount of cash on the balance sheet. The remaining amount owed to creditors is called Net debt = Total debt – Cash.

Shareholders are the owners of equity. For most companies, shareholders' equity consists of preferred shares and common shares. These shareholders have a claim on the assets after all creditors are repaid. In legal terms, we say the creditors have a higher priority claim than shareholders. By rearranging equation (4), we see that the value of the Equity = EV - Net debt.

If there is a SAFE or convertible note outstanding, we assume they are converted into equity for the purposes of valuation, called the as-converted basis. Remember that we need to take into account any accrued but unpaid interest on the convertible notes, and other features such as the valuation cap and conversion discount.

Let's assume we calculate the EV of a start-up as $2.7 million. We arrived at this EV by discounting future cash flows using equation (3). Let's also assume the business has the following capital structure:

- Venture debt of $300,000
- Cash of $100,000
- Convertible note of $500,000, with a valuation cap of $3 million and accrued unpaid interest of $100,000
- 250,000 common shares outstanding, of which the founders own 200,000 shares

Table 4.1 shows the calculation of the value of the equity, the pre-money price per share prior to conversion of the note, and the post-money price per share after conversion (as-converted basis).

The convertible note is treated as equity, so the only debt is the venture debt of $300,000. Net debt after subtracting cash is $200,000 = $300,000 − $100,000. The value of the equity using equation (4) is:

$$Enterprise\ value = [Total\ debt - Cash] + Equity$$

$$\$2.7\ million = [300,000 - 100,000] + Equity$$

$$Equity = \$2.5\ million$$

We use this equity value and the pre-money shares outstanding to find the pre-money price per share:

$$Pre\text{-}money\ price\ per\ share = Equity \div Pre\text{-}money\ shares\ outstanding$$

$$\$10.00 = \$2.5\ million \div 250,000$$

Table 4.1. Calculation of Pre-Money and Post-Money Price Per Share

Enterprise value	$ 2,700,000
– Net debt	200,000
= Equity	$ 2,500,000
÷ Pre-money shares outstanding	250,000
= Pre-money price per share	$ 10.00
Convertible note, accrued value	$ 600,000
÷ Pre-money price per share	$ 10.00
= New shares created	60,000
+ Pre-money shares outstanding	250,000
= Post-money shares outstanding	310,000
Equity	$ 2,500,000
÷ Post-money shares outstanding	310,000
= Post-money price per share	$ 8.06

The convertible note has a valuation cap of $3 million, above the current EV of $2.5 million, so the cap is not used. The convertible's accrued value is the face value of $500,000 plus the unpaid interest of $100,000 = $600,000. This accrued value is used for calculating the number of shares created upon conversion. We use the pre-money price per share, so the note converts into 60,000 shares:

New shares = Convertible note, accrued value ÷ Pre-money price per share

60,000 = $600,000 ÷ $10.00

Now we can calculate the post-money shares outstanding and the post-money price per share.

Post-money shares outstanding = 250,000 + 60,000 = 310,000 shares

Post-money price per share = $2.5 million ÷ 310,000 = $8.06

ANGEL VALUATION OF PRE-REVENUE START-UPS

Now that we have valuation principles and some idea of how to divide the pie, let's look at how angel investors assign a value to a start-up. Since seed investing in pre-revenue start-ups is so difficult, various high-profile angels have developed their own approaches that have become industry standards. We will look at the methods developed by Bill Payne, Dave Berkus, and the Ohio TechAngels.

Recall from Chapter 3 that angel investors are high net–worth individuals who invest in start-ups at the seed stage. Angels are experienced entrepreneurs or business executives who are motivated to give back by financing and mentoring young founders. Early-stage investing is risky, so angels either invest in a portfolio of start-ups or diversify their holdings by pooling their money in angel groups and investing together. Research for the US found that 10% of angel investments accounted for 90% of total returns. A diversified portfolio returned an average of 2.6x the original investment over 3.5 years, which equates to an IRR of about 27%.

Let's look at the four approaches.

The Bill Payne Scorecard Method

Bill Payne is a successful US angel investor who has been active since 1980. According to his online profile, he has invested in over 50 start-up companies.[1] He founded four angel groups and is the author of *The Definitive Guide to Raising Money from Angels* (2011), which can be downloaded free online.[2]

Table 4.2 illustrates Bill Payne's Scorecard method, which is a form of relative valuation. It works by comparing a start-up to recent angel-funded deals in each region and sector, then adjusting the valuation up or down based on seven dimensions. Payne starts with an average pre-money valuation of $2 million. He then adjusts this valuation up or down using the seven categories. The angel needs to conduct due diligence and use their experience to decide this starting point and the weighting for each of the seven categories. The value will be different in Silicon Valley, New York, Chicago, and Detroit. The final value is the sum of the seven components.

Let's say you are an experienced angel. Your value for a start-up is shown in Table 4.2. You start with a pre-money valuation of $2 million and adjust the seven categories from Bill Payne's starting weights. You decide the start-up's founder and team are better than average, so you increase this weighting by 1.25x to 37.5%, which leads to 37.5% × $2.0 million = $0.75 million. The market opportunity is better than average (1.50x), adding 37.5% × $2.0 million = $0.75 million. The product and technology are average (1.00x), adding 15% × $2.0 million = $0.30 million. This start-up is weaker than its competition (0.75x) and needs to work on building its sales channels and partnerships (0.80x). The need for additional investment is average (1.00x). In the "Other" category, early customer feedback on the product is good (1.00x). Based on these adjustments, the scorecard adds up to 115.5% of $2.00 million, or $2.31 million. This is the pre-money valuation.

Table 4.2. Bill Payne Scorecard Valuation

Scorecard	Average Weight	Increase / Decrease	Adjusted Weight	Pre-Money Valuation (in millions)
Average pre-money valuation in region				$ 2.00
Adjustments:				
x Strength of entrepreneur and team	30%	1.25 x	37.5%	0.75
x Size of the opportunity	25%	1.50 x	37.5%	0.75
x Product/technology	15%	1.00 x	15.0%	0.30
x Competitive environment	10%	0.75 x	7.5%	0.15
x Marketing, sales channels, partnerships	10%	0.80 x	8.0%	0.16
x Need for additional investment	5%	1.00 x	5.0%	0.10
x Other (e.g., early customer feedback)	5%	1.00 x	5.0%	0.10
Pre-money valuation	100.0%		115.5%	$ 2.31

The Payne Scorecard is subjective and relies on expert judgment. Like a relative valuation, it starts from a comparison of recent deals. But other start-ups may not be comparable, and two angels may reach different conclusions. The Payne Scorecard illustrates how early-stage valuation is an art, not a science.

The Dave Berkus Method

Dave Berkus is another successful US investor who has invested in more than 100 start-ups and founded an angel group.[3] Berkus first published his valuation method in 1996 and updated it in 2016.[4] Berkus assigns a pre-money valuation by rating how the start-up is managing the risks faced by all young companies. Starting from a base of $500,000 for having a sound business idea, Berkus adds up to $500,000 for each of four categories:

1 Does the start-up have a working prototype (reducing technology risk)?
2 Does the start-up have a quality management team (reducing the risk of failure on execution)?
3 Does the start-up have product rollout or sales (reducing production risk)?
4 Does the start-up have strategic relationships (reducing market risk)?

Berkus answers these questions by speaking to the founders, management team, developers, key employees, and customers. His maximum pre-money valuation is $2.5 million = $500,000 + (4 × $500,000).

Table 4.3. Dave Berkus Method

Category	What?	Speak to?	Maximum	Pre-Money Valuation
Sound business idea	Base value	Founders	$ 500,000	$ 500,000
Risk addressed:				
+ Quality team	Execution	Management	500,000	500,000
+ Working prototype	Technology	Developers	500,000	500,000
+ Product rollout/sales	Production	Key employees	500,000	150,000
+ Strategic relationships	Marketing	Customers	500,000	250,000
Pre-money valuation			$ 2,500,000	$ 1,900,000

Table 4.3 provides an example. The base valuation is $500,000. The start-up has a quality team and working prototype, but they have poor production and are weak on marketing. The pre-money valuation is therefore $1.9 million, which is below the highest recommended valuation of $2.5 million.

The Risk Factor Summation Method

The Risk Factor Summation method is not attributed to any individual angel, although it is described by Bill Payne as "described by the Ohio TechAngels."[5] Like the Payne Scorecard method, it starts from an average valuation based on similar start-ups in the region. The angel then adjusts this pre-money valuation upward or downward based on their assessment of 12 risks.

Anything that lowers the risk increases the pre-money valuation, while anything that increases the risk reduces it. The angel assigns a number from –2 to +2 to each risk category, where negative is a reduction and positive is an increase in risk. Lowering risk by 1 unit increases the pre-money valuation by $250,000, while increasing risk by 1 unit reduces it by this amount.

In the example in Table 4.4, the base valuation for a start-up is $2.0 million. The angel makes subjective risk adjustments that mostly cancel each other out. Overall, they increase the pre-money valuation to $2.25 million.

VENTURE CAPITAL VALUATION OF GROWTH COMPANIES

We have been looking at how an angel investor assigns a valuation to a pre-revenue start-up at the seed stage. Now we look at how VCs assign a value when the start-up is entering the growth stage. By the time the founder is ready to pitch a VC for a

Table 4.4. Risk Factor Summation Method

Risk Category	Assessment (negative = lower, positive = higher)	Pre-money Valuation
Base valuation		$ 2,000,000
Management	−2	500,000
Stage of the business	1	−250,000
Legislation/political risk	0	0
Manufacturing risk	2	−500,000
Sales and marketing risk	−1	250,000
Funding/capital-raising risk	1	−250,000
Competition risk	0	0
Technology risk	−1	250,000
Litigation risk	1	−250,000
International risk	0	0
Reputation risk	0	0
Potential lucrative exit	−2	500,000
Pre-money valuation	−1	$ 2,250,000

Series A funding round, the start-up will have a product, its first customers, and some monthly recurring revenue (MRR). The start-up will have a capitalization table detailing the existing shareholders, shares outstanding, and capital raised in prior funding rounds. Unlike angel investors, VCs will have the benefit of the start-up's brief operating history when assigning a valuation. But this process is still an art, not a science. And the VC will likely be in a stronger bargaining position than the founders.

The key driver of the VC valuation is the size of the market opportunity. In Chapter 2, we talked about the total addressable market (TAM), serviceable available market (SAM), and serviceable obtainable market (SOM). Recall that TAM is the whole market (e.g., wealth management industry), SAM is the segment targeted by the start-up (e.g., market for robo-advice), and SOM is the market share a start-up can realistically achieve (e.g., 10% of the market for robo-advice). A VC may like an entrepreneur's idea, but they will not invest unless the start-up has the potential to become a "billion-dollar company." It is not enough to have a good idea – there also need to be a lot of customers willing to pay for it.

The VC Valuation Method

VCs are looking for investments with the potential to generate an IRR of 25% to 35% over a 6- to 10-year horizon. To achieve this lofty goal, a start-up must go after a large market and grow sales exponentially.

Let's look at a quick example. Assume a start-up will be sold for a price-to-earnings (P/E) multiple of 15x earnings after eight years. This future value for the business is called the terminal value (TV) and the 15x P/E multiple is called the exit multiple. Let's assume a start-up is forecast to generate $400 million of sales in year 8 with a net margin of 10% of sales, implying net income of $40 million. What is the TV?

$$TV = Earnings \times \frac{Price}{Earnings} = \$40 \text{ million} \times 15 = \$600 \text{ million}$$

In this case, we have used a P/E multiple and found the value of the equity. We can also find the enterprise value (EV) using a multiple of EV-to-EBITDA, where EBITDA is earnings before interest, taxes, depreciation, and amortization. To use this exit multiple, we would need to forecast EBITDA in the terminal year. We could then back out the value of the equity by deducting net debt.

The exit multiples used to forecast the TV of a start-up are typically based on comparable firms in the same industry. While no two firms are ever alike, the average (or median) multiple of several comparable companies should be used. Even this process may be difficult when a start-up is creating a new market and, therefore, is not comparable to any existing firms. We discuss this problem below.

If the start-up has a TV of $400 million in year 8, what is the equity worth today? The PV depends on the discount rate. If we use a discount rate of 25%, then $600 million discounted for 8 years is equal to $100 million today:

$$PV = \frac{FV}{(1+r\%)^n} = \frac{\$600 \text{ million}}{(1+25\%)^8} = \$100 \text{ million}$$

This example illustrates how VCs think about valuation. The VC valuation method works backward from the exit value of the investment, or TV, and applies a discount rate to calculate the value today. The VC's exit may take the form of an IPO, where shares are sold to the public, or an acquisition by a competitor. Either way, the VC valuation method forecasts what they think the start-up will be worth in the future and the funding required to get there. Then the VC figures out how much to invest today to generate their desired IRR of 25% to 35%. In other words, the VC generates a forecast and backs out the size of their investment today.

The VC will use an IRR at the higher end of the 25% to 35% range for a higher-risk start-up, and an IRR at the lower end for a lower-risk one. This venture capital valuation method also generates a price per share based on backing out the value of the equity and dividing by the number of shares outstanding.

Of course, a VC knows that not every investment will reach exit, as many will fail. So, we need to modify the discount rate, taking into account the probability of exit. Let's assume the probability of any start-up surviving each year is 20%, or a 1-in-5 chance. The discount rate to use in the VC valuation method is based on equation (5):

$$r\% = \frac{(1+target\ IRR)}{(1-probability\ of\ failure)} - 1 = \frac{(1+25\%)}{(1-20\%)} - 1 = 0.5625\ or\ 56.25\% \tag{5}$$

In other words, the discount rate is increased to 56.25% per annum to achieve a 25% IRR with a probability of bankruptcy in any year of 20%.

Let's work through another example to calculate the price per share in a Series A round. We start with some assumptions:

- The founders and angels hold 1 million shares.
- The start-up is forecast to earn a profit of $2 million when it is sold in five years' time.
- The exit multiple is 20x P/E.
- The VC's target IRR is 25%.
- The probability of the start-up surviving each year is 20%, or a 1-in-5 chance.
- The VC invests $2.5 million in Series A.
- Net debt is $0.

Using these initial assumptions, we can determine the share price using these steps:

1 Calculate the TV at exit.

$$TV = \$2\ million \times 20\ P/E = \$40\ million$$

2 Calculate the discount rate adjusted for the risk of bankruptcy.

$$r\% = \frac{(1+target\ IRR)}{(1-probability\ of\ failure)} - 1 = \frac{(1+25\%)}{(1-20\%)} - 1 = 56.25\%$$

3 Calculate the post-money valuation required to achieve the required IRR. In this case, a TV of $40 million discounted at 56.25% for 5 years has a present value of $4.3 million.

$$PV = \frac{FV}{(1+r\%)^n} = \frac{\$40\ million}{(1+56.25\%)^5} = \frac{40\ million}{(1.5625)^5} = \$4.3\ million$$

4 Calculate the pre-money valuation before the VC invests. If the post-money valuation is $4.3 million and the VC invests $2.5 million, the pre-money valuation is

$$Post\text{-}money\ valuation = Pre\text{-}money\ valuation + VC\ investment$$

$$\$4.3\ million = Pre\text{-}money\ valuation + \$2.5\ million$$

$$Pre\text{-}money\ valuation = \$1.8\ million$$

5 Calculate the VC's ownership stake as a percentage of the post-money valuation.

$$VC\ ownership\ \% = VC\ investment \div Post\text{-}money\ valuation$$

$$58.2\% = \$2.5\ million \div \$4.3\ million$$

6 Calculate the post-money number of shares. Recall the sum of ownership stakes must total to 100%. If the VC has 58.2%, then the founders and angels own 41.8%. If the founders and angels have 1.0 million pre-money shares, the post-money shares are

$$\frac{Founders\ and\ angel\ shares}{VC\ shares} = \frac{1\ million}{X} = \frac{41.8\%}{58.2\%}$$

$$X = 1\ million \times \frac{58.2\%}{41.8\%} = 1.39\ million$$

The post-money shares are, therefore, 2.39 million = 1 million held by founders and angels and 1.39 million held by the VC.

7 Determine the price per share.

$$Price\ per\ share = \frac{Post-money\ valuation}{Post-money\ shares\ outstanding} = \frac{\$4.3\ million}{2.39\ million} = \$1.79$$

Based on a post-money valuation of $4.3 million and post-money shares outstanding of 2.39 million, each share is worth $1.79.

This example is based on a single funding round (i.e., Series A only) prior to exit. In practice, start-ups usually require multiple rounds of funding over many years. The capitalization table, discussed in the previous chapter, shows the shares held by different investors (e.g., founders, angels, VCs) and their ownership at each funding round.

These calculations become more complicated when the founders use stock options to attract and reward current and future employees. The cap table will need to take account this pool of shares for employees, called the Employee Share Ownership Plan (ESOP).

VALUATION OF MATURE COMPANIES

The two main ways that a VC can exit an investment is through an IPO or an acquisition. When a company goes public through an IPO, the shares are sold to institutional investors and the public. The VC may sell some shares at the time of the IPO and sell the remainder after their lock-up period ends. An acquisition provides a potentially quicker exit as a competitor or other financial buyer (i.e., an asset manager) buys all the start-up's shares. The VC may receive cash for their shares or new shares in the acquirer that the VC can hold or sell later.

Let's examine how to value a mature fintech that is going public through an IPO. We will use two valuation approaches: relative valuation using market multiples of comparable companies and fundamental valuation using a DCF model. Our discussion will be brief, as there are excellent books that examine both approaches in detail. One authoritative source is *Investment Banking: Valuation, LBOs, M&A, and IPOs*, third edition, by Joshua Rosenbaum and Joshua Pearl, listed under additional reading at the end of this chapter.

Relative Valuation Using Market Multiples

Relative valuation is based on comparing the value of similar things. We use it all the time without realizing it. When looking to buy a used car or a house, we look at similar cars or properties to see what other people paid for them. Of course, no two cars or houses are the same, which is why we look at an average of three to five comparables. The same is true with the valuation of companies.

Relative valuation of companies takes two forms: market multiples of comparable companies and precedent transactions.

Market multiples are a way of standardizing the value for a company's common share. The multiple compares a market-based measure in the numerator (stock price P or enterprise value EV) to an accounting-based measure in the denominator (sales, EBITDA, cash flow, earnings). The multiple may be backward-looking or forward-looking depending on the accounting-based measure. A backward-looking multiple covers a recent fiscal period, such as a fiscal year or quarter. You may see the term *last 12 months* (LTM) to indicate the most recent 4 quarters. Or the multiple may cover a future fiscal period, including the *next 12 months* (NTM) for the next 4 quarters.

Table 4.5. Common Market Multiples

Equity Multiples	Enterprise Multiples	
$\dfrac{Price\,per\,Share}{Earning\,per\,Share}$	$\dfrac{Enterprise\,Value}{Sales}$	$\dfrac{Enterprise\,Value}{EBITDA}$

Table 4.5 shows the most used market multiples: P/E, EV/Sales, and EV/ EBITDA. We say P/E is an equity multiple because it is based on the price of one common share. EV/Sales and EV/EBITDA are enterprise multiples because they take the perspective of all investors in the enterprise. Any of these multiples can be used to generate a value for one common share, directly using P or indirectly using EV. This value does not take into account a control premium. Market multiples fluctuate because the market prices used to calculate the numerators are always changing.

Precedent transactions are the multiples paid when a company is acquired. Precedent transactions give a snapshot at a point in time when a change of control takes place, which happens infrequently. A precedent transaction is the price to acquire 50% or more of the common shares, incorporating a control premium.

Both forms of relative valuation rely on three steps:

1 Identify comparable companies or transactions
2 Choose the valuation multiple
3 Generate an implied value for the target company

We start by identifying companies that are like the target company, called comparable companies (or "compcos"). We look for companies in the same industry, line of business, geography, and company size as our target company. Just like comparing used cars, we need companies that are as close as possible to our target, if they exist. We don't compare a sports car to a dump truck, or a motorcycle to a sports utility vehicle. If we are valuing a BMW, we would look at other BMWs, Audis, Mercedes, and high-end cars. But if we are valuing a Honda Civic, we compare it to Hondas, Fords, Toyotas, and other mid-price compact cars.

For the valuation to be useful, we need to find three to five comparable companies or precedent transactions. One or two comparables are not useful, as they may be outliers. Similarly, it is unlikely we can find ten companies that are like our target.

Once we have our comparables, we will calculate the average and the median, dropping any outliers that cause these two metrics to diverge. We want the average and median to be as close as possible.

Second, we calculate both equity and enterprise multiples for the comparable companies or precedent transactions. Other equity multiples to consider are price-to-sales and price-to-book value per share (also called market-to-book). Another enterprise multiple to consider is EV-to-EBIT. We do not compare EV to earnings as this would mix an enterprise multiple with an equity multiple. We can also use multiples that compare the EV to features of the company, such as the number of employees, the number of customers, or some other metric.

The analyst calculates the average (or median) multiple across the three to five comparable companies for the LTM and NTM. The assumption is that a reasonable buyer will offer the same multiple for the target company. If the average NTM P/E multiple of the comparable companies is 15x earnings, then this is a reasonable assumption when valuing our target company.

Third, the analyst uses this average or median multiple to generate an implied valuation for the target company. If the earnings of the target company are $10 million, then a 15x P/E multiple would imply a valuation of $150 million = 15 × $10 million. Relative valuation is imprecise, so analysts often calculate a variety of equity and enterprise multiples and generate a range of valuation. For example, we might calculate the implied valuation based on LTM and NTM P/E, EV-to-sales, and EV-to-EBITDA.

The key difference between market multiples and precedent transactions is that a market multiple is based on prices today, whereas a precedent multiple is based on the price paid in completed acquisitions. Precedent transactions are historical. We use this approach when buying a house. The buyer collects a list of recent sales in the neighborhood and compares the price with reference to square footage, number of bedrooms, or some other metric.

Let's look at an example of using precedent multiples to value a target company. We see that comparable companies were acquired at the following multiples of EV-to-sales: 3x, 2x, 4x, 5x, and 8x. The average of these precedents is 4.4x sales. If your target company has sales of $50 million, its implied value would be $220 million = 4.4 x $50 million.

Dropping outliers may affect the implied value. Dropping the 8x multiple and averaging the remaining 4 precedents generates an implied value of $175 million = 3.5 x $50 million. This value is 20% lower, showing how sensitive relative valuation can be to outliers.

We should also only consider transactions that happen in recent years. If the first two acquisitions happened too long ago, the average of the last three precedents is

Table 4.6. Market Multiples of Comparable Companies for Adyen

Company	Market Cap (US$ billions)	Price-to-Earnings		EV-to-Sales		EV-to-EBITDA		EBITDA Margin
		LTM	NTM	LTM	NTM	LTM	NTM	
Adyen	44.0	75.5	50.2	4.9	20.3	50.5	33.1	10%
VISA	386.8	29.3	23.8	13.4	12.0	19.0	17.0	71%
MasterCard	329.7	34.3	28.2	15.5	13.5	25.5	22.1	61%
Intuit	108.7	59.0	26.7	8.5	7.7	34.3	18.9	18%
PayPal	78.4	35.0	14.4	2.9	2.6	15.2	10.2	19%
Square	36.7	–	36.4	2.1	1.8	–	28.5	2%
Average		39.4	25.9	8.5	7.5	23.5	19.4	34%
Median		34.6	26.7	8.5	7.7	22.2	18.9	19%

Source: Refinitiv. As of December 20, 2022. LTM = Last 12 months, NTM = Next 12 months

5.67x and the target's implied value is $283 million = 5.67 × $50 million. Again, we see that relative valuation is an art, not a science.

Example: Adyen's Market Multiples for Payments

Table 4.6 shows the market multiples for the Dutch payments fintech Adyen (ticker: ADYEN) and select comparable companies. Adyen was founded in 2006 and went public on the Amsterdam stock exchange in 2018. We see the price in USD per share and the 52-week change, the market capitalization and the LTM and NTM market multiples. The EBITDA margin is EBITDA as percentage of revenues. In your opinion, is Adyen undervalued, overvalued, or correctly valued?

Fundamental Valuation Using Discounted Cash Flow (DCF)

The alternative valuation methodology is called fundamental (or intrinsic) valuation. It tries to value the company bottom-up by forecasting cash flows and finding the present value. The most widely used model is a discounted cash flow (DCF) model. The goal of a DCF valuation is to calculate the present value of free cash flows generated by the firm, which are cash flows that can be distributed to creditors and shareholders. We forecast the company's operating performance over a 5- to 10-year horizon. The projected free cash flow to the firm in each year is discounted to today, then summed up, generating an EV for the business.

Before continuing, we note that a DCF valuation cannot be used to value a bank, an insurance company, or some other financial intermediaries. These businesses do not generate cash flows and do not report a measure equivalent to EBITDA. We will return to the valuation of banks and similar financial intermediaries later in this chapter.

A DCF model is built starting with a forecast of sales, margins, and EBIT. We generate this forecast in an Excel spreadsheet using many assumptions (or guesses). The most important assumptions are sales growth, operating margins, investments in short-term assets (i.e., working capital), and investments in long-term assets (i.e., capital expenditures). These inputs are used to forecast excess cash that is generated by the business and can be paid out to investors, called free cash flow to the firm (FCFF). FCFF represents cash flows that do not need to be reinvested for the business to grow. In theory, they are excess and can be paid out to debt holders and shareholders.

Equation (6) shows the calculation of FCFF. This equation recognizes that a growing, profitable business is required to pay corporate taxes to the government. While accounting rules allow depreciation and amortization (D&A) to be deducted before calculating taxes, D&A is a non-cash expense so is added back when calculating FCFF. But cash needs to be invested in capital expenditures (CAPEX) to maintain assets. D&A and CAPEX are taken from the statement of cash flows. And cash needs to be invested in working capital in the form of inventory, receivables, and payables.

FCFF = EBIT(1 – tax rate) + D&A – CAPEX – Change in net working capital   (6)

Notice FCFF is not EBITDA. FCFF starts with EBIT, which includes both operating income and non-operating income. The calculation of FCFF does not consider how assets are financed, so there is no deduction of interest expense when calculating taxable earnings. For this reason, the appropriate amount of pre-tax income is measured using earnings before interest expense and taxes (EBIT).

FCFF deducts a theoretical amount of cash required to pay corporate taxes. We do not use actual taxes, which may be artificially low in any year due to accounting choices and capital structure choices. Instead, we use a forward-looking estimate based on the marginal (or statutory) tax rate paid by a business in each country. The assumption is that the marginal tax rate is most representative of what will be paid by the business over the future. You may see EBIT(1 – tax rate) called net operating profit after tax (NOPAT) or EBIT after-tax.

Net working capital (NWC) measures cash tied up in current assets minus current liabilities, excluding cash and short-term debt. Equation (7) is the formula for NWC. (We exclude cash and debt to avoid double counting because they are part of the calculation of EV.) Notice FCFF subtracts the change in NWC in each period, not the total amount shown on the balance sheet. Change in NWC from one year to the next captures the additional cash required to support the growth in sales.

$$NWC = (Current\ assets - Cash\ \&\ equivalents) - (Current\ liabilities$$
$$- Short\text{-}term\ debt) \tag{7}$$

When we value a business, we assume it goes on forever. This perpetuity assumption creates a problem for a fundamentals-based valuation such as a DCF model. Technically we need to forecast FCFF forever. To address this problem, we use a shortcut. We assume the business is sold at the end of our forecast horizon (after 5 to 10 years). This value in the future value is the terminal value (TV). Terminal means end point. In other words, TV is the market value of the assets at the end of our forecasting horizon. We call it TV to avoid confusion with EV, which is the market value of the assets today.

There are two approaches to calculate TV. The first approach uses a perpetuity growth formula, shown in equation (8):

$$TV_t = \frac{FCFF_t \times (1 + g\%)}{(r\% - g\%)} \tag{8}$$

where TV in the year t is calculated by forecasting FCFF in year $t+1$, divided by the discount rate r% minus the perpetuity growth rate g%, both expressed as decimals. The discount rate r% is typically the weighted average cost of capital (WACC), a value around 10% for mature companies. The perpetuity growth rate g% is the sustainable growth rate of earnings. This growth rate is typically close to the long-term nominal growth rate of GDP, or 2% to 4%. Using equation (8), a FCFF in year 5 of $10 million, WACC of 7%, and perpetuity growth of 3% generates a TV of $257.5 million = [$10 million × (1 + 0.03)] ÷ (0.07 − 0.03).

The second approach to calculate TV is to use a multiple of future EBITDA, shown in equation (9):

$$TV_t = EBITDA_t \times \frac{EV}{EBITDA} \tag{9}$$

Notice this method uses future EBITDA, not FCFF. Notice also that we use a relative valuation method, namely a multiple of EV-to-EBITDA. The choice of this future multiple is subjective, based on the analyst's judgment, but is often based on the current EV-to-EBITDA multiple for this business. So, if EBITDA in year 5 is $20 million and the EV-to-EBITDA multiple is 12x, then TV = $240 million = $20 million × 12. In general, it's a good idea to make sure both approaches lead to a similar TV.

Once we have a forecast of FCFF in each year and a TV at the end of our horizon, we calculate EV by discounting each of these cash flows and summing them up. The discount rate is the WACC. Equation (10) shows this formula based on a five-year forecast horizon:

$$EV = \frac{FCFF_1}{(1+WACC\%)^1} + \frac{FCFF_2}{(1+WACC\%)^2} + \frac{FCFF_3}{(1+WACC\%)^3} + \frac{FCFF_4}{(1+WACC\%)^4} + \frac{FCFF_5}{(1+WACC\%)^5} + \frac{TV_5}{(1+WACC\%)^5} \quad (10)$$

Notice in year 5, we discount both the final year FCFF and the TV. The TV represents all FCFFs from year 6 onwards in perpetuity. The DCF is, therefore, a perpetual forecast, although we use the TV as a shortcut for future years. As a result, this TV usually represents a sizable portion of the EV, typically 70% to 80% of the present value. For this reason, it is important to check the sensitivity of these calculations to different assumptions about sales growth, margins, WACC, and perpetuity growth rates.

We back out the value of the equity from EV using equation (4). Recall that Common equity = EV – Net debt – Preferred – NCI. If we want a price per share, we divide common equity by the number of common shares outstanding, Price = Equity ÷ Shares outstanding. The convention is to use fully diluted common shares outstanding, not basic shares outstanding.

ARK Invest and Adjusted EBITDA

ARK Invest's Cathie Wood is a high profile and controversial asset managers. She founded ARK Invest in 2014 after her employer, Alliance Bernstein, thought her proposed investment strategy was too risky. ARK Invest's family of disruptive innovation funds caught the public's imagination and rose to $50 billion of assets under management by February 2021. After generating a 100%+ return over the previous 12 months, these funds then collapsed by mid-2022 to $16 billion – a decline of close to 70%. This fall reflected the collapsing share prices of the underlying holdings and the withdrawal of funds by disappointed investors.

Let's look at ARK's Fintech Innovation ETF (ticker: ARKF). At the end of the third quarter of 2022, ARKF had $0.76 billion of assets under management and around 30 holdings. The share price rose dramatically over the first two years, from 2019 to 2021, then dropped by almost 80% from the peak. Figure 4.2 shows the performance of ARKF versus the Standard & Poor's 500 Index (S&P500) over the same period. Both series are indexed to 100 when the ARKF launched in February 2019. Over the same period, the S&P500 has increased by 50% while ARKF is down 10%, a dramatic underperformance versus the market.

Figure 4.2. ARKF Fintech Innovation ETF vs. S&P500 Index

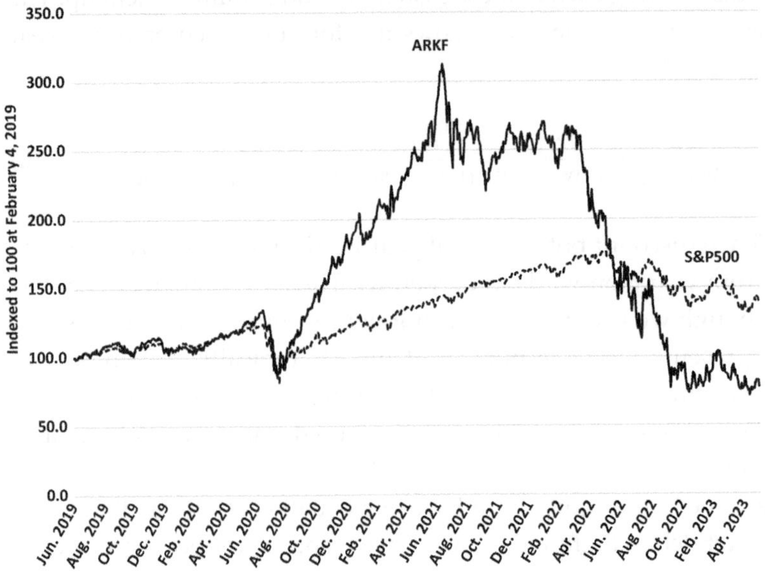

Source: Author, data from Refinitiv Eikon.

Table 4.7 shows 10 of these fintechs with their market multiples. This table high-lights the difficulty of using relative valuation for disruptive fintech companies. These disruptive fintech companies are different from traditional listed equities. We see many outliers. The P/E multiples are artificially high due to low earnings per share (EPS), or negative EPS in two cases. The same problems plague the EV multiples. Eight out of 10 companies are outliers in EV/EBITDA, either unreasonably high (above 20x) or negative for 2 fintechs with negative EBITDA. While the EV/Sales multiples are more reasonable (between 2x and 10x), this multiple is negative for Robinhood Markets. How is this possible? Robinhood has positive sales but has a negative EV. Its stock market capitalization is lower than the value of cash holdings on the balance sheet.

Wood argues that traditional accounting metrics penalize disruptive technology companies that are investing aggressively to transform industries and scale into mass market opportunities. In the article "Disruptive Innovation and Profitability," Wood makes the case that US Generally Accepted Accounting Principles (GAAP) are not reasonable for valuing what critics call "profitless tech" companies.[6] These younger companies sacrifice short-term profits to achieve exponential growth and capture highly profitable opportunities.

Table 4.7. ARK Fintech Innovation ETF Holdings

Company	Business	Country	P/E[1]	EV/ Sales[1]	EV/ EBITDA[1]
Shopify	E-commerce	Canada	60.5	8.5	415.6
Square	Payments	US	41.5	2.5	126.1
Mercado Libre	E-commerce	Uruguay	473.2	4.7	104.3
Coinbase	Crypto	US	2.7	1.4	14.0
Robinhood Markets	Wealth	US	Neg	Neg	Neg
Adyen	Payments	Netherlands	97.7	5.6	106.5
Discovery Ltd.	Insurtech	South Africa	1,418.6	1.4	6.7
Intuit	Personal finance	US	36.2	9.4	39.9
Nubank	Digital bank	Brazil	970.0	7.7	Neg
Zillow Group	Real estate	US	Neg	1.3	59.4

1. Sales, EBITDA, and earnings are for the past fiscal year. Neg = negative. Stock price as of December 15, 2022.
Source: ARK Fintech Innovation ETF, Refinitiv.

Now you may be thinking, "Cathie Wood is just trying to justify why the price of ARK ETFs should be worth more than what the market is currently paying for them." That may indeed be the case. Remember how we talked about incentives in earlier chapters? Wood's incentive is to increase the value of her ETFs. It is important to be skeptical whenever someone is selling something. Keeping that in mind, let's see what she says.

Wood argues for making five adjustments to GAAP-based EBITDA for disruptive tech companies. The five areas are research and development (R&D), sales and marketing expense, stock-based compensation, deferred revenue, and asset impairment. Each of these areas reduces EBITDA under US GAAP and profitability. Wood argues that they also have the potential to generate significant cash flow and profits in the future.

First, disruptive technology companies invest heavily in R&D. Wood highlights that the ARK disruptive companies have a median R&D expense of 28.5%, which is 2.5x higher than the 12% for the median company in the Nasdaq 100.[7] Under US GAAP, R&D is expensed on the income statement. But International Financial Reporting Standards (IFRS) allows a portion of R&D to be capitalized as an asset on the balance sheet. Wood argues for adding back R&D expense, which will increase EBITDA and earnings.

Second, disruptive technology companies spend heavily on sales and marketing to grow their customer bases. The ARK disruptive companies have a median sales and marketing expense of 33.2% of sales, twice as high as the 17.2% for the median Nasdaq 100 company. Part of this expense is normal to maintain market share. But as we discussed earlier, fintech companies need to invest heavily to acquire customers and grow their business. Wood argues for adding back part of sales and market expense to EBITDA.

Third, disruptive technology companies reward employees with stock-based compensation. Stock-based compensation is a non-cash reward for employees, such as the issuance of restricted shares and equity options. The ARK disruptive companies have a median stock-based compensation of 22.6%, which is 7x higher than the 3.2% for the median Nasdaq 100 company. US GAAP requires stock-based compensation to be included in cost of goods sold and expensed when awarded. Wood argues for adding back this non-cash expense to EBITDA, like depreciation and amortization.

Fourth, deferred revenue is a liability created when customers prepay for products and services. Many disruptive technology companies sign multi-year contracts and collect cash up front from customers. Under US GAAP, these revenues are not recognized. Instead, the cash is offset by a liability on the balance sheet. Wood argues that deferred revenue is a sign of validation of the business, indicating higher growth and declining cost curves in the future. It should, therefore, be counted in EBITDA when received.

Fifth, asset impairment is a non-cash expense reflecting the marking down of assets to their fair market value. When a company makes an acquisition, the cost of the acquired assets over fair value is goodwill on the acquirer's balance sheet. Under US GAAP, these assets are tested for impairment each year by comparing the book value against the market value. If the book value is higher, there is an asset impairment expense that reduces EBITDA and earnings. Wood argues that one-time asset impairment charges triggered by the decline in stock markets do not impact the long-term growth and cash flow of companies. Instead, this non-cash charge should be added back to EBITDA.

In summary, ARK Invest adjusts EBITDA for disruptive technology companies in five ways:

1 Add back R&D expense
2 Add back incremental sales and marketing spent on gaining market share
3 Add back stock-based compensation
4 Add back deferred revenue
5 Add back one-time non-cash asset impairments

Using adjusted EBITDA, Wood illustrates that the disruptive technology companies in the ARK ETFs have positive cash flows, which is a better reflection of their longer-term growth and profitability profile. This example illustrates the problem of market multiples. They can be manipulated by adjusting sales, EBITDA, and earnings per share. So, always check how these metrics are calculated!

VALUATION OF BANKS AND FINANCIAL INTERMEDIARIES

Bank equity analysts use financial ratios to evaluate how a bank is doing, relative to its peers, and value the stock using market multiples of earnings and book value. But the nature of bank accounting means that sales and EBITDA are not available. As a result, it is not possible to use enterprise multiples or a DCF model.

Let's start by looking at the financial statements for a typical bank. Table 4.8 shows the balance sheet for the largest US bank, JPMorgan, for the years 2020 to 2022. We see the totals in billions of US dollars on the left and the common-size balance sheet on the right. A common-size balance sheet shows each of the categories as a percentage of total assets.

In general, a bank's profitability is driven by how it uses its balance sheet, how it is leveraged, and how it manages risks. Loans made up 30% of total assets in 2022, with other interest-earning assets at 41%, cash at 15%, and other assets at 13%. JPMorgan financed its assets in 2022 primarily with deposits (64%), debt (14%), other liabilities (14%), and then equity (8%). These figures reflect JPMorgan's diversified business model, which combines commercial and retail banking with investment banking and asset management businesses.

Table 4.8. JPMorgan Balance Sheet, 2020 to 2022

	2020	2021	2022	2020	2021	2022
Fiscal year ending Dec. 31	$ in Billions			% of Assets		
Cash & due from banks	503	721	540	15	19	15
Loans, net	985	1,061	1,116	29	28	30
Other interest-earning assets	1,470	1,516	1,515	43	41	41
Other assets	427	445	494	13	12	13
Assets	3,385	3,744	3,666	100	100	00
Deposits	2,144	2,462	2,340	63	66	64
Debt	528	538	531	16	14	14
Other liabilities	433	449	502	13	12	14
Liabilities	3,105	3,449	3,373	92	92	92
Equity	279	294	292	8	8	8

Source: JPMorgan Annual Reports.

Table 4.9. JPMorgan Income Statement, 2020 to 2022

	2020	2021	2022	2020	2021	2022
Fiscal year ending Dec. 31	$ in Billions			% of Revenues		
Net interest income	55	52	67	45	43	52
Noninterest income	65	69	62	55	57	48
Total revenues	120	122	129	100	100	100
Less: Provision for credit losses	5	–9	6	4	–8	5
Less: Noninterest expense	79	71	76	66	59	59
Less: Income taxes	7	11	8	6	9	7
Net income	29	48	38	24	40	29
Net interest margin %	2.2	2.0	2.5			
Efficiency ratio %	66	59	59			

Source: JPMorgan Annual Reports.

Table 4.9 shows JPMorgan's income statement for the years 2020 to 2022. We see the totals in billions of US dollars on the left and the common-size income statement on the right. A common-size income statement shows each of the line items as a percentage of total revenues.

JPMorgan earned revenues from two sources: net interest income (52% of 2022 revenues) and noninterest income (48%). Net interest income is the profit from lending and investing businesses, calculated as interest income minus interest expense. A typical bank issues loans funded with deposits and earns a spread between the lending and borrowing rates. If we charge 5% on a loan (interest income) and pay 2% on a deposit (interest expense), we generate a gross profit of 3%. Banks like JPMorgan also earn interest income from investing in bonds and dividend-paying stocks.

Analysts measure the profitability of this interest-earning part of a bank's business using the net interest margin (NIM) ratio. NIM is total net interest income divided by average interest-earning assets. The typical NIM ratio for a North American bank ranges from 1% to 3%, with JPMorgan earning 2.5% in 2022, an increase over the previous two years due to the rise in interest rates.

Noninterest income is generated from fees and commissions. Fees and commissions are charges for bank accounts and debit transactions, for credit cards, for underwriting and advisory mandates, for originating and servicing mortgages, and for managing assets. Noninterest income includes profits (or losses) from trading and risk-taking businesses. Noninterest expenses include salaries, marketing, and other costs of running the bank. A bank must deduct provisions for credit losses, which is an estimate of loans that will not be repaid. Net income (or profit) is then pre-tax profit less income taxes.

We measure a bank's ability to manage its costs using the efficiency ratio. It is the ratio of noninterest expense to total revenues. JPMorgan's efficiency ratio in 2022 was 59%, an improvement over 2020.

We evaluate the bank's profitability using the return on assets (ROA) and the return on equity (ROE). ROA is the ratio of net income to total assets. Given that bank balance sheets are large and competition among banks is high, ROA ratios are low, typically below 2%. Bank shareholders tend to focus on ROE, which is the ratio of net income available to common shareholders divided by common equity (at book value).[8] ROE provides a measure of the return earned in a given year for every dollar of common equity. Bank ROEs average from 8% to 18%. ROE is sensitive to the amount of financial leverage measured as the ratio of total assets to common equity. The relationship between ROE, ROA, and financial leverage can be illustrated using equation (11):

$$ROE = \frac{Net\ Income}{Common\ Equity} = \frac{Net\ Income}{Assets} \times \frac{Assets}{Common\ Equity} = ROA \times Financial\ Leverage \quad (11)$$

This decomposition of ROE shows that a bank can transform low ROA into high ROE using financial leverage. For example, when a bank with total assets of $100 is funded using $10 of common equity, then an ROA of 1% equates to an ROE of 10% = ROA × Leverage = 1% × (100 ÷ 10). One obvious way to increase ROA is to take greater risks on loans, which may lead to higher profitability in the short run but larger losses in the long run. Investors carefully monitor bank risk taking to make sure it is not excessive.

We value bank stocks by comparing the market multiples of similar banks to each other. Bank analysts focus on two multiples: the price-to-earnings (P/E) and price-to-book (P/Book) ratios. We saw the P/E multiple earlier. The P/Book, also called market-to-book, is the ratio of the share price to the book value per common share. Analysts typically consider both backward-looking (LTM) and forward-looking (NTM) multiples.

Table 4.10 compares JPMorgan to comparable global banks. JPMorgan has a larger stock market capitalization and earns an above average ROE of 15% (relative to the peer average of 9.7%). This ROE reflects an above average ROA of 0.6% (versus peers of 0.3%) and above average financial leverage of 12.5x (versus peers of 11.5x). JPMorgan has a similar price-to-earnings multiple to its peers but a higher price-to-book multiple. Notice that JPMorgan has a Tier 1 regulatory ratio of 13.5%, above its peers.

Table 4.10. JPMorgan vs. Comparable US Banks

Company	Market Capitalization (US$ billions)	ROE %	ROA %	Assets to Equity	Price to Equity	Price to Book	Tier 1 Capital Ratio %
JPMorgan	410	15.2	0.6	12.5	9.9	1.3	13.5
Bank of America	243	10.6	0.1	11.2	9.1	0.9	11.2
Wells Fargo	155	8.6	0.0	10.4	10.0	0.9	10.6
Morgan Stanley	149	11.1	1.4	11.8	14.1	1.5	15.3
Goldman Sachs	113	10.5	−0.1	12.3	11.2	1.0	15.1
Citigroup	97	7.8	0.1	12.0	7.3	0.5	13.0
Average of 5 peers	152	9.7	0.3	11.5	10.4	0.9	13.0
Median of 5 peers	149	10.5	0.1	11.8	10.0	0.9	13.0

Source: Refinitiv Eikon, as of April 15, 2023.

Table 4.11. Valuation Multiples and Financial Ratios for Select Fintech Companies

Company	Market Capitalization (US$ billions)	ROE %	ROA %	Assets to Equity	Price to Earnings NTM	Price to Book NTM	EV to EBITDA NTM
Square	38.6	−5.3	−2.4	1.8	32.7	2.1	25.7
Kakao Pay	6.1	3.1	0.8	1.8	226.1	4.4	143.1
Paytm	5.0	−22.4	−17.7	1.3	−38.9	3.4	−55.1
PayPal	86.8	11.5	3.1	3.9	14.9	3.8	11.0
Robinhood	8.9	−14.4	−4.8	3.4	−22.4	1.3	17.2
SoFi	5.6	−7.5	−2.3	3.4	−43.9	1.1	16.4
Wise Plc	7.4	14.4	0.6	18.5	38.0	11.0	22.1
Average	22.6	−2.9	−3.2	4.9	29.5	3.9	25.8
Median	7.4	−5.3	−2.3	3.4	14.9	3.4	17.2

Source: Refinitiv, as of April 15, 2023.

Example: Financial Ratios and Market Multiples

Table 4.11 shows the market multiples for the next 12 months and the financial ratios for a range of publicly listed fintechs, listed alphabetically. We see lots of variation and some potential outliers. In your opinion, which one is most attractive as an investment and why?

Key Terms

comparable companies (compcos)

discounted cash flow (DCF) model

efficiency ratio

enterprise value (EV)

financial leverage

free cash flow to the firm (FCFF)

last 12 months (LTM)

market multiples

net interest margin (NIM)

net working capital (NWC)

next 12 months (NTM)

noninterest income

perpetuity growth formula

precedent transactions

price-to-book (P/Book)

price-to-earnings (P/E)

return on assets (ROA)

return on equity (ROE)

terminal value (TV)

QUESTIONS FOR DISCUSSION

1   What are the four steps in valuation? How do they work together?

2   What is enterprise value (EV) and how is it calculated? How do you use EV to arrive at a valuation of the equity in a business?

3   What do the Bill Payne Scorecard and the Risk Factor Summation method for pre-revenue start-ups have in common? How are these angel valuation methods different from the Dave Berkus method?

4   What roles do the terminal value and target IRR play in the VC valuation method? How does a VC use this method to arrive at a pre-money valuation for a start-up?

5   What is the main difference between a relative valuation and a fundamental valuation for a mature company?

6   Why do market multiples of comparable companies not work for younger fintech companies?

7   What is the goal of a discounted cash flow (DCF) valuation? What is free cash flow to the firm (FCFF)?

8   What are the five ways in which ARK Invest recommends adjusting EBITDA for disruptive technology companies?

9   What is the logic behind ARK Invest Cathie Wood's five adjustments to EBITDA for disruptive tech companies? In your opinion, are they justified or not?

10   What methodology is used for valuing a bank like JPMorgan? What are the main multiples used?

ADDITIONAL READING

Angel Resource Institute, "2020 ARI HALO Report," https://angelresourceinstitute.org/.

Anshuman, V. Ravi, John Martin, and Sheridan Titman, 2012, "An Entrepreneur's Guide to Understanding the Cost of Venture Capital," *Journal of Applied Corporate Finance* 24, no. 3 (2012): 75–83.

Hellmann, Thomas, Paul Schure, and Dan H. Vo, "Angels and Venture Capitalists: Substitutes or Complements?" *Journal of Financial Economics* 141, no. 2 (2021): 454–478.

Rosenbaum, Joshua, and Joshua Pearl, *Investment Banking: Valuation, LBOs, M&A, and IPOs*, 3rd ed. (New York: Wiley Finance, 2020).

VC University, "Democratizing Access to Venture Capital Education," accessed December 15, 2021, https://venturecapitaluniversity.com/.

Wood, Cathie, "Disruptive Innovation and Profitability," ARK Invest, December 1, 2022, https://ark-funds.com/articles/commentary/disruptive-innovation-and-profitability/.Table 4.11. Valuation Multiples and Financial Ratios for Select Fintech Companies

5

Bitcoin, Blockchain, and Cryptocurrencies

SUMMARY

- The first cryptocurrency Bitcoin was launched in 2009, providing an innovative solution to the double-spend problem known as hashing.
- Ownership of bitcoins is recorded in an electronic distributed ledger called the blockchain, so-named because transactions are batch processed in blocks and secured using cryptography in an immutable, append-only, public ledger.
- Other developers soon launched alternative cryptocurrencies to Bitcoin ("altcoins"), and later digital tokens. The common feature of these cryptoassets is they are all recorded on separate blockchains.
- Many cryptoassets were pre-mined and sold to the public through initial coin offerings (ICOs), before regulators shut down this market in mid-2018 due to the large number of frauds.
- As the cryptocurrency market has grown, innovations such as cryptowallets for storage and cryptoexchanges for trading of cryptoassets have emerged to address pain points.
- Academic researchers have studied the economics of Bitcoin as a means of payment, the ability to conduct arbitrage across cryptocurrency exchanges, and the returns from investing in cryptocurrencies versus traditional assets.

The previous chapter outlined how angel investors and VCs value a fintech and the methods used to value more mature fintechs and financial intermediaries using market multiples of comparable companies.

This chapter dives into the world of Bitcoin, cryptocurrencies, and other digital tokens. These electronic forms of money are recorded on an electronic ledger called a blockchain that records ownership and is secured using cryptography. The emergence of the blockchain technology is driving innovations in how companies are organized, contracts are set up, and incentives are established, known as the field of cryptoeconomics.

THE RISE (AND FALL) OF CRYPTOECONOMICS

Cryptoassets are arguably the purest form of fintech innovation, as they are made possible by technology. A cryptoasset is a digital asset that ownership of is recorded on an electronic, distributed ledger known as a blockchain. (Blockchain is a generic term and not a proper noun, so it is not capitalized.) A blockchain is secured against alteration using cryptography.

The science of cryptography is based on mathematics using computer algorithms to encode and protect information (data) and communications (messages). The word *crypto* comes from the Greek word *kryptos*, which means hidden. Cryptography was already used more than 2,000 years ago by the Ancient Egyptians and the Roman Empire, who both used ciphers to encode messages.

The most widely known cryptoasset is a form of digital money called a cryptocurrency. The first cryptocurrency, Bitcoin, emerged in 2009 and was quickly followed by competing digital coins known as Alternatives to Bitcoin (or altcoins). Cryptocurrencies were soon joined by other digital assets known as tokens: utility tokens, securities tokens, governance tokens, and non-fungible tokens (NFTs). The total value of cryptocurrencies was around $1.3 trillion in April 2023, a sharp decline from $2.0 trillion at year-end 2021.

A utility (or service) token records a claim to a product or service. A security token represents an ownership claim to the cash flows generated by a business or asset (such as real estate). A governance token provides the holder with the ability to vote. A non-fungible token (NFT) is a cryptographically secured data file that is non-interchangeable but can be bought or sold, such as a digital piece of art, a photo, a video, or an audio clip. All these digital assets are recorded on some form of blockchain and secured against tampering using cryptography.

Cryptocurrencies and tokens are a fascinating, volatile landscape. Prices go up and down through different "crypto winters." Cybersecurity is always an issue, particularly with the increase in hacking and emerging technologies such as quantum computing. Like the broader financial markets, the crypto markets have seen their share of fraud and scams. The bottom line for anyone interested in cryptoassets is *caveat emptor*, which is Latin for "buyer beware." We all need to be informed and educated when making investment decisions and avoid behavioral biases such as FOMO (fear of missing out).

BITCOIN: THE FIRST CRYPTOCURRENCY

The digital currency bitcoin, or BTC, is the creation of an anonymous individual (or group) known as Satoshi Nakamoto, who posted a nine-page working paper on the internet in 2008 titled "Bitcoin: A Peer-to-Peer Electronic Cash System."[1]

Satoshi Nakamoto is a pseudonym and not the inventor's real name. To this day, Satoshi's true identify is unknown. While some have claimed to be the fabled creator and others are rumored, the consensus is that the real individual or group of individuals has yet to be revealed. Contrary to standard practice, we refer to the Bitcoin founder using the first name "Satoshi," not the surname "Nakamoto."

Satoshi's motivation was to create a currency not controlled by a central authority. Satoshi explained that a purely peer-to-peer (P2P) version of electronic cash would allow online payments to be sent directly from one party to another without going through a central intermediary, such as a central bank.

Bitcoin was a response to a loss of confidence in the traditional financial system after the 2008–2009 Global Financial Crisis. The second block in the Bitcoin blockchain includes the date and headline from a leading British newspaper: "The Times 03/Jan/2009 Chancellor on Brink of Second Bailout for Banks."[2]

We need to clarify some spelling. Purists use the uppercase "B" in Bitcoin when referring to the concept of Bitcoin or the network for transacting in this digital coin. But individual coins and the currency unit are spelled with a lowercase "b" as bitcoins. There is even controversy over whether the plural form is bitcoins or bitcoin, although Satoshi reportedly used both in bitcointalk posts![3] The bitcoin symbol is either ₿ or BTC. The Bitcoin network is open and transparent, with the core software freely available for download online.[4]

The Bitcoin network was launched over the internet in 2009, with Satoshi mining the first coins. Bitcoin has gone through many boom-and-bust cycles over the past decade, with dramatic price volatility and crypto winters. A crypto winter is a period of negative sentiment when prices have fallen, then remained low for an extended period. Typically, the winter ends with bitcoin tokens rallying to new heights, although the most recent crypto winter has been deeper than past episodes.

Figure 5.1 shows the BTC price in US dollars from CoinMarketCap, a leading website for data on cryptocurrencies.[5] The bitcoin price rose from below $1 to a peak of $35 in June 2011, before dropping again to $4. It then rose to almost $1,150 by late

Figure 5.1. Bitcoin Price and Crypto Winters

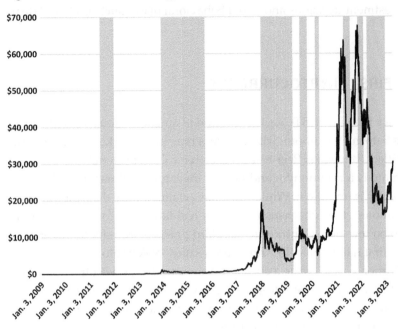

Source: Author, data from CoinMarketCap.

2013, crashed to a low of $177 in 2015, then bounced back to end 2015 at $428, before doubling again to end 2016 at $952.

Bitcoin exploded in price throughout 2017, rising from $1,000 to peak above $19,000 in mid-December, only to fall back to $15,000 two weeks later. In 2018, it continued falling to a low below $4,000 by March 2019. It rallied over the spring above $12,500, then fell back to $7,000 by year-end 2019.

With the onset of the COVID-19 pandemic, BTC continued to experience extreme volatility. After bouncing around $7,000 for the first quarter of 2020, it skyrocketed above $60,000 in April 2021, fell below $30,000 by July 2021, then rose again above $60,000 by November 2021!

In 2022 the cryptocurrency markets witnessed a series of shocks and scandals that drove the market downward: Terra-Luna, Three Arrows Capital, Celsius, and FTX. Bitcoin entered another crypto winter, falling by 75% over 2022 to end the year below $17,000. At this point, the market capitalization of all cryptocurrencies had declined from a peak of almost $3 trillion to around $800 billion, of which BTC was $324 billion. But Bitcoin experienced a thaw in early 2023 and rose to around $30,000 by mid-April 2023. Clearly HODLers of BTC have experienced a wild ride over the years!

Table 5.1. Bitcoin Statistics

Year	Average Price (USD)	Min Price (USD)	Max Price (USD)	St. Dev. Price (USD)	Average Daily Return (%)	Bitcoins in Circulation
2010	0.17	0.06	0.37	0	4.81	4,378,243
2011	6.05	0.30	35.00	6	2.45	6,604,402
2012	8.47	4.33	15.40	3	0.68	9,371,011
2013	189	13	1,151	242	2.86	11,380,586
2014	525	314	896	145	−0.33	12,960,176
2015	272	177	459	58	0.31	14,342,474
2016	566	373	967	137	0.50	15,641,818
2017	4,018	785	19,290	4,078	1.74	16,425,120
2018	7,561	3,271	17,319	2,436	−0.53	17,125,076
2019	7,383	3,395	12,933	2,642	0.24	17,796,539
2020	11,057	4,830	28,857	4,213	0.46	18,399,414
2021	47,386	28,983	67,562	9,827	0.22	18,750,821
2022	28,387	15,787	47,466	10,165	−0.23	19,242,081

Source: CoinMarketCap, author's calculations.

Table 5.1 provides a snapshot of the ups and downs of bitcoin's price from 2010 to 2022, the number of bitcoins in circulation, and the network difficulty over time. Given Bitcoin's origin as a response to the instability of the global financial system, we have to wonder what Satoshi would think of how the original vision has been perverted.

The Double-Spend Problem

While others had dreamed of creating a digital money, earlier efforts failed as no one could solve the "double-spend" problem: how to allow for the electronic exchange of money without a trusted intermediary to verify that the money had not been spent twice.[6]

The abstract to the 2008 working paper explains:

> The problem of course is the payee can't verify that one of the owners did not double-spend the coin. A common solution is to introduce a trusted central authority, or mint, which checks every transaction for double spending ... The problem with this solution is that the fate of the entire money system depends on the company running the mint, with every transaction having to go through them, just like a bank. (Nakamoto, 2008)

Satoshi's solution to the double-spend problem was to use a time-stamped electronic record-keeping system to record creation and transfers of bitcoins. This electronic ledger was secured against alterations using cryptography. The ledger itself would remain public and transparent, with copies widely available for verification. This solution relied on a P2P network of independent computers (called nodes) where transactions were collected in blocks and hashed to make these records immutable. Identical copies of this ledger are distributed across the Bitcoin network, which had more than 46,000 nodes in 2023.

Blockchain

The blockchain is an electronic distributed ledger that records ownership of a single asset, Bitcoin. When bitcoins are transferred from one owner to another, these transactions are collected and batch-processed in blocks, rather than verifying each transaction one at a time. Each block contains a timestamp, a reference to the previous block, a list of transactions that have been verified since the previous block, and a numerical value (called a nonce). A block is like a page of transactions in a book. Blocks are appended to the digital ledger like pages in a book. The pages are chained together and secured using a cryptographic hash, like binding a book. This system of processing transactions in blocks and chaining them together using hashes is why this electronic ledger is called the blockchain.

The Bitcoin blockchain is public and permissionless. It is fully transparent, so anyone can connect to the blockchain network, download the blockchain from the internet, view the contents, and confirm new transactions according to the rules of the system. No one needs permission of a central intermediary to view or alter the transactions. The ledger shows every bitcoin created, with each coin (or part of a coin) identified by a digital address. The blockchain also records the date and time when ownership of a bitcoin (or part of one) changes.

The owners of bitcoins are listed using the digital address associated with their account. This digital address is the hashed version of a public key (or hexadecimal number) assigned to each owner. Each owner also has a private key (similar to a password) used for unlocking and transferring bitcoins. The owner's real-life identity is hidden, so this setup is described as pseudo-anonymous.[7] Theoretically, the owner's digital address could be traced back to their computer or their account or a digital exchange. Owners may have multiple addresses, but each one is unique, and these accounts cannot be combined.

The first public key recorded in the genesis block of the Bitcoin blockchain belongs to Satoshi Nakamoto, the inventor. By searching someone's public key, you can add up all the bitcoins they control. So, Satoshi's public key in the ledger (1A1zP1eP5QGefi2DMPTfTL5SLmv7DivfNa) is associated with 1,125,150 bitcoins.

Hashing and SHA-256

Satoshi proposed a solution that relied on a P2P network of independent computers (called nodes) where transactions were time-stamped, collected in blocks, and hashed to make these records immutable. A cryptographic hash function, or simply "hash," is a mathematical algorithm that maps data of arbitrary size to a string of a fixed size. A hash is a one-way function – it cannot be decrypted or inverted to reveal the source data.

You can think of a hash as a form of compression where a string of data of any size – such as the text of the Bible, a digital image, or an electronic recording – is converted into a string of a fixed size. Anyone who enters the same data into a specific hash algorithm will receive the identical string, but it is almost impossible to decrypt a hash and restore the original data given current computing power. (This will change when quantum computing becomes commercially available.)

Satoshi chose to encrypt blocks using the widely available Secure Hash Algorithm 256-bit, or SHA-256. This statistical function converts data of any size into a 256-bit representation.[8] Anyone putting the exact same data into a SHA-256 algorithm will receive the identical 256 bits (or 32 bytes) hash, allowing the comparability of the data to be checked. This system of time-stamping each block and including a hash of the previous block makes it impossible to alter previous blocks without redoing all of them.

The Bitcoin network operates according to rules established by Satoshi, called protocols. He arbitrarily set the maximum number of bitcoins that would be created at 21 million. Transactions in Bitcoin would be collected and batched every 10 minutes into 1-megabyte (MB) blocks. Due to this size constraint, the average block in 2018 contained around 1,500 transactions. In other words, the throughput on the Bitcoin network was approximately 1,500 transactions every 10 minutes, or 2.5 transactions per second. By comparison, the VISA network can reportedly process up to 24,000 transactions per second, although the actual throughput is much lower.

FEATURES OF THE BITCOIN BLOCKCHAIN
Blockchain has become a generic term describing distributed electronic ledgers that are secured using cryptography. Electronic ledgers can be distinguished based on a variety of characteristics. Here are nine key features of the Bitcoin blockchain:

- **Form**: Electronic (digital).
- **Contents**: Data on ownership and transactions in Bitcoin. This data only shows one side of every transaction. It does not show the price paid for a bitcoin or what was exchanged (e.g., fiat currency or cryptocurrency).

- **Security**: Encrypted through cryptographic hashing using the Secure Hash Algorithm 256-bit (SHA-256). Identities are pseudo-anonymous, with the owner's digital address shown.
- **Transparency**: Public. Anyone can view the contents.
- **Access**: Permissionless. Anyone can download and view the Bitcoin blockchain.
- **Consensus mechanism**: Proof-of-work (PoW) through a process called mining where nodes race to find a hash with certain features that meets a specific level of difficulty.
- **Transaction processing/throughput**: Transactions are processed in batches of roughly 1 block every 10 minutes. Each block contains between 1,200 and 2,400 transactions, leading to a throughput of 2 to 4 transactions per second.
- **Interoperability**: The Bitcoin blockchain is a closed ledger that represents the complete state of the Bitcoin network. It only records bitcoins and it is not compatible or interconnected with other distributed ledgers.
- **Governance**:[9] The Bitcoin network is governed by Bitcoin owners and miners. Changes to the main features of Bitcoin require support from a majority of the hash power on the network. The client software, called Bitcoin Core, is open-source and maintained by a community of developers who contribute to the codebase. The release notes for each Bitcoin Core software release contain a credits section to recognize all those who have contributed to the project.

Proof-of-Work and Mining

The process of verifying and confirming transactions is called proof-of-work (PoW). PoW is one of many ways to reach consensus on the truth, or consensus algorithms.

A node on the Bitcoin network would be selected at random to update the blockchain, receiving new bitcoins as a reward for this work. To ensure fairness in distributing these block rewards, nodes on the network known as miners compete against each other to confirm transactions and receive the reward. They search for a random number called the nonce that – when hashed with the contents of a block – generates a 256-bit hash beginning with a specific number of zeros (e.g., 00000000839a8e6886ab…). The process of searching for the nonce is called mining. It might also be called random number guessing. These design choices were written into the Bitcoin code and the software, which is free to download from the internet.

Miners run the Bitcoin software that randomly searches for the nonce using trial and error. The software repeatedly increments the nonce and hashes the contents of a block and checks if the hash has the desired number of leading zeros. If it does not, the software iterates and tries again. The first miner to find the nonce and receive confirmation that it works from another miner on the Bitcoin network receives the block reward. This process of searching for the nonce, hashing a block, and receiving the reward is known as "proof-of-work."

A miner is rewarded for being the first to find the nonce and create a block with newly minted bitcoins. Given that only 21 million bitcoins will ever be created, this block reward is halved every 210,000 blocks (or roughly every four years). The block reward started at 50 bitcoins per block in 2009, and as of 2019 it was 12.5 bitcoins per block. As of May 2020, the block reward was 6.25 bitcoins per block.

The Bitcoin software adjusts the probability of finding the nonce so that the creation of blocks remains constant at 6 blocks per hour, or roughly 1 every 10 minutes. The probability of finding the hash, known as the difficulty level, is proportional to the amount of computing power on the Bitcoin network, known as the hash rate. As more computing power is devoted to mining bitcoins (measured in total hashes per second across all nodes), difficulty level is adjusted dynamically to maintain a fixed rate of block creation. The hash rate has risen exponentially as more and more miners apply more computing power to search for the nonce (Figure 5.2). Satoshi never explained these architectural choices, but they have come to dominate the operation of the Bitcoin network.

Mining is a wasteful activity, as the many computers and servers searching for the hash consume electricity. The annual consumption of electricity as of year-end 2022 was estimated at 73 terawatt-hours, or the equivalent annual electricity usage of Austria.[10] This electricity consumption generates the same carbon footprint as Switzerland. The energy consumption of cryptocurrencies has declined from a peak above 200 terawatt-hours in early 2022, with the decline explained by the fall in value in bitcoins and the move by the Ethereum network to the energy-efficient proof-of-stake consensus mechanism.

The proof-of-stake (PoS) protocol is a set of rules to reach consensus and verify transactions on a blockchain. It changes behavior by changing the incentives. PoS does not require mining to verify transactions. Instead of mining, a holder of a given cryptocurrency must deposit or "stake" cryptocurrency with the network to be entered into a pool of validators. Validators are then randomly chosen to verify transactions on the blockchain and receive the block reward. The probability of being selected is proportional to the amount of coin they have staked.

Unlike PoW, PoS validators do not need to use significant amounts of computational power because they are not competing but are selected at random. They do not mine blocks; they create blocks when chosen. This validation process is called attesting. You can think of attesting as saying, "This block looks good to me." A validator

Figure 5.2. Bitcoin Price vs. Hash Rate

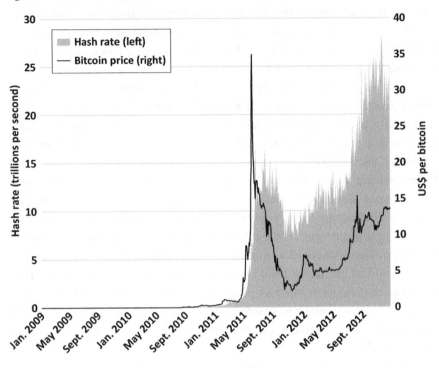

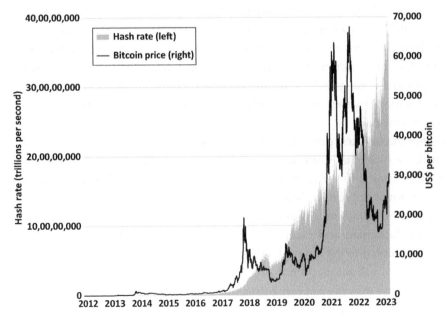

Source: https://blockchain.info/stats

that attests (or verifies) malicious blocks loses their stake as a penalty. Researchers have studied PoS cryptocurrencies and find that their prices are more stable in the long run, as PoS does not create the incentive for investors to accumulate coins and gamble seen with PoW.

In September 2022, the Ethereum network completed its transition from PoW to PoS, reducing its energy consumption by 99.95%. This transition from PoW to PoS – known as "The Merge" – took two years to complete as two blockchains were run in parallel to test the stability of PoS.[11] We will return to a discussion of this event in Chapter 6 when we take a deeper look at Ethereum.

Transaction Fees

An interesting feature of Bitcoin is that the network does not impose any official transaction fees to process transactions. Users just have to wait patiently for their transaction to be added to a successful block by a miner. The only official reward is the block reward. But the block reward is being cut in half roughly every four years as the number of bitcoins in circulation approaches the 21 million limit. While an increase in the price of each bitcoin has increased the dollar value of the reward for a smaller block reward, the difficulty of finding the nonce and receiving the block reward has increased exponentially. So, what will happen when all 21 million bitcoins have been created? How will miners be incentivized to confirm transactions through the costly process of mining when there are no more bitcoins to reward them?

The answer is voluntary transaction fees. Bitcoin's system of confirming transactions worked fine until mid-2016, when the network started to get crowded. Up to that point, the number of Bitcoin transactions waiting to be confirmed in any 10-minute period could all fit in a 1-MB block. But as Bitcoin's popularity increased, the number of transactions waiting to be confirmed exceeded this block size, leading to congestion and longer wait times.

Technically, verified transactions that were waiting to be confirmed were stored in a memory pool or "mempool." There they would wait until a miner chose them for a block. A miner racing to find the nonce is free to choose any transactions they want from their mempool. But given that only one block is randomly confirmed every 10 minutes, transactions took longer to confirm as the network became more and more crowded.

What happened next illustrates the power of economic incentives. Senders who wanted quicker confirmation of their transactions started offering a voluntary fee to incentivize miners to pick their transactions first. In other words, users paid to get to the front of the line, just like a FastPass at Disney World! Miners began choosing transactions from the mempool that would maximize their profitability. They chose transactions with the highest fee-to-size ratio to generate the highest aggregate fee for each block. While this fee started off as voluntary and small, it has risen in size and become de facto mandatory as the Bitcoin network has become more crowded. The transaction fee for Bitcoin is known as the "feerate" and is measured in Satoshis-per-byte, where 1 bitcoin is divisible into 100,000 Satoshis.

Fees remain voluntary, but Bitcoin's decentralized design does eliminate the possibility of monopoly pricing. Bitcoin fees are highly volatile, with significant variation over time and even across transactions within a single block. The physical limit on the block size at 1 MB leads to higher fees when transactions are more urgent, blocks are fuller, and congestion and waiting times on the Bitcoin network are greater.

It is puzzling, therefore, to learn that a significant portion of Bitcoin blocks are empty or not filled to capacity. Researchers who have studied all blocks from the genesis block on January 3, 2009, through late 2018 suggest that mining pools – which dominate the hash rate – may be colluding to extract higher fees from Bitcoin users.[12] This profit-maximizing behavior is undermining Satoshi Nakamoto's vision of building a decentralized P2P electronic cash system that users can trust.

BITCOIN'S FIVE BUILDING BLOCKS

- **Blockchain**: A distributed public ledger that maintains a continuously growing list of ownership records called blocks. It is append-only, permissionless, and transparent. If blockchain is a massive accounting ledger, then the blocks are its pages.
- **Cryptographic hashing**: A mathematical algorithm used to secure, compress, store, and retrieve data on the blockchain. A time-stamped hash pointer connects each block to the previous one.
- **Peer-to-peer (P2P) network**: A series of computers called nodes connected over the internet, each of which stores a copy of the blockchain, and racing to confirm transactions through a process called mining. This consensus algorithm is known as proof-of-work (PoW).
- **Digital keys**: A public and a private key that are unique to a user. They are a cryptographic way to prove ownership, like your name and physical signature or a username online with a password.
- **Bitcoin script**: A programming language used to execute different actions (i.e., send, receive).

CRYPTOCURRENCIES

Due to the popularity and spectacular rise in price of Bitcoin, it did not take long for other cryptocurrencies to be created and launched. At year-end 2021, Bitcoin was only one of more than 17,000 coins, tokens, and other cryptoassets with a total market capitalization around US$ 2 trillion.[13] By April 2023, the number of coins, tokens, and other cryptoassets had risen above 23,000 but the total market capitalization had dropped to US$1.3 trillion.

Alternatives to Bitcoin

Satoshi Nakamoto generously posted the Bitcoin source code on the web-based hosting site GitHub in 2009.[14] As Bitcoin caught on in popularity, programmers began to modify this code to create alternative cryptocurrencies with different features and use cases. The early imitators were known as "Alternatives to Bitcoin," or altcoins, because they were simple modifications of the Bitcoin code with different features and governance. Many of these competing cryptocurrencies were pre-mined and sold to the public through initial coin offerings, or ICOs. When regulators around the world effectively shut down ICOs in mid-2018, crypto innovators found other ways to distribute their digital tokens.

The first altcoins to appear were the cryptocurrencies Litecoin and Namecoin in 2011, Peercoin in 2012, and Dogecoin, Gridcoin, Primecoin, Nxt, and Ripple XRP in 2013.

- Litecoin was an alternative digital currency that used a different hash algorithm called Scrypt that relied more on a computer's memory than its computational power, making it more difficult and costly to mine than Bitcoin.
- Namecoin uses a Bitcoin-like blockchain to allow users to register internet domain names in a public database. The blockchain is censorship-resistant and not controlled by the main governing body for internet domains, ICANN.
- Peercoin combined proof-of-work (PoW) with proof-of-stake (PoS) consensus mechanisms. Under PoS, the right to confirm transactions and receive new coins is allocated in proportion to the quantity of the coin held by miners. In other words, a miner holding 1% of Peercoin will be rewarded by confirming 1% of all Peercoin blocks.
- Dogecoin was introduced as a joke currency that featured the dog from the "Doge" internet meme as its logo. The founders wanted to provide a fun cryptocurrency that would reach a different audience.

Table 5.2. Top 10 Cryptocurrencies by Market Capitalization

Rank	Name	Symbol	Price (US$)	Market Capitalization ($ billions)	Supply	Use-Case
1	Bitcoin	BTC	29,521	571	Proof of work (PoW)	Digital currency
2	Ethereum	ETH	2,080	248	Pre-mined, then PoW	Smart contract
3	Tether	USDT	1.00	81	Minted	Stablecoin
4	Binance Coin	BNB	341	53	Pre-mined	Digital currency
5	USD Coin	USDC	1.00	32	Minted	Stablecoin
6	Ripple XRP	XRP	0.51	27	Pre-mined	Payments
7	Cardano	ADA	0.44	15	PoS	Digital currency
8	Dogecoin	DOGE	0.09	13	PoW	Joke coin
9	Polygon	MATIC	1.16	11	PoS	Ethereum platform
10	Solana	SOL	24.78	10	Pre-mined	DeFi dapp

Source: CoinMarketCap, April 17, 2023.

Many coins followed, some with names taken from popular movies (Tron and Neo), while others had names that tried to capture their use-case (Dash, PotCoin).

As of April 2022, the top 10 cryptocurrencies on CoinMarketCap had a market capitalization of $1.5 trillion (Table 5.2). This represents 79% of the total cryptocurrency market capitalization of $1.9 trillion, with Bitcoin alone making up 41%. These figures have fluctuated widely as cryptocurrency prices have gyrated over the past two years.

The most innovative and transformational cryptocurrency is ether (ETH), which is the token used to run decentralized applications programmed on the Ethereum blockchain. Ether was launched through a crowdsale in mid-2014.[15] A crowdsale is where coins or tokens are pre-mined and sold to the public for the first time in what is called an ICO. We will have much more to say about the Ethereum blockchain and ether in Chapter 6.

The most important innovation in cryptocurrencies of recent years is the stablecoin. Stablecoins are tokens backed by fiat currencies (such as the US dollar), commodities (such as gold or oil), other cryptocurrencies (such as bitcoin or ether), or nothing at all (algo stables). The first stablecoin appeared in 2014 and then attracted many imitators in 2018 following the wild swings in the cryptocurrency markets.[16] The goal of a stablecoin is to provide businesses and individuals with a payment token that acts as a store of value and medium of exchange and does not feature the volatility experienced by other cryptocurrencies. We will return to the topic of stablecoins in Chapter 6 on decentralized finance.

Trading and HODLing Cryptocurrencies

We hear many different names used to describe cryptocurrency investors. The news site CoinDesk refers to "natives," "newbies," and "the curious." Websites refer to the most successful crypto investors as "whales." Investors who hold crypto but do not transact are called "HODLers," in reference to a 2013 Bitcoin forum post by an apparently inebriated user who wrote, "I AM HODLING."[17] Given the volatility of cryptocurrencies over the years, HODL has also been translated to mean "Hold On for Dear Life!"

Cryptocurrencies have become a major traded asset class, with retail and institutional investors buying, selling, and making markets in these digital assets. A cryptocurrency can be exchanged for a fiat currency (such as US dollars, euros, or Japanese yen) or other cryptocurrency (such as bitcoin, ether, or XRP). These cryptoassets can be traded 24 hours per day, 7 days per week on over 400 unregulated exchanges globally, with the leaders being Binance, Coinbase, and Kraken.[18]

A key development was the launch of futures contracts on bitcoins, which began trading on the Chicago Mercantile Exchange (CME) in December 2017.[19] Other innovations such as the creation of Bitcoin margin trading, exchange traded funds (ETFs), and cryptocurrency pooled investment vehicles and derivatives have followed.

Cryptocurrency markets are unregulated so there is no single data feed similar to what is available for stock markets. The lack of a consolidated and comprehensive data history, together with the increased size and depth of the cryptocurrency markets, means that any research findings based on earlier periods or shorter time windows may no longer apply.

Academics have published a number of findings on cryptocurrencies. More recent studies have overturned earlier results as market liquidity and volumes increase and more data becomes available. Academics are now focused on explaining the risks and returns from this new asset class, applying traditional finance theories and empirical techniques. In the final section of this chapter, we will examine some of the leading research on trading in cryptocurrencies.

Cryptocurrencies have gained notoriety due to their association with criminal activity and fraudsters, and the subsequent regulatory crackdown in many countries. With cryptoexchanges unregulated and operating over the internet, it is difficult for investors to choose the best location for trading and hedging with prices diverging and markets segmented, creating arbitrage opportunities for more sophisticated investors.

Hard Forks

It may come as a surprise to learn that there is more than one cryptocurrency with Bitcoin in the name: Bitcoin, Bitcoin Cash, Bitcoin SV, and Bitcoin Gold. What's going on? This situation happens when there is a hard fork in a cryptocurrency. A hard fork should not be confused with a fork in a blockchain, which is a natural occurrence due to having many nodes confirming blocks simultaneously.

A hard fork signals a disagreement among holders of a cryptocurrency that leads to a divorce. If you picture a fork standing on its handle, it looks like a tree with a trunk that divides into different branches. When a minority of owners of a cryptocurrency want to change the rules but cannot get the majority of holders to agree, the minority may break away to create their own digital coin. This division is known as a hard fork, which creates a new branch from the same trunk. At the point when transactions start, these new coins are no longer recognized as valid by the original blockchain. A new blockchain is created to reflect this hard fork between the original and the new coin.

Interestingly, both coins share the same transaction history up to the point of the fork. Coins in existence prior to the fork now appear on both blockchains and remain valid. Effectively the old coin is split into two parts, much like a stock spin-off for a publicly listed company. While, in theory, each coin should drop in value to reflect that the coins have been divided in two, in practice no one appears to notice! The sum of the parts is greater than the whole.

The hard fork that created Bitcoin Cash took place on August 1, 2017, at block 478,558 on the Bitcoin blockchain. A minority of Bitcoin owners wanted to increase the block size to 8 MB to increase the number of transactions that could be processed over a 10-minute period. Immediately before the hard fork, a Bitcoin was worth approximately $2,746. The next day one Bitcoin was worth $2,741 and one Bitcoin Cash was worth $380, for a total of $3,121. Magic! Another hard fork in the Bitcoin blockchain occurred on October 24, 2017, at block 491,407 to create Bitcoin Gold. Then on November 15, 2018, there was a hard fork in Bitcoin Cash to create Bitcoin SV. And so it goes.

Initial Coin Offerings (ICOs)

Cryptocurrencies and tokens are created in two main ways: through mining like Bitcoin, and through a crowdsale of pre-mined tokens known as an initial coin offering, or ICO.

While Ethereum pioneered the sale of pre-mined tokens in mid-2014, the expression "initial coin offering" first appeared in the September 2014 press release

Table 5.3. Capital Raised in Initial Coin Offerings (ICOs)

Period	Number of ICOs	Capital raised (US$ millions)	Media mentions of ICOs[2]
2014	7	30.4	7
2015	7	8.6	0
2016	43	256.4	50
2017	343	5,482.0	3,069
2018, first half [1]	460	14,295.4	7,397
Total	860	$ 20,072.8	10,523

1. January 1 to July 31, 2018. 2. Search in Factiva for "initial coin offering" or ICO w/10 (crypto* or crowdsale) Source: CoinDesk ICO Tracker; Factiva.

announcing the sale of the Breakout Coin (BRO) by Breakout Gaming.[20] The sale of cryptocurrencies and tokens through ICOs exploded in mid-2016.

An ICO is analogous to an initial public offering of a stock, except buyers subscribe to cryptocurrencies that are pre-mined and sold by the founders. By selling a digital token to the public through an ICO, the creator of a pre-mined coin can cut out financial intermediaries who would typically run the capital-raising process. With an ICO, all the marketing, book building, and pricing takes place over the internet. Instead of an offering document, the founders would post a "whitepaper" online – a document that described the new coin's use-case and unique features. Purchasers would subscribe during a month-long offering period, placing buy orders using fiat currency (aka paper money) or other cryptocurrencies (bitcoin, ether). These new coins and tokens then begin trading online on any number of electronic exchanges, called cryptoexchanges.

According to CoinDesk's ICO tracker, 2014 saw seven ICOs raising $30.4 million, of which the Ethereum crowdsale of ETH was $18.4 million (Table 5.3).[21] In 2015, seven more ICOs raised $8.6 million. In the first five months of 2016, five ICOs raised $17.6 million. Then in May 2016, the German internet company Slock.It launched an ICO to finance a project called The DAO, which raised $150 million.

Capital raising via ICOs then took off, with 37 more issues over the remainder of 2016 raising $86.8 million. The full year of 2017 saw 343 ICOs raising $5.5 billion, with another 460 ICOs raised $14.3 billion over the first seven months of 2018. CoinDesk stopped reporting on ICOs on July 31, 2018, following the regulatory crackdown. In total, more than $20 billion was raised in 860 ICOs from 2014 to mid-year 2018.

The largest ICO was $4.2 billion, raised in June 2018 through the sale of the cryptocurrency EOS by its developers, Block.one (Table 5.4). The funds are intended to finance development of an open-source software called EOS.io that can be used to build a fast, scalable, and easy-to-use blockchain for enterprises.[22] The messaging app

Table 5.4. Top 10 Largest Initial Coin Offerings

Rank	Name	Close Date	ICO Size (US$ millions)
1	EOS	1-Jun-18	4,200
2	Telegram	29-Mar-18	1,700
3	TaTaTu (TTU)	20-Jun-18	575
4	Dragon	15-Mar-18	320
5	Huobi	28-Feb-18	300
6	Filecoin	10-Sep-17	262
7	Tezos	13-Jul-17	232
8	Sirin Labs	26-Dec-17	158
9	Bancor	12-Jun-17	153
10	The DAO	1-May-16	152

Source: CoinDesk ICO Tracker.

developer Telegram raised $1.7 billion in a two-phase ICO of the gram coin in February and March 2018. The funds will be used to develop the Telegram Open Network (TON), an ambitious blockchain meant to decentralize multiple facets of digital communication, ranging from file sharing to browsing, to transactions.[23]

CASE STUDY: RIPPLE XRP'S SEARCH FOR A USE-CASE

The Silicon Valley fintech Ripple Labs developed and runs an interbank payments network called the RippleNet. The start-up was originally called Opencoin and was founded in 2011 by three engineers – Jed McCaleb, David Schwartz, and Arthur Britto. Opencoin changed its name to Ripple in 2013.

McCaleb had founded the Bitcoin exchange Mt. Gox in 2010, which he sold in 2011, but remained a minority investor until its collapse in 2014. He was fascinated by Bitcoin but recognized the limitations and waste of mining, voicing his concerns in a post on the Bitcoin forum.[24] McCaleb wanted to develop a digital currency system in which transactions were verified by consensus. He approached developers Britto and Schwartz to build this alternative distributed ledger suitable for global payments. McCaleb also recruited Chris Larsen, the CEO of P2P lender Prosper and previous co-founder of the online mortgage company E-LOAN (sold to Banco Popular in 2005).

McCaleb, Larsen, and Powell launched Opencoin in 2012. They acquired a software called Ripplepay from a Canadian developer, Ryan Fugger, who had developed a protocol back in 2004 for securely transferring money over the internet.

Following the acquisition, the team launched the XRP ledger, which was originally called "ripples" but later took the name of its cryptocurrency, XRP.

Between October 2012 and September 2016, Ripple raised $55 million in funding, including backing from leading venture capitalists such as Andreessen Horowitz and Google Ventures, as well as the Spanish multinational bank Santander.[25]

In 2013, Larsen told the media, "We want to create a free PayPal for the world."[26]

Around this time, McCaleb left the firm following an internal dispute. Larsen took over as CEO, a role he retained until 2017 when he stepped down, continuing as chairman of the board. McCaleb went on to create the competing decentralized payment network Stellar and the token lumen.

Despite the revolutionary ideals of Bitcoin's early believers, Larsen never thought blockchain technology should be used to overthrow the existing financial system.[27]

Ripple partnered with banks globally to build an interbank payments network called the RippleNet. RippleNet was built on a permissioned distributed ledger, where transactions are verified by 35 trusted third parties, not by mining. This private, permissioned distributed ledger allows bank customers to transfer money across borders with minimal costs. Transfers are executed within five seconds with users able to see the exchange rate they receive and track the transfer end-to-end on a mobile app. This performance solved a major pain point for consumers, who were used to paying $35–$50 in fees plus a large FX spread to execute cross-border transfers that might take weeks to arrive.

Ripple's original design envisaged a cryptocurrency to facilitate interbank settlement, providing the rationale for the XRP coin. A sender's fiat currency (e.g., US dollars) would be converted into XRP by their bank, transferred to the recipient's bank as XRP, then converted into the recipient's desired currency (e.g., British pounds).

The founders pre-mined 100 billion XRP tokens and kept 20 billion for themselves. They gave away or sold XRP privately through 2013 and 2014, a process that led to a $700,000 fine from the US SEC in 2015 for failing to follow anti-money laundering (AML) rules and register as a money services business. By mid-2015, 31 billion XRP were in circulation with a market capitalization of $256 million.

By mid-2017, 75 banks had joined RippleNet, and XRP was trading on 30 crypto-exchanges. This news, together with the growing popularity of Bitcoin, contributed to XRP's dramatic rise in price over 2017. XRP skyrocketed from $0.00647 at the start of the year to $2.21 by year-end, an increase of 340 times (or 34,000%). The 20 billion XRP held by the founders increased in value from $129 million to over $44 billion! XRP continued to climb through year-end despite the fall in Bitcoin, hitting a peak of $3.36 on January 7, 2018.

There was just one problem: RippleNet's bank members were not using XRP for money transfers. They preferred to use fiat currencies, leaving the XRP without a use-case. This fact became clear in early January 2018 when the *Financial Times* published a critical article reporting that, of the 16 banks interviewed, "Most had not yet gone beyond testing."[28] This fact was confirmed by a senior Ripple executive while giving testimony to the UK government. The price of XRP began to fall as questions mounted about its *raison d'être*.

While Ripple has been marketing XRP as an alternative reserve asset to fiat currencies, banks and central banks have not adopted it. XRP has proven to be a purely speculative asset – not backed by any assets but driven by speculators. XRP crashed in 2018, hitting a low at close of $0.25, then falling to $0.14 in March 2020. XRP began rising again in early 2021 and finished the year at $0.84, before falling to $0.34 at year-end 2022.[29] Whether the wisdom of the crowds proves to be true or not remains to be seen with XRP.

CRYPTOCURRENCY GROWING PAINS

Like any radical innovation, cryptocurrencies have faced growing pains. These pain points led to more innovations to smooth the way for growth and mainstream adoption. Two pain points that have been overcome are the problems of storage and the problems of trading. The storage problem was addressed by the creation of cryptowallets, while the problem of trading was resolved by the emergence of cryptoexchanges. Unfortunately, these innovations have generated honey pots of valuable information that have attracted their share of hackers, scammers, and criminals, which is also true of the traditional financial system.

Of course, any disruptive threat generates a response from the incumbents who strike back at some point. In this case, the incumbents who have been painfully slow to respond are monetary authorities, who have promised but not delivered their own alternative to Bitcoin called the central bank digital currency (CBDC). We look at these three developments in this section.

Cryptowallets: From Paper to Hardware

Many types of software and financial intermediaries have emerged to help store and trade bitcoins and other cryptocurrencies. We focus on only two of them: cryptowallets and cryptoexchanges.

The Bitcoin Core software creates a "wallet" where the user can store bitcoins, creates an individual node in the P2P Bitcoin network accessed over the internet, and provides access to the blockchain for verifying Bitcoin transactions. A Bitcoin "user" (a participant in the network) stores the addresses associated with each parcel of bitcoin that they own in a "wallet." Like a conventional cash wallet, a bitcoin wallet balance is the sum of the balances of all the addresses inside the wallet. While individual bitcoin addresses are designed to be anonymous, it is possible to link addresses belonging to the same wallet when more than one address is used to make a purchase.[30]

In the early years, the only way to own and transfer a bitcoin was P2P from one node to another, using each bitcoin's unique address in combination with the owner's public and private keys. Holders secured their bitcoins against theft by storing this information offline, encrypted on a computer or USB key or – more commonly – in a "paper wallet." A paper wallet is basically what it sounds like. The owner would print off the information on a literal piece of paper that was then folded up and locked away somewhere.

Over time, paper wallets, computers, and USB keys have been shown to be unsafe, leading to the loss of many bitcoins. They were thrown away, lost, stolen, or hacked. Some paper wallets were accidentally destroyed. Clearly the problem of securely storing bitcoins was difficult for many novice users as it required a good deal of knowledge and IT skills.

This pain point led to the creation of cryptocurrency wallets. A cryptocurrency wallet is a software application or hardware device used to receive and send cryptocurrencies. Unlike a real-world wallet, a cryptocurrency wallet doesn't hold any cryptocurrencies. Instead it stores a small secret in the form of a seed (or individual private key), which is used to generate addresses for incoming transactions and to authorize outgoing transactions. The hundreds of cryptowallets available differ in features like security, privacy, interoperability, ease of use, backups, and support. Cryptocurrency wallets can be divided into two groups based on their level of security: software wallets that are less secure and hardware wallets that are more secure.

A software wallet is a cryptocurrency application that runs on a desktop, tablet, or smartphone. Software wallets represent the most widely used cryptocurrency software among users and are typically free of charge. A software wallet has an address and stores both the user's private key and the recovery seed for the wallet. An address is a unique alphanumeric identifier used to receive payments.[31] It can be shared with other users in the same way an email address would be shared. Addresses can also be transformed into the QR code format, so they can be scanned by a mobile device or camera.

A private key is a randomly generated secret number that is unique to the owner at a specific address. Private keys are mathematically linked to the corresponding public keys used to transfer cryptocurrencies. A user needs this private key to transfer coins and, therefore, needs to keep it secure. Sharing a private key with someone allows them to access your coins. A recovery seed, or seed, is a list of words in a specific order that stores all the information needed to recover a wallet if it is lost. From a security point of view, software wallets are "hot wallets" because they are connected to the internet and expose the seed, making it vulnerable to attacks.

A wallet that is not connected to the internet is a cold wallet, also called cold storage. The most secure form of cold wallet is a hardware wallet. The first cryptocurrency hardware wallet was the Trezor, created in 2013 by two Bitcoin pioneers who collaborated to provide a solution.[32] One of the creators, Marek Palatinus, had created the first mining pool called the Slush Pool in late 2010. He recognized that he needed a better way to store his bitcoins than a paper wallet and collaborated with Pavol "Stick" Rusnák to build one.

The Trezor was a small, single-purpose USB key that would keep the private keys protected in an isolated environment. It was built using open-source hardware and software to allow auditing and included a way to backup and recover lost passwords. The first model, Trezor One, was launched in mid-2014 by Satoshi Labs. It included two-factor authentication using a PIN and a passphrase, which was any word, sequence of words, or set of letters. It was easy to use and connected to a computer using a USB port. Later versions of the Trezor added additional features, such as compatibility with over 1,000 cryptocurrencies, color displays, and encrypted storage in the cloud.

Cryptoexchanges: Marketplaces or Honey Pots?

Cryptoexchanges are electronic exchanges that facilitate buying and selling of Bitcoin and other cryptocurrencies for a fee. Thousands of cryptoexchanges and marketplaces have popped up online, mostly unregulated and providing trading in the top 100 most actively traded coins. These exchanges are two main types: ones that exchange fiat currencies for cryptocurrencies (fiat-to-crypto) and others that exchange only cryptocurrencies (crypto-to-crypto). Most large exchanges offer both options.

Three of the most active and widely used cryptocurrency exchanges are Binance, Coinbase, and Kraken (see Table 5.5). In each case, Bitcoin dominates in terms of its price, market capitalization, and trading volume.[33]

While prices across exchanges used to vary widely, these differences have now been arbitraged away for the most actively traded coins. Any variation in prices lies within a band created by different exchange fees and hedging costs. In late 2017 the Chicago Mercantile Exchange (CME) began trading in Bitcoin futures, further facilitating hedging and arbitrage in this coin.[34]

Table 5.5. Leading Cryptocurrency Exchanges

Binance	Founded in 2017, Binance is the world's largest cryptocurrency exchange by reported volume. Originally headquartered in China, it moved its servers to Japan to avoid government restrictions and is registered in the Cayman Islands. At one point it traded 1,600 crypto pairs across spot, derivatives, and DeFi markets, although most of its volume is in Bitcoin. See https://www.binance.com/.
Coinbase	Founded in 2012, Coinbase is the largest cryptocurrency exchange based in the United States. It went public on Nasdaq in 2021 via an $86 billion direct listing. It is regulated by the New York Department of Financial Services with a virtual currency license, serves 44 US states, and has a NY state banking charter. It offers the largest number of coins and markets among US cryptoexchanges. See https://pro.coinbase.com.
Kraken	Kraken was founded in 2011 and was the first US crypto firm to receive a state-chartered banking license, as well as one of the first exchanges to offer spot trading with margin, regulated derivatives, and index services. Kraken is the world's largest global digital asset exchange based on euro volume and liquidity. Globally, Kraken's client base trades nearly 90 digital assets and 7 different fiat currencies, including GBP, EUR, USD, CAD, JPY, CHF, and AUD. See: https://www.kraken.com.

Source: CoinMarketCap; Forbes.

Most (but not all) cryptocurrency exchanges require customers to register and go through a verification process to authenticate their identity ("know your customer," or KYC). Once authentication is complete, an account is opened and the customer transfers funds into their account to start trading. It is important to know that coins in an account with an exchange are effectively owned by the exchange, which holds the private keys. While owners retain a nominal claim, the cryptoexchange is listed as owner on the blockchain until such times as the coins are withdrawn.

This standard set-up creates a risk of theft that many users may not be aware of. The cryptoexchange becomes a honey pot that may be easier to breach than the blockchain recording ownership of a cryptocurrency or token. The earliest and most notorious cryptoexchange was Mt. Gox, which was set up in 2010 by an American programmer in Japan. He sold it a year later to a French programmer, Mark Karpales, who ran the exchange until its collapse in 2014. Early in its life, Mt. Gox was the victim of a small hack in June 2011, when 2,000 bitcoins with a value of $30,000 were stolen from internet-connected wallets at a price of $0.01. The Bitcoin price collapsed from over $35 to below $2, then recovered. Mt. Gox continued to operate, but this incident foreshadowed a much bigger hack to come.

Trading activity on Mt. Gox grew fast. By 2014 the exchange was estimated to be managing over 70% of the Bitcoin transactions worldwide. Problems began to appear as users could not access their coins, and calls to the exchange went unanswered. In February 2014 Mt. Gox filed for bankruptcy after revealing that hackers had stolen approximately 850,000 bitcoins valued at $460 million over a period of years. The news caused a

20% drop in the market price of Bitcoin. Most of the Mt. Gox coins were never recovered, and the exchange's owner was later found guilty in court of fraud and embezzlement. The episode revealed a major security weakness inherent in the Bitcoin ecosystem, not to mention highlighting how much trust owners were placing in cryptoexchanges.

After the collapse of Mt. Gox, other cryptoexchanges around the world rose to take its place. These cryptoexchanges have names like BitMEX, Binance, Bitfinex, Bitstamp, Coinbase, Gemini, Huobi, Kraken, and OKEx.

The largest exchange by trading volume in 2018 was Binance (named for *Binary + Finance*), surpassing $10 billion in daily volume. Originally founded in China, Binance moved to Japan in 2017 in advance of the Chinese ban on cryptocurrency trading and later moved to Taiwan. Binance charges a 0.1% trading fee, with a discount for transactions using the Binance coin (BNB). While it is free to deposit coins, there is a cost to withdraw that varies by coin (e.g., 0.0005 BTC for Bitcoin). In its annual recap for 2018, Binance reported average daily trading volume of US$1.2 billion across 151 coins, with over 10 million Binance users spread across 180 countries.[35]

Unfortunately, security remains an issue for even the biggest cryptoexchanges. In May 2017 Binance revealed that it had been the victim of a "large scale security breach," with hackers stealing 7,000 bitcoins worth US$40 million. Many cryptoexchanges have been hacked over the years, with the incidents becoming more frequent: $72 million from Bitfinex in August 2016, $60 million from Nicehash in December 2017, $535 million from Coincheck in January 2018, $195 million from BitGrail in February 2018, $40 million from Coinrail and $32 million from bithumb in June 2018, and $60 million from Zaif in September 2018.[36] With the difficulty and cost of mining increasing over time, many talented individuals will continue to view hacking a cryptoexchange as a better reward for their effort.

Scams, Bans, and Criminal Cases

The dramatic growth of ICOs soon caught the attention of securities regulators in the United States and abroad. Following an investigation, the US Securities and Exchange Commission (SEC) concluded that some tokens offered and sold in ICOs were securities and therefore subject to federal securities laws. Any future sales through an ICO (or initial token offering, ITO) would need to be registered, and the exchanges that traded in them would need to be regulated. The co-director of the SEC's Enforcement Division stated,

> The innovative technology behind these virtual transactions does not exempt securities offerings and trading platforms from the regulatory framework designed to protect investors and the integrity of the markets.[37]

With ICOs raising so much money in such short periods of time, it was inevitable they would also attract criminals and scam artists, as well as the scrutiny of securities regulators. The turning point came on July 25, 2017, when the US SEC asserted its jurisdiction over the ICO market, arguing that digital tokens – regardless of the terminology or technology used – were a form of security known as an "investment contract." The SEC applied the "Howey test" – a three-part test based on an earlier US Supreme Court case. The SEC began applying the test to determine if a digital token is an investment:[38]

1 It is an investment of money
2 It is an investment in a common enterprise
3 It is an investment where profits come solely from the efforts of others

On September 25, the SEC established a Cybersecurity Unit to focus on "violations involving distributed ledger technology [i.e., blockchain] and initial coin offerings." Speaking several days later, SEC chairman Jay Clayton said ICOs were likely a breeding ground for fraud. "It would shock me if you don't see pump-and-dump schemes in the initial coin offering space," Clayton says. Other jurisdictions also acted, with securities regulators in China and Korea banning ICOs and trading on cryptoexchanges, while regulators in Europe, Singapore, Australia, and Japan issued warnings to retail investors.

The SEC wasted no time cracking down on fake ICOs and other scams over 2017 and 2018:

- August 28, 2017: The SEC issued an alert to warn investors about potential scams involving ICOs and suspended trading in the securities of several publicly traded blockchain-related businesses.
- September 30, 2017: The SEC brought its first enforcement action in connection with an ICO against a businessperson and his two companies, which were charged for defrauding investors.
- December 4, 2017: The SEC's Cybersecurity Unit froze the assets on an alleged ICO fraud.
- December 12, 2017: The SEC issued a cease-and-desist order to stop the launch of an ICO where the company had failed to register the security.
- January 30, 2018: The SEC halted an ICO scam for a fake business backed by executives with criminal backgrounds that claimed to have raised $600 million toward the purchase of an FDIC-insured bank.
- April 3, 2018: The SEC charged two co-founders of a celebrity-endorsed ICO that had raised more than $32 million with orchestrating a fraud. The duo created

fictional executives with impressive biographies, posted false or misleading marketing materials to the company's website, and paid celebrities (including boxer Floyd Mayweather and music producer DJ Khaled) to promote the ICO on Instagram.

- May 16, 2018: The SEC launched a website promoting a fake ICO, "HoweyCoin," using the same tactics employed by scammers, including celebrity endorsements and guaranteed returns on investment. People who clicked on "Buy Coins Now!" were redirected to an SEC webpage that said, "If you responded to an investment offer like this, you could have been scammed – HoweyCoins are completely fake!"
- May 21, 2018: The SEC halted an ongoing fraud involving an ICO that had raised $21 million from investors in and outside the US. The founder fraudulently claimed to have business relationships with reputable companies and fabricated testimonials from corporate customers.

The list goes on. Investigations into ICOs by consultants and the media uncovered more disturbing facts. Studies found that 80% of ICOs in 2017 were scams.[39] A blockchain analytics firm reported that investors had been duped out of nearly $100 million in ICO exit scams, where the ICO seller disappears with the funds either before or during the project. A study by the US market regulator FINRA argued that ICO valuations were often based on a fear of missing out (FOMO) rather than on market or business fundamentals.

The *Wall Street Journal* reviewed the whitepapers of 3,291 ICOs and found that 2,000 of them showed signs of fraudulent activity, improbable returns, and plagiarism. They contained sentences such as "nothing to lose," "guaranteed profit," "highest return," and "no risk." Finally, the US Federal Bureau of Investigation (FBI) felt compelled to issue a report that outlined the key strategies of scam ICO offerings: misrepresentations of directors' professional experience, an engineered false impression of how much traction the ICO has garnered in the industry, and unrealistic promises about prospective returns on tokens.

In summary, as the SEC warns, "If the investment sounds too good to be true, it probably is."[40]

Central Bank Digital Currencies

The current monetary system is based on fiat money, which are pieces of paper issued by a country's monetary authority, typically the central bank. Since the 1970s, fiat money is not backed by gold. Instead it is backed by a promise from a government authority that the note is legal tender within a given jurisdiction. You will see this promise written on banknotes accompanied by the signature of the head of the monetary authority. Each note bears a serial number and other devices to prevent counterfeiting, with the monetary authority keeping a centralized digital ledger of notes in circulation.

The public's trust in this fiat currency is based on the government's monopoly over taxation of its citizens. If the government needs more money, it can always print more notes, but this increase in the money supply is inflationary. Modern governments commit not to use this power, but they have reneged on their promises in the past when faced with economic, financial, or political difficulties, such as economic downturns, hyperinflation, or wars. For this reason, believers in Bitcoin and cryptocurrencies argue that fiat money is a fiction that can break down at any time.

All articles about electronic money start by reminding the reader that money serves three purposes. It is a unit of account that allows products and services to be compared using a single pricing system. It is a medium of exchange that can be used to pay for these products or services, allowing the economy to function efficiently without the need for barter. And it is a store of value, allowing households to save and delay consumption to a future date. Inflation erodes purchasing power over time, which is why the monetary authority seeks to control the amount of money in circulation and influence the rate of interest for borrowing and lending money.

Critics argue Bitcoin is not money because it does not meet all three functions. While Bitcoin may function as a unit of account, it has been unsuccessful as a medium of exchange, with few merchants willing to accept Bitcoin for payment. The problem is the time and cost it takes to verify Bitcoin transactions using mining, which can take hours to days. The price of a bitcoin has been extremely volatile, undermining its usefulness as a store of value. If the value constantly fluctuates, this uncertainty will prevent many users from using it.

Bitcoin purists reply that the original purpose has been perverted by market forces. Satoshi envisaged an electronic money that would allow online payments to be made directly between two parties without the need of a trusted financial intermediary. These transfers would be possible for small, casual transactions with minimum transaction costs. Instead, the Bitcoin network is now dominated by a handful of mining pools controlling around 75% of hashing and charging variable, high transaction fees.[41]

This history of money and its criticism brings us to central bank digital currencies (CBDCs). Like incumbents in other areas of the financial system, central banks and monetary authorities are responding to the threat from Bitcoin and other cryptocurrencies by issuing digital versions of their fiat currencies. These digital forms of fiat currencies are called CBDCs. The idea is to provide an electronic version of paper money that can compete with cryptocurrencies. Unlike cryptocurrencies, however, this electronic money is centrally controlled by a monetary authority like the central bank. According to the Bank for International Settlements, more than 80 countries are looking at the feasibility of a CBDC.

There are many open questions about CBDCs, of which we raise three. First there is the question of whether CBDCs should be recorded on a blockchain or not. A CBDC that is centrally controlled by a central bank does not require a blockchain, because it has a trusted party to verify transactions. But to be an attractive alternative to a cryptocurrency, a CBDC should not be controlled by a central bank but should be decentralized and transacted P2P with ownership recorded on a blockchain.

Second, critics of CBDCs express concern that this digital money may undermine fiat currency, hamper the ability of central banks to implement monetary policy, and destabilize the financial system. Researchers have dismissed these concerns, showing that digital currencies will not choke off credit, crowd out investment, or undermine financial stability.[42]

Third, the question is whether a CBDC should be created for retail customers or only for wholesale customers (e.g., banks). Most countries are not looking at retail CBDCs. Instead, they are focused on a wholesale version that can improve efficiency of payments by reducing the settlement time and costs. This wholesale CBDC would be exchanged P2P between banks but not available to the public.

At this point crypto enthusiasts are probably no longer interested in CBDCs. They may increase the efficiency of the payment system, but they are not decentralized or available to individuals. So, let's leave this topic to the central banks who have written volumes on this topic.[43]

CASE STUDY: THE COLLAPSE OF THE FTX CRYPTOEXCHANGE

Just when crypto appeared to be gaining legitimacy, the collapse of the cryptocurrency exchange FTX has destroyed the public's trust. Year-end 2022 saw 30-year-old Sam Bankman-Fried, the founder of FTX, being extradited in handcuffs from the Bahamas to the United States to face a list of criminal charges, including fraud, conspiracy, and money laundering.[44]

Bankman-Fried, widely known by his initials SBF, had been the face of crypto for the previous three years. In 2019, SBF launched FTX Trading Ltd. and its native cryptocurrency token, FTT. FTX specialized in trading of derivatives, allowing holders to take leveraged positions in bitcoin and other cryptocurrencies without the need to post margin. At its peak in 2021, FTX had over 1 million users and was the third largest cryptoexchange by volume. The token FTT peaked at US$80. And SBF had a personal worth estimated at US$26.5 billion. By the end of 2022, it was all gone, along with US$1 billion of missing client funds.

Born in 1992, SBF graduated in 2014 with an undergraduate degree from MIT, then went to work for a proprietary trading firm in New York City. In 2017 he quit to work briefly for the Centre of Effective Altruism in California before founding Alameda Research, a hedge fund focused on quantitative trading. Alameda earned high profits arbitraging Bitcoin prices between US and Japanese exchanges. SBF founded FTX in April 2019 to provide a platform for trading crypto derivatives, which are financial contracts whose value is based on underlying movements in cryptocurrency prices.

SBF received tremendous media attention through his speaking engagements and efforts to lobby regulators and politicians. He gave testimony before the US House Committee on Financial Services about the cryptocurrency industry and acquired a stake in Robinhood Markets. He made political donations of nearly $45 million during the 2020 election, primarily to Democrats.[45] He was an investor in venture capital funds managed by Sequoia Capital. Sequoia was also an investor in FTX, along with the Ontario Teachers' Pension Plan, the Singaporean sovereign wealth fund Temasek, BlackRock, and Binance CEO Changpeng Zhao.

FTT was a token that rewarded holders for transactions on the FTX exchange and for liquidity staking. FTT was a deflationary coin with a buy-and-burn mechanism that reduced coins in circulation. The most active exchanges for trading FTT were FTX, Binance, and Bitcoin.com. Shortly before its collapse, the FTT token had a market capitalization of $5 billion.

On November 2, 2022, an article appeared on CoinDesk that questioned the ties between FTX and Alameda.[46] The reporter pointed out that $5.8 billion of the $14.6 billion in assets on Alameda's balance sheet was the token FTT, issued by FTX, financed by $7.4 billion in loans. On November 6, several days after the CoinDesk story broke, Changpeng Zhao, the CEO of rival exchange Binance and an investor in FTX, disclosed that Binance had liquidated its $2 billion position in FTT.

As seen in Figure 5.3, the price of FTT fell as other holders took their lead from Binance, creating a liquidity crunch at Alameda. Cryptocurrency markets also fell, with bitcoin dropping by 26% from around $21,300 to $15,800.

At this point, the links between the exchange FTX and the hedge fund Alameda became apparent. Regulated exchanges are arms-length from trading and required to hold customer funds in special escrow accounts. This arrangement protects investors on an exchange in case the exchange collapses. This set-up was not followed by FTX.

FTX halted trading on November 8, freezing customer accounts, while SBF disclosed he was negotiating a sale of the exchange to Binance, subject to due diligence. FTT continued to plummet as news stories began to circulate of an

Figure 5.3. FTT vs. Bitcoin

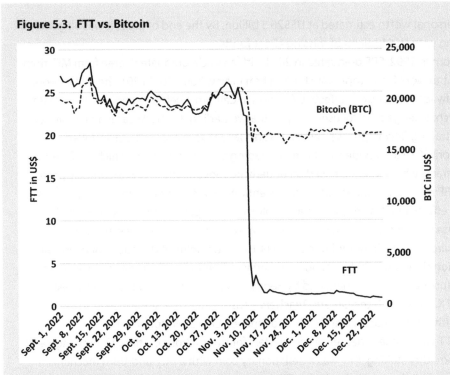

Source: Author, data from Refinitiv Eikon.

investigation by the US SEC and FTX's legal team quitting. On November 10, Binance announced it was walking away from the deal after finding a $9.4 billion hole.

On November 22, FTX and Alameda filed for bankruptcy. The filings revealed that SBF had been using customer funds from FTX to finance trading by Alameda – much of it in the token FTT. With FTT worthless, the loans could not be repaid and the customer funds were lost. Commenting on the bankruptcy filing, a CoinDesk article reported,[47]

> [The law firm Sullivan and Cromwell] described the FTX empire – at its height valued at $32 billion – as the "personal fiefdom of Sam Bankman-Fried," the former CEO of the exchange. The lawyer told the court that Bankman-Fried and a small group of executives ran the company "with a lack of corporate controls that none of us in the profession … have ever seen."

CRYPTO RESEARCH FINDINGS

The growth in Bitcoin and cryptocurrencies is matched by a growing body of published papers that study Bitcoin as a means of payment, price arbitrage across cryptocurrency exchanges, and the returns of cryptocurrencies versus traditional assets. This research falls broadly under the fields of cryptoeconomics, market microstructure, and asset pricing. We will wait to discuss the research on tokens until the next chapter after we introduce the Ethereum network and describe the various types of tokens.

Cryptoeconomics

A first body of academic research applies the tools from economics to the study of Bitcoin, cryptocurrencies, and blockchain. This new field is know as cryptoeconomics. Researchers in cryptoeconomics are building theoretical models, running experiments, and conducting empirical studies that address questions such as:

- Can Bitcoin become a viable global currency and/or means of payment?
- What are the incentives of the different actors in the Bitcoin network? What governance mechanisms can resolve any moral hazard problems?
- What is the impact of information asymmetry between miners and users?
- Which consensus mechanism maximizes welfare for the crypto ecosystem?
- What determines the value and volatility of Bitcoin or other cryptoassets?
- What explains the returns from investing in cryptocurrencies over time?

This field of cryptoeconomics is growing each year as more academics turn their attention to it. While many researchers broadly support this project, they have identified a number of obstacles, which we will classify as trust, operational efficiency, and stability. These features are necessary for Bitcoin to become widely adopted as a means of payment, unit of account, and store of value.

TRUST IN BITCOIN

The public's trust in Bitcoin has been undermined by its association with illegal activity on Silk Road and the darknet, incidents of price manipulation, hacks and frauds, and high price volatility. While suspicious activity may be expected to decline as Bitcoin matures, the stigma associated with these early events lingers and undermine the public's trust in Bitcoin.[48]

One group of researchers studying all Bitcoin transactions from January 2009 to April 2017 concluded that one-quarter of Bitcoin users and one-half of Bitcoin transactions over this period were involved in illegal activity.[49] The researchers reached this conclusion by mapping transactions to users based on Bitcoin addresses revealed through various hacks. This figure has been disputed by subsequent research that suggests illegal transactions, scams, and gambling made up less than 3% of volume.[50]

Despite the massive market capitalization of Bitcoin, market manipulation is also a concern. One study has documented episodes where suspicious transactions from a small number of addresses were used to manipulate the Bitcoin price.[51]

It is important to remember that similar illegal activities and risks exist in the traditional financial system. Just try searching these notorious names: Bre-X Minerals, Enron, WorldCom, Bernie Madoff, the 2007 Subprime Crisis, and the 2012 price-fixing scandal in the London interbank market (LIBOR). Financial markets and banking have a spotted history.

OPERATIONAL EFFICIENCY AND STABILITY

For Bitcoin to be useful as a means of payment, its users must be able to conduct transactions cheaply, quickly, and with certainty. To serve as a unit of account and store of value, it needs to be stable and preserve its value. This objective motivates central banks in the conduct of monetary policy and the fight against inflation, where the goal is to provide a stable currency that reduces uncertainty, allows households and businesses to make spending and investing decisions, and supports the economy.

A first set of studies examine these issues using general equilibrium models or game theory. One study argued that Bitcoin will never reach the scale and speed required to support modern payments due to limited block size of 1 MB and the incentives of miners.[52] Miners effectively control the verification of blocks and can collude to strategically leave blocks partially empty, crowding out low-value payments. A related study concluded that Bitcoin is a natural oligopoly controlled by miners due to the concentrated production and ownership of Bitcoin mining hardware.[53]

A second set of studies argues that Bitcoin's limited adoption is an equilibrium outcome rather than a short-lived problem.[54] As the Bitcoin network expands, network delays grow, increasing the time needed for generating consensus, delaying transaction settlement, and leading users to abandon the system.

A third set of studies concludes that high volatility is a feature of the Bitcoin system. One study argues Bitcoin's design leads to multiple equilibria with sharply different price and security levels.[55] Price feedback amplifies volatility, leading to booms and busts unconnected to fundamentals. A competing study reaches the same conclusion about multiple equilibria, with two sources of volatility – one linked to the

Table 5.6. Risks to HODLers of Cryptocurrencies

Risk	Description
Price risk	Users face market risk due to the extreme volatility in Bitcoin prices versus fiat currencies and other coins.
Counterparty risk	Unregulated cryptoexchanges are a source of counterparty risk for cryptocurrency holders, along with wallets, smart contracts, and other protocols. Any protocols that act as financial intermediaries on a cryptocurrency network are a honey pot for thieves.
Settlement risk	Bitcoin transactions may be delayed, and payments are irreversible, creating transaction (or settlement) risk. If bitcoins are sent due to error or fraud, the system offers no built-in mechanism to undo this event.
Operational risk	Bitcoin's technical infrastructure and security creates operational risk. A user's private key may be lost through human error, hacks, or malware that steals wallet credentials and private keys. The arrival of quantum computing will undo the security provided by hashing algorithms.
Governance risk	Bitcoin is governed by a pro bono group of programmers who maintain the code and network, posting updates and dealing with technical problems. This group was responsible for the Segregated Witness (SegWit) protocol update, where the format of a Bitcoin transaction was changed to remove the witness information from the input field of the block.[56] The breakdown of consensus can lead to forks, such as the August 2017 fork that led to the creation of Bitcoin Cash. Other forks led to Bitcoin SV, eCash, and Bitcoin Gold.
Legal and regulatory risks	Bitcoin is subject to legal and regulatory risks that vary across countries and over time. Many users believe Bitcoin transactions are anonymous. They are in fact pseudonymous, with each transaction linked to the user's public key published on the blockchain. The user's identity may be revealed through a hack of an exchange, when they convert Bitcoin into fiat currency, or when paying retailers with Bitcoin.

changes in the future stream of net transactional benefits captured by miners, and one unrelated to any fundamentals that is analogous to sunspots.[57]

Overall, cryptoeconomics research highlights a number of risks facing HODLers of Bitcoin and other cryptocurrencies, which are summarized in Table 5.6.

Faced with these obstacles, some researchers conclude that Bitcoin is an intrinsically worthless, non-dividend-paying object that will never replace the US dollar.[58] Even if we adopt this view, this conclusion does not imply that blockchain-based tokens do not offer advantages over fiat currency or traditional financial securities such as stocks and bonds. Rather than throwing out the baby with the bathwater, researchers have looked at how a more efficient crypto economy can be built on a different blockchain. In particular, there is a growing body of research focused on the Ethereum network and decentralized finance (DeFi), which is discussed in the next chapter.

Market Microstructure and Trading

A second body of academic research examines the functioning of cryptocurrency markets and exchanges. This field, called market microstructure, is concerned with how prices are determined, information is created, and trading takes place. Researchers have studied these questions as well as the drivers of high fees and the ability of certain actors to move prices and volatility.[59]

A study of Bitcoin returns and trading volume using hourly and daily data over a five-month sample in early 2018 found substantial commonality in hourly trading volume for four Bitcoin-fiat currency pairs across exchanges located around the world.[60] Trading volume across Bitcoin exchanges is higher on exchanges during local working hours, similar to foreign exchange markets. This study suggests that Bitcoin trading is dominated by individuals, not institutional investors, as seen in the substantial trading on weekends.

Another study of price discovery in cryptocurrency markets found that changes in the Bitcoin price explain 80% of movements in other cryptocurrencies from September 2017 to January 2018.[61] All Bitcoin exchanges contribute to price discovery when Bitcoin price deviations across trading locations are small. But when Bitcoin markets become segmented, price movements are dominated by transactions on the largest exchanges.

A number of market microstructure papers have identified profitable opportunities to arbitrage Bitcoin prices across exchanges located around the world.[62] Arbitrage opportunities were large, profitable, recurring, and followed consistent patterns. Using tick-level or high-frequency data from 2013 through mid-2018, researchers find significant average price differences (also called spreads) that persist for a minute or longer. These spreads increased during the early hours of a trading day when Asia-Pacific and European exchanges opened, then decreased in the late hours when exchanges in North America were active. Price deviations grew larger as the Bitcoin price rose sharply in 2017 and 2018. Certain events created arbitrage opportunities, such as the entry of a new Bitcoin exchange or the aftermath of a bitcoin heist, such as the 2014 Mt. Gox hack or the 2016 Bitfinex breach.

Bitcoin arbitrage opportunities continued despite the introduction of futures and margin trading in bitcoin. By the end of May 2017 the major exchanges (Bitfinex, Bitstamp, Coinbase, Coincheck, Kraken) had introduced margin-trading services, and bitcoin futures trading has been available since December 2017 at both the Chicago Board Options Exchange (CBOE) and the CME. The research suggests that Bitcoin traders did not take advantage of these arbitrage profits due to a lack of capital and a lack of sophistication.

Asset Pricing and Crypto Returns

The final body of academic research focuses on explaining asset price movements (called returns), the volatility or variability of prices and returns, and trading and

Table 5.7. Cryptocurrency Index vs. US Stocks

Period: 2011 to 2018	Daily		Weekly		Monthly	
	Crypto-currency	US Stock Market	Crypto-currency	US Stock Market	Crypto-currency	US Stock Market
Average return	0.46%	0.05%	3.44%	0.22%	20.44%	0.94%
Standard deviation	5.46%	0.95%	16.50%	1.98%	70.80%	3.42%
Sharpe ratio[1]	0.08	0.05	0.21	0.11	0.29	0.27

1. The Sharpe ratio shown is the average return ÷ standard deviation.
Source: Liu and Tsyvinski, 2021.

investment strategies. A study of the returns from investing in an index of over 1,700 cryptocurrencies from 2011 to 2018 documented a monthly return of 20.4% over this period, compared to 0.94% for US stocks (Table 5.7).[63] The standard deviation of cryptocurrency returns was many times higher, leading to comparable Sharpe ratios – a measure of the return divided by the standard deviation, providing the risk-adjusted return.

While earlier studies argued Bitcoin prices could not be predicted, these researchers find that cryptocurrency returns over this period were driven by user adoption, such as the number of wallet users, active addresses, transactions, and payments on the Bitcoin network. Surprisingly, cryptocurrency returns were unrelated to the costs of electricity or computing power used in mining and verifying transactions. These researchers also found that both investor attention and momentum predict cryptocurrency movements. Google searches of the word "Bitcoin" predict returns over one to six weeks ahead, while past weekly cryptocurrency returns predict returns over the coming one to five weeks.

In a related study, researchers use the methods developed in the extensive stock return literature to explain the cross-section of cryptocurrency returns and to test trading strategies that generate excess returns.[64] By *cross-section*, we mean the performance of one cryptocurrency versus another, such as bitcoin versus ether, not the absolute performance. Starting with 24 possible factors, the researchers isolate 3 factors that explain most of the variation in returns across cryptocurrencies: movements in the cryptocurrency market, the size of a coin (measured by its unit price or market capitalization), and price momentum over the previous one to four weeks.

The crypto market factor picks up the co-movement of an individual coin with the overall market, similar to the beta of a stock. The cryptocurrency market tends to follow Bitcoin, in much the same way that the US dollar dominates movements in foreign exchange markets. They show that small coins have higher average returns than large coins, and low-price coins have higher average returns than high-price coins. These size factors may pick up both greater liquidity and the convenience yield for larger, more mature cryptocurrencies. Finally, they find that a portfolio of coins that have risen the most over the past one to four months will outperform relative to a portfolio of coins with the lowest return over the same window. This momentum factor works for the coming one to four weeks.

Finally, several papers look at how investors react to blockchain-related announcements from publicly listed companies.[65] Both studies find that equity markets overreact, with stock prices initially outperforming the overall stock market but then reversing later. The rise in blockchain disclosures coincided with the rise of Bitcoin prices in the last quarter of 2017. The fact that abnormal stock returns were linked to the performance of bitcoin suggests that investors did not understand the difference between bitcoin and blockchain. Caveat emptor!

Key Terms

altcoin	mining
blockchain	mining pool
central bank digital currency (CBDC)	nodes
cryptoasset	nonce
cryptocurrency	pre-mined
cryptography	private key
distributed ledger technology (DLT)	proof-of-work (PoW)
double-spend problem	public key
hard fork	Secure Hash Algorithm 256-bit (SHA-256)
hashing	security token
HODLer	stablecoin
Howey test	token
initial coin offering (ICO)	utility token
mempool	whitepaper

QUESTIONS FOR DISCUSSION

1 What is cryptoeconomics and why use the term *crypto*?
2 What is Bitcoin? How did its creator Satoshi Nakamoto address the double-spend problem?
3 What is blockchain? What are its main differences relative to traditional ledgers?
4 What is hashing and SHA-256? How are these two concepts related to proof-of-work and mining of Bitcoin?
5 What are the transaction fees associated with Bitcoin and how are they determined and allocated among miners?

6 What are altcoins and what were the first ones created? Were they mined or sold through an initial coin offering?

7 What is a hard fork and how did one lead to the creation of Bitcoin Cash?

8 What are cryptowallets? What are cryptoexchanges?

9 What are the risks of using Bitcoin as a means of payment?

10 What have researchers found explains price changes and the cross-section of returns in Bitcoin?

ADDITIONAL READING

Foley, Sean, Jonathan R. Karlsen, and Tālis J. Putniņš, "Sex, Drugs, and Bitcoin: How Much Illegal Activity Is Financed through Cryptocurrencies?" *Review of Financial Studies* 32, no. 5 (2019): 1798–1853.

Jain, Pankaj K., Thomas H. McInish, and Jonathan L. Miller, "Insights from Bitcoin Trading," *Financial Management* 48, no. 4 (2019): 1031–1048.

Liu, Yukun, and Aleh Tsyvinski, "Risks and Returns of Cryptocurrency," *Review of Financial Studies* 34, no. 6 (2021): 2689–2727.

Liu, Yukun, Aleh Tsyvinski, and Xi Wu, "Common Risk Factors in Cryptocurrency," *Journal of Finance* 77, no. 2 (2022): 1133–1177.

Nakamoto, Satoshi, "Bitcoin: A Peer-to-Peer Electronic Cash System," Bitcoin.org, October 31, 2008, https://bitcoin.org/bitcoin.pdf.

6

Ethereum and Decentralized Finance

SUMMARY

- Ethereum is building an internet of value where peer-to-peer (P2P) transactions take place securely without a trusted intermediary.
- Smart contracts are coded on the Ethereum blockchain, automating execution. Like LEGO blocks, developers combine them to create decentralized applications (dapps) and decentralized autonomous organizations (DAOs).
- To run smart contracts and dapps, users buy "gas" using the cryptocurrency ether (ETH), one of many ERC-20 tokens that can be exchanged on the Ethereum network.
- A stablecoin is a cryptocurrency whose value is kept stable by pegging it to another asset, with the token backed by fiat currency, commodities, cryptocurrencies, or nothing at all.
- Decentralized finance (DeFi) is a new financial system and "internet of money" built on blockchain that allows P2P trading that is faster, cheaper, more personalized, and secure.
- An estimated 10% of cryptocurrencies are locked into DeFi smart contracts used for decentralized exchanges, borrowing or lending, liquidity staking, yield farming, stablecoins, service tokens, and derivatives.

The previous chapter outlined the digital currency Bitcoin, which spawned many imitators known as altcoins. We saw how transactions in cryptocurrencies are recorded on a blockchain and verified through a consensus protocol called mining.

This chapter takes us into the world of Ethereum, smart contracts, and decentralized applications. *Decentralized* is a magic word in the crypto world. It means no single entity has control; decision making is distributed across a network of computers.

THE ETHEREUM NETWORK

The most transformational blockchain is the Ethereum network ("Ethereum"), which is the brainchild of Russian-Canadian programmer Vitalik Buterin. He saw the need for an open-source, programmable blockchain that would support smart contracts, decentralized applications (dapps), and decentralized autonomous organizations (DAOs). The native currency of Ethereum is ether (ETH), which is used to buy "gas" required to run dapps on the network. Ethereum is the foundation for decentralized finance (or DeFi), a disruptive innovation transforming financial services.

We have a lot of ground to cover. Programmable blockchains, smart contracts, dapps, DAOs, ether, gas, and DeFi – this jargon may seem overwhelming, particularly as much of it is new and borrows terminology from computer science, mathematics, and cryptography. But it's not as complicated as you think. Just think of DeFi as crypto LEGO.

Yes, LEGO – those colorful plastic blocks loved by children and used to build different things. LEGO comes in different shapes, colors, and sizes. With a little imagination, you can build a car, plane, or boat. If you are ambitious, you can build a house, tower, or town. LEGO is practically indestructible. Denmark has a whole amusement park built out of LEGO, including a hotel.[1] LEGO is fun and creative. Its potential is only limited by your imagination.

DeFi is LEGO for programmers. The LEGO pieces are called smart contracts, executable pieces of code that do things without human intervention. With a little imagination, you can use smart contracts to build dapps, which are software applications that run autonomously and securely over the internet. If you are ambitious, you can use smart contracts to build a virtual company called a DAO that is programmed to make decisions based on computer code. Smart contracts are embedded on a blockchain, making them practically indestructible. When it comes to DeFi, its potential is only limited by your imagination.

Vitalik Buterin: Crypto Visionary

Vitalik Buterin was born in Russia in 1994 and emigrated with his family to Toronto, Canada, when he was 6 years old. In 2011, the 17-year-old Buterin first learned about Bitcoin from his father, a computer programmer, and began writing about it online. He went on to launch *Bitcoin Magazine,* one of the first publications to take cryptocurrencies seriously.[2]

Buterin authored many articles in *Bitcoin Magazine* that explained the intricacies of Bitcoin and tracked the evolving ecosystem. He interviewed and debated with leading software developers internationally, wrote spirited defenses of Bitcoin, and educated a growing audience on this innovation.

After finishing high school in 2012, Buterin went to the University of Waterloo to study computer science. He continued advocating for Bitcoin while recognizing that its potential was limited by certain design choices. Bitcoin transactions were slow to process due to the limited block size and the time-consuming mining process. The Bitcoin blockchain only recorded transactions in BTC and could not accommodate other cryptoassets. And the Bitcoin scripting language was too simplistic.

So, in November 2013, the 19-year-old Buterin posted a whitepaper with a new solution titled "Ethereum: A Next-Generation Cryptocurrency and Decentralized Application Platform."[3] He described his vision for Ethereum in an article published in *Bitcoin Magazine*:[4]

> [A] group of developers including myself have come up with a project that takes the opposite track: a cryptocurrency network that intends to be as generalized as possible, allowing anyone to create specialized applications on top for almost any purpose imaginable. The project: Ethereum.

Ethereum was an evolution of Satoshi Nakamoto's vision that addressed Bitcoin's shortcomings. Buterin described Bitcoin as the foundation on which crypto developers were trying to build next-generation protocols, much like SMTP for email and HTTP for webpages had been built on the TCP/Internet protocol. A protocol is a set of rules that allows data to be shared between computers. For cryptocurrencies, they establish the structure of the blockchain – the distributed database that allows digital money to be securely exchanged on the internet. Protocols are the standards that govern how a network like Ethereum operates.

Buterin described what he was thinking when he developed the idea for Ethereum in a 2014 blog post:[5]

> I first wrote the initial draft of the Ethereum whitepaper on a cold day in San Francisco in November, as a culmination of months of thought and often frustrating work into an area that we have come to call "cryptocurrency 2.0" – in short, using the Bitcoin blockchain for more than just money. In the months leading up to the development of Ethereum, I had the privilege to work closely with several projects attempting to implement colored coins, smart property, and various types

of decentralized exchange. At the time, I was excited by the sheer potential that these technologies could bring, as I was acutely aware that many of the major problems still plaguing the Bitcoin ecosystem, including fraudulent services, unreliable exchanges, and an often surprising lack of security, were not caused by Bitcoin's unique property of decentralization; rather, these issues are a result of the fact that there was still great centralization left, in places where it could potentially quite easily be removed.

Buterin concluded that Bitcoin – as visionary as it was – was not a good foundation for Web3, the internet of value. Bitcoin was inefficient, lacked scalability, and had a limited scripting language. So, rather than asking developers to build on a faulty foundation, Buterin proposed a new one:

> Ethereum aims to be a superior foundational protocol and allow other decentralized applications to build on top of it instead of Bitcoin, giving them more tools to work with and allowing them to gain the full benefits of Ethereum's scalability and efficiency.[6]

The Ethereum whitepaper described the concept of smart contracts with examples of use-cases such as savings accounts, peer-to-peer gambling, financial derivatives, and new cryptocurrencies. While financial applications might attract attention early on, Buterin saw the potential for Ethereum to enable non-financial use-cases such as decentralized data storage, email, and digital identity. Initially, Figure 6.1 shows that Bitcoin has continued to dominate media attention, but over time public awareness and interest in Ethereum has grown.

Ethereum Timeline and Key Milestones

In early 2014, 20-year-old Buterin received the means to pursue his vision when he was chosen for a Thiel fellowship – a $100,000, two-year award offered by PayPal founder and tech billionaire Peter Thiel. Buterin dropped out of university to work on Ethereum full-time.

In mid-2014, Buterin relocated to Zug, Switzerland – a tax haven in the Swiss Alps. It has been given the nickname Crypto Valley due to the ecosystem of blockchain and crypto start-ups that emerged there. Buterin was joined by the seven other Ethereum co-founders that he had met along the way.[7]

Out of the eight co-founders, arguably the second most influential one is Gavin Wood.[8] A British programmer, Wood is credited with coding the first technical implementation of Ethereum in the C++ programming language. He also

Figure 6.1. Google Search Popularity – Bitcoin and Ethereum

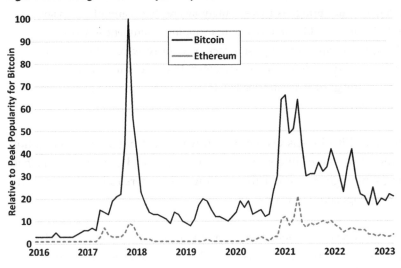

Source: Author, data from Google.

proposed Ethereum's native programming language Solidity for developing smart contracts that run on the Ethereum Virtual Machine (EVM). And he was the first chief technology officer of the Ethereum Foundation until his departure in January 2016.

In mid-2014 Buterin and the Ethereum team raised $18.4 million through a crowd-sale of ETH, the native token that would be used on the Ethereum network.[9] While 72 million tokens were pre-mined, only 60 million were sold over the 42-day crowdsale at prices between 1,327 and 2,000 ETH per Bitcoin, or roughly $0.311. Of the un-sold tokens, 9 million were allocated to the approximately 100 developers behind the project and 3 million to the non-profit foundation set up to govern it, the Ethereum Foundation.

Buyers of ETH at this initial coin offering were told explicitly that it was a prod-uct, not a security or investment. ETH tokens could not be transferred until after the launch of the genesis block, which happened in early 2015. With this capital infusion, Ethereum gained wide publicity even beyond the crypto community.

Table 6.1 shows the milestones for the Ethereum blockchain from 2013 to 2023. The Ethereum Foundation officially launched its blockchain on July 30, 2015, under the prototype Frontier.[10] Since then, there have been several network updates that altered the way transaction fees are calculated and set the stage for the transition to proof-of-stake in September 2022.

Table 6.1. Milestones for the Ethereum Blockchain

Date	Event	Note
Nov. 27, 2013	Whitepaper	The introductory paper by Vitalik Buterin, the founder of Ethereum, before the project's launch in 2015.
Apr. 01, 2014	Yellowpaper	A technical definition of the Ethereum protocol, authored by Dr. Gavin Wood.
July – Sept. 2014	Ether sale	Ether crowdsale lasting 42 days that raised $18.4 million.
July 30, 2015	Frontier	Launch of a live, barebone implementation of the Ethereum project. It followed the successful Olympic testing phase. It was intended for technical users, specifically developers.
Sept. 7, 2015	Frontier thawing	Lifted the 5,000 gas limit per block and set the default gas price. Introduced the difficulty bomb (called the Ice Age) to ensure a future hard fork to PoS.[11] This change was originally planned for Oct. 2017 but delayed until Sept. 2022.
July 20, 2016	DAO fork	The DAO fork was in response to the 2016 DAO attack where an insecure DAO contract was drained of over 3.6 million ETH in a hack.
Oct. 16, 2017	Byzantium	Reduced block mining rewards from 5 to 3 ETH and delayed the difficulty bomb by a year.
Feb. 28, 2019	Constantinople	Ensured the blockchain didn't freeze before PoS was implemented. Optimized the gas cost of certain actions in the EVM.
Dec. 8, 2019	Istanbul	Optimized the gas cost of certain actions in the EVM, and improved denial-of-service attack resilience. Allowed contracts to introduce more creative functions.
Dec. 1, 2020	Beacon Chain	The Beacon Chain is a parallel blockchain introduced as a first step to the transition to PoS.
Apr. 15, 2021	Berlin	Optimized gas cost for certain EVM actions, and increased support for multiple transaction types.
Aug. 15, 2021	London	Reformed the transaction fee market, along with changes to how gas refunds are handled and schedule for introduction of the difficulty bomb.
Oct. 27, 2021	Altair	First scheduled upgrade for the Beacon Chain, preparing for The Merge.
Sept. 6, 2022	Bellatrix	Second scheduled upgrade for the Beacon Chain, preparing for The Merge.
Sept. 15, 2022	Paris (The Merge)	Move from PoW mining algorithm to PoS. Introduced a new set of internal API methods.
Apr. 12, 2023	Capella, Shanghai	Third major upgrade for the Beacon Chain, enabling staking withdrawals. Upgraded execution layer Shanghai to enable staking withdrawals.

Source: Ethereum, https://ethereum.org/en/history/.

Ether: The Crypto Fuel for Ethereum

Ethereum created the token ether (ETH) to pay for running dapps on the Ethereum network. If Ethereum is a toll road, then ETH is the cost to use it. Buterin describes ether as the internal crypto fuel of the Ethereum network. While coding and hosting a dapp on Ethereum is free, running this dapp has a cost due to the servers and computational power required. If you think of the Ethereum network as a virtual computer, the cost to run it is paid in ETH.

Users who want to run a dapp must buy "gas" to run it, the same way that a car requires gas for its engine. With a car, the amount of gas depends on how far you drive, your speed, and other factors. On the Ethereum network, the amount of gas depends on the computational resources required to run a program. If you want to run a simple dapp, it doesn't require much gas. But if the program is complex, the user must buy more gas using ETH. This system ensures developers write efficient applications that do not waste computing power and keep the network healthy. It also creates a disincentive for malicious behavior that would tie up the Ethereum network.

Transactions using ETH were verified using the same proof-of-work (PoW) consensus mechanism as Bitcoin until September 2022. Under PoW, miners were incentivized to verify blocks of transactions on the Ethereum network in exchange for receiving ETH. Whereas Bitcoin uses SHA-256 for hashing blocks, the hash algorithm for Ethereum is Ethash, a computationally demanding algorithm that relies more on memory.

A new block is created every 12 to 15 seconds, with miners initially receiving 5 ETH per block. This reward was reduced to 3 ETH in late 2017 and to 2 ETH in early 2019. The average time it takes to mine an Ethereum block is around 13 to 15 seconds. Ethereum miners choose which transactions to confirm based on the amount of gas offered, so this system provides an incentive for both coders and miners to be efficient.

While more research needs to be conducted, one study of transaction fees on the Ethereum blockchain found that the price of "gas" responded to economic theories of supply and demand, rising and falling based on network utilization and computational power required to process different transaction types.[12]

There is no limit on how many ETH can be created. In April 2022, there were around 120 million ETH coins in circulation. Subtracting the 72 million created at the time of the crowdsale, around 48 million ETH have been awarded as block rewards to miners.

Proof-of-Stake (PoS) Consensus Mechanism

Buterin always recognized the PoW consensus mechanism based on mining was inefficient and wasteful. He wrote a blog on the Ethereum website in 2014 where he outlined how proof-of-stake (PoS) would work and why it was needed.[13] Then, in 2015, Ethereum announced plans to switch from PoW to PoS for verifying ETH transactions.[14] This switch took place in 2022, with Ethereum officially abandoning PoW and mining. Ethereum's transition to PoS reduced energy consumption for verifying transactions on the Ethereum network by 99.95%.

Under PoS, transactions continue to be processed in blocks by validators, not miners. As the name suggest, validators check that new blocks propagated over the network are valid and occasionally create new blocks themselves in exchange for the block reward. Under PoS, the time to create new blocks is fixed. One validator is randomly selected to be a block proposer in every 12 second slot. This validator is responsible for creating a new block and sending it out to other nodes on the network. Also in every slot, a committee of validators is randomly chosen, whose votes are used to determine the validity of the block being proposed. The first block in every 32 slots, called an epoch, is a checkpoint block triggering a vote by the validators. This mechanism provides finality on the previous blocks.

To become a validator, a node must stake (or deposit) 32 ETH into a smart contract on Ethereum. On a PoS blockchain, staking means to post cryptoassets as collateral to earn the right to verify transactions. The staked crypto is held in an escrow account, where it continues to be owned by the validator. This smart contract then monitors the validators.

Any malicious behavior by validators leads to a penalty called slashing where their escrowed coins are lost ("burned"). In most PoS networks, slashing is triggered by one of two conditions: validator downtime or double signing.[15] Downtime may lead to a very small penalty (e.g., burn 0.1% of tokens), whereas double signing can incur a much higher one (e.g., burn 5% of tokens).

Ethereum's transition to PoS took place on September 15, 2022, in an event known as "The Merge." The Merge happened after two years of experimentation and testing where multiple blockchains were run in parallel. As described on the Ethereum website,

> The Merge was the joining of the original execution layer of Ethereum (the Mainnet that has existed since genesis) with its new proof-of-stake consensus layer, the Beacon Chain. It eliminated the need for energy-intensive mining and instead enabled the network to be secured using staked ETH. It was a truly exciting step in realizing the Ethereum vision—more scalability, security, and sustainability.[16]

For supporters and skeptics of cryptocurrencies and blockchains, The Merge was an important milestone that showed Ethereum was able to evolve to achieve its vision. The Merge set the stage for further scalability upgrades not possible under PoW, bringing Ethereum one step closer to achieving the full scale, security, and sustainability required to support a DeFi system. We will discuss DeFi in a moment.

Smart Contracts and Decentralized Applications

Two of the most important innovations of the Ethereum network are smart contracts and decentralized applications (dapps). We described a smart contract as a piece of

LEGO and a dapp as something you can build with it. Smart contracts and dapps are central to the purpose and utility of the Ethereum blockchain, making possible direct P2P transactions without a trusted intermediary.

Smart contracts are computer code that execute a transaction without human intervention. The code is kept secure by encrypting it on the Ethereum blockchain to prevent alterations. This form of decentralized automation removes the need for a financial intermediary to execute a contract. As Buterin explains,

> [A] smart contract is a mechanism involving digital assets and two or more parties, where some or all of the parties put assets in and assets are automatically redistributed among those parties according to a formula based on certain data that is not known at the time the contract is initiated.[17]

Smart contracts reduce costs by automating and speeding execution of an agreement between parties. For example, a smart contract may be programmed to transfer your money to a vendor after receiving confirmation of delivery of a product. Or you might use a smart contract as part of a car sharing plan. When the smart contract receives your payment, it unlocks the car so that you can use it. By removing human decision making, smart contracts can increase the speed of execution, minimize mistakes, increase transparency, and generate cost savings.

Smart contracts can be written using the programming language Solidity, an object-oriented language for implementing smart contracts on the Ethereum platform.[18] It is a statically typed, high-level scripting language developed to run on the EVM. Solidity was influenced by C++, Python, and JavaScript. Other smart contract languages are Vyper, Yul, Yul+, and any curly-bracket language.[19]

Solidity is Turing-complete, meaning it is possible to write a computer program that will find the answer to any problem. This expression is named for Alan Turing, a British mathematician credited with theorizing and then building the first computer. Developers coding in a Turing-complete language can in principle solve any problem, with no guarantees regarding runtime or memory usage.

When we say Ethereum is a programmable blockchain, it is because the code for a smart contract resides at a specific address on the blockchain, known as a contract address. Other applications can call the smart contract functions, change their state, and initiate transactions.

Smart contracts can be used to program different types of applications that run without human interference. This type of application is called a decentralized application, or dapp (also spelled Dapp or dApp).[20] A dapp is a web application built on top of an open, decentralized, P2P infrastructure service such as Ethereum. Many dapps combine a smart contract with a front-end user interface.

Early crypto developers posted a manifesto on GitHub that sets out the rules for dapps, titled "The General Theory of Decentralized Applications, Dapps."[21] A dapp must have the following characteristics:

1 It must use open-source code and work without third-party intervention. It must be user-controlled, as in they propose and vote on changes that are automatically implemented.
2 All information must be held in a publicly accessible blockchain network. Decentralization is key, as there cannot be a central point of attack.
3 Dapps must have some sort of cryptographic token for access, and they must reward contributors in the said token, such as miners and stakers.
4 A dapp must have a consensus method that generates tokens, such as proof-of-work (PoW) or proof-of-stake (PoS).

Programmers write dapps for everything. We can broadly distinguish financial and non-financial dapps. A financial dapp transfers payment on a blockchain. Examples are digital wallets, decentralized exchanges, and crypto derivatives. A non-financial dapp does not transfer payment; instead it executes a contract such as online voting, decentralized governance, or a game. Or a dapp can combine both a financial and a non-financial transaction.

One of the earliest, high-profile non-financial dapps was CryptoKitties. It was launched in October 2017 by the developers at Dapper Labs in Vancouver, Canada. CryptoKitties is a game on a blockchain that allows players to purchase, collect, breed, and sell various types of virtual cats. Each digital cat is unique and is stored as a non-fungible token (NFT). As the website explained, "Breed your rarest cats to create the purrfect furry friend. The future is meow!"[22] This lighthearted program was designed to introduce the world to the possibilities of the Ethereum blockchain and the potential for dapps.

CryptoKitties quickly went viral. In fact, it was so popular that it caused a sixfold increase in pending transactions and slowed the Ethereum network, generating media headlines like "Loveable Digital Kittens Are Clogging Ethereum's Blockchain."[23] The most expensive CryptoKitty ever purchased sold for $110,707. In total, people had spent over $24 million on CryptoKitties by early 2022.

Types of Tokens

A dapp requires a token to run. The word *token* in the crypto world refers to a digital asset whose ownership is recorded on a blockchain or, more accurately, a cryptographic token. So, *token* is an umbrella term that covers many types or flavors. We will see that a cryptographic token can represent virtually anything. But the key is that a token is created to do something.

Because tokens are so important for dapps, Ethereum created programming standards for tokens so that they could be used by all smart contracts and dapps. These standards are called "Ethereum Request for Comments" (ERC). These standards specify the application programming interface (API) required to transfer tokens between smart contracts.

ERC-20 is Ethereum's standard for fungible tokens. A fungible token is a token that is defined by its value and is interchangeable. With fiat money, two coins of the same value (25 cents; i.e., a quarter) are fungible because you can replace one with another. A fungible token is divisible into parts, the same way that a $1 bill can be replaced by 100 cents. There are four types of fungible tokens:

- **Payment token**: A payment token is used as money to buy things online. Cryptocurrencies are payment tokens. Bitcoin can be used to pay for e-commerce. The cryptocurrency (or coin) ETH is used to pay for the gas required to run applications on Ethereum.
- **Utility (or service) token**: A utility token represents a claim to a service on a given network. Brave's Basic Attention Token (BAT), for example, is used to tip content creators through the Brave browser.
- **Security token**: A token that represents ownership in a business, or a claim to its cash flows, is known as a security token. It is the digital equivalent of a common stock or other financial security.
- **Governance token**: A governance token provides holders with voting rights, such as the Marker token used for voting on decisions related to the stablecoin DAI.

ERC-721 is the most commonly used standard for non-fungible tokens. A non-fungible token (NFT) represents ownership of unique items that are not divisible. In the real world, a piece of art or a house are non-fungible, because they have unique qualities that make them different from other houses or pieces of art. In the crypto space, NFTs are used to record digital ownership on a blockchain of unique items: houses, art, photographs, collectibles, or anything else that is not divisible. NFTs on Ethereum can only have one official owner at a time and are not divisible. So NFTs make it possible to create real-world scarcity for digital objects.

In March 2021, an investor paid $69.3 million for a digital piece of art sold by the auction house Christie's – the highest price ever paid for an NFT.[24] The token represented ownership of the digital artwork "Everydays: The First 5000 Days" by Mike "Beeple" Winkelmann, a US graphic designer. It was purchased by an investor using cryptocurrency to draw attention to this space and illustrate how anyone can use cryptocurrency for payment.

The jury is out on whether NFTs are more than a fad and will retain their value over time. CoinMarketCap tracks more than 100 "NFTs and collectibles," with a total market capitalization in mid-April 2023 of $25 billion.[25] Statista reports that close to $14 billion of NFTs were sold on the Ethereum blockchain in 2021 across collectibles, games, art, metaverse, utility, and DeFi.[26]

Decentralized Autonomous Organizations

One of the transformation ideas proposed in the Ethereum whitepaper was the decentralized autonomous organization (DAO). Buterin had a vision of a world where an organization existed electronically and operated according to a set of rules programmed in computer code. This DAO would be created by coding smart contracts on the Ethereum blockchain.

A DAO allows individuals to come together virtually to support a common enterprise without the need for a physical corporation, paper documents, or a management team. Like a corporation, a DAO controls an asset that it uses for some purpose or mission. To make this work without human intervention, a DAO must codify and program its governance framework – the rules, protocols, and other institutional features needed to operate. Buterin describes Bitcoin as the first DAO because it features decentralized decision making without a central authority to verify and confirm transactions.[27]

CASE STUDY: THE DAO HACK

On April 29, 2016, the German internet company Slock.It launched the first DAO on the Ethereum platform. The plan was to raise funds through the crowdsale of DAO tokens, then to use decentralized voting to decide which projects to fund using the wisdom of the crowd. Smart contracts were programmed to allocate funds when a certain percentage of voters agreed to fund a project.

The crowdsale ran for 28 days starting April 30, 2016, at a price of 100 DAO tokens for 1 ETH. It was widely successful, raising $150 million of ETH from 11,000 members by May 28, 2016. This total represented 12 million ETH, or 15% of all the tokens in circulation. This success far exceeded the expectations of its creators and gained widespread public attention. Basking in this success, by mid-June the DAO had 50 projects waiting to be voted on by its members. Then it was robbed.

Unfortunately, the computer code written to create this DAO was breached by hackers, who, on June 17th, siphoned off $40 million of ETH.[28] The coins were sent to the address of a new DAO, where they could not be accessed for 27 days. This hack was detected while in progress by members of the Ethereum community, who alerted Buterin and his team.[29]

The DAO Hack led to a high-profile and pivotal debate in the crypto community about the principle that a blockchain is immutable and its entries cannot be changed over time. It sparked a crisis in the Ethereum community that culminated in a hard fork between Ethereum (ETH) and Ethereum Classic (ETC).

The Ethereum team could see the hack in progress on the Ethereum blockchain. While Ethereum network hosted the DAO, the vulnerability for the breach was in the smart contract used to create the DAO. Because the Ethereum blockchain is public and transparent, everyone could watch as the DAO's ETH was transferred from the original owners to the hackers. But the hackers were following the Ethereum network's rules with the ETH transferred in blocks using PoW.

The central question was whether the hack should be stopped by modifying the Ethereum blockchain to return the ETH to its rightful owners. In other words, is a blockchain capable of being modified or not?

The purists argued that modifying a blockchain was against all principles of cryptocurrencies. In this view, a blockchain is censorship-free and immutable, and it should never be altered. Transactions could be appended using the accepted protocols but not rewritten and the hackers had the right to keep the stolen tokens as a reward for their ingenuity and work to reveal the flaw in the DAO's code.

The opposing view was that the DAO Hack was theft and not acceptable. If more than 50% of the holders of ETH agreed to alter the ledger, then it should be modified and the tokens returned to their rightful owners.

The debate raged for weeks until the vote was held in late June 2016. Many individuals posted opinions through online forums such as Reddit. The vote was close. The majority of ETH holders, backed by Buterin, voted in favor of modifying the Ethereum ledger to return the stolen tokens. So, on July 20, 2016, the Ethereum team took steps to return the funds to their owners, creating a rift in the Ethereum community.

On that day, the purists who opposed this decision proceeded with a hard fork, creating Ethereum Classic (ETC) as of block 1,920,000 on the Ethereum ledger. Following this hard fork, holders of ETH also held ETC on two different blockchains.

In December 2017, holders of Ethereum Classic voted to cap the maximum supply at 210,700,000 ETC, roughly 10 times that of Bitcoin (BTC). ETH continues to have no cap. Ethereum Classic cannot be used to pay for gas on the Ethereum network. But that hasn't prevented people from speculating in it. As of late April 2022, Ethereum Classic was trading around $30, up from its price of $1.60 at the time of the hard fork in July 2016.

Table 6.2. Stablecoins and Market Capitalization

Name (Creator)	Ticker	Collateral	Price	Market Cap ($ in billions)
Tether (Bitfinex)	USDT	USD securities	$1.00	66.2
USD Coin (Centre Consortium)	USDC	USD securities	$1.00	44.2
Binance USD (Binance, Paxos)	BUSD	USD securities	$1.00	17.5
DAI (MakerDAO)	DAI	Cryptocurrencies	$1.00	5.9
Pax Dollar (Paxos)	USDP	USD fiat	$1.00	0.9
TrueUSD (TrustToken)	TUSD	USD securities	$1.00	0.8

Source: CoinMarketCap, as of December 24, 2022.

Stablecoins

Anyone who has followed bitcoin (BTC) knows cryptocurrencies are volatile. Between 2015 and 2022, BTC ranged in price from $313 to $46,310, hitting a high of $69,000 on November 10, 2021. While the average daily price change was only 0.3%, the daily standard deviation was 4.1%, pointing to days with extreme movements, both positive and negative. This volatility has undermined Bitcoin's role as a means of payment and unit of account. It has also undermined the credibility of cryptocurrencies as digital money.

The crypto community has solved this problem by creating stablecoins. A stablecoin is a payment token whose value is kept stable by pegging it to another asset. Stablecoins are typically pegged at $1.00, with most backed by some form of asset (or collateral). The first stablecoins were backed by reserves of fiat currencies, such as the US dollar (Tether, USD Coin, TrueUSD). There are also stablecoins backed by euro, British pound, and Australian dollar. Stablecoins have been issued backed by cryptocurrencies such as Bitcoin or Ethereum (DAI) and commodities like gold (Digix Gold Tokens). And a new class of algorithmic stablecoins are not backed by any reserves or collateral at all (TerraUSD).

Stablecoins are like other cryptocurrencies, with ownership recorded on a blockchain providing transparency, security, and pseudo-anonymity. But not all stablecoins are created equal. Some are controlled by a company, while others are minted by a smart contract that controls the collateral. The leading example of a centralized stablecoin is Tether (USDT), which is controlled by the founders of the Bitfinex cryptoexchange. The leading decentralized stablecoin is DAI, controlled by the MakerDAO smart contract. We will talk more about the MakerDAO and DAI below. Table 6.2 shows the largest stablecoins by market capitalization at year-end 2022.

Tether first appeared in July 2014 under the name RealCoin, issued on the Bitcoin blockchain via the Omni Layer Protocol. The name was changed, and it became available as an ERC-20 token issued on the Ethereum blockchain. The whitepaper claimed that Tether would be backed one-for-one by holdings of the US dollar. Despite the promise to offer stability, Tether's value has been volatile, especially after questions emerged about whether the Tether outstanding was fully backed by US dollar reserves or not.

In 2019 a lawyer for Tether reported that each coin was backed by $0.74 of cash and securities, with the remainder backed by bank loans.[30] The value of Tether fell from parity to $0.92 per USDT, and the founders were fined by US regulators for misrepresenting to customers that it had "sufficient US dollar reserves" to back every token.[31] Despite this setback, Tether has the largest market capitalization, at $83 billion in April 2022.

CASE STUDY: THE INSTABILITY OF TERRAUSD AND LUNA

TerraUSD (UST) was an algorithmic stablecoin launched in September 2020 by Terra, a South Korean company founded in 2018 by Do Kwon and Daniel Shin. The founders wanted to drive adoption of blockchain technology by providing a stable cryptocurrency. Terra was a blockchain with its own native governance token, LUNA, that was linked to the stablecoin UST. These links were ultimately responsible for the downfall of both.

An algorithmic stablecoin is pegged to the US dollar but is not backed by US dollar or fiat reserves. Instead, it was backed by its sister coin, LUNA, with an algorithm automatically adjusting UST supply to keep the price at $1. UST holders were promised passive income of 20% through a decentralized savings protocol called Anchor whose yield was derived from staking on PoS blockchains and from interest paid by borrowers. UST was initially widely popular and rose to have a market capitalization of $60 billion.

In May 2022 LUNA and UST crashed following a run on the stablecoin, destroying $45 billion in market capitalization. In hindsight it became clear the ecosystem was a Ponzi scheme built on the illusion of value for LUNA. UST were created by burning LUNA; if 1 LUNA was worth $85, it could be replaced with 85 UST at $1 each. The algorithm controlled the supply of UST to maintain the peg at $1. If UST rose above $1, more LUNA would be burned to increase the UST supply. If UST fell, the algorithm would remove UST from circulation and issue new LUNA. But LUNA was not backed by any asset or use-case.

The flaw in this model was exposed following the run on UST on May 7. The algorithm increased the supply of LUNA to protect the peg, causing the price of LUNA to crash from $119 to $0. The price of 1 UST fell to $0.10. Cryptocurrency exchanges ceased trading in both worthless tokens and the Terra blockchain was suspended. Ultimately this crash is blamed for wiping out $300 billion in market capitalization from the cryptocurrency markets.[32] At year-end 2022, Kwon was facing legal charges in various jurisdictions for his role in this crash.

Tokenomics

Researchers studying the economics of tokens (or tokenomics) are building the theoretical foundations for a token-based economy. This research considers how token-based capital raising differs from traditional equity financing (such as initial public offerings) and when tokens may be a better way to raise capital. It also considers how to optimally create and allocate tokens in a platform economy to address moral hazard and liquidity.

One study argues that tokens are a hybrid of money and investable assets.[33] Tokens are a means of payment on digital platforms allowing users to pay for transactions. For example, Filecoin is a digital marketplace that allows users to exchange data storage space using the token FIL. Users pay for transactions in FIL tokens, while miners post FIL as collateral. As the users on a platform increase, it becomes easier to find a transaction counterparty and the usefulness and value of the FIL token increases.

These researchers show that the equilibrium price of a token is determined by the total volume of user demand, rather than by the standard valuation model of discounting cash flows. Tokens can lower transaction costs paid by users by allowing them to capitalize on platform growth. The resultant feedback between user adoption and token price accelerates adoption and dampens price volatility.

A number of studies compare token financing with traditional equity financing, focusing on the agency problems, information asymmetry, and risk sharing between entrepreneurs and investors.[34] While not ideal for all use-cases, tokens are likely to dominate equity for start-ups where entrepreneurial effort is crucial and when signaling quality to outside investors. A token works better for technology businesses where the moral hazard problem between the founder and the investors is greater. This research concludes that the optimal design of a token contract combines a crowdsale through an ICO with a revenue-sharing agreement that replicates the payoffs from issuing equity.

Another study disagrees, concluding there is a fundamental paradox with issuing tokens to finance a platform business. The mechanics of miner compensation increases the supply of tokens and lowers the amount investors are willing to pay for them, limiting the value of utility tokens as an alternative to traditional financing options.[35] A competing study argues this problem can be addressed by burning tokens when there is over-supply, which will boost their value.[36]

Various papers agree that blockchain solves a moral hazard problem between founders, investors, and users of a platform.[37] The blockchain eliminates the ability of owners to create more tokens without investing effort. In other words, tokenization acts as a commitment device that prevents a platform from exploiting users by diluting their stake. The founder is motivated to invest effort in a platform business because the payoff depends on profit, whereas the payoff to token investors depends on transaction volume, which is less sensitive to effort.

To summarize, the decentralized governance provided by issuing tokens on a blockchain to finance a platform business reduces the moral hazard problem between insiders and outsiders and aligns their incentives, encouraging adoption of the platform by users.

DECENTRALIZED FINANCE (DEFi)

Decentralized finance (DeFi) is a movement to build a global, decentralized financial system based on cryptoassets, blockchains, and smart contracts.[38] The goal is to disintermediate the traditional financial intermediaries that control the current financial system by allowing secure P2P transactions over the internet. DeFi is built on open-source technology that anyone can download and use for free.

DeFi does not refer to a specific financial product or service, but rather an ecosystem, an infrastructure, and a marketplace. Some people call it the "internet of money," "network of value," or "Web3" – a cryptocurrency term that refers to a decentralized version of the internet run solely on a blockchain. DeFi is enabling many different categories of activities, as shown in Figure 6.2. We will discuss these categories further on.

Figure 6.2. DeFi Categories

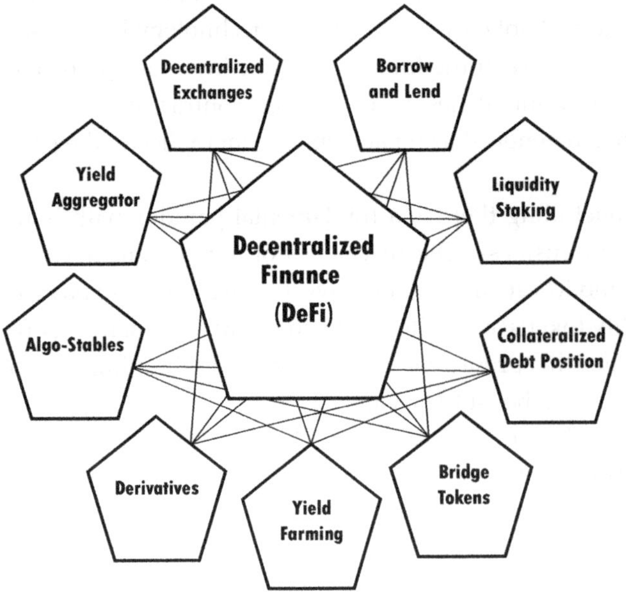

DeFi is creating a financial system that is open, permissionless, transparent, and automated. DeFi markets are always open, and there are no centralized authorities who can block payments or deny access to anything.[39] Services that were previously slow and at risk of human error are automatic and safer. This new ecosystem is built to be faster, cheaper, more personalized, and secure without requiring trusted intermediaries.

Believers in the transformational paradigm of fintech argue that DeFi will dramatically alter how financial markets operate. Holders of the traditional paradigm agree that DeFi may attract some market share and establish itself as an alternative financial system, but the old and the new will co-exist, and the traditional system will continue to dominate.

CASE STUDY: CURVE FINANCE – A DECENTRALIZED EXCHANGE

Curve Finance is a leading decentralized exchange (DEX) and liquidity pool for swapping stablecoins on the Ethereum network.[40] It had locked valued close to $25 billion at the end of 2021, but this total had fallen to $3.6 billion by year-end 2022. Curve Finance has coded an automated market maker (AMM) that allows users to engage in arbitrage across smart contracts and decentralized exchanges.

The AMM operates like a securities lending facility with different pools of stablecoins. Users provide liquidity by depositing stablecoins into a pool and collecting a fee charged by other users who borrow one or more of the stablecoins for some period. Depositors were promised an annual percentage rate (APR) of 10% to 50% per annum by earning interest and sharing in trading fees, although this claim has now disappeared from its website.

For example, the 3CRV liquidity pool allows users to swap between the stablecoins DAI, USDT, and USDC. Each of these stablecoins should have a value of US$1, but their prices may vary from this underlying value due to market supply and demand on different exchanges. The 3CRV liquidity pool provides a way to arbitrage these price differences through borrowing in each of these stablecoins.

Users connect their digital wallet to the Curve AMM, set up a savings account, and deposit one of these stablecoins into the liquidity pool. Another user borrows from this pool for some period and is charged a rate of interest. The depositor receives a share of this interest charged based on their pro-rata contribution to the liquidity pool. Curve collects a fee of 0.04% from each transaction, of which half goes to the liquidity providers (depositors) and half goes to the owners of the Curve DAO.

Market Size: Total Value Locked

There are no official statistics on the DeFi market. Most knowledge is on websites and blogs, on social media sites (such as Twitter), and in the collective memories of participants. When it comes to market size, the main metric is total value locked, or TVL. TVL is the dollar value of cryptocurrencies locked up in a smart contract for any project, in a liquidity pool for lending, or staked on a PoS blockchain. TVL is the most widely used measure of the health of crypto.

Figure 6.3 shows the growth of the DeFi market based on TVL according to the website DefiLlama. The DeFi market size was close to $40 billion at year-end 2022, a dramatic fall from a year earlier, when the TVL was above $175 billion.[41] DeFi represents 5% of the value of all cryptocurrencies, which had a market capitalization of $800 billion at year-end 2022. We see a dramatic rise in DeFi over 2021 and the equally spectacular collapse in 2022 associated with the fall in value of bitcoin, the failure of Terra LUNA/UST, the fraud at FTX, and other crypto scandals.

DeFi transactions take place securely on a blockchain without the need for banks, brokers, asset managers, or insurers. Any product or service traditionally available through one of these incumbents can be coded using smart contracts and exchanged

Figure 6.3. Total Value Locked in DeFi

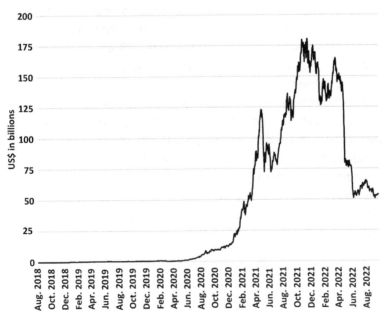

Source: DefiLlama.

P2P between counterparties. You can set up a deposit account and transfer money, take out a loan or mortgage, raise capital by issuing bonds or equity, trade crypto-currencies and derivatives on decentralized exchanges, engage in margin trading, and take out insurance against some risk. Any financial use-case can be coded using a smart contract.

Dominance of Ethereum

According to DefiLlama, more than half of the DeFi market is built on the Ethereum blockchain, with close to 60% of TVL at year-end 2022.[42] The next largest blockchains were Tron, with 10.8%, and BSC, with 10.5%.

Ethereum's dominance is no surprise given DeFi was always part of the vision. Writing in the preface to *DeFi and the Future of Finance* by Harvey et al., Ethereum founder Vitalik Buterin explains,

> Decentralized finance (or DeFi) has always been a big part of what I hoped to see people build on Ethereum. Ideas around user-issued assets, stablecoins, prediction markets, decentralized exchanges, and much more had already been at the top of my mind as well as the minds of many others trying to build the next stage of blockchain technology in those special early days of 2013–14. But instead of creating a limited platform targeting a set of known existing use cases, as many others did, Ethereum introduced general-purpose programmability, allowing blockchain-based contracts that can hold digital assets and transfer them according to pre-defined rules, and even support applications with components that are not financial at all.[43]

The Ethereum network was custom built to enable DeFi. It is open source and has created a global community of developers. It supports multiple programming languages. It allows coders to write smart contracts that contain the necessary logic for complex transactions. It has established an industry standard for fungible tokens, ERC-20. It has built the most developed ecosystem of smart contracts, dapps, and DAOs across blockchain networks.

Ethereum also combines a transparent governance structure with transparent fees (or gas). It has a liquid and widely available token (ETH) and is improving the rate at which it processes transactions. Finally, Ethereum has succeeded in creating network effects, attracting the highest value locked of cryptoassets among competing blockchain networks.

Finally, Ethereum has shared a vision and tracked its progress, reporting on all milestones and providing programmers and developers with advance notice of forks

Table 6.3. DeFi Categories Ranked by Total Value Locked, Year-End 2022

Category	Protocols	TVL	% of DeFi TVL	Description
DEXes	655	$15.9	40	Swap/trade cryptocurrency
Lending	199	$10.8	27	Borrow and lend assets
Liquidity staking	61	$8.9	22	Rewards for staked assets
Collateralized debt position	60	$8.1	20	Mint stablecoin using collateral
Bridge token	36	$7.8	20	Bridge token from one network to another
Yield farming	365	$4.7	12	Pay reward for staking on their platform
Services	62	$2.2	6	Provide a service to the user
Derivatives	53	$1.3	3	Smart contracts based on underlying asset
Algo-stables	99	$1.3	3	Algorithmic stablecoins
Yield aggregator	78	$1.1	3	Aggregate yield from diverse protocols

Source: DefiLlama.

and network upgrades. The vision is to bring Ethereum into the mainstream and serve all of humanity.

To accomplish its vision, Ethereum recognizes the need to be scalable, secure, and sustainable. Ethereum needs to support thousands of transactions per second, to make applications faster and cheaper to use. As the adoption of Ethereum grows, the protocol needs to become more secure against all forms of attack. Recognizing the importance of the climate emergency, Ethereum needed to reduce its energy-intensity, accomplished in the fall of 2022 by the transition to PoS that reduced network energy use by 99.95%.

DeFi Categories

Figure 6.2 and Table 6.3 show the most popular DeFi categories and the number of associated protocols. Each protocol is associated with a smart contract, a dapp, or a DAO. The biggest DeFi categories were decentralized exchanges (DEXes), borrowing and lending against cryptocurrencies, and liquidity staking. As we look at these activities, remember our LEGO analogy. With LEGO, you can build anything by putting the bricks together in different combinations. With DeFi, many developers have built dapps and DAOs by combining smart contracts in new and interesting ways.

A DEX is a smart contract that allows users to buy, sell, or trade cryptocurrencies or other tokens. Because they run on the Ethereum blockchain, DEXes operate without a central authority. Instead, the smart contracts enforce the rules, execute trades, and securely handle funds when necessary. Many DEXes use liquidity pools to help maintain fair market values for the tokens they trade. These liquidity pools are managed by an AMM, a smart contract that maintains the price of tokens relative to one another within a specific pool. The leading DEXes are Curve, Uniswap, and PancakeSwap.

Cryptocurrency investors can borrow and lend assets using DeFi protocols such as Anchor, AAVE, and Compound. We mentioned the Anchor protocol earlier when discussing the stablecoin TerraUSD. AAVE is a smart contract for depositing and lending crypto. Rather than providing a P2P loan between one borrower and a group of lenders, AAVE uses a pool where lenders deposit cryptocurrencies and borrowers take out collateralized loans. The deposit and loan pool are run by a smart contract. Borrowers pay interest to the pool, which is paid pro rata to depositors' contribution to the liquidity of the pool. Borrowers take out a debt token called aToken, which can be moved and traded like other ERC-20 tokens on the Ethereum blockchain.

Liquidity staking has been extremely popular with the crypto community. Liquidity staking is pledging crypto to increase the liquidity of a pool and earn a reward. Staked crypto can be borrowed by other users, much like securities lending and repo markets for traditional financial securities. The user staking crypto receives a liquidity provider (LP) token, representing the share of the liquidity pool owned by the user. This token appreciates in value reflecting the interest earned.

Lido is a leading DeFi application for liquidity staking. Lido is a DAO that allows users to double-dip on liquidity returns. Users stake ETH, Solana (SOL), or other tokens, and receive liquidity tokens (called stToken) one-to-one to their deposits. These stTokens can then be staked elsewhere across the DeFi ecosystem to earn more returns. Lido launched its staking app at the end of 2020 and attracted TVL of $18.7 billion in 18 months.

Yield farming builds on liquidity staking. Yield farming is the practice of maximizing returns on liquidity staking.[44] Yield farming is risky as users execute complex strategies, adding leverage by moving cryptoassets between lending marketplaces. A yield farmer may deposit tokens into a liquidity pool run by a DEX, then flip the LP token to another pool such as Convex Finance. Despite its risk, liquidity mining has become a norm and most DeFi projects offer this program to attract users.

Bridging tokens were created to solve a pain point with blockchains. Most blockchains are closed to other cryptoassets by design, meaning they cannot communicate with one another. We say they lack interoperability. For example, the Bitcoin blockchain is standalone and only records transactions in bitcoin. It cannot record transactions in ETH or other cryptocurrencies. This lack of interoperability creates a problem for users who hold both cryptocurrencies and want to move them across blockchains.

Bridge tokens allow crypto from one blockchain network to be used on another. The leading bridging tokens are Wrapped Bitcoin, Multichain, and Wormhole. The largest, Wrapped Bitcoin (WBTC), is a stablecoin backed one-to-one with Bitcoin deposits. By "wrapping" BTC in an ERC-20 token, WBTC bridges bitcoin to the Ethereum network. It allows decentralized exchanges, cryptowallets, and payment services to support both cryptocurrencies using a single node on Ethereum, instead of having to run two separate nodes for ETH and BTC networks. WBTC also combines the greater liquidity of bitcoin with the faster processing times of the Ethereum blockchain.

Another innovation is a collateralized debt position (CDP). A CDP is a loan of a stablecoin collateralized by cryptocurrencies and controlled by a smart contract. The smart contract records the deposits and provides the loan against some portion of the collateral. Below we will look at the MakerDAO smart contract, which dominates this market with its stablecoin DAI.

CASE STUDY: MAKERDAO – A DECENTRALIZED CENTRAL BANK

One of the earliest and highest profile DeFi projects is MakerDAO, launched in 2015. Table 6.4 shows that MakerDAO was the largest DeFi application with close to $6 billion of TVL across blockchains at year-end 2022.

Table 6.4. Total Value Locked by DeFi Protocol, Year-End 2022

Rank	Protocol	US$ billions	%
1	MakerDAO	6.0	15
2	Curve	3.7	9
3	AAVE V2	3.2	8
4	JustLend	2.7	7
5	Uniswap V3	2.5	6
6	PancakeSwap	2.2	6
7	Balancer	1.5	4
8	Compound	1.4	4
9	JustStables	0.9	2
10	Uniswap V2	0.9	2
	DeFi TOTAL	39.7	100

Source: DefiLlama.

MakerDAO is a smart contract that allows users to deposit cryptocurrencies (such as ETH) and borrow the stablecoin DAI against that collateral. This system of borrowing in a stablecoin against collateral held in a smart contract is called a collateralized debt position (CDP). Once the borrower gets the DAI tokens, they can freely transact with them while leaving their collateral locked but exposed to market volatility. Like similar stablecoins, DAI is linked to the US dollar with an exchange rate of 1:1. Unlike other stablecoins, DAI is decentralized and not managed by an intermediary.

> MakerDAO effectively acts like a decentralized central bank that creates money backed by reserves (collateral) but is not operated by a government. The collateralized stablecoin DAI allows users the ability to borrow against their cryptocurrency holdings, providing liquidity without the need to sell. And this liquidity supports other DeFi projects on the Ethereum network.
>
> To borrow DAI, a user deposits ETH or other ERC-20 tokens into a vault managed by the smart contract. The user can then borrow DAI up to some percentage of the USD value of this collateral. MakerDAO requires a high collateralization rate to offset the high price volatility of cryptocurrencies. With a 200% collateralization rate, a user depositing $100 can withdraw $100 ÷ 2 = $50 of DAI. The borrower is charged an interest rate on the loan that changes to maintain the 1:1 peg between the DAI in circulation and the US dollar. A drop in the value of the posted collateral may trigger liquidation, so borrowers need to monitor their exposures as crypto prices change.

The second largest CDP token is Abracadabra, described by its creators as "a spell book that allows users to produce magic internet money."[45] Users post collateral and borrow a USD-pegged stablecoin called Magic Internet Money (MIM). Unlike other stablecoins, Abracadabra accepts interest-bearing tokens as collateral instead of cryptocurrencies. An interest-bearing token is minted by platforms to reward users for posting collateral. The token accrues interest and increases in value in proportion to their share in a lending pool. Abracadabra allows users to get more bang for their buck by reposting these tokens, creating leverage by stretching their collateral twice. Abracadabra is not a DAO, but it does employ smart contracts to open, borrow, leverage, and repay these loans.

Derivatives are a financial contract between two parties with a value determined (or derived) by price changes in an underlying asset. This area of financial engineering is perfect for smart contracts, which can be used to create an endless variety of derivatives without the need for intermediaries. The leading DeFi derivatives protocol is Synthetix. Synthetix launched in September 2017 and allows users to gain on-chain exposure to a range of off-chain assets. Users trade and exchange "synths," derivative tokens that track price movements of cryptocurrencies, fiat currencies, stocks, and commodities. For example, a user can purchase synthetic bitcoin (sBTC) to profit from increases in the BTC price and only pay a fee of 0.30% to Synthetix for this service. Derivatives are new to DeFi, and the value locked to Synthetix was only $1.1 billion as of spring 2022.

Now that we have looked at the various categories, let's take a closer look at two DeFi activities: a stablecoin backed by a smart contract and a DEX for swapping cryptocurrencies.

CASE STUDY: R3 CORDA BUILDS A DLT FOR REGULATED FINANCIAL SERVICES
In early 2012, American David Rutter decided to leave the British brokerage firm ICAP Plc where he had been CEO of the electronic brokerage businesses Brokertec and EBS. For more than a decade Rutter had overseen the introduction of electronic trading platforms that disrupted the traditional voice brokerage business for foreign exchange and fixed income trading. He saw the paradigm shifting and chose to become a pioneer in the world of cryptocurrencies, long before DeFi was conceived.

Rutter founded R3CEV, a venture capital firm investing in technology ventures, and recruited Jesse Edwards and Todd McDonald as partners. R3CEV combined the R from Rutter's name, 3 for the number of partners, and CEV for the focus on crypto, exchanges, and ventures. In late 2016 the initials were dropped, and the fintech became simply known as R3.[46]

In early 2014, R3's partners visited California's Silicon Valley to scout out potential investments among the bitcoin and blockchain start-ups. Rutter was amazed at the number of young, inexperienced entrepreneurs with a shallow PowerPoint deck who believed they could disrupt the biggest banks and infrastructure of Wall Street. Despite having no understanding of how markets worked, these crypto entrepreneurs were raising millions of dollars from Silicon Valley VCs at ridiculous valuations. Rutter was amazed but recognized a market opportunity.

Rutter knew clearing, settlement, and record keeping of financial securities was a major pain point for financial institutions.[47] There was a tremendous opportunity to move this non-proprietary, back-office function out of individual banks and into the cloud, where the expense could be shared across firms. And blockchain provided the cryptographic solution to create trust among financial market participants.

Returning to New York City, Rutter assembled a small team of blockchain experts and convened a series of roundtables with the biggest banks to pitch his solution. R3 would build a blockchain for securities issuance, clearing, and settlement that would dramatically reduce back-office costs using smart contracts. One estimate put the potential savings at $15 billion to $20 billion per year![48]

On September 15, 2015, R3 announced that nine leading global banks had formed a joint venture to build a proprietary blockchain for global financial markets. Using an innovative model, each bank paid an annual membership and provided staff to R3 to work on the project. By year-end 2015, a total of 42 banks had joined the club, each paying up to $5 million for the privilege. In a stroke, Rutter had raised over $100 million and secured the best talent without giving up any equity.

Being a pragmatic businessman, Rutter cared more about solving the pain point than the technology to do it. Guided by the mantra "adopt, adapt, or build," he divided the R3 staff into two working groups that began sprinting as fast as they could to find a solution. The first working group tested five existing blockchains (including Ethereum) and concluded none was enterprise-grade and capable of processing the high volumes required for financial markets.

Starting in mid-September 2015, the second working group began developing an open-source, financial services blockchain from scratch. The first version of R3 Corda was released in March 2016. Corda was not a traditional blockchain, but instead was a permissioned distributed ledger. It did not bundle transactions in blocks but validated each transaction individually, speeding up the processing time. No wasteful mining was required to reach consensus on transactions; instead, trusted intermediaries (called notaries) verified transactions.

The Corda ledger was immutable and encrypted. Corda was permissioned and private with no unnecessary sharing of data; only counterparties to a trade were sent the data. Consensus occurred between counterparties, not between all participants. And smart contracts allowed settlement to occur directly on the ledger without the need for human intermediaries.

As of year-end 2022, hundreds of regulated financial institutions – central banks, commercial banks, fintechs, financial market infrastructure providers, and exchanges – were using R3 Corda, its connected networks, and its industry expertise in their businesses. Corda enabled up to 20,000 transactions per second and worked seamlessly with many business databases including Azure SQL, SQL Server, Oracle, and the Java Virtual Machine.[49]

While not strictly part of DeFi, Corda illustrates how entrepreneurship, agile thinking, and partnerships can be used to build a solution that solves a customer pain point while meeting the needs of the regulated financial system.

Key Terms

automated market maker (AMM)	ERC-20 token
bridge token	ether (ETH)
the DAO Hack	Ethereum
decentralized application (dapp)	fungible token
decentralized autonomous organization (DAO)	interest-bearing token
	liquidity provider (LP) token
decentralized exchange (DEX)	liquidity staking
decentralized finance (DeFi)	MakerDAO

non-fungible token (NFT)

permissioned

proof-of-stake (PoS)

protocol

slashing (burning)

smart contract

stablecoin

staking

token

total value locked (TVL)

Web3

yield farming

QUESTIONS FOR DISCUSSION

1 What is the Ethereum network and who created it?
2 What problems did Vitalik Buterin see with the Bitcoin network for the future of the internet of value (Web3)?
3 What is ether (ETH) and what role does it play on the Ethereum network?
4 What is a smart contract? What is a decentralized application (dapp)? How are smart contracts and dapps related to LEGO?
5 What is a token and what are the different categories used by dapps?
6 What is a decentralized autonomous organization (DAO) and what happened to the one created by Slock.It?
7 What is the purpose of a stablecoin and what are the different types? What distinguishes Tether from DAI?
8 What is decentralized finance (DeFi) and what are the main activities across different blockchains?
9 What is total value locked and how it is measured?
10 Which DeFi activities do you find most interesting and why?

ADDITIONAL READING

Buterin, Vitalik, "DAOs, DACs, DAs and More: An Incomplete Terminology Guide," Ethereum Foundation Blog, May 6, 2014, https://blog.ethereum.org/2014/05/06/daos-dacs -das-and-more-an-incomplete-terminology-guide/.

Buterin, Vitalik, "Ethereum Whitepaper: A Next-Generation Smart Contract and Decentralized Application Platform," Ethereum, accessed April 25, 2022, https:// ethereum.org/en/whitepaper/.

Harvey, Campbell R., Ashwin Ramachandran, and Joey Santoro, *DeFi and the Future of Finance* (Hoboken, NJ: John Wiley & Sons, 2021).

7

Alternative Finance, Online Lending, and Crowdfunding

SUMMARY

- Crowdfunding platforms allow individuals, businesses, and social causes to raise capital directly from individuals and institutional investors. Activity is concentrated in the United States and Europe.
- These portals are categorized as investment and non-investment. Investment portals issue debt (loans) and equity. Non-investment portals are donation-based and rewards-based.
- P2P/marketplace lending and balance sheet lending represent 90% of all money raised. Equity crowdfunding represents only 3%, with donation-based and rewards-based crowdfunding at 7%.
- Online portals charge a variety of fees but feature high operating expenses. Losses have forced some of the biggest pioneers to pivot their business away from retail, move into financial services, or allow themselves to be acquired.
- The main benefit of digital capital raising for borrowers is ease of application, speed, and access to capital, but costs are high and success is uncertain. The main risks for investors are illiquidity, principal-agent problems, and fraud.
- In theory, alternative finance may be able to increase financial inclusion, but for now most capital is raised by borrowers and issuers who have access to traditional sources but prefer to use fintechs.

The previous chapter described how crowdsales of cryptocurrencies allowed developers like Ethereum to raise the capital required to create an alternative financial system called decentralized finance (DeFi).

This chapter looks at how individuals, small businesses, and social causes can raise capital through more traditional, centralized portals that connect them to the crowd. We will talk about how technology companies such as Alibaba and Amazon are providing financing in Chapter 11. We already discussed initial coin offerings (ICOs) in Chapter 5.

THE MOST DISRUPTIVE WAY TO RAISE MONEY?

Crowdfunding allows individuals, businesses, and social causes to raise capital directly from the crowd in the form of debt, equity, donations, or rewards. The fintechs that function as financial intermediaries are called online portals or crowdfunding platforms.[1] Debt crowdfunding platforms are commonly called peer-to-peer (P2P) lenders or marketplace lenders. You may hear crowdfunding called "alternative finance."

Historically, capital raising has been monopolized by banks and venture capitalists who help individuals and businesses raise money, charging a hefty price for this service. As with other areas of fintech, technology has made it possible for individuals, businesses, and social causes to bypass traditional financial intermediaries and raise money directly over the internet from the crowd. The money raised might finance an artist's creative project, a charitable cause in the community, or an entrepreneur's new idea. Crowdfunding is faster and simpler, avoiding the delay, costs, and screening required by banks, broker/dealers, and other incumbents. In 2015, the investment bank Goldman Sachs stated that crowdfunding was potentially the most disruptive of all the new models in finance.[2]

Online crowdfunding platforms were first launched in the United States and United Kingdom in the 2000s, before spreading around the world. The UK lender Zopa, launched in 2005, is seen as the pioneer among online portals.[3] It was followed in the US by OnDeck and Prosper in 2006, Credit Karma and LendingClub in 2007, Indiegogo and GoFundMe in 2008, and Funding Circle (UK), Kabbage, and Kickstarter in 2009.

Dedicated crowdfunding platforms were technologically feasible and economically viable due to the existence of the internet, mobile phones, software, APIs, cloud computing, and social media. With low barriers to entry, the number of crowdfunding portals grew rapidly over the first decade. The data provider Crunchbase reported close to 1,500 active crowdfunding platforms headquartered in the United States in 2022, with another 200 that had closed.[4]

Traditional crowdfunding was described as P2P because online portals connected individuals looking to raise capital with large numbers of individuals, known as the crowd, who each contributed a small amount. But instead of borrowing from the crowd, the majority of this funding is coming from institutional investors such as hedge funds, pension funds, insurance companies, banks, and professional investors. For example, around 85% of the funds on Prosper are supplied by institutional investors, while LendingClub and Funding Circle shut down their retail channel and work only with institutional investors.

With money coming from both individuals and institutional investors, this is not truly P2P lending. To reflect this broader source of capital, the term *marketplace lending* is used. We will continue to describe it as crowdfunding, but keep in mind that money is coming from many sources.

Crowdfunding and P2P/marketplace lending platforms are multi-sided markets that have users on various sides – borrowers, issuers, or campaign sponsors on one side; lenders, investors, and backers on another; and third parties such as advertisers, service providers, and consultants on a third. As with all multi-sided platforms, a higher number of active participants increases the value to the platform operator, the entity raising capital, and the crowd. Network effects are crucial.

In theory, a campaign sponsor can quickly and easily post a campaign on a platform such as Kickstarter or GoFundMe to raise capital quickly. In practice, it is harder, slower, and more expensive than its sounds. Most campaigns do not reach their funding goals, and the amounts available are typically small. Looking at volumes raised globally, around 90% of dollars raised takes the form of online loans and credit. The crowdfunding platforms that are most widely recognized by the public and raise equity or donations are less than 10% of the total dollars raised.

As alternative finance has matured, the early hope that online portals would disrupt traditional financial intermediaries and transform capital raising has faded. Running a crowdfunding platform is a tough business. Online portals have struggled to monetize users and cover the high cost of customer acquisition, which is estimated at $500 to $1,000 per customer. The financial disclosures of the largest, publicly listed online portals show years of losses, with share prices that have underperformed the overall stock market.

Many of the biggest online platforms have pivoted from their initial vision. Pioneers such as Zopa and Prosper have closed to retail investors to focus on institutions. Some have changed their business to become full-service digital banks, such as LendingClub. And others have sold themselves to large financial institutions, such as Kabbage and OnDeck. Many online platforms shut down in the early 2020s, driven out of business by the COVID-19 pandemic or regulators.

Rather than disrupting traditional capital raising, online portals have become an alternative digital channel for raising money, albeit offering some of the advantages of other fintech business models. In terms of the five dimensions of financial intermediation, online portals have succeeded in some areas but failed in others. They have reduced information asymmetry between savers and borrowers/investors by increasing disclosure, transparency, and monitoring for this micro-segment of the financial system.

Crowdfunding platforms may reduce transaction costs by lowering the cost and increasing the speed to post a campaign. But they still charge high underwriting/ origination fees for this service, as well as high interest rates for lower-rated borrowers.

These online platforms have not solved the problem of liquidity; there is little ability to resell securities purchased on a crowdfunding platform. They do not provide risk sharing as many online platforms have no skin in the game (except balance sheet lenders). Investors bear the risks of investing in a brand-new business or lending to someone of unknown credit quality.

Many of these online platforms have not built trust. Instead, there have been the same episodes of fraud, misrepresentation, and other principal-agent problems found in the traditional financial system.

CROWDFUNDING BASICS

We divide crowdfunding into two broad types: investment and non-investment. The difference is what the contributor expects for their money. Investors and lenders on investment crowdfunding portals raise money from expecting a financial return on their money. The investment may take the form of debt or equity securities, where debt is a loan to be repaid and equity is an ownership stake in the business. Contributors to non-investment crowdfunding have different motivations, using the portal to donate money to charities and individuals or to raise money for community-building projects. Table 7.1 shows these four models of crowdfunding with the capital raised and market share in 2020.

The two models of investment crowdfunding are debt and equity. Let's look at each in turn.

Online Lending

Online lending, also called debt crowdfunding, provides unsecured loans or other forms of credit to individuals and small businesses through a digital portal. This online portal acts as a financial intermediary, matching borrowers with lenders. The borrower may be an individual looking to take out a loan to consolidate their debts or a small business looking to finance an expansion.[5] Like a traditional loan or bond, the

Table 7.1. Types of Crowdfunding Portals and Investors

Category	Capital Raised In 2020[1]	Description	Parties to Transaction
Investment Crowdfunding			
1. Debt	$101 billion (89% share)	Portal issues a loan to an individual or small business. Two types: P2P/marketplace lending or balance sheet lending.	Lender ➜ Borrower
2. Equity	$4.4 billion (4% share)	Portal sells ownership stakes in a business, real estate, or stream of cash flows from a business (revenues, profit-sharing, or royalties).	Investor ➜ Issuer
Non-investment Crowdfunding			
3. Donation-based	$7.0 billion (6% share)	Portal asks individuals to contribute to a fundraising campaign with no promise of any benefit to the donor.	Donor ➜ Sponsor (or recipient)
4. Rewards-based	$1.3 billion (1% share)	Portal raises money to finance development of a new product or service.	Backer (or supporter) ➜ Sponsor (or recipient)

1. Cambridge Centre for Alternative Finance.

borrower has a contractual obligation to make regular interest payments and repay the money borrowed at some future date.

Online portals leverage technology to provide loans faster than traditional sources. Borrowers can complete an application online in minutes. In theory, the lending decision is quick, possibly days, providing faster access to capital. Online lending is also more flexible than bank credit, with no penalty for early repayment on loans. The catch? Online loans may cost more depending on the riskiness of the borrower.

Online lending portals feature two business models, distinguished based on who holds the loan. P2P/marketplace lenders are financial intermediaries, matching borrowers with lenders and collecting fees for this service. Balance sheet lenders are principals and act like a bank, supplying loans directly to consumers and businesses. The online portal provides the funding itself and holds the loan on its balance sheet.

In practice, many online lending portals combine both business models, with the larger, more established platforms offering both P2P/marketplace and balance sheet lending.

Who is borrowing from these fintech lenders? The borrowers are individuals or small businesses. Individuals can borrow up to $50,000 and small businesses up to $500,000 for terms up to 5 years. A study of 4 million consumer loans from 2 million US borrowers between 2012 to 2017 found that the average loan size was $8,500 with a maturity of 3.25 years.[6] The average borrower was 49 years old and had a credit

Table 7.2. Terms for Consumer Loans on US P2P/Marketplace Lenders

Company	Interest Rate (APR)	Minimum FICO Score	Term	Loan Amounts
Prosper	7.0% to 36%	640	3 to 5 years	$2,000 to $50,000
Happy Money	10.5% to 30%	640	2 to 5 years	$5,000 to $40,000
Peerform	6.0% to 30%	600	3 to 5 years	$4,000 to $25,000
Upstart	6.7% to 36%	600	3 to 5 years	$1,000 to $50,000

Source: Company websites, as of April 2023.

score of 654, lower than the average US credit score. This study found that fintech lenders built a foothold initially by lending to higher-risk borrowers and then grew their market share by targeting lower-risk borrowers.

Table 7.2 provides examples of the loan terms for unsecured consumer loans from four US P2P/marketplace lenders. Individuals apply online with no application fees. The platforms promise a quick turnaround of as little as several days. Each platform specifies a minimum FICO credit score, with the borrowing rate tied to the risk of default. When applying for the loan, the borrower specifies the reason, which falls under one of these categories: consolidate debt, home improvement, medical or dental expense, car purchase, household expense, special occasion, business loan, pay taxes, pay for vacation, or other. Loans can be prepaid at any time with no penalty. P2P/marketplace platforms are transparent about the interest rates charged and the fees that go with loans.

Small businesses have increasingly turned to online lenders to access capital, raising $43 billion or 43% of online lending globally in 2020. This segment has been growing while consumer lending has been shrinking. Many online lenders specialize in small business lending, including Kabbage and OnDeck in the US, Lendified and Lending Loop in Canada, and Funding Circle in the UK.

Who is buying loans from P2P/marketplace platforms? The original P2P platforms raised money from the crowd, with individual investors committing a small part to each loan (such as $100). These individuals would log on to the platform and find a list of borrowers looking to raise capital. Each borrower would have a borrowing target and description of how they would use the proceeds. The online platform would assign a credit rating and interest rate on the loan, which was the return (or yield-to-maturity) to the lender. The retail investor could buy some of the loan during the subscription period, with a dashboard showing how much had been committed. In all-or-nothing loans, the borrower would only receive the funds if their loan was fully subscribed. By investing small amounts in any given loan, individual investors could diversify their exposure by holding a portfolio and reduce the exposure to any given borrower.

From P2P to Marketplace Lending

As demand for borrowing grew, the capital available from individuals was insufficient to meet demand. Online portals therefore expanded to accept investments from institutional investors such as hedge funds, money managers, banks, and insurance companies. These institutional investors viewed online loans as an alternative asset class to bonds, allowing them to diversify by contributing to a portfolio of borrowers. In some cases, the platform may fund the loan itself, known as balance sheet lending, with the online portal becoming just another channel for traditional lending.

Sophisticated institutional investors soon automated their investment process. By connecting to the online portal using an API connection, they can download and screen postings in real-time. This data is analyzed by proprietary computer algorithms (or robots) that make the decision to invest or not. One study of LendingClub found that these robot investors systematically outperformed less sophisticated investors, but only when the online portal provided sufficient information on borrowers to assess the likelihood of default.[7]

The market for alternative finance has been growing and innovating, leading to other debt-based models. There are now loans backed by invoices and trade finance, unsecured mini bonds, consumer finance/buy-now-pay-later (BNPL), and crowd-led microfinance.

As with any type of credit, there is a risk the borrower cannot repay and may default, known as credit risk. The portal addresses the asymmetric information problem by screening borrowers and providing investors with information on the risk of a loan and the borrower. The online portal collects both traditional hard data and alternative soft information from the borrower and assigns a credit rating that shows the risk of default. This credit risk is then reflected in the interest rate charged on the loan.

While fintech lenders claim they use alternative data to evaluate borrowers, researchers disagree on whether this is true or not. Some studies look at how fintech lenders use machine learning to evaluate and price credit risk and conclude that P2P/marketplace lenders can find "invisible prime" borrowers who may be turned down by traditional lenders due to low FICO scores.[8] Using alternative data allows these creditworthy "subprime" borrowers to access credit at a much lower cost than they otherwise would.[9] But one study of 4 million US online loans did not support this claim, showing instead that the online portal's credit ratings were mostly explained by the hard information contained in credit reports.[10]

Some research supports the view that investors use soft information when deciding to invest. Retail lenders avoid borrowers who make spelling errors in loan applications or where the description of the borrower and their loan request is either too short or too long.[11] Retail lenders are more likely to fund applications with keywords that evoke emotions. They also avoid loans with a higher interest rate, which is a signal of higher risk of default.

Researchers have looked at what predicts default using data made available by leading online lenders. US borrowers are more likely to default if they rent their accommodation, use loans to finance medical expenses or a small business, or borrow for a five-year maturity.[12] Borrowers are less likely to default if they are employed in a professional position or take out the loan to finance a wedding, buy a car, or consolidate their debts.

Another study concluded that fintech loans were significantly more likely to default than bank loans for borrowers with the same risk.[13] The explanation was based on what happened after the online loan was taken out. Borrowers who took out online loans to pay down their higher-cost debt later spent more and ran up their debt again, leaving them worse off than before.

Finally, a study found that sending text messages to borrowers that expressed positive expectations for repayment increased the likelihood borrowers would repay their loans.[14] But messages that reminded borrowers of the negative consequences of not repaying their debts did not work and, in fact, had the opposite effect!

CASE STUDY: LENDIFIED – USING ARTIFICIAL INTELLIGENCE TO LEND TO SMALL BUSINESSES

Lendified is a fully automated online lending platform for small to medium-sized enterprises (SMEs). The company was founded in Toronto in 2015 by two former Canadian bank executives to supply fast and affordable funding to small businesses. Lendified was acquired by Merchant Growth in January 2023.

Co-founders Troy Wright and Kevin Clark noticed that many small business owners couldn't get the funding they needed from the large Canadian banks. These small businesses were then stuck without funding or forced to overpay for expensive merchant advance financing. Recognizing the importance of supporting this economic engine of Canada, Wright and Clark left their jobs at a large bank and started Lendified.

Lendified's value proposition is to take the pain out of applying for a loan by offering a simple and fast decision with rapid access to capital. Through Lendified's simple online process, business owners can apply online in under 10 minutes, get an instant decision, and receive funding in as little as 48 hours. Lendified offers loans up to $150,000 with terms up to 24 months. The borrower must be a profitable business with at least 6 months of operations, $100,000 in revenue, and a credit score of the owners of 610 or higher. Rates are based on the unique risk profile of each business and are often lower than other private lenders. A one-time origination fee of 3% is charged to cover processing and servicing. Loans have fixed biweekly payments and no prepayment penalty if paid from cash flow.

Lendified is a balance sheet lender, meaning they originate and hold the loans through the portal. Funding is provided by credit facilities and mezzanine financing from a variety of institutional and high net worth investors.

Lendified's competitive advantage over traditional bank lenders is technology, specifically the online loan application and the proprietary credit platform. The application process is entirely online and completed in minutes for a frictionless borrower experience. Lendified's software, Judi.ai, connects via API to the applicant's bank account and automatically generates a cash flow forecast. This forecast is analyzed by a proprietary credit engine to evaluate the ability to finance the loan. The loan may be collateralized by working capital, such as inventory or accounts receivable, to reduce the risk and the cost of borrowing.

Lendified licenses its Judi.ai software to financial institutions, first-party lessors, and supply management organizations across North America. Judi.ai can cut loan adjudication costs by 90% and improve customer service by making loan decisions in minutes rather than weeks. Using this tool, lenders can manage their credit risk and build a quality loan book quickly and efficiently.

Source: https://www.lendified.com/.

Equity Crowdfunding

Equity crowdfunding, also called investment crowdfunding, allows founders to sell ownership stakes (i.e., common shares) in their business. Individual investors become shareholders in the business with a legal claim on the company's profits and assets in case of bankruptcy. Equity crowdfunding allows entrepreneurs to get an idea of market demand for their business idea before incurring high start-up costs, allows them to advertise their product, and can generate feedback on product design from potential customers.[15]

Crowdfunding platforms may be distinguished by whether they are all-or-nothing or keep-it-all. With all-or-nothing crowdfunding, the money is only collected if the campaign meets its funding target. If the goal is to raise $100,000 but only $90,000 is pledged, the campaign is unsuccessful. The money is then returned to the backers. For keep-it-all crowdfunding, any money pledged is passed to the campaign sponsor, which would be $90,000 in this example. Research has shown that all-or-nothing crowdfunding campaigns force the entrepreneur to bear greater risk but raise more capital on average, with higher quality and more innovative projects having greater success rates.[16]

Real estate crowdfunding and profit-sharing crowdfunding are variations on equity crowdfunding that raise money from the crowd to invest in real estate or the royalties, accounts receivable, or profits from a business. The key feature is that the investors have an ownership stake and share in the cash flows generated by specific assets. Real estate crowdfunding has been growing fast, offering investors exposure to retail or commercial real estate projects (like a publicly listed real estate investment trust or REIT). Royalty-based crowdfunding is an innovative funding model where companies give up a percentage of their future revenues in exchange for capital to grow.

Investing in new business is risky, as most start-ups fail. For this reason, regulations in various countries set limits on how much retail investors may invest in any given crowdfunding campaign. In the United States, Regulation Crowdfunding sets a limit based on annual income or net worth, capped at the greater of $2,200 or 5% of annual income up to $150,000 (or 10% of annual income above $150,000). In Canada, the same regulation sets a cap at CA$2,500 per deal, or CA$10,000 if a registered dealer has supplied advice. Some equity crowdfunding platforms, such as Wefunder or StartEngine, may be open to retail investors but impose restrictions on how much can be invested in a single campaign.

Other equity crowdfunding platforms may only be accessed by high net worth investors, who are accredited and can afford to lose their investment. For example, AngelList specializes in early-stage funding for technology start-ups and is only open to accredited investors who meet minimum thresholds for income or net worth. Venture capitalists may also look at retail-backed projects to pick up signals on where to invest. Researchers found that a successful equity crowdfunding campaign helps raise venture capital later.[17]

Crowdfunding platforms perform various levels of due diligence, such as background checks, site visits, credit checks, cross-checks, account monitoring, and third-party proof upon funding projects.[18] The extent of due diligence is related to legislation requirement, platform size, and type or complexity of crowdfunding campaigns. Greater due diligence is associated with a higher percentage of successful campaigns, more fund contributors, and a larger amount of capital raised on platforms.

Leading platforms also encourage greater disclosure to reduce the information asymmetry between entrepreneurs and investors. Issuers who provide detailed disclosure of qualitative business information have more success raising money through equity crowdfunding.[19] Examples of qualitative business information are the description of the business model, competitive strategy, product market, drivers and barriers for product/service adoption, and milestones. This study also found that sophisticated investors are turned off by excessive use of promotional language or self-praise on business quality without factual support. Unfortunately, the same is not true of unsophisticated retail investors, who are undeterred.

Researchers have used data from leading online portals to examine what factors contribute to the success of an equity crowdfunding campaign. Entrepreneurs benefit by disclosing costly, reliable information that could be used by potential investors to assess the credibility of that information and inform their decisions.[20] Entrepreneurs in equity crowdfunding can signal quality and increase their chances of success by disclosing higher quality information about the risks of the project and by ensuring the founders have skin in the game.[21] Serial crowdfunding entrepreneurs are more successful because they leverage social capital from previous successful campaigns.[22]

Donations and Rewards Crowdfunding

The two models of non-investment crowdfunding are donation-based and rewards-based. These models may also be called community-based crowdfunding. Some observers include microfinance (or micro-credit) platforms in this category in cases where profits from existing projects are donated to new entities.

Donation-based crowdfunding asks individuals to contribute to a fundraising campaign with no promise of any benefit to the donor. Donors are motivated because they want to help, not because of financial returns. Common donation-based causes include artistic projects, civic projects, charities, medical expenses, and disaster relief. So a community organization may run a fundraising campaign to build a community hall. GoFundMe is the largest donation-based crowdfunding portal in the United States, having acquired its main competitor Crowdrise in 2017.

Rewards-based crowdfunding raises money to finance the development of a new product or service. The entrepreneur or business effectively pre-sells a future product to backers (or supporters), who are promised a reward when the project is completed. Kickstarter and Indiegogo are rewards-based crowdfunding platforms that primarily support artistic projects. For example, a musician may seek funding to record an album, where backers receive a copy once the album is completed.

Entrepreneurs can use rewards-based crowdfunding to finance innovation projects and get valuable feedback from customer investors on product development, with greater involvement from customer investors increasing funding success.[23]

A study found that after Kickstarter introduced a mandatory but unverified "risks and challenges" section to all project pages in 2012, backer support for high-risk projects decreased.[24] Longer risk disclosures, however, were associated with other non-risk disclosures, which increased backer support. This evidence illustrated how reducing information asymmetry can increase access to capital.

To launch a crowdfunding campaign, an individual advertises a project on a crowdfunding portal with a specific funding target and subscription period. Individuals pledge some amount of money, which is collected at the end of the subscription period. Kickstarter provides advice on how to run a successful campaign, including building your community, demonstrating your product at events and meetups, creating a compelling project page, and pitching your product to the media.[25]

CASE STUDY: KICKSTARTER'S MISSION TO BRING CREATIVE PROJECTS TO LIFE

Kickstarter's mission is "to bring creative projects to life." Kickstarter is a crowdfunding portal for creative projects: art, comics, crafts, dance, design, fashion, film and video, food, games, journalism, music, photography, publishing, technology, and theater. Kickstarter is an all-or-nothing portal. Creators only receive donations if their funding goal is met.

Running a crowdfunding campaign on Kickstarter is straightforward. The creator sets the funding goal and funding period, which can last from 1 to 60 days. The creator sets up a project page with a video and description that explains the story behind the creative project. The project page clearly outlines the rewards that backers will receive when the project is completed. The creator also needs to communicate with backers and keep them informed of progress while the project is underway. Once the project is completed, the creator needs to deliver the reward to the backers.

Kickstarter projects must abide by five rules:

1 Projects must create something to share with others. Every project needs a plan for creating something and sharing it with the world.
2 Projects must be honest and clearly presented. Projects cannot mislead people or misrepresent facts, and creators should be candid about what they plan to accomplish.
3 Projects cannot fundraise for charity. Funds raised on Kickstarter must go toward facilitating the project outlined by the creator on the project page.
4 Projects cannot offer equity. Investment is not permitted on Kickstarter. Projects cannot offer incentives like equity, revenue sharing, or investment opportunities.
5 Kickstarter prohibits projects that are illegal, heavily regulated, or potentially dangerous for backers, as well as rewards that the creator did not make.

As of spring 2023, Kickstarter had hosted more than 589,000, projects of which 40% were successful in reaching their funding goal. Statistically, projects lasting 30 days or fewer have the highest success rates. Total dollars pledged to successful

Kickstarter projects was $6.6 billion, with a successful campaign receiving an average of $27,800. Some campaigns have gone viral, however, with more than 700 projects raising $1 million or more, notably the Pebble Time smartwatch ($20 million), the *Veronica Mars* movie project ($6 million), and the *Reading Rainbow* project ($5 million).

It is free to set up a campaign on Kickstarter. Kickstarter only charges fees for successful campaigns: a platform (underwriting) fee of 5% of total funds raised, plus a payment processing fee of 3% + $0.20 per pledge. Pledges under $10 have a discounted micro-pledge fee of 5% + $0.05 per pledge.

Assume you raise $10,000 from 100 backers who each contribute $100, with half paying by credit card. Kickstarter would charge a $500 underwriting fee and $260 for payment processing fees for a total of $760, or 7.6% of the funding amount. You would receive $9,240. Funds raised on Kickstarter for a creative campaign are subject to taxes in the year in which the funds were received. If your $10,000 creative project incurred $8,000 in total expenses (including Kickstarter fees), then the profit of $2,000 would be taxable income for you in that year.

THE RISE AND FALL OF CROWDFUNDING GLOBALLY

Crowdfunding and online lending has grown rapidly over the past 15 years. The Cambridge Centre for Alternative Finance estimates that the alternative finance market raised US$418.6 billion globally in 2017.[26] China was the dominant market, raising more than $350 billion in 2017, or 86% of the market. In that year, the United States raised $42 billion (10%) and Europe including the UK raised $12 billion (3%). As seen in Figure 7.1, Chinese retail investors had embraced unregulated P2P lending, with more than 6,600 online portals by 2018 raising a cumulative $1.2 trillion.

The growth of alternative finance in China was too good to be true. Widespread fraud and the bankruptcies of hundreds of portals in 2016 and 2017 were followed by a regulatory crackdown that effectively halted most online portals. Millions of investors lost their life savings after founders liquidated the platform or made off with their money, with more than 84% of the platforms failing.

For example, Ezubao, established in 2014, became one of China's largest P2P platforms, raising $8 billion within two years.[27] In early 2016, news outlets reported that 20 people associated with the platform had been arrested for fraud. Chinese retail investors staged protests in front of police stations, publicly blaming the platform operators and lax regulators for their losses.

Figure 7.1. Rise and Fall of Global Crowdfunding

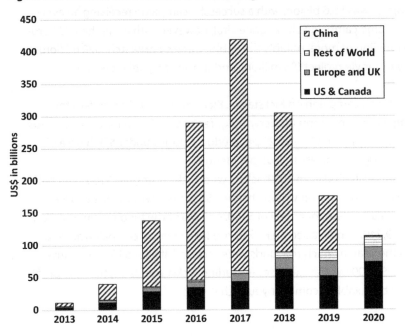

Source: Cambridge Centre for Alternative Finance.

Due to the Chinese collapse, the global market for alternative finance appears to have shrunk each year from 2018 to 2020. In fact, most regions around the world have continued to grow. By 2020, $113.7 billion in alternative finance was raised globally, with the United States raising $73.6 billion for a 65% market share, followed by Europe and the UK with $22.6 billion, or a 20% market share.[28] By this year, the Chinese market accounted for only 1% of the global volume, raising just $1.2 billion.

Despite the dramatic rise and fall, alternative finance has raised close to $1.5 trillion over the past eight years, with a compound annual growth rate of 33%. This growth in alternative finance has been made possible by low interest rates and the search for yield among institutional investors who view crowdfunding as a new asset class.

Many crowdfunding and online lending portals have pivoted their businesses in response to market forces. A handful of the largest online lenders have moved away from their initial P2P/marketplace lending roots to become digital banks offering a range of financial services, such as the LendingClub in the US and Zopa in the UK. Other online lenders have closed their retail operations to focus exclusively on institutional lenders, such as the UK small business lender Funding Circle.

Table 7.3. Global Crowdfunding Volumes, 2019–2020

	2019		2020		Y-O-Y
	US$ billions	%	US$ billions	%	Growth (%)
DEBT:					
P2P/marketplace lending	128.5	73.1	53.2	46.8	−59
Balance sheet lending	34.6	19.7	42.9	37.7	24
Other debt-based	5.0	2.8	5.0	4.4	0
SUBTOTAL	168.1	95.7	101.0	88.9	−40
EQUITY:					
Real estate crowdfunding	2.9	1.6	2.8	2.4	−3
Equity-based crowdfunding	1.1	0.6	1.5	1.3	39
Other equity-based	0.1	0.0	0.1	0.1	92
SUBTOTAL	4.0	2.3	4.4	3.9	9
INVESTMENT	172.1	98.0	105.4	92.7	−39
Donation-based crowdfunding	2.7	1.5	7.0	6.2	161
Rewards-based crowdfunding	0.9	0.5	1.3	1.1	39
NON-INVESTMENT	3.6	2.0	8.3	7.3	131
TOTAL RAISED	175.7	100.0	113.7	100.0	−35

Source: Cambridge Centre for Alternative Finance, 2021.

Alternative Finance Market Size and Growth

From its start about a decade ago, the global crowdfunding industry has grown rapidly. While comprehensive data is hard to find, the Cambridge Centre for Alternative Finance conducted a comprehensive survey of crowdfunding and online lending in 2020.[29]

Table 7.3 provides a breakdown of data on global crowdfunding volumes for 2019 and 2020. Total capital raised in 2020 was $114 billion, a 35% decline from 2019. We see the continued dominance of debt crowdfunding, representing an 89% share of alternative finance volumes at $101 billion. The single largest category is P2P/marketplace lending, which accounted for 47% of capital raised by alternative finance in 2020. This segment shrank by 59% relative to 2019, while balance sheet lending has increased by 24%. These changes reflect the COVID-19 pandemic, where government support for households in many advanced economies squeezed out platforms focused on consumers. Some jurisdictions, such as the United Kingdom, funneled support via online portals to small businesses, boosting this category. In 2020 equity investment raised $4.4 billion across categories, or 4% of total capital raised, which represented a 9% increase over 2019. Finally, we see that non-investment crowdfunding more than doubled to $8.3 billion, driven by an increase in donation-based volumes.

Figure 7.2. US Crowdfunding (US$ in Billions)

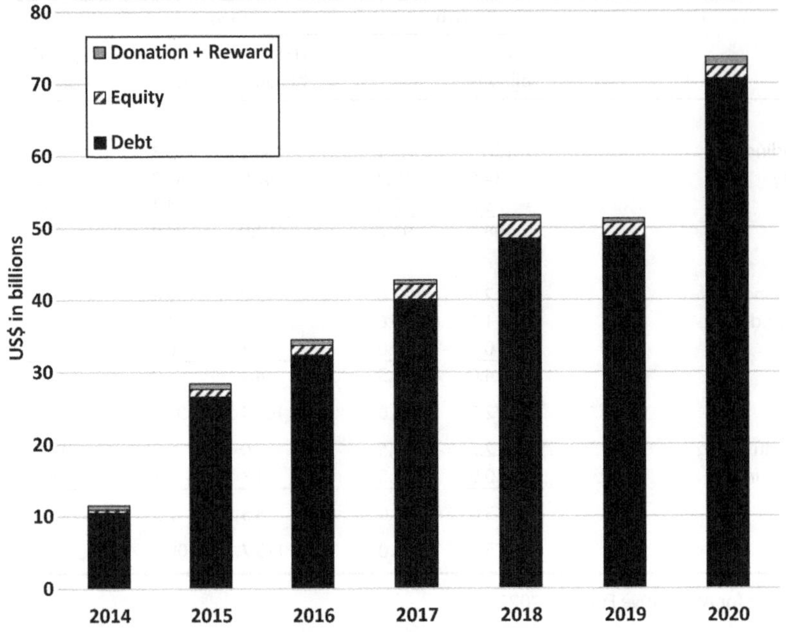

Source: Cambridge Centre for Alternative Finance.

Globally, the United States was the largest market for alternative finance in 2020 with a 65% market share, more than double its share in 2019. Europe and the UK were the second largest at 20%, then Asia Pacific (excluding China) at 8%, and Latin America and the Caribbean at 5%.

Figure 7.2 looks more closely at crowdfunding in the United States. We see that 96% of crowdfunding dollars raised come from P2P/marketplace and balance sheet lending to individuals and small businesses. Equity crowdfunding represented only 2.5%, and non-investment crowdfunding (donation and rewards) was 1.5%. For debt crowdfunding, 53% of loans went to consumers, 44% went to businesses, and 3% to real estate. Lending to consumers slowed during the COVID-19 pandemic, while lending to business has been growing, doubling in 2020 versus 2019.

Regulations and Crowdfunding Logistics

Online portals are subject to the same rules for investor protection, risk management, and capital and/or liquidity requirements as other financial service intermediaries.

Figure 7.3. LendingClub Structure for Issuing Notes (2014)

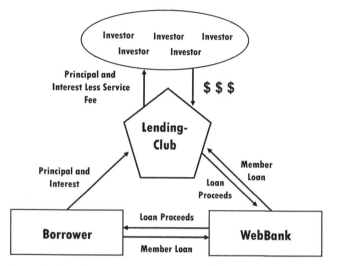

Source: LendingClub IPO prospectus dated December 10, 2014.

While regulators around the world see a rationale for regulating online portals, there is no internationally agreed standard or approach.[30] Some countries include online portals under existing legislation for banks, non-bank credit providers, collective investment schemes, and securities issuers (e.g., Germany, Hong Kong SAR, the Netherlands, Singapore). Other countries have introduced new regulations specifically for fintech credit (e.g., Switzerland, France, Spain, the UK).

In Canada, for example, online loans are typically classified as securities and are regulated as such using existing rules. This includes the need to provide a prospectus to retail investors. This added cost has effectively meant that only institutional investors and accredited (high net worth) investors can invest through online portals in Canada.

With so much variation across countries and complexity within countries, the rules have changed as the industry evolves. Regulatory risks remain a top concern for online portals, particularly for debt portals that serve consumers.

Let's look at how an online portal is set up in the United States.

Online portals typically partner with a regulated bank to issue loans, which are then repackaged and sold to investors on the platform. The dominant US P2P/marketplace lending platforms during the 2010s, LendingClub and Prosper, had a combined 90%+ market share. Interestingly, both partnered with Utah's WebBank, a state-chartered bank that facilitated the issuance of consumer loans. Figure 7.3 is based on a 2014 bond prospectus for LendingClub.[31] The notes sold to LendingClub lenders are backed by loans issued to borrowers by WebBank.

LendingClub borrowers must be US citizens or permanent residents and at least 18 years old with a US social security number, bank account, and valid email account. Most importantly, they must meet LendingClub's credit criteria. The borrower (a consumer or a small business owner) enters into a loan agreement with WebBank, not LendingClub. The loans are unsecured and not guaranteed by any third party or government guarantee. The borrower makes monthly payments of principal and interest to LendingClub, who passes these cash flows to lenders.

If a borrower fails to make a payment within 30 days of the due date, LendingClub will do its best to pursue reasonable collection efforts and may refer the loan to a collection agency. But any loss is suffered by the investor, not LendingClub or WebBank. The lender has no recourse to the borrower and does not know their identity.

In the United States, crowdfunding and lending platforms are covered by federal and state licensing requirements, consumer protection laws, securities laws, anti-money laundering (AML) laws, and the national securities association FINRA's rules for funding portals. A funding portal must register with the US Securities and Exchange Commission (SEC) and become a member of FINRA. Under the 1933 Securities Act, a funding portal cannot offer investment advice, solicit purchases or sales of securities displayed on its platform, or hold customer funds or securities. If it wishes to engage in these activities, it must register as a broker-dealer, which is a more arduous process. FINRA maintains a list of registered funding portals, as well as former portals that have shut down or were banned.[32] Registered online portals must meet ongoing reporting and disclosure requirements and report their gross revenue to FINRA each year.

These regulations and reporting requirements pose a high barrier to entry. To encourage the fintech industry, the US Office of the Comptroller of the Currency (OCC) announced plans in late 2016 to issue a special purpose national bank charter – called a fintech charter – that would allow online portals to be supervised federally by the OCC without the need for state licensing and oversight. In 2018, before any fintech companies applied, the New York state regulator moved to block it, challenging the OCC's authority in the courts. After this challenge was rejected, the OCC granted its first fintech charter in January 2022 to Social Finance Inc. (SoFi). The OCC press release stated,

> Today's decision brings SoFi, a large fintech, inside the federal bank regulatory perimeter, where it will be subject to comprehensive supervision and the full panoply of bank regulations, including the Community Reinvestment Act. This levels the playing field and will ensure that SoFi's deposit and lending activities are conducted safely and soundly, including limiting the bank's ability to engage in crypto-asset activities.[33]

Some online portals are unregulated because they are restricted to accredited investors and only sell private securities. An accredited investor is an individual who meets an annual income threshold or a net worth requirement. These online portals sell securities that are not registered and therefore illiquid and higher risk. An example of an unregistered online portal is AngelList Venture, which is dedicated to venture capitalists that invest in start-ups. Since founding, AngelList has raised over $10 billion in capital for over 12,000 start-ups, which their internal marketing reporting that their platform participated in over 50% of all top-tier US venture capitalist (VC) deals over this period. AngelList may not be regulated in the United States, but it was forced to register and face regulation to enter the UK market.

Benefits and Risks of Crowdfunding

Like any financial product or service, there are benefits and risks to alternative finance. The benefits are mostly earned by the individuals or businesses raising money through crowdfunding. Most of the risks are faced by the individuals providing the money.

EASE, SPEED, AND ACCESS TO CAPITAL

For an individual or business that needs money, the main value proposition of crowdfunding and online lending is the ease of the application process, the speed of the fundraising, and the access to capital.

For many entrepreneurs, the hardest part of starting a business is raising capital. (The same is true for musicians, writers, or other artists who want to create something new.) When an entrepreneur has an idea but no product or service yet, the typical sources of capital are the founder's own savings and investments from family and friends. A bank will not lend to a start-up until it has stable revenues or some collateral to secure the loan. Nor will venture capitalists invest at this early stage – not until they see sales are growing and the path to a future exit.

The entrepreneur's typical alternatives are to work out of home or a shared workspace, such as an incubator, while conducting market research and developing a prototype or minimum viable product (MVP). Once they reach the seed stage with an MVP and their first customers, the entrepreneur can apply to an accelerator, such as Y Combinator, or find wealthy angel investors who are willing to invest once they see the business plan and some traction in the market.

With the arrival of crowdfunding, an entrepreneur has an alternative way to raise money at the pre-seed and seed stage. By pitching the idea through a crowdfunding website using only a brief description and a video, the entrepreneur may be able to raise money quickly from large groups of individuals. Better still, these individuals may pre-purchase a product or service to finance its development or donate money to see a creative or civic project come to life.

Small businesses are financed differently than big ones. Most small businesses have neither the credit history nor the collateral to secure a loan from a bank. For these reasons, online lenders are becoming an important source of financing for small businesses. Data from the US Federal Reserve's annual Small Business Credit Survey shows the growing importance of online lenders. The 2019 edition reported that applications to online lenders continue to trend upward, with 32% of small businesses seeking funding turning to online lenders in 2018, up from 24% in 2017 and 19% in 2016.[34]

Interestingly, this growth occurred despite small business applicants expressing *lower* satisfaction with online lenders compared to satisfaction levels with large and small banks. When asked why they applied, small businesses reported that the main factors for choosing online lenders were speed of decision or funding (63%), chance of being funded (61%), and no collateral requirement (45%). The least important reason cited was the cost or interest rate on the funding (13%).

ILLIQUIDITY, POOR DISCLOSURE, AND FRAUD

Crowdfunding may be a wonderful way for social causes to raise donations or entrepreneurs to finance the development of a new product through rewards-based crowdfunding. But it is not necessarily a great place for individuals looking for a financial return to invest their money.

There are many risks for individuals when purchasing debt or equity from an online portal. Four principal risks are credit risk, liquidity risk, poor disclosure, and the risk of fraud.

Credit risk is the risk that a lender will default and not repay their loan. To help lenders understand the credit risk, a lending platform posts financial information provided by the borrower and assigns a letter or number rating indicating the risk of default (like a credit rating for a company). The lending platform then sets the interest rate on the loan to reflect this risk. A higher-risk loan will pay a higher interest rate. A retail investor needs to understand that a higher return only comes with higher risk.

If a lender defaults on a loan and misses an interest or principal payment, a P2P/marketplace platform passes the losses to the lender. The investor suffers a loss, not the platform. While a lender might have a portfolio with only a small stake in any given loan, the loss of principal on any given loan may wipe out the interest received from the remainder of the portfolio if any position is too large. For this reason, online portals encourage lenders to spread their bets and avoid large exposures to any single borrower.

This situation is a classic principal-agent problem. The platform (the agent) is rewarded with an underwriting commission if a loan is sold, giving them an incentive to increase loan volumes. But the platform does not bear the risk of default, which is passed through to the lender (the principal).[35] In finance, we say the incentives are misaligned in this setting. The situation is different for a balance sheet lender, as the credit risk stays with them. The incentives are aligned, as the balance sheet lender bears any losses on loans that they originate.

Liquidity is the ability to sell an asset near its fair-market value. If an investor holds shares in a publicly traded company, such as Apple Inc. (Ticker: AAPL), they can see the market price each day and can expect to be able to sell their shares at close to this price quickly and easily. In the case of equity purchased in a crowdfunding campaign, however, there is no public market and no guarantee that anyone may want to buy it at any price. The same is true for a portion of an online loan. In both cases, the investment is illiquid and cannot be sold in a reasonable amount of time without offering a large discount.

Disclosure risk is a risk that a borrower or issuer will not share material information in a timely fashion. Companies that sell securities to the public are required by securities regulators to make frequent disclosures about the business, its performance, and other material facts. These disclosures are verified by lawyers and accountants, as any misrepresentation can lead to fines, penalties, and even prosecution. Such disclosures may be limited or non-existent for securities purchased through crowdfunding. While the online portal may collect financial statements for up to three years, this data is not necessarily audited or updated in a timely fashion. Researchers have found, however, that entrepreneurs benefit by disclosing material information that allows potential investors to assess the credibility of the business and inform their decisions.[36]

The risk of fraud is best illustrated by an example from crowdfunding in China. China's online lending industry experienced rapid growth from 2007 to 2017 without significant regulation. The number of P2P/marketplace lending platforms rose dramatically, fueled on one side by a shortage of funding for individuals and small businesses and speculation from retail investors on the other side.[37] China's alternative finance market reached US$358 billion in 2017, of which one-third was borrowing by small businesses. Online portals also provided campus loans to students and payday loans to individuals at sky-high interest rates.

At its peak, China's P2P lending market had attracted $200 billion in investments from 50 million savers enticed by returns of 10% or more.[38] In 2016 and 2017, China's P2P market experienced widespread fraud, the exposure of Ponzi schemes, and the collapse of hundreds of portals, leaving nothing for retail investors. As we discussed earlier, the P2P lender Ezubao, founded in 2014, collapsed after it was exposed as a Ponzi

Table 7.4. Risks in Crowdfunding

Type of Risk	Description
Credit risk	Investments in start-ups and early-stage ventures are speculative, and these enterprises often fail. The success of a start-up or early-stage venture often relies on the development of a new product or service that may or may not find a market. Be prepared to lose your entire investment.
Illiquidity	You will be limited in your ability to resell your investment for the first year and may need to hold your investment for an indefinite period. You may have to locate an interested buyer yourself when you do seek to resell your investment.
Limited disclosure	The company must disclose information about the company, its business plan, the offering, and its anticipated use of proceeds, among other things. An early-stage company may be able to provide only limited information about its business plan and operations. The company is also only obligated to file information annually, including financial statements. You may have only limited continuing disclosure.
Possibility of fraud	Certain opportunities may turn out to be money-losing fraudulent schemes. There is no guarantee crowdfunding investments are immune from fraud.
Cancelation restrictions	Once you make an investment commitment for a crowdfunding offering, you will be committed to make that investment (unless you cancel your commitment within a specified period). The ability to cancel your commitment is limited.
Valuation	The valuation of private companies, especially start-ups, is difficult. You may risk overpaying for the equity stake you receive. There may be additional classes of equity with rights superior to the class of equity sold through crowdfunding.
Investment in personnel	An early-stage investment is also an investment in the entrepreneur or management of the company. Being able to execute on the business plan is often a key factor in whether the business is viable and successful. You should also be aware that a portion of your investment may fund the compensation of the company's employees, including its management.
Lack of professional guidance	Many successful companies partially attribute their early success to the guidance of professional early-stage investors (e.g., angel investors and venture capital firms). An early-stage company primarily financed through crowdfunding may not have the benefit of such professional investors.

Source: US Securities and Exchange Commission.

scheme where 95% of the investments were fakes; over 900,000 investors lost the equivalent of US$7.6 billion.[39] In 2017, Chinese regulators stepped in to regulate the market, forbidding student loans and restricting payday loans. From a peak of more than 6,000 online portals, the number in operation tumbled below 1,600 by August 2018.[40]

Table 7.4 summarizes the risks for retail investors from the US SEC.

How Crowdfunding Portals Make Money

Crowdfunding portals are financial intermediaries that operate as multi-sided platforms. By centralizing capital raising through their platform, they can charge fees to users on both sides of the platform – issuers or borrowers on one side, investors or lenders on the other. The party raising money, known as the issuer or borrower, pays the most fees. But there are also fees for servicing investors/lenders, as well as management fees. Some fees may be contingent on "success," which means the platform only collects its fee if the campaign reaches its funding goal within a specific time frame.

Distinct categories of crowdfunding use different monetization strategies and label their fees differently. Let's look at two examples.

Equity, rewards-based, and donation-based crowdfunding portals only charge the party raising the cash, namely the issuer or campaign sponsor. The platform is free to the people who provide money, called the backer, donor, or investor. The fees charged by these online portals are

- **Sign-up fee**: Portals may charge a listing fee regardless of the success or failure of the campaign.
- **Subscription fee**: Alternatively, a portal may offer a monthly or annual subscription fee that allows issuers to run a pre-determined number of campaigns over a fixed period.
- **Underwriting fee**: The platform may charge a fee of 1% to 5% of any capital raised, whether the funding target is reached or not. This fee is subtracted from the loan proceeds before the money is disbursed. Alternatively the platform may charge a success fee only if the funding target is reached. This fee may be called an underwriting fee, a platform fee, or a fundraiser fee.
- **Management fee and carry percentage**: The platform may collaborate with the lead investors who source and vet deals. In this case, the platform makes an investment in the campaign and has skin in the game, allowing them to share upside if the deal is successful.
- **Payment processing fee**: The portal will charge a payment processing fee of 3% plus an amount per pledge paid, with some of these fees transferred to third parties (such as a credit card issuer).
- **Management fee**: Some platforms charge a management fee as a percentage of assets under management (AUM), like an asset manager.

Online lending portals charge fees to both the borrower and the lender. Their fees are the following:

- **Loan interest rate**: The portal collects a periodic interest payment from the borrower that is passed to the lenders. The interest rate charged varies with the riskiness of the borrower and the term (or maturity) of the loan. The annual percentage rate (APR) may range from a low of 6% to a high of 30% or more. On its financial statements, the portal may report this fee as interest income.
- **Origination fee**: Borrowers are not charged to apply for a loan. Instead, the platform charges an origination (underwriting) fee of 3.0% to 6.5% of the total amount raised, like the underwriting fee paid when issuing a bond in debt capital markets.

- **Late or missed payment fee**: Late or delinquent borrowers that miss a payment are charged a fee that varies by portal but is specified in the loan contract (called an indenture). One Canadian platform charges an overdue payment fee equal to 15% of the missing loan payments if they are not rectified within seven days of notification. In addition, the borrower is charged a $50 non-sufficient funds (NSF) fee.
- **Servicing fee**: Lenders are charged a servicing fee that is collected whenever a borrower makes a repayment. The servicing fee may be an annualized rate of 1% to 3%, which is collected monthly on the outstanding balance of principal at the time of the payment.
- **Early repayment fee**: Unlike banks, most online lenders allow loans to be repaid early without any fees or penalties.
- **Marketing (or transaction) fee**: Some portals originate loans on behalf of a third party, such as a bank, a hedge fund, or a high net worth individual. The portal may charge these lenders a marketing fee or a transaction fee to cover the expense of acquiring customers. LendingClub in the US charges banks that issue a loan through its portal a transaction fee of 1% to 6% of the face amount of the loan.

While online portals charge many types of fees, there are many costs associated. A crowdfunding portal has similar expenses to a traditional financial intermediary. The important expenses of online portals are

- Sales and marketing expenses (known as the cost of customer acquisition)
- Technology costs
- Research and development
- Salaries, benefits, and employee compensation
- General and administrative expenses (e.g., overhead)
- Distribution, processing, and servicing costs to third parties
- Corporate taxes
- Funding costs for balance sheet lenders
- Write-downs on non-performing loans for balance sheet lenders

Most online portals are private companies and do not disclose their financial statements. But we can get an idea by looking at the financial statements and stock market performance of portals that have gone public through an initial public offering (IPO). In the United States, three examples are LendingClub (IPO in 2014), OnDeck (2014), and Credible Labs (2017). In the UK, two examples are Trufin (2018) and Funding Circle (2018). Despite the excitement about fintech, these stocks have all been bad investments for shareholders. The share price of every single portal fell below its initial listing price either immediately or within a year of its listing.

CASE STUDY: LENDINGCLUB'S MARKETPLACE LENDING PLATFORM

LendingClub (ticker: LC) was at one point the largest American P2P lender. Lending-Club was founded in 2007 and listed on the New York Stock Exchange in December 2014 at $15.00 per share. The IPO prospectus showed that LendingClub had origi-nated $6 billion in loans for consumers and small businesses over its seven-year life, although it was still unprofitable.

Figure 7.4 shows the total return of LendingClub benchmarked against the S&P500 Composite Index. The stock price rose over the first month to $25.74, then declined steadily for the next six years. LC was down -93% over this period while the S&P500 was up 119%.

Figure 7.4. LendingClub vs. S&P500 Composite Index

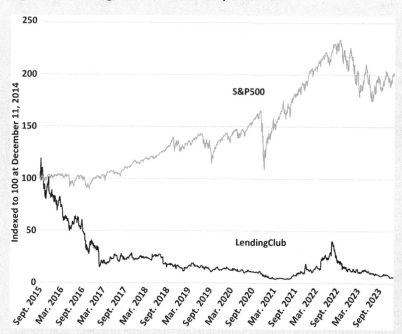

Source: Author, data from Refinitiv Eikon.

In July 2019 LendingClub completed a 1-to-5 reverse stock split, whereby every 5 shares were consolidated into 1 share. So, the $15 IPO price became $75. As of year-end 2022, LendingClub had a market capitalization of $890 million, and its share price was $1.70 (or $8.50 compared to the IPO price of $15). While there are many reasons for this decline (including a lawsuit against the founder and CEO), a principal explanation was the terrible performance of the underlying business.

LendingClub lost money in every fiscal year since it was founded until 2021. And its success in 2022 is linked to the decision to exit P2P/marketplace lending entirely.

Table 7.5 provides selected financial data on LendingClub for the fiscal years 2020 to 2022. The main source of revenues was non-interest income, made up mostly of origination fees charged to borrowers. Operational expenses were high, dominated by sales (marketing), general and administrative, engineering, and product development expenses, which in aggregate represented 158% of revenues in 2020!

Table 7.5. LendingClub Selected Financial Statements, 2020–2022

	2020	2021	2022	2020	2021	2022
INCOME STATEMENT		US$ millions			% of Revenues	
Net interest income	59	213	475	19	26	40
Noninterest income	259	606	712	81	74	60
Revenues	318	819	1,187	100	100	100
Less: Provision for credit losses	3	139	267	1	17	23
Less: Noninterest expense	502	661	767	158	81	65
Less: Income tax	0	0	−137	0	0	−12
Net income (loss)	−188	19	290	−59	2	24
BALANCE SHEET		US$ millions			% of Assets	
Cash and securities	771	1,027	1,470	41	21	18
Loans and other assets	1,093	3,873	6,510	59	79	82
Assets	1,863	4,900	7,980	100	100	100
Liabilities	1,139	4,050	6,815	61	83	85
Equity	724	850	1,164	39	17	15

Source: LendingClub Annual Report, various years.

LendingClub had a massive loss in 2020 and was forced to pivot its business model. In 2020, it closed its retail business to focus on institutional investors. In 2021 LendingClub shut down its P2P/marketplace lending program entirely and relaunched as a challenger bank. These changes allowed it to turn around its fortunes, with the new business generating a profit in 2021 and 2022. The fortunes of LendingClub are mirrored across many online portals that have not been able to make a success of P2P lending.

CROWDFUNDING RESEARCH FINDINGS

Let's look at the findings from academic research on online lending and crowdfunding. These studies have focused on US and European online lenders, because these online portals have given researchers access to large quantities of data to study.

Competition and Financial Inclusion

One set of research studies asks whether online lenders are disrupting traditional banks. Online portals have entered markets where bank branches are fewer and competition is lower,[41] in underbanked rural communities,[42] in communities where complaints about bank misconduct are higher,[43] and areas where banks have pulled back during past economic downturns.[44] This research suggests online lenders are filling a gap in the market, providing underbanked consumers with access to credit at a lower cost. Another study found that competition from fintechs increases financial inclusion by disrupting monopolistic banks that use payment data to learn about consumers' credit quality.[45]

Several papers focus on fintech lending to US small businesses. One study found that fintechs and other non-bank lenders increased lending to small businesses after the 2008 financial crisis when the larger banks were reducing lending, with greater effects in regions where banks had larger market share prior to the crisis.[46] By stepping up when banks stepped back, these sources of alternative finance supported employment, wages, and new business creation for the next eight years covered by the study.

A second study found that fintechs increase access to credit in areas with fewer bank branches, lower incomes, and more minority households, and in industries with fewer banking relationships.[47] This research also found that fintech lending was greater in US counties where the economic effects of the COVID-19 pandemic were more severe.

Another body of research contradicts this story of financial inclusion. These studies of US data suggest that online lenders compete with domestic banks to provide loans and mortgages to the most creditworthy borrowers. Online lenders do not target risky or marginal borrowers who have low access to finance, but instead target borrowers who already have access to bank credit.[48]

Online lenders may provide smaller loans than banks[49] and charge a lower interest rate than banks to individuals with higher credit scores.[50] But fintech lenders charge a higher rate to lower-rated borrowers, making it a stretch to argue they increase access to capital.

Take the example of the US residential mortgage market, where fintech lenders have rapidly gained market share.[51] Fintech mortgage lenders have used technology to process mortgage applications 20% faster than other lenders, adjusting mortgage supply more quickly to meet demand.[52] But these lenders charge a premium interest rate relative to banks and serve more educated populations and older borrowers with good access to finance. Not surprisingly, this same study finds that fintech lenders have lower default rates than traditional lenders.

A less positive picture is provided by a recent study that suggests fintechs may have facilitated fraud under the $800 billion US Paycheck Protection Program established to help businesses keep their workforce employed during the COVID-19 crisis.[53] The research found that fintech loans were more associated with misreporting and inconsistencies, such as nonregistered businesses, multiple businesses at residential addresses, abnormally high implied compensation per employee, and inconsistent jobs numbers. Fintechs increased their market share over time, with suspicious lending in 2021 four times the level at the start of the program.

Non-US Effects of Fintech Lending

This story about financial inclusion is hopeful, but the research so far is largely focused on the United States. At a global level, we see that fintech lending has grown in advanced economies, not emerging ones. Fintech lending is greater in countries with higher GDP per capita, in countries where banks earn higher profit margins, and in countries where banking regulation is weaker.[54] This same study found that alternative finance is also more developed where the ease of doing business is greater, investor protection and the efficiency of the judicial system are more advanced, and equity and bond markets are more developed. In other words, fintech credit builds on an existing developed financial system.

A study of online lending in China looked at how Alibaba's Ant Group was affecting the fortunes of micro, small, and medium-sized enterprises.[55] Credit access significantly reduces the firm's volatility, particularly for credit-constrained firms, reducing the likelihood of bankruptcy. Instead, these firms invest more in advertising and product/sector diversification, particularly during business downturns.

Discrimination and Bias in Alternative Finance

Researchers have studied gender, racial, or other biases in crowdfunding. A study of Kickstarter found that female entrepreneurs represented only 35% of campaigns, but both sexes set similar funding goals and women enjoyed higher funding success rates than men.[56]

A second study examined whether backers fund entrepreneurs of their own gender. It found that experienced male and female investors show no gender preferences when investing in projects, but inexperienced female investors favored female founders.[57]

Finally, a third study found that entrepreneurs with trustworthy faces receive more pledges and attract more backers on Kickstarter than those who are deemed to look untrustworthy, with a stronger effect for female entrepreneurs.[58]

In equity crowdfunding, African American men are significantly less likely than similar white founders to receive funding, with potential prospective supporters rating identical projects as lower in quality when they believe the founder is an African American male.[59] This bias can be reduced by including third-party endorsements and evidence of prior success, and removing indicators of the founder's race.

A study of online lending found that after adjusting for risk, Latinx (Latin American origin) and African American borrowers were charged significantly higher interest rates on mortgages.[60] These authors highlight that algorithmic decision-making tools such as machine learning may incorporate bias when trained on data that itself incorporates human biases based on gender, race, income levels, and other factors. Data scientists need to be vigilant and consider using training sets that have been pre-treated to remove or counter these biases.

CASE STUDY: SOFI'S EVOLUTION FROM ONLINE LENDER TO FULL-SERVICE BANK
SoFi, short for Social Finance Inc., was founded in San Francisco in 2011 by four Stanford business school students. From its roots as a P2P lender to MBA students at leading US universities, SoFi has grown to become a one-stop shop for financial services that allows members to borrow, save, spend, invest, and protect their money.

The original use-case was to provide loans to Stanford business school students funded by alumni. The inaugural loan program saw 40 Stanford alumni lend $2 million to 100 students. This P2P model relied on the social connection between current and future alumni and proved to be extremely successful.

The founders took this model to leading universities across the United States. By September 2013, SoFi had funded $200 million in loans to 2,500 borrowers at 100 eligible schools. Undergraduate and graduate students were eligible for loans from $5,000 to $100,000 at a low fixed rate.

Over the next few years, SoFi moved away from alumni-funding, raising equity, debt, and lines of credit from individual investors including PayPal founder Peter Thiel, venture capitalists such as Third Point Management and Silver Lake, and banks such as JPMorgan Stanley and Japan's Softbank. They also began securitizing their loan book, receiving a AAA credit rating. They worked on building relationships with former borrowers (called members) through singles events, wine tastings, career counseling, and home-buying workshops.[61] By 2018, SoFi had attracted 300,000 members.

In mid-2021, SoFi went public in a SPAC-related IPO that valued the fintech at $9 billion. By this point, it was the largest non-bank unsecured consumer lender in the United States. It described itself as a member-centric, one-stop shop for financial services that allows members to borrow, save, spend, invest, and protect their money. Its value proposition is speed, product selection, content, and convenience. SoFi's IPO prospectus states,

> Our mission is to help our members achieve financial independence to realize their ambitions … to have the financial means to achieve their personal objectives at each stage of life, such as owning a home, having a family, or having a career of their choice – more simply stated, to have enough money to do what they want.

SoFi's product offering included student loans, personal loans, and mortgages; a deposit (cash) account and credit card, made possible by bank partners; wealth and asset management, commission and fee-free trading in stocks and exchange traded funds, a robo-advisor service, and cryptocurrency trading (in partnership with Coinbase); a credit score monitoring and budgeting tool; and insurance (life, auto, home, renters) through partnerships with insurance companies. In early 2022, SoFi received regulatory approval to become a bank-holding company following the acquisition of Golden Pacific Bank.

SoFi is targeting an underserved, younger customer segment of millennials and Gen Z called HENRYs (high earners not rich yet) and HENWS (high earners not well served). These customers are 25 to 45 years old with $100,000+ of income and a high credit score (700+). SoFi emphasizes building trust and a relationship with consumers as the best means to monetize a customer, by increasing lifetime value and reducing the cost of customer acquisition.

Despite this success and media attention, SoFi has lost money in its last three fiscal years due to operating expenses exceeding revenues by a large margin.

Table 7.6. SoFi Selected Financial Statements, 2020–2022

	2020	2021	2022	2020	2021	2022
INCOME STATEMENT	US$ millions			% of Revenues		
Net interest income	178	252	584	31	26	37
Noninterest income	388	733	989	69	74	63
Revenues	566	985	1,574	100	100	100
Less: Provision for credit losses	0	8	54	0	1	3
Less: Noninterest expense	894	1,458	1,838	158	148	117
Less: Income tax	−104	3	2	−18	0	0
Net income (loss)	−224	−484	−320	−40	−49	−20
BALANCE SHEET	US$ millions			% of Assets		
Cash and securities	873	495	1,422	10	5	7
Loans and other assets	7,691	8,682	17,586	90	95	93
Assets	8,563	9,176	19,008	100	100	100
Liabilities	5,510	4,479	13,479	64	49	71
Equity	3,054	4,698	5,528	36	51	29

Source: SoFi IPO Prospectus.

Key Terms

all-or-nothing	investor
alternative finance	issuer
backer	keep-it-all
balance sheet lending	lender
borrower	marketplace lending
campaign	origination fee
credit risk	peer-to-peer (P2P) lenders
donation-based crowdfunding	rewards-based crowdfunding
equity crowdfunding	underwriting fee

QUESTIONS FOR DISCUSSION

1 What are the two types of online portals for alternative finance?
2 What are the two types of investment crowdfunding and how are they different?
3 What are the key differences between rewards-based and donation-based crowdfunding?
4 Why are peer-to-peer (P2P) platforms now called marketplace platforms?

5   What is a balance sheet lender and why are the incentives different from a P2P/marketplace lender?

6   Who is borrowing from online lenders and who is providing funding? How do lenders assess the risk of default for online loans?

7   What has been the growth of alternative finance globally and where is the most capital raised? What has happened in China?

8   How is crowdfunding regulated and what are the risks to individual investors or lenders?

9   How successful have crowdfunding platforms been in disrupting traditional financial intermediaries such as banks?

10   Has crowdfunding increased access to capital for underbanked communities? Are there biases based on gender, race, or other factors?

ADDITIONAL READING

Bartlett, Robert, Adair Morse, Richard Stanton, and Nancy Wallace, "Consumer-Lending Discrimination in the FinTech Era," *Journal of Financial Economics* 143, no. 1 (2022): 30–56.

Cornelli, Giulio, Jon Frost, Leonardo Gambacorta, P. Raghavendra Rau, Robert Wardrop, and Tania Ziegler, "Fintech and Big Tech Credit: A New Database," BIS Working Paper No. 887, September 25, 2020.

Di Maggio, Marco, and Vincent Yao, "Fintech Borrowers: Lax Screening or Cream-Skimming?" *Review of Financial Studies* 34, no. 10 (2021): 4565–4618.

Jagtiani, Julapa, and Catharine Lemieux, "Do Fintech Lenders Penetrate Areas That Are Underserved by Traditional Banks?" *Journal of Economics and Business* 100 (2018): 43–54.

Tang, Huan, "Peer-to-Peer Lenders versus Banks: Substitutes or Complements?" *Review of Financial Studies* 32, no. 5 (2019): 1900–1938.

8

Robo-advisors and Digital Wealth Management

SUMMARY

- Robo-advisors are the most visible fintechs driving innovation and disruption in investing and financial planning. These new entrants have faced an uphill battle to acquire customers, with many start-ups pivoting to serve incumbents or being acquired.
- Incumbent financial institutions have been fast-followers, launching successful robo-advisor services that have captured most of the assets under management (AUM) in the robo segment.
- The wealth management industry manages $100 trillion in investments with three distinct activities: financial planning, investing, and operations.
- Digital wealth management uses technology to automate and improve the customer experience, while generating fees and commissions from asset acquisition, portfolio management, and automation of back-office operations.
- Many successful fintechs in wealth management are working behind the scenes to partner with incumbents and provide business-to-business (B2B) products and services.
- The future of digital wealth management is a hybrid model of a human advisor supported by computer algorithms that automate boring tasks and improve the customer experience.

The previous chapter examined ways fintechs are allowing individuals and small businesses to raise capital from the crowd in the form of debt, equity, rewards, or donations.

This chapter follows the rise and stumble of robo-advisors, the online investment portals that automate retail investment in a portfolio of exchange traded funds. It also looks more broadly at how technology is transforming the wealth management industry.

SPOILER ALERT: GOLIATH BEATS DAVID

Robo-advisors have captured the attention of both the media and the public with catchy advertising, innovative designs, and their low-cost approach to investing. These fintechs offer automated online investment portals that use computer algorithms to provide customized portfolio recommendations to individual investors. Robo-advisors first emerged in 2008 and gained popularity as a low-cost and simple alternative for investors unwilling to pay for the services of an investment advisor and for do-it-yourselfers.

Everyone loves a David versus Goliath story with an entrepreneurial start-up defeating a larger incumbent. Unfortunately it didn't work out as planned; Goliath won.

The following quote from the industry newsletter, Backend Benchmarking, summarizes the state of the robo-advisor industry: "In the end, robo advice is a story of adoption at major firms, not one of disruption by independent start-ups."[1]

Robo-advice began as a disruptive, niche fintech product. It has now consolidated around a few large players owned by incumbents, with only a few independent fintechs still standing. This outcome reflects a hard fact: It takes economies of scale to survive in robo-advice given low fees, the high cost of customer acquisition, low barriers to entry, and the high degree of competition.

The fate of independent robo-advisors highlights an important lesson: Technology by itself does not provide a sustainable competitive advantage, because fast-followers can replicate it or acquire it. The biggest barrier to entry is customers.

Despite the fate of robo-advisors, fintechs continue to disrupt the broader wealth management industry. Globally this industry manages over $100 trillion of investments.[2] Wealth management covers many activities from financial planning to portfolio management, to back-office operations. Technology has always been a key success factor in this industry. But its importance has only increased due to aging populations, globalization, regulatory changes, and the increasing demands from end-customers. Many fintechs are attracted to this industry, as a first, second, or third use-case, by the large profit pools and many customer pain points.

We use the term "digital wealth management" to describe how technology is changing the way that financial advisors serve customers and the wealth management industry functions. Fintechs are leveraging technology to lower costs, increase productivity, and improve the customer experience using cloud computing, data science, application programming interfaces (APIs), cryptography, blockchain, and artificial intelligence (AI). Fintechs are active in both the business-to-consumer (B2C) and business-to-business (B2B) channels. They are providing much more than simply investing algorithms and mobile apps. There are sophisticated analytics, software for customer onboarding and relationship management, risk management and cybersecurity tools, and special apps for regulatory compliance (known as regtech).

Professionals working in wealth management may wonder what this disruption means for them. Initial fears that robots were going to take their jobs have been dispelled. Many individual investors still want to speak to a person, particularly among baby boomers. But technology has raised customer expectations and changed the competitive dynamics of the industry. The result is better service, lower fees, and greater transparency that benefit consumers but lower industry profitability.

There is no question technology is transforming the wealth management industry. It is leading to fee compression and greater transparency that will lower profitability for incumbents and benefit consumers. Let's take a look.

The Rise of the Robo-advisor

Robo-advisors automate the investment process for retail customers and charge a low fee for their services, typically 0.25% to 0.50% of assets under management (AUM). You connect to the robo over the internet or a mobile app. You answer a series of questions about your savings goals, return expectations, and risk tolerance. The robo-advisor's algorithm maps your answers to a portfolio recommendation that can be implemented automatically once funds are transferred into an account.

The portfolios are constructed using low-cost exchange traded funds (ETFs) traded on stock exchanges. The base recommendation is a balanced fund of equities and bonds, where more risk tolerance or a longer horizon increases the allocation to equities.

If you decide to invest, you set up an investment account by entering your personal information online. While some robo-advisors have fully automated the customer onboarding process, others may use a human advisor. To complete the process, you transfer funds into your account by linking your robo-advisor account with your bank account. Once the funds are received, they are invested automatically in the chosen portfolio. The portfolio is automatically rebalanced on a quarterly, monthly, or daily basis to maintain the target asset allocation. You can see portfolio and performance online any time using a simple, clean, and attractive dashboard.

While the original robo-advisors were fully automated to minimize costs, the majority of robo-advisors now offer a hybrid service, with access to a salesperson or a registered financial advisor available for a higher fee. From this initial foothold in investing, robo-advisors have been expanding into brokerage, financial planning, personal finance, tax reporting, and even banking.

Despite their high profile, most independent robo-advisors have been acquired by incumbents or shut down. We will look at how these disruptors failed to transform the industry, but first we need to understand the rise in passive investing and ETFS.

Passive Investing and ETFs

Over the past three decades, the wealth management industry has seen a rise in the share of passive investing relative to active investing and the increasing share of ETFs relative to mutual funds. These trends laid the groundwork for the robo-advisor industry.

The modern portfolio theory developed by Nobel Prize laureates Harry Markowitz, William Sharpe, and their peers laid the groundwork for the growth of passive investing, also called index investing.[3] Passive investing does not rely on skill or technical analysis to beat the markets through security selection or timing, but instead focuses on tracking broad market indices and minimizing fees. John Bogle, founder of Vanguard Group, created the first index mutual fund in 1975. He also created an industry. Vanguard's low-cost, passive mutual funds and ETFs now manage more than $8 trillion across 422 funds.[4]

Passive index funds have grown in popularity globally driven by the decline in interest rates following the 2008–2009 Global Financial Crisis. With lower returns, investors have put greater emphasis on the fees charged by asset managers. This focus coincided with new regulations that forced greater transparency on the industry, requiring asset managers to disclose and explain their fees more clearly.

Investors learned that active managers were collecting 1% to 2% of AUM each year, as well as other non-transparent fees (front-end and back-end load), even though most active managers failed to beat the market. Only one-quarter of all active funds delivered a higher return than their passive rivals over the decade ending in 2021.[5] Not surprisingly, actively managed funds fell from 81% of the market in 2010 to 60% in 2020.[6]

The success of passive investing has contributed directly to the growth of ETFs. An ETF is an investment fund that trades on a stock exchange, just like a share. Each ETF holds a portfolio of securities such as stocks, bonds, or some other asset class. The earliest ETFs were created to mimic stock market indices. State Street Global Advisors launched the Standard & Poor's Depository Receipts (SPDR) in 1993 to track the S&P500, a market capitalization weighted index of 500 large US companies. The SPDR has consistently been the largest ETF in the world, with over $450 billion AUM at year-end 2022.

Figure 8.1. Growth of Exchange Traded Funds

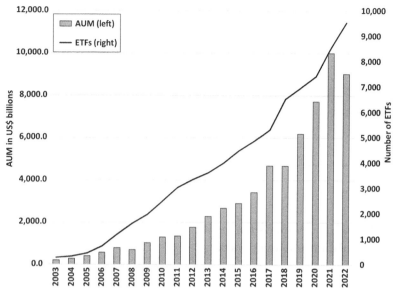

Source: ETFGI.

ETFs were created as a cheaper, more liquid substitute to traditional mutual funds. Mutual funds are investment trusts created by an asset management firm (like Fidelity or Vanguard) to hold a portfolio of securities. Mutual funds require minimum investments of $500 to $1,000. A mutual fund is illiquid and trades only once a day based on their closing price. They charge a high management expense ratio (MER) of 1% to 2%. MER is based on a fund manager's annual operating expenses, expressed as a percentage of the fund's average net assets. The MER includes management salaries, marketing and administration costs, and distribution costs. It does not include advisory fees, front- or back-end loads, or fees to purchase or redeem a fund.

ETFs are better than mutual funds on every dimension. An EFT is also created by an asset manager (like BlackRock), charges a much lower MER between 0.03% and 1.00%, has no minimum investment amount, and trades throughout the day like a stock. Figure 8.1 shows that the value of assets managed through ETFs passed $10 trillion with more than 8,500 ETFs traded globally.[7] The largest managers are Black-Rock, Vanguard, and State Street Global Advisors.

While most ETFs are created to replicate the performance of market indexes, there are now thousands of ETFs available that offer exposure to different asset classes (stocks, bonds, commodities, precious metals, bitcoin, real estate), sectors (health

Table 8.1. The US Robo-advisor Pioneers

Robo	Launch	2022 AUM (US$ billions)	Account Minimum	Advisory Fee
Betterment	2010	33.8	None	0.25%–0.40%
Wealthfront	2011	24.9	$500	0.25%
Personal Capital	2011	22.9	$100,000	0.89%
FutureAdvisor (BlackRock)	2012	1.8	$5,000	0.50%
Vanguard Personal Advisor Services	2013	268.0	$50,000	0.30%
Schwab Intelligent Portfolios	2014	76.1	$5,000	Free
Acorns	2014	6.2	None	$3 per month
SigFig	2014	2.3	$2,000	0.25%

Source: Backend Benchmarking.

care, technology), markets and regions (emerging markets, Japan), and strategies (currency hedged, low volatility, dividend income).

The Early Disruptors

The first US robo-advisor, Betterment, was founded in 2007 and launched in 2010.[8] Table 8.1 shows that it was quickly followed by similar start-ups: Wealthfront (2011), Personal Capital (2011), and FutureAdvisor (2012). Over the next years, robo-advisors appeared around the world: in Canada (Nest Wealth, Wealthsimple), the UK (Nutmeg), Australia (Stockspot, Raiz), and continental Europe (MoneyFarm, OwlHub).

The robo-advisor pioneers followed a textbook disruptive innovation strategy, gaining a foothold in the asset management industry by targeting two customer segments:

Underserved customers: The early robo-advisors targeted millennials, particularly young professionals who were high earners but not rich yet (HENRYs). These digital natives were tech-savvy with low savings to invest (e.g., $10,000 or less). They tended to distrust the motives of banks and investment advisors. They were attracted to an automated service that allowed for low minimum investments and was transparent about fees. They liked the digital interface that could be accessed 24/7 on a laptop or smartphone. And they were not being targeted by traditional wealth managers yet due to their small savings, which made it uneconomic to serve them given the expensive cost structure of the incumbents.

Price-sensitive customers: The early robo-advisors also targeted price-sensitive, mass-affluent customers. These tended to be older individuals who had more savings to invest (e.g., $100,000 to $1,000,000) but were unwilling to pay the high advisory fees charged by financial advisors. They also didn't want to pay for ancillary services that were typically bundled together by the financial advisor. These customers were do-it-yourself (DIY) investors, not by choice but due to cost, although they would benefit from professional investment advice.

The Robo-advisor Value Proposition

The robo-advisor value proposition for these target customer segments had four parts: a delightful customer experience; transparent, low fees; state-of-the-art technology; and return-enhancing strategies (such as tax-loss harvesting). Eventually most leaders have added the human touch by creating an option to speak with a person.

First, robo-advisors promise a delightful customer experience that is fast, easy to use, and enjoyable. Their digital platforms feature eye-catching design, with attractive images and graphics. The websites are uncluttered and feature clear statements about the company's goals and value proposition. Being digital, the site is open 24/7 and runs on multiple devices – a laptop, tablet, or smartphone.

The process of asking questions and generating a portfolio recommendation is fast, maybe 5 minutes or less. It features easy-to-follow instructions and choices. The process of onboarding a customer can be completed in 20 minutes or less. The website answers frequently asked questions and provides educational articles or blogs about investing.

Second, robo-advisors have capitalized on the distrust toward investment advisors by offering full transparency and lower fees. When setting up an account, there is typically a low or no minimum investment. The advisory fee is either set as a percentage of AUM or a fixed dollar amount that may vary for higher investment amounts and for different levels of service. The starting fee may be as low as 0.25% of AUM or $2 per month for Acorns, increasing to 0.35% to 0.50% for premium services. Many robo-advisors had a teaser campaign to get customers onboard, offering no advisory fee for some initial amount, while others waived the fee for some initial period.

To be fair, this fee is only the robo-advisor's advisory fee. Because robo-advisors build portfolios using ETFs, the customer also pays the MER of the third-party ETF, which covers its costs and profit margin. So, if a robo like Canada's Wealthsimple charges an advisory fee of 0.50% of AUM, the customer also pays an ETF MER ranging from 0.12% to 0.23% of AUM. The all-in cost to the customer is therefore 0.62% to 0.73% of AUM.[9] For an investment of $10,000, this means an annual cost of only $62 to $73.

To drive home the importance of minimizing fees, robo-advisors like Canada's Nest Wealth have interactive features on their websites that simulate the future account balance for a specified investment and time horizon for a traditional account charging a 2.0% fee versus their low monthly subscription fee.

Third, robo-advisors use state-of-the-art technology and are not encumbered by the legacy computer systems of incumbents. Robo-advisors have coded their software platforms from scratch using the latest programming languages and technologies.

Incumbents were held back by older programming languages and operating systems that are difficult to maintain and impossible to integrate. Worse still, these incumbents held customer data in different silos across the organization that were not being exploited to understand their customers.

Fourth, the most innovative robo-advisors generate value for customers by adding return-enhancing strategies at little to no additional cost. For example, they might offer tax-loss harvesting to minimize taxes by recognizing losses on investments that have fallen to offset taxable gains on other investments in the portfolio. While human investment advisors typically implement tax-loss harvesting on an annual basis, computer algorithms can be programmed to execute this strategy monthly, weekly, or daily. This high frequency is simply not possible with a human financial advisor.

Wealthfront introduced daily tax-loss harvesting at the portfolio and stock level as early as October 2012. They showed that it increased pre-tax portfolio returns by an average of 4.0% per annum and after-tax returns by 1.6%, assuming a marginal tax rate of 40%. This gain more than offset Wealthfront's annual advisory fee. In June 2017, Wealthfront began offering multi-factor smart beta portfolios that delivered an additional return of 0.70% per annum. Finally, in February 2018, Wealthfront offered risk parity portfolios, made famous by the hedge fund Bridgewater Associates, for accounts with more than $100,000 in AUM.

As time went by and robo-advisors wanted to attract a broader demographic, they began to offer the ability to speak to a sales representative by phone or online chat. Many older or conservative customers want to speak with a representative before investing their savings. The robo-advisor may, therefore, connect customers to a human agent. It may be a registered financial advisor or simply a customer service representation, but this option is attractive to many customers. Robo-advisors typically charge a fee for this human option and may require investing a minimum in assets.

Wealthfront never offered this human option, preferring to stick to a fully automated process. But Betterment pivoted to add access to a human advisor in 2017. This difference may partly explain how Betterment moved from second place to being the largest independent robo-advisor in the space of 18 months. A newcomer into the robo space, SoFi offers access to a team of financial planners without requiring a higher minimum account balance or subscribing to a more expensive plan option.

Vanguard Personal Advisor Services offers access to live planners for accounts with a minimum balance of $50,000. Schwab Intelligent Portfolios Premium charges a one-time planning fee of $300 and a $30/month advisory fee after that to get unlimited one-on-one access to a Certified Financial Planner.

The Response by Incumbents

While entrepreneurial start-ups have driven innovation in the robo-advisor segment, some of the largest mutual fund companies and broker-dealers have been fast-followers. These incumbents have either developed a robo offering in-house or licensed the software from a start-up. Despite their later start, the leading wealth managers quickly captured a large share of the robo-advisory market.

The first to respond in 2013 was Vanguard Group, followed by discount brokerage Charles Schwab in late 2014. Other incumbents were slower, either watching the market or struggling to build their own robo offering. Then, in 2016, in-house robo-advisors were launched by Bank of America Merrill Lynch, Capital One, E*Trade, Fidelity Investor Services, and TD Ameritrade.

This response by incumbents followed the strategy outlined by Harvard Business School's Clayton Christensen.[10] Christensen argued that incumbents should not overreact to the threat of disruption. Disruption is a process that can take time, and incumbents can get quite creative in defense of their franchises. It is important to respond, but the incumbent should not abandon their existing profitable customers. Instead, they should invest to improve their primary product while at the same time launching a new division to compete directly with the disruptive new entrant, offering a low-cost, no-frills service of their own.

CASE STUDY: VANGUARD'S MOVE INTO ROBO-ADVICE

The Vanguard Group is the largest US mutual fund company, with $7 trillion of AUM. In mid-2013 it began piloting an in-house robo-advisor called Personal Advisor Services. It combined the client-friendly online experience of a fintech with the ability to speak with a team of investment advisors.

Personal Advisor Services was launched in 2015. It required a minimum account size of $50,000 and charged an annual advisory fee of 0.30% for the first $5 million in AUM, with rates declining for higher account balances. It recommended portfolios built using low-fee Vanguard ETFs. It also included a financial planning feature. Clients with more than $500,000 in assets had access to a dedicated financial advisor.

At the time of launch, Personal Advisor Services had attracted a remarkable $7 billion in AUM.[11] Growth was explosive. By year-end 2018, it was managing over $112 billion of AUM, more than half of all funds managed by robo-advisors in the United States. At this point, Betterment was managing $14.1 billion and Wealthfront $11.5 billion.

By year-end 2022, Vanguard's robo had $268 billion, more than 3.5 times its closest competitor Charles Schwab and 4.6 times the combined AUM of Wealthfront and Betterment. Vanguard's remarkable success demonstrated the power of its brand and its distribution model. Table 8.2 compares two of Vanguard's robo-advisors.

Table 8.2. Vanguard US Robo-advisor Options and Services

Robo Offering	Personal Advisor Services	Vanguard Digital Advisor
Launched	2015	2019
Minimum account balance	$50,000	$3,000
Advisory fee	0.30%	0.15%–0.20%
Source of ETFs	Vanguard	Vanguard and third-party
ETF management expense ratio	0.03%–0.22%	0.03%–0.40%
Tax-efficient investing	Yes	Yes
Portfolio tracking	Yes	Yes
Online experience	Yes	Yes
Customized portfolio	Yes	No
Access to an advisor	Yes	No
Support for complex financial planning	Yes	No

Source: The Vanguard Group.

Some incumbents chose to white label robo-advisor software from fintechs as an alternative or interim solution. In 2014 Betterment launched a robo-advisor for advisors called Betterment Institutional (later renamed Betterment for Advisors) and signed up 25 asset managers. Fidelity Institutional Wealth Services chose this option to bridge a gap while it built an in-house robo, which launched in 2016.

Many incumbents have licensed robo-advisor software from start-ups such as SigFig. Founded in 2007, SigFig initially targeted retail customers but then pivoted to a B2B business model.[12] Among its clients is the Swiss bank UBS, which took an equity stake in SigFig in 2016. UBS Wealth Management began offering this robo-advisor to its 7,000 brokers in the United States. By 2018 UBS had abandoned plans to build its own robo-advisor, viewing SigFig's platform as a better solution. Other clients of SigFig are JPMorgan Stanley, New York Life, Santander Bank, and Wells Fargo.

Other incumbents preferred to acquire, rather than build, a robo capability. In 2015 BlackRock acquired the fifth largest independent robo-advisor, FutureAdvisor, for a price estimated between $150 million and $200 million. FutureAdvisor had been founded in 2010 by two ex-Microsoft engineers and had acquired $600 million in AUM by the time of the acquisition. Following the takeover, BlackRock began to license FutureAdvisor to a range of financial intermediaries, including BBVA, US Bank, RBC Wealth Management, and LPL Financial Holdings.

Lessons for Aspiring Disruptors

Despite fintechs like Betterment and Wealthfront having a seven-year head-start, incumbents like Vanguard and Charles Schwab have now captured most of the robo-advisor market. What lesson should we take away from Goliath beating David in this case?

First, it highlights that the main obstacle for a fintech start-up is acquiring customers.

For North American robo-advisors, the cost of customer acquisition is estimated at upwards of $500 in advertising and marketing expense per new customer. Similar figures are reported in the UK.[13] If the average robo-advisor advisory fee is 0.35% of AUM with an account size of $10,000, a customer would generate only $35 in advisory fees each year, leading to a payback of 14.4 years = $500 / $35. Increasing the average account size to $50,000 reduces this payback to 2.9 years = $500 / $175. But that is still a long time to be burning cash as a start-up.

By contrast, incumbents have massive existing customer bases to whom they can market this new, lower-cost digital service. While this might cannibalize their existing customer base, this strategy recognizes that price-sensitive customers will inevitably switch to a robo-advisor. An incumbent is better to offer this service in-house than to lose customers to a start-up.

Second, it demonstrates that technology is not a source of sustainable competitive advantage.

The flaw with some start-up business models is they view technology as the ultimate value proposition for customers. But technology is widely available and can be copied by competitors. Incumbents have massive technology and marketing budgets, scale, and the ability to hire talent and acquire intellectual property. They have well-recognized brands and well-developed distribution networks that employ tens of thousands of salespeople and investment advisors. They have the ability to cross-sell a variety of products and services to subsidize their robo-advisory service. They also have the ability invest in or acquire successful robo-advisors, as seen by the equity stakes of UBS in SigFig and BlackRock in FutureAdvisor. Fidelity Go offers a lower fee to its robo clients because it recommends in-house Fidelity funds, allowing it to be competitive.

Third, the experience of robo-advisors illustrates that it may be smarter to work with incumbents instead of attacking them.

Pivoting to a B2B model and partnering with an incumbent is an attractive growth opportunity. In 2018, for example, Canada's Wealthsimple launched a premium robo-advisor service called Wealthsimple for Advisors.[14] The service provides an all-in-one wealth management platform for financial planners, investment advisors, portfolio managers, and dealers. It has front- and back-office solutions to help advisors optimize and scale their business. The success of Wealthsimple's B2B business provided the capital to invest in the B2C business and grow internationally.

Similarly, Canada's number two robo-advisor, Nest Wealth, pivoted to offer its technology to incumbents. Nest Wealth's founder recognized that it could not compete with Wealthsimple's marketing budget in the B2C space, so chose to focus instead on targeting underserved financial advisors who needed a robo offering.

CASE STUDY: WEALTHFRONT'S SOPHISTICATED FINANCIAL ADVICE AT A LOW COST

The US robo-advisor Wealthfront launched in 2011 with the goal of making sophisticated financial advice available to everyone at a low cost using technology. Wealthfront was founded by Silicon Valley venture capitalist Andrew Rachleff and ex-bond trader Dan Carroll.

Rachleff came up with the idea sitting in an investments course. The portfolio modeling was being done in Excel. He realized this process could be automated, like the tools he was using at the venture capital firm where he worked. So Rachleff left in 2005 to start an automated investing business. He also began teaching a course on technology disruption to Stanford MBAs.

Rachleff and Carroll spent three years trying different ideas – first a crowd-based social investing site on Facebook where users could post fantasy stock trades, then a site where users could follow the trades of professional investors. After both ideas failed to gain traction, they pivoted to the robo-advisor model in 2011.

The co-founders hired three software engineers and built Wealthfront's platform in just three months. They didn't have to invent mean-variance portfolio investing; they just had to write the software to implement it. To keep costs low, they would construct portfolios using low-cost ETFs to match a client's risk-return profile.

Prior to opening an account, Wealthfront asked prospective customers to complete a questionnaire. The answers pointed to 1 of 20 risk profiles, each associated with a different target asset allocation of US stocks, developed market stocks, emerging market stocks, dividend growth stocks, corporate bonds, treasury inflation-protected securities, US government bonds, and municipal bonds.

Rachleff based Wealthfront's strategy to grow its business on the theory of disruptive innovation he was teaching at Stanford: Target a set of underserved consumers with a low-cost product before adding features and moving up-market to target mainstream customers. So Rachleff and Carroll targeted millennials working at successful tech start-ups like Facebook and LinkedIn. These young professionals were comfortable with technology and were becoming rich quickly but did not trust bankers. They told Rachleff they would pay money for someone to manage their wealth if they didn't have to talk to a person. Wealthfront signed their first customers after posting a PowerPoint presentation explaining their value proposition on Facebook and LinkedIn.

Wealthfront grew through word-of-mouth. They spent no money on marketing and focused all their resources on product development. Around one-third of new clients were acquired through a customer referral system; for every person a customer invited, they got an additional $5,000 of AUM managed for free. With no cost for advertising, Wealthfront was able to charge fees that were one-quarter the amount of their competitors and still generate a gross margin of 90%.

Rachleff's long-term vision was to automate all of a customer's financial life in one app. Wealthfront expanded their investment services but only offered products that could be fully automated: tax-loss harvesting, multi-factor smart beta, and risk parity strategies. They automated customer insights and investment recommendations by combining customer data with third-party sources. As they gained scale, Wealthfront lowered account minimums and fees. Wealthfront diversified into financial planning including retirement, college, real estate, and time-off-to-travel planning. They added an automated line of credit allowing a customer to borrow up to 30% of their portfolio and receive the funds within a day.

In early 2022 the Swiss bank UBS made an offer to buy Wealthfront for $1.4 billion. Wealthfront had $27 billion of AUM and more than 470,000 clients, so the price was $20 per $1 of AUM, or $3,000 per client. UBS was not after Wealthfront's advisory fees. UBS wanted Wealthfront's award-winning, state-of-the-art technology platform. UBS planned to use Wealthfront as the foundation of its new digital offering to serve UBS's core affluent clients and target millennials and Gen Z. Then, in September 2022, UBS withdrew its offer after its shareholders protested about the price tag. Wealthfront remains independent and managed close to $25 billion of AUM at year-end 2022.

Robo-advisor Research Findings

Few empirical studies of robo-advice have been published in leading academic journals, although there have been theoretical models and experimental papers.[15] The most prominent study assessed how moving to a robo-advisor affected investor performance and trading behavior.[16] The impact depended on how diversified an investor was prior to switching. Under-diversified investors benefited; they increased their portfolio diversification and experienced higher market-adjusted returns. The investors who were already highly diversified did worse; they traded more, and this higher trading activity did not translate into better performance. Both groups benefited by reducing well-documented behavioral trading biases (such as trend chasing), but these biases did not disappear.

THE WEALTH MANAGEMENT INDUSTRY

At an estimated $1.8 trillion of AUM in 2022, robo-advice is less than 2% of the $100 trillion wealth management industry.[17] Before looking deeper at how fintechs are transforming wealth management, we need to cover some introductory concepts.

This vast industry employs a dizzying list of professionals with job titles like financial advisor, financial planner, relationship manager, salesperson, portfolio manager, trader, research analyst, private banker, private equity specialist, risk manager, and more. And this brief list does not include the many head-office and back-office support staff.

The wealth management industry has a wholesale and a retail side. The wholesale side is dominated by financial intermediaries called institutional investors who are paid to manage portfolios of investments. This category includes asset management firms, pension funds, mutual fund companies, insurance companies, and banks. The underlying investments belong to individual savers, who may be called beneficial owners or beneficiaries in the case of a pension fund.

Institutional investors are paid a fee based on AUM or assets under administration (AUA). The distinction refers to who makes decisions. AUM describes funds where the institutional investor makes decisions on behalf of clients. AUA describes funds where the institutional investor holds the money but decision making remains with the client. The fees for managing investments may be as high as 3.50% of AUM or AUA.

The retail side of the industry consists of individual investors and professionals who advise them. They may be called financial advisors, registered investment advisors (RIAs), financial planners, wealth managers, or investment counselors. To advise the public, a financial advisor must be registered and demonstrate their knowledge of securities laws by passing an exam, such as the US Series 7 or the Canadian Securities Course. Financial advisors may also have a professional designation such as Chartered Financial Analyst (CFA) or Chartered Financial Planner (CFP).

While anyone can invest on their own, many retail investors pay for investment advice. Wealth managers distinguish these retail investors based on their wealth. Individuals with $1 million or more in investments are called high net worth (HNW) and with $30 million are ultra-high net worth (UHNW).

Over the past 30 years, UHNW individuals have increasingly set up a family office to manage their wealth. A family office is a dedicated team of professionals with different specializations – financial advisors, portfolio managers, bankers – who manage the wealth and business affairs of a wealthy family or individual. The family office hires other professionals, such as accountants, insurance, and lawyers.

So, what does fintech have to do with HNW individuals and family offices?

The answer is that fintechs are using technology to provide retail investors with many of the same sophisticated and personalized services as HNW individuals receive. Who doesn't want to receive personalized service? Until recently, it was not economically feasible to offer a retail customer this level of service because the salary required by the professional advisors was too high.

Technology changes this equation by allowing professional services to be written in code with computer algorithms (not robots) serving customers. As we saw earlier, robo-advisors like Wealthfront have been able to provide daily rebalancing and tax-loss harvesting at the stock level, multi-factor smart beta and risk parity investment strategies, and other services normally reserved for HNW customers.

Digital wealth managers are providing better service to retail customers at a lower cost. The retail side of the wealth management industry is guilty of providing low transparency around the fees charged to investors. Customers are typically charged 2% to 3% of AUM, with other fees that may be hidden or not disclosed.

Take the example of stock trading. A broker might disclose a fixed charge of $10 per trade, but not provide transparency on the bid-ask spread or the length of time the trade was held on the broker's order book. Unless a customer used a limit order, the dealer could watch the market and trade when it suited their position. Overall, retail customers face many pain points when investing or working with financial advisors. These underserved and overcharged customers are the target market for the fintech entrants into this industry.

Digital Wealth Management

Digital wealth management leverages technology to automate and improve the customer experience, while generating fees and commissions from asset acquisition, portfolio management and automation of back-office operations. By automating standard, repetitive tasks, fintechs can lower costs, increase productivity, and offer more value to investors. Fintechs in wealth management are applying all of the same

Figure 8.2. Wealth Management Value Chain

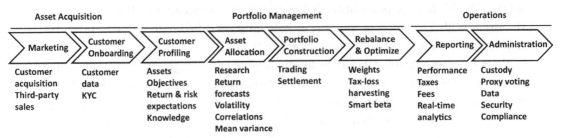

tools as other lines of business: the internet and smartphones, big data and cloud computing, APIs and AI, blockchain and cryptography, among many others.

Besides the obvious use-cases for portfolio construction and management, fintechs are addressing many use-cases including customer relationship management (CRM), digital identity, cybersecurity, and regulation and compliance.

To understand the opportunities and pain points for fintechs in wealth management, it helps if we look at the wealth management value chain. Figure 8.2 breaks down this value chain into three main activities, each of which consists of several activities.

The first activity is acquiring customers and their investments. Marketing and advertising attract clients, either directly or through third parties who are paid a commission for client referrals. The high costs of customer acquisition explain the need for economies of scale. These costs are even higher when customer acquisition is outsourced to third-party sales teams.

Once a customer is acquired, the process of onboarding involves collecting basic customer data and billing information. Importantly, they must satisfy the regulatory requirement to know your customer (KYC), or know your client. KYC means verifying the identity of a client, evaluating their financial knowledge and risk tolerance, and establishing what investments are suitable. The financial advisor must also comply with anti-money laundering (AML) laws by conducting due diligence to ensure the funds are not the proceeds of criminal activity.

The second activity is portfolio management. Portfolio management is building and executing an investment strategy to meet a client's long-term financial goals. The wealth manager creates a customer profile based on their assets and wealth, investment objectives, return expectations, risk tolerance, and investor knowledge. This customer profile determines the recommended asset allocation.

Research on modern portfolio theory has established diversification and mean-variance analysis as the industry standards for constructing portfolios. The inputs to this mean variance optimization are return and volatility forecasts and correlations among asset classes. The wealth manager constructs the portfolio by buying and/or selling assets, with settlement taking place over one to two days.

Once established, this portfolio is rebalanced and optimized to respond to modify weights based on asset price movements, to take advantage of tax-loss harvesting, or to execute investment strategies such as smart beta designed to outperform market benchmarks.

The third category of tasks is operational, completed by the back office on a regular basis. There is reporting to clients and to tax and regulatory authorities on portfolio performance, taxable gains or losses, and fees. The customer or financial advisors can access real-time analytics via dashboards or other software tools. The administration of assets involves custody of securities, proxy voting, data capture, ongoing security, and compliance with regulations.

Digital Financial Advice: The Future Is Hybrid

Professionals working in the wealth management industry may wonder – will they be replaced by robots? The answer is no.

According to research by Chuck Grace and Andrew Sarta, the future of digital wealth management is a hybrid model. In "Next-Generation Financial Advice: Reimagining Wealth Management in the Age of Technology," they argue that human advisors will be supported by computer algorithms and software that assist with customer onboarding, portfolio optimization, and reporting.[18] Technology will automate boring tasks and improve the customer experience.

Customers will have access 24/7 to a well-designed web portal or mobile app for tracking their investments. These apps will feature clean dashboards with easy-to-read graphs of portfolio allocation and returns, news and research, a chat function, and online support via a chatbot. And a human advisor will be available for important life decisions, particularly when it comes to financial planning and avoiding behavioral biases. After all, many investors still want to speak to a person, particularly retirees and baby boomers.

The consultancy firm EY agrees with Grace and Sarta and calls their hybrid model "Advisor 2.0":

> We see Advisor 2.0 as an evolution of delivering wealth management to investors. Technology and tools are changing the ways that human financial advisors market themselves, interact with clients, optimize processes, and develop and implement investment strategies. Firms will continue to develop their channels to suit investors' preferences, and these will coexist for the foreseeable future.[19]

Rather than taking away jobs, computers and software will increase human productivity and provide more personalized, timely customer support at a lower cost. Technology will allow the wealth management industry to meet the needs of an aging population despite a decline in the number of financial advisors.

The Technology-Enabled eAdvisor

Until now, most retail customers have been underserved and forced to manage their own investments, even if they are willing to pay for advice. Why is that?

The answer is math. It has not made economic sense for a financial advisor to focus on most retail customers. Financial advisors face high overhead costs and time constraints. A traditional financial advisor can manage around 200 customers. If this advisor charges 2.0% of AUM and the average customer has $100,000, the advisor will collect $400,000 in fees before expenses. But if the average customer has only $10,000 to invest, the same advisor will only generate $40,000. So it makes economic sense for a financial advisor to focus on HNW customers with large AUM.

Research by Fidelity in 2016 illustrated how technology can make financial advisors more productive, allowing them to manage a larger book of clients. These technology-enabled advisors are called eAdvisors. Fidelity found that eAdvisors have a median AUM that is 42% higher, with 35% more AUM per client.[20] The typical eAdvisor is younger and makes greater use of social media and email to stay in touch with clients.

eAdvisors communicate and collaborate with clients via video conferencing or online conferencing and use automated email alerts for client updates. Most offer clients e-signature options, and nearly all provide electronic delivery of statements and reports, as well as online access to such documents. They use data aggregation tools to provide the total picture of clients' assets and liabilities. More than half have client segmentation strategies and are serving more Gen X and Gen Y clients.

The Fidelity study points out that demographics are creating a looming supply-demand imbalance in the wealth management industry. Retiring advisors are not being replaced rapidly enough to serve this aging population. Technology may be one way to increase the productivity of fewer eAdvisors to meet this rising market demand.

These demographic changes create an important role for technology going forward. And leading fintechs have been capitalizing on the market opportunity, establishing a foothold by targeting pain points in the wealth management value chain. Let's take a look at a few examples.

Digital Customer Onboarding

Customer relationship management is a key success factor in wealth management. But financial advisors face major pain points due to manual workflows, administration, and legacy information technology (IT) systems. The process of onboarding a new customer can be particularly painful, as it takes up the time of both the customer and the financial advisor, who needs to capture lots of valuable customer information while complying with KYC and AML requirements. Believe it or not, most financial advisors still use paper forms and require physical (wet) signatures.

Canada's Nest Wealth seemed like an unlikely candidate to solve this financial advisor pain point. Launched in 2014, Nest Wealth was Canada's first robo-advisor.[21] Former trader and TV show host Randy Cass wanted to democratize access to sophisticated financial advice while reducing the fees. Nest Wealth charged a fixed monthly fee of $40 for accounts between $40,000 and $75,000, with no charge for smaller accounts and $80 per month above $75,000. Like Wealthfront, Nest Wealth used no marketing but attracted customers by word of mouth.

When Nest Wealth's main competitor Wealthsimple raised CA$30 million in mid-2015 from a major Canadian financial institution, Cass had to rethink his business model. Nest Wealth had never raised external capital and could not match Wealthsimple's budget or distribution channel in the B2C space.

Cass saw a silver lining to this dark cloud. Such a large investment validated the disruptive threat from robo-advisors. Other incumbents would be forced to respond, and soon Nest Wealth's phone was ringing off the hook. But rather than wanting to license Nest Wealth's investing algorithms, these incumbents were interested in the state-of-the-art technology platform that allowed for paperless digital onboarding and easy administration of back-office functions.

Cass heard that financial advisors were struggling to find time for client meetings and business development, because up to 15 hours each week was consumed by unproductive activities: faulty paperwork, compliance tasks, and administration. Paperwork received by dealers that was not in good order could not be entered into the administration systems, resulting in delays in placing trades. Approximately 40% of paperwork submitted by financial advisors was returned for corrections and often required a follow-up meeting with the client. One financial advisory firm estimated that the administration costs for each client were $15 per month.

Seeing a business opportunity, Cass pivoted Nest Wealth into the B2B market. Nest Wealth rebuilt their technology platform to focus on the pain points of financial advisors. Within two years, they launched Nest Wealth Pro and signed licensing agreements for this technology platform with six partners, including two of the six largest banks in Canada. Nest Wealth continues to run a B2C robo-advisor, but the majority of its revenues now come from the B2B business.

CASE STUDY: BLACKROCK'S ALADDIN PLATFORM FOR FINANCIAL ADVISORS

Not all technological innovation is created by fintechs. The world's largest asset manager, BlackRock, has hopes to become the largest technology provider for the wealth management industry. With this goal in mind, BlackRock has been licensing its in-house portfolio management platform, Aladdin, to institutional investors, corporations, and financial advisors.[22]

The name Aladdin is short for "Asset Liability and Debt and Derivative Investment Network." This software was initially created to run BlackRock's business but was then licensed to hedge funds and other institutional investors to manage risks in their investment portfolios. Following an internal hackathon where a team came up with the idea, BlackRock created a version for wealth managers. Aladdin Wealth has since been licensed to 16 retail wealth management firms, including JPMorgan Stanley and UBS Group.

Aladdin Wealth uses the same portfolio, construction, and risk management capabilities that BlackRock uses to manage its own business. The platform combines front-, middle-, and back-office functions for managing client portfolios in one place. A financial advisor can build portfolios aligned with investors' goals and risk tolerance. They can show clients their investments, exposure to risk, and performance.

Aladdin Wealth provides the ability to rebalance portfolios as market views and client needs change. They can explain how their portfolios might perform across different market and economic conditions using stress tests built on BlackRock's global risk models.

Aladdin Wealth allows a financial advisor to analyze a client's total household wealth by including external assets held by third parties. This data is accessed using secure APIs. The client can see their portfolio exposures across asset classes, geographies, and risk factors. And Aladdin Wealth simplifies administration such as workflow, client reporting, and regulatory compliance.

Sustainable Investing to Tackle Climate Change

More and more customers want to invest their savings to do good for society and the planet. Over the past decade, sustainable investing has emerged as the fastest growing and most socially important trend in the asset management industry. In 2020, global sustainable investments reached $35.3 trillion, or more than one-third of total AUM – a 54% increase since 2014.[23] Sustainable investing is the integration of environmental, social, and governance (ESG) factors into asset selection and portfolio construction. It may also be called responsible investing or ESG investing.

While sustainable investing started as a tool for screening investments, it is now seen as a distinct risk factor, return generator, and source of resilience during downturns. A survey by BlackRock found that 54% of global respondents consider sustainable investing to be fundamental to investment processes and outcomes.[24] The respondents planned to double their sustainable AUM by 2025, from an average of 18% of AUM in 2020 to 37% on average by 2025.

UK retail investors can invest in sustainable companies that are fighting climate change through the UK fintech Clim8 Invest.[25] Founded in 2019 by serial cleantech entrepreneur Duncan Grierson, Clim8's mobile app provides a simple way to invest in businesses engaged in clean energy, clean technology, sustainable food, clean water, smart mobility, and recycling. Clim8's two investment funds hold stocks, bonds, and ETFs screened based on their sustainability credentials, impact, and performance. UK investors can download the mobile app and invest with as little as £25, choosing one of three risk profiles (Cautious, Balanced, and Adventurous). The management fee is 0.60% of AUM. As of early 2022, Clim8 had raised £12 million and built a team of 42 employees.

CASE STUDY: ROBINHOOD'S COMMISSION-FREE TRADING FOR RETAIL

In 2014 the fintech Robinhood launched a mobile trading app with the mission to democratize finance. Robinhood began offering zero-commission trading for retail investors at a time when discount brokerages were charging $5 to $10 per trade. This innovation addressed a major pain point facing retail customers.

Robinhood's founders, Vlad Tenev and Baiju Bhatt, were roommates at Stanford University, then both worked for hedge funds writing algorithms for high-frequency trading. They saw first-hand the discrepancy between costs charged to institutional versus retail traders. Robinhood explicitly targeted younger, less wealthy millennial investors. These price-sensitive DIY investors were unhappy paying fees that bundled services they did not want, such as equity research, market commentary, and customer support. No surprise, then, that 75% of the 150,000 customers who signed up for a Robinhood account at launch were born after 1980.[26]

When asked how they planned to monetize their business without charging fees, the founders explained that Robinhood's no-frills, electronic trading platform had very low overhead. Robinhood would offer margin trading and earn income from lending to traders and premium subscriptions.[27] Leading venture capitalists were convinced, with Robinhood closing a $3 million seed-round funded by Andreessen Horowitz and Google Ventures. And the regulator FINRA granted Robinhood approval to operate as a securities broker-dealer – no small feat for a start-up.

Following launch, Robinhood grew rapidly. It had 2 million customers by year-end 2017, 6 million by 2018, and 10 million by 2019. In July 2019, it raised $323 million in a Series E round that valued the company at $7.6 billion. Faced with this viral success, much of the US brokerage industry was forced to offer zero-commission fee structures.

In December 2019 Robinhood was fined $1.25 million by FINRA for violations related to customer equity orders between October 2016 and November 2017. Robinhood had failed to satisfy its best execution obligations when it directed trades to four broker-dealers that paid for the order flow.

The story did not draw much attention, likely because it was overshadowed by the start of the COVID-19 pandemic a month later. Online trading by retail investors exploded. In May 2020 Robinhood raised $280 million in a Series F funding round, valuing the company at $8.3 billion.

In August 2020 *Fortune* magazine ran a cover story titled "The Inside Story of Robinhood's Billionaire Founders, Option Kid Cowboys and the Wall Street Sharks That Feed on Them."[28] The story exposed Robinhood's monetization strategy, called payments for order flow. It explained that Robinhood's main source of revenues was selling information on retail customer trades to hedge funds and other sophisticated investors.

Robinhood described this revenue on their website as "rebates from market makers and trading venues." While the impact on any given investor was small, these sophisticated investors were making millions, particularly using the order flow from retail trading in stock options.

The negative publicity did not deter the faithful. Retail investors continued to flock to Robinhood, with customers hitting 12.5 million by year-end. Nor did it deter venture capitalists. Robinhood raised another $200 million in a Series G, implying a valuation of $11.2 billion. It seemed that any news was good news for Robinhood's owners.

In January 2021 the meme stock craze hit the headlines. Stocks such as GameStop rose dramatically following a short squeeze orchestrated by retail investors on Reddit. Downloads of the Robinhood app were five times greater than the previous month, reaching around 3.3 million downloads in January 2021 alone. The sharp rise in GameStop stock led Robinhood to restrict trading for several days.

Figure 8.3. Robinhood vs. S&P500 Composite Index

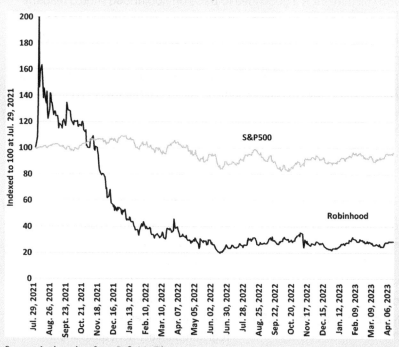

Source: Author, data from Refinitiv Eikon.

Angry customers argued their platform was colluding with hedge funds against its loyal user base.

The Depository Trust and Clearing Corporation, Wall Street's main clearinghouse for stock trades, demanded that Robinhood post $3 billion in cash collateral to cover risky trades by its customers – an extraordinary amount that was raised from existing investors over the February 1 weekend.[29]

The public backlash saw Robinhood's founders called before the US Congress and Senate in February and March to give testimony at investigations into the meme stock frenzy. As this controversy swirled around the company, Robinhood announced plans to go public through an initial public offering (IPO).

In July 2021 Robinhood priced its IPO at $38 per share, valuing the company at $31.7 billion, and the co-founders were worth $5 billion.[30] Figure 8.3 shows that the fairy tale has not ended well. By year-end 2022 Robinhood's share price had fallen by 78% to $7.70, compared to the S&P Composite Index down 11%. It looks like Robinhood robbed from the poor to become rich!

Anyone who still thinks it is a good idea to trade on Robinhood should read the study titled "Attention Induced Trading and Returns: Evidence from Robinhood Users."[31] It shows that Robinhood investors engage in more attention-induced trading than other retail investors, which means they trade more in high-attention stocks. Attention-induced trading is not a good strategy; the top stocks purchased each day by Robinhood users decline by almost 5% more than the market on average over the next month.

Key Terms

assets under administration (AUA)

assets under management (AUM)

back office

beneficial owners

customer onboarding

customer relationship management (CRM)

eAdvisor

ESG investing

exchange traded funds (ETFs)

financial advisor

high net worth (HNW)

know your customer (KYC)

management expense ratio (MER)

mutual fund

passive (index) investing

payment for order flow

portfolio management

registered investment advisor (RIA)

regtech

robo-advisor

sustainable finance

wealth management

QUESTIONS FOR DISCUSSION

1 What is a robo-advisor and how do they create a personalized portfolio for a customer? What does it cost to use a robo-advisor?

2 What is passive investing and how does it explain the growth of exchange traded funds (ETFs)?

3 What is the business strategy of robo-advisors and what customers are they targeting?

4 What has been the experience of incumbent asset managers as they respond to the threat of disruption from robo-advisors?

5 What are the main lessons from the David-vs.-Goliath battle between robo-advisors and incumbents?

6 What is the wealth management industry, how big is it, and who works in it?

7 What is the difference between institutional investors and retail customers? What are high net worth customers?

8 What is meant by digital wealth management? What technologies are being used to transform this industry and how?

9 What are examples of fintechs attacking different parts of the wealth management value chain?

10 What is a technology-enabled eAdvisor, and why is a hybrid model so important for the future of the wealth management industry?

ADDITIONAL READING

Backend Benchmarking, "The Robo Report Fourth Quarter 2022," accessed April 1, 2023, https://www.backendbenchmarking.com/the-robo-report/.

Grace, Chuck, and Andrew Sarta, "Next-Generation Financial Advice: Reimagining Wealth Management in the Age of Technology," in *The Technological Revolution in Financial Services: How Banks and Fintech Customers Win Together*, eds. Michael R. King and Richard W. Nesbitt (Toronto: University of Toronto Press, 2020).

Heredia, Lubasha, Simon Bartletta, Joe Carrubba, Dean Frankle, Chris McIntyre, Edoardo Palmisani, Anastasios Panagiotou, Neil Pardasani, Kedra Newsom Reeves, Thomas Schulte, and Ben Sheridan, "Global Asset Management 2021: The $100 Trillion Machine," BCG, July 2021, https://web-assets.bcg.com/79/bf/d1d361854084a9624a0cbce3bf07/bcg-global-asset-management-2021-jul-2021.pdf.

Investment Company Institute, "2021 Investment Company Fact Book," May 2021. https://www.ici.org/system/files/2021-05/2021_factbook.pdf.

Lo, Andrew W., and Stephen R. Foerster, *In Pursuit of the Perfect Portfolio* (Princeton, NJ: Princeton University Press, 2021).

9

Payments and Insurtech

SUMMARY

- Payments is a $2 trillion industry that generates an estimated 40% of bank revenues. It is complex, with many players collaborating and competing in overlapping networks.
- The large profit pools and many customer pain points in payments have attracted many successful fintechs, with more fintech unicorns born in payments than any other area of financial services.
- These fintechs started with a single use-case (such as a new form of mobile money or a fair exchange rate on currency transactions) and have expanded their product offering over time.
- Successful payment fintechs have solved pain points around e-commerce, money transfers, foreign exchange, international remittances, and cashless means of payment.
- Insurance is a $6 trillion industry broken down into life insurance, property and casualty insurance, and health insurance.
- Insurtechs are exploiting mobile apps, cloud computing, biometrics, sensors, data science, and artificial intelligence (AI) to disrupt this industry.
- Insurtechs leverage technology and big data to develop customized insurance products that meet the needs of underserved and niche customers.
- Digital-only insurance companies are using AI and machine learning to develop and price innovative products that formerly were not possible given the underwriting history required and the high distribution costs.

The previous chapter showed how economies of scale and the cost of customer acquisition have proved to be the biggest stumbling blocks to fintechs in wealth management.

This chapter shows that fintechs can successfully attack the profit pools of the payments and insurance industries, both of which are complex, regulated, and fragmented. The secret is to develop apps that solve customer pain points and automate processing.

PAYMENTS, MONEY TRANSFER, AND FOREIGN EXCHANGE

Payments, money transfer, and foreign exchange (FX) have been the front line in the battle between fintech companies and incumbents. This $2 trillion industry has grown, fueled by e-commerce and the digital economy. The industry is complex, with many players collaborating and competing in overlapping networks. More $1 billion+ fintech unicorns have been born in payments than in any other area of financial services.

For the rest of this chapter, we will use the term *payment* to refer to both payments and money transfers even though they are slightly different. If you are not quite sure of the difference, the textbox "Payments and Money Transfer Jargon" defines some of this terminology.

Consumers and businesses face many pain points in this part of the financial system. Payments and money transfers can be slow, non-transparent, and costly, particularly when they cross national borders. A bank wire from one bank to another, for example, costs around $35 and takes several business days to arrive even when it is sent within the same country and the same currency. Sending a remittance overseas may incur costs representing around 10% of the proceeds and could take weeks to arrive.[1] Existing financial intermediaries provide poor customer service and charge many fees with little transparency.

PAYMENTS AND MONEY TRANSFER JARGON

You may already be familiar with much of the jargon used in payments, but just in case, let's define a few terms: payment, method of payment, money transfer, remittance, cross-border payment, and FX transaction.

A *payment* is a transfer of money from one party to another in exchange for goods and services. A *method of payment* (or payment method) is how you pay. Consumers mostly pay with cash, debit cards, credit cards, checks, and prepaid cards (including gift cards and loyalty/points cards).[2] Businesses primarily pay with electronic fund transfers (EFTs), followed by checks and credit cards. You can make larger payments using a bank wire, which is a variation on an EFT. Bitcoin and cryptocurrencies are the newest digital methods of payment.

A *money transfer* is the movement of money from one place to another. It may be a payment, or it may also simply be moving money between two financial institutions. You might transfer money between your bank accounts or send money to a friend using Venmo in the United States or Interac e-Transfer in Canada. A *remittance* is when you send money to relatives abroad.

When money crosses national borders, it is called a *cross-border payment*. A cross-border payment involves an *FX transaction*. One currency is exchanged for another, such as Canadian dollars for US dollars, or Japanese yen for Swiss francs. The rate to convert from one currency to another is the exchange rate. An FX transaction involves a fee or commission, which may be a fixed amount or a percentage of the transaction.

The payments industry, therefore, represents a vast opportunity for disruption. Over the past decade, fintechs have found innovative ways to speed up payments and lower their cost while providing a better customer experience. Fintechs are providing new payment methods, targeting underserved customers, automating billing, reducing FX costs, and facilitating international remittances. These innovations are creating trust, reducing friction, and bringing valuable services to unbanked populations.

The payments industry has generated many fintech success stories: PayPal, Square, and Stripe in the US; Lightspeed in Canada; Adyen, Klarna, and Wise (formerly TransferWise) in Europe; Paytm in India; and Ant Group (formerly AliPay) and Tencent WePay in China. These fintechs have used technology to provide payments, money transfers, and FX transactions that are faster, cheaper, and easier, leading to a better customer experience. People who use these companies don't ever want to go back.

Many technology companies that are also moving into financial services have targeted payments as a first entry point to gain a foothold with end-customers. By processing payments and money transfers, companies such as Alibaba, Amazon, and Google are able to collect transaction data that can be mined to reveal customer insights. These insights may lead to innovative new product offerings.

A $2 Trillion Industry

The payments industry is big, profitable, and complicated. The strategy consultant McKinsey & Company estimates that this industry generates close to 40% of bank

Figure 9.1. Global Payments Revenues (2020)

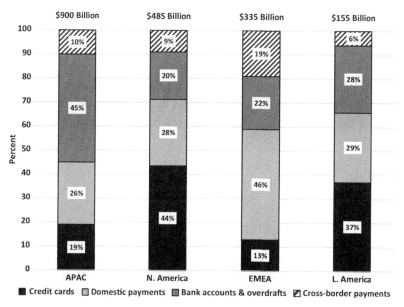

Source: McKinsey & Company.

revenues.[3] McKinsey reported total revenues of US$1.9 trillion from payments glob-ally in 2020, with revenues forecast to grow to $2.5 trillion by 2025. Roughly half of global revenues are in Asia Pacific, with North America making up one-quarter, and the rest spread around the rest of the world.

Why are payments such a large percentage of bank revenues? The answer is fees and interest charges. Figure 9.1 shows the distribution of payments revenues across four categories of payments for different regions. In North America, fees from pay-ments totaled a whopping $485 billion in 2020, of which 44% was interest and fees from credit cards, 28% was fees charged on domestic payments and bank accounts, 20% was interest and fees from bank accounts and overdrafts, and 9% was fees charged on cross-border transactions.

Figure 9.1 shows the largest market for payments is Asia Pacific at $900 billion, of which 45% of revenues are from bank accounts and overdrafts. It is clear why fintechs are disrupting this line of business given this high profitability. Domestic payments were 26%, credit cards 19%, and cross-border payments 10%.

The largest US bank, JPMorgan, recognizes the importance of digital payments. Its 2018 Investor Day presentation explained that 65% of clients would consider leav-ing a firm if digital channels were not integrated.[4] The presentation revealed that

47 million Chase customers made an average of 5 automated teller machine (ATM) transactions per month, 6 digital wallet transactions, 32 debit card and 21 credit card transactions, 3 peer-to-peer (P2P) money transfers, and 2 online deposits. That's 69 fee-generating transactions per customer and 3.2 billion per month.

JPMorgan laid out its strategy to retain its dominant market position in the payment ecosystem. It has signed multiple partnerships and made large acquisitions, such as the fintech WePay. JPMorgan is involved in payments all around the world, with dedicated teams and innovative products across the value chain in each region.

THE PAYMENT RAILS

Payments travel through a network of computers known as the *payment rails*. While payments are electronic, these rails are a physical network of cables and wires connecting computers globally. Bytes of data are transmitted as electronic pulses on wired and wireless networks, or as beams of light on fiber optic networks. Insiders call this infrastructure "the plumbing" because it exists where no one sees it. But the payment rails are critical to the functioning of the economy. And control of the plumbing brings wealth.

Think of the payment rails as a network of roads. In most countries, the payment rails are owned by the government and – until recently – were operated solely by the major banks or an industry association controlled by banks. There are separate roads based on size: highways for large payments and local roads for small payments.

Business-to-business payments travel on the large value transfer system (LVTS). The LVTS is the fastest way to get around, with payments completing the journey in one day or even intraday. LVTS is used to transfer large sums of money and financial securities between banks, businesses, and the government. Many countries have upgraded their LVTSs in recent years, making the trip nearly instantaneous. This is known as real-time gross settlement (RTGS).

The United States has two LVTSs. One is operated by the central bank, known as the Fedwire (after the Federal Reserve), and the other is run by a private entity known as the Clearing House Interbank Payments System (CHIPS). In Canada, the LVTS is called Lynx and is operated by an industry association controlled by the banks. Europe's most important LVTS is the TARGET2 system, which is overseen by the European Central Bank and operated by the national central banks.

Consumer payments travel along the local roads, which are slower. These roads were designed to manage high volumes of small payments made using paper checks, credit cards, and debit cards. Driving cross-country on smaller roads can take days. The US small payments system is the Automated Clearing House (ACH) network. In Canada we have the Automated Clearing Settlement System (ACSS). And in Europe it is the European Automated Clearing House Association (EUCHA).

Each country controls its own payments network. When the roads cross between countries, there are border crossings and checkpoints. Just like physical goods, cross-border payments are checked by customs agents, who verify the origin and contents of money transfers. The most important reason is to prevent the transfer of funds originating from criminal activity, known as anti-money laundering (AML). Just as vehicles are searched to prevent drug smuggling, payments are checked to prevent crime and money laundering.

In the United States, payments and money transfers are regulated by the Federal Reserve and federal and state regulators. The US Treasury's Financial Crimes Enforcement Network (FinCEN) keeps a list of registered money service businesses (MSBs). In Canada, payments are regulated by the Bank of Canada. The government agency FINTRAC regulates AML and anti-terrorist financing and maintains a registry of all MSBs operating in Canada.

The Payment Players

Banks can be found everywhere in payments. They provide cash accounts, and they issue means of payment such as checks, debit cards, and e-Transfers. Banks provide money transfer services including bank drafts, bank wires, and EFTs. Banks operate interbank networks to facilitate and process electronic payments (e.g., CHIPS, Interac, Moneris). They act as brokers and dealers in currency markets. And they provide letters of credit for trade finance.

But banks are not the only players in the payments industry. There are other businesses called a money service business (MSB) or a payment service provider (PSP). Both acronyms refer to the same thing, so we will stick with MSB. An MSB handles all forms of payments, money transfers, and FX transactions. An MSB may also cash checks and other money-related instruments, paying out money in the form of cash, a bank deposit, a check, or a money order. Or the MSB may deposit the money in a digital wallet on a mobile phone.

Figure 9.2. The Payment Players

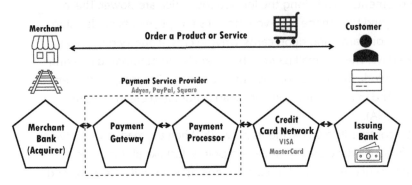

MSBs are regulated and required to collect customer identification (i.e., know your customer, or KYC), keep records, and comply with anti-money laundering (AML) regulations. While a bank may be registered as an MSB, there are also non-bank financial institutions, such as Money Mart and Western Union, or fintechs such as PayPal, Square, Stripe, and WePay.

In addition to banks and MSBs, there are a variety of other payment players. It is easiest to explain what they are by looking at an example of a payment and how it travels along the payment rails.

Figure 9.2 illustrates what players are involved when you use a credit card to make an online or in-store purchase. You are the customer. You get approved for a credit card by an issuing bank. This bank may be where you hold your deposits, but not necessarily. The issuing bank lends you money when you make a purchase, sends you a credit card bill each month, and collects your payment. They may charge an annual fee, collect interest on any outstanding unpaid balances, and reimburse you in case you return something (called a chargeback).

The credit card is branded with the name of a company that operates a proprietary credit card network. The credit card networks are owned by VISA, MasterCard, and American Express. These companies set the rules for their networks, including the interchange fee. The interchange fee is a cost deducted from the sale price for transacting with a credit card and is shared between the players that process and settle the transaction. Think of it as a toll for using their network. The credit card companies may also capture and analyze customer data to provide insights to their payment partners.

The merchant where you shop has its own bank, called the merchant bank (or acquirer).[5] For in-store purchases, the merchant bank provides the point-of-sale (POS) machine used to transmit data and authorize purchases. This POS machine sends a message to the issuing bank to ask if funds are available. For online purchases, the merchant connects via a payments gateway such as PayPal.

The other players in this process are the payment gateway and the payment processor. The payment gateway transmits information securely, ensuring it travels via the correct network to its destination. The payment processor is like the postal service, delivering messages between the gateway and the two banks. Some fintechs operate as both a payment gateway and a payment processor, such as Adyen, PayPal, and Square.

Now that we know the players, let's walk through a transaction. There are two parts to processing a payment: authorization and settlement.

First, authorization is approving a transaction and takes one to two seconds:

1 You buy an item online or in-store with a credit or debit card. If online, you enter your credit card details onto a form. If in-store, you tap your card at a POS machine. Both methods involve data that is transmitted along a network of computers.

2 Details of the transaction are sent via an application programming interface (API) to a payment gateway. The gateway encrypts this data to keep it private, then sends it to a payment processor and waits for authorization.

3 The payment processor is a messenger that routes the encrypted information via the appropriate network to the customer's issuing bank. The processor asks, "Does this customer has enough credit to pay for the transaction?" Examples of payment processors are Chase Merchant Services, First Data, FIS, Moneris Solutions, and WorldPay (formerly Vantiv).

4 The issuing bank responds to the payment processor with a yes (an approval) or a no (a denial). The payment processor sends the answer to the payment gateway.

5 The payment gateway decrypts the information and sends it to the merchant, either authorizing or denying the transaction. If online, you see that your transaction has been approved. If using a POS machine, you get a message and a receipt of your transaction.

6 If the transaction is authorized by the issuing bank, the payment processor instructs the merchant bank to transfer funds into the merchant's account for the sale. So the merchant gets paid immediately, and you have now borrowed money from your issuing bank.

Next, settlement is transferring money from your account at the issuing bank to the merchant's account at the merchant bank. It can take up to two business days for the funds to arrive:

1 The issuing bank receives the authorization and sends the transaction to be processed. Transactions are typically processed in batches at the end of the day. That
is why your credit card bill has two dates: transaction date and posting date.

2 The funds are transferred from the issuing bank to the merchant bank within one
to two days.

3 This merchant bank deposits the money in the merchant's bank account, minus
fees. The service fee consists of a processing cost and an interchange fee.

4 The issuing bank posts the transaction on your credit card account and sends you
a bill each month. Because the money has already been sent to the merchant bank,
the issuing bank has lent you the funds and has a credit exposure to you.

How Payment Players Make Money

Now that we understand the steps, let's look at how payment players make money
(i.e., their monetization strategy). Payment fintechs generate revenues by charging
fees and earning income for taking risk exposures. Table 9.1 gives an example of the
fees that may be charged for a $100 credit card purchase.

From the $100 paid by the customer, the merchant bank deducts a merchant dis-
count of $2.00 and a processing fee of $0.50, for a total of $2.50 or 2.5%. The merchant
will also be charged a monthly assessment by the credit card company of 0.11% based
on their aggregate sales. In the end, the merchant receives $97.39. How is the total fee
of $2.61 split up?

The merchant discount is a combination of a merchant bank's surcharge (profit)
and the interchange fee. The interchange fee of 1.75% is set by the credit card network, either VISA or MasterCard. The merchant bank deducts the interchange fee

Table 9.1. Fees Charged for $100 Credit Card Payment

Who	Amount	%	Notes
Customer pays	$ 100.00		
Less: Merchant discount	$ 2.00	2.00	Merchant fee + interchange
Less: Assessment fee	$ 0.11	0.11	VISA, MasterCard
Less: Processing fee	$ 0.50	0.50	$0.50/transaction
Merchant receives	$ 97.39		
Who gets what?			
Issuing bank	$ 1.75	1.75	Interchange fee
Merchant bank	$ 0.25	0.25	Merchant fee (surcharge)
Card network	$ 0.11	0.11	Assessment fee
Payment gateway/processor	$ 0.50	0.50	Processing fee

when depositing funds into the merchant's account. This interchange is then sent to the issuing bank that acquired the customer. Interchange covers risks such as customer default (bad debt), fraud, and handling costs, among others. Interchange fees vary by card network, as well as by type and size of transaction.

On top of the interchange fee, the merchant pays the credit card company an assessment fee of 0.11%. This assessment is charged monthly based on the volume of transactions. Together, the interchange fee and the assessment are called the swipe fee. The swipe fee allows a merchant to accept and process credit cards at their store.

The payment gateway and payment processor share a processing fee, in this example $0.50 per transaction. This is a flat rate; if the transaction is larger, the percentage is smaller. For a $1,000 purchase, a $0.50 processing fee is only 0.05%.

This example is a domestic transaction without any currency conversion. Cross-border payments are charged a fee for converting from one currency to another, such as Canadian dollars for US dollars. This conversion fee is charged by the issuing bank. It may be disclosed, or it may be hidden in the exchange rate chosen by the issuing bank. This fee can be substantial, as high as 3% for consumer transactions.

Banks and other MSBs also earn interest income from taking risk exposures, specifically FX risk, liquidity risk, and credit risk. FX markets are volatile, with exchange rates moving continuously. A bank trading in FX will pay one rate to buy US dollars (called the bid) and receive a different rate to sell (called the ask). The difference between these two prices, called the bid-ask spread, compensates the FX dealer for holding inventories of currencies whose prices are changing. The FX conversion can occur at any time of the day when it is most profitable for the bank or MSB to transact.

Banks provide liquidity by depositing cash with other banks as collateral against future payments. This cash has a cost that is passed on to customers. A bank with a credit exposure to a customer may lose money if the customer defaults on their debts, called credit risk. Credit risk is compensated by charging fees to all customers for overdrafts and credit cards. While these sources of income may appear small in isolation, they add up fast when trillions of dollars are being transferred through payment networks.

In addition to direct charges associated with a payment or money transfer, banks make money by charging other indirect fees: annual account fees, maintenance fees, fees for non-sufficient funds, and more. For business clients, banks charge fees for trade finance, including fees for issuing and confirming letters of credit, document handling fees, return document fees, handling fees, and many more associated with exports and imports.

CASE STUDY: PAYTM'S BUSINESS MODEL AND DIGITAL PLATFORM

Let's look at how the Indian payments fintech Paytm makes money. Paytm is an acronym for "pay through mobile." It was founded in 2010 in New Delhi by Vijay Shekhar Sharma, who invested $2 million into his start-up called One97 Communications. Large equity investments from Ant Financial, Alibaba, and Softbank Ventures allowed Paytm to scale and grow rapidly.

In November 2021, Paytm went public through India's largest initial public offering (IPO). The sale of $2.5 billion in shares set Paytm's market capitalization at $18.5 billion, with Sharma worth $1.7 billion.[6] The stock plunged 27% on its first day of trading, however, making it one of the worst initial showings by a major technology IPO since the 1990s dot-com bubble. Since the IPO, Paytm's shares are down 66%, while the MSCI India index is flat.

From its roots as a service to top up prepaid mobile phones and recharge direct-to-home satellite TV, Paytm expanded into digital payments and financial services and began offering credit and access to financial products and services through many financial partners. By the time of the IPO, Paytm was India's largest payments platform, offering payment solutions, commerce, and cloud solutions to 337 million consumers and 22 million merchants.

Consumers use Paytm's mobile app for P2P money transfers, in-store and online payments, mobile phone top-ups, and utility bill payments. They can access personal loans, credit cards, and insurance from financial partners. These use-cases allow Paytm to monetize its users at little or no incremental cost.

Paytm reports revenues under two segments: payment and financial services and commerce and cloud services. The payment business has two drivers: payment processing and subscription revenues. Payment processing revenues are the sum of transaction fees charged to merchants and the convenience fees charged to consumers.

Payment processing revenues are measured using the take rate, which is the percentage of gross merchant volume (GMV) for processing transactions. So payment processing revenue = GMV × Take rate. Paytm had GMV of $137 billion and revenues of $159 million, or a take rate of 12 bps for the 12 months ending at the second quarter of fiscal year 2022.

Paytm collects recurring subscription fees from merchants for use of the Paytm QR code, Soundbox (a voice-activated smart device for payments), POS devices, and the all-in-one payment gateway. Paytm charges from $1.2 to $3.1 per month per active device.

Paytm launched financial services platform in 2019 that provides mobile banking, lending, insurance, and wealth management. Paytm mobile banking operates through Paytm Payments Bank, which is 49% owned. The products are bank accounts, fixed deposits, and debit cards. Paytm launched a co-branded credit card with 300,000 active cards by Q2 2022.

Paytm runs an online lending platform that provides consumers loans (including buy-now-pay-later) and merchant loans sourced from partner banks and non-bank financial institutions. Paytm earns 2.5% to 3.5% of the loan value for distribution and 0.5% to 1.5% for collections. Consumers can also access insurance and wealth management from financial partners through the Paytm platform.

Despite these many promising developments, Paytm continues to experience enormous losses, as shown in Table 9.2. While sales and marketing have declined as a percentage of revenues, operating expenses remain above 100% of revenues.

Table 9.2. Paytm Financial Statements, as of March 31

	2020	2021	2022	2020	2021	2022
INCOME STATEMENT	Indian rupees (millions)			% REVENUES		
Revenues	32,808	28,024	49,742	100	100	100
Less: Processing charges	22,659	19,168	27,538	69	68	55
Less: Sales and marketing	13,971	5,325	8,554	43	19	17
Less: Other expenses	27,314	23,234	39,482	83	83	79
Total Operating expenses	63,944	47,727	75,574	195	170	152
Less: Tax + excep. items	-2,714	-2,742	-1,903	-8	-10	-4
Net income (loss)	-28,422	-16,961	-23,929	-87	-61	-48
BALANCE SHEET	Indian rupees (millions)			% ASSETS		
Assets	103,031	91,513	179,916	100	100	100
Liabilities	21,979	26,165	38,400	21	29	21
Equity	81,052	65,348	141,516	79	71	79

Source: Refinitiv.

The Fintech Value Proposition in Payments

The fintech value proposition is to provide payments faster, cheaper, and more conveniently with greater transparency around fees and a better customer experience.

To illustrate this value proposition, let's imagine a Canadian business, Beaver Inc., which wants to make a cross-border payment to a US contractor, Eagle Ltd. This payment will incur a transaction fee for the money transfer, a currency conversion fee, and a bid-ask spread for the currency conversion. The transfer could take as little as one working day to as long as several weeks, with little transparency on the actual fee or where the payment stands while in progress.

First, Beaver could get its bank to wire the funds to Eagle's bank. A Canadian bank wire costs CA$25 for the sender and CA$10 for the recipient, plus a 3% currency conversion fee. So a payment of CA$1,000 costs $25 + $10 + $30 = $65 (or 6.5% of the transfer amount). A payment of CA$10,000 costs CA$25 + $10 + $300 = CA$335 (or 3.35%), which is getting cheaper as a percentage of the total. The fixed costs make a bank wire uneconomic for smaller amounts.

Second, Beaver could send the payment using PayPal, which transfers funds cross-border via the LVTS-ACH rails. The funds must come from a PayPal account, a connected bank account, or a debit or credit card. The funds are then transferred into Eagle's PayPal account. From there, it can be transferred into a local bank account for free. A PayPal transfer takes from one to five working days to be completed.

PayPal charges a fixed fee and a currency conversion fee that vary with the country of origin (2.9% to 3.9% for advanced economies; more for emerging market economies) and a bid-ask on the currency conversion. In this example, Beaver is charged a fixed fee of CA$2.98 per transfer plus a currency conversion fee of 3.5%. A CA$1,000 payment costs $37.98, and a CA$10,000 payment costs $352.98. PayPal is cheaper than a bank wire for smaller transfers but more expensive for larger ones.

Third, Beaver could send the payment on RippleNet, which connects many Canadian banks directly to US banks. RippleNet was created by the Silicon Valley start-up Ripple as a private interbank network for money transfers. If both Beaver and Eagle's banks are RippleNet members, the money transfer is nearly instantaneous and costs the banks close to nothing. The final cost to Beaver should in principle be lower than a bank wire or PayPal.

Fourth, Beaver could make the transfer using a cryptocurrency like bitcoin (BTC). Cryptocurrencies allow transfers directly from one computer to another computer (P2P) over the internet. The transaction is recorded and encrypted on the blockchain to avoid theft and provide security. This process seems secure, low cost, and anonymous on the surface. In practice, a cryptocurrency transfer involves several intermediaries (cryptowallets, cryptoexchanges, payment processors) who see the identity of the parties. These intermediaries may have low security, making them honey pots for hackers. And the fees and delays for processing transactions can be very high and not transparent.

Beaver would start by converting Canadian dollars into bitcoin through a cryptoexchange like Coinbase. Then the bitcoin could be transferred to Eagle, who would need to convert it back into US dollars to use it. The price of bitcoin, the fees charged by miners, and the time for verification vary with the traffic on the bitcoin network. It could take hours or days to complete, and the cost could vary widely. While bitcoin is not economically viable for small transactions, other cryptocurrencies could be used that are cheaper and quicker to transfer.

Fintechs Disrupting Payments

Many new entrants have been attracted to the payments industry by the large profit pools and many customer pain points. We may think of fintechs like Adyen, Klarna, Paytm, Square, Stripe, and Wise. But this industry is increasingly dominated by technology companies, like the bigtech firms Amazon, Apple, Google, and Samsung, and the Chinese techfins Ant Group (formerly Alipay) and Tencent WePay.

These new entrants have followed the same disruption strategy seen in other financial lines of business. Start with a single use-case. Build a foothold with core customers in one part of the value chain. Expand the product offering to capture other parts of the value chain and appeal to mainstream customers.

A single use-case might be a trustworthy and convenient means of payment, a new form of mobile money, a fair exchange rate on currency transactions, or a quick and inexpensive remittance.

An expanded product offering might be to combine a payment gateway and payment processor in one app. It might be to roll out better data analytics, customer insights, and reporting using big data, artificial intelligence (AI), and machine learning. These improvements and innovations will keep customers sticky and grow monthly recurring revenue.

These new entrants had good strategy but also good timing, benefiting from the following technological and regulatory changes:

1 Improvements in communications systems including the internet, smartphones, 3G/4G/5G networks, and cloud computing.
2 Improvements in payment networks around the world to allow real-time gross settlement.
3 Developments in payment technologies such as Near Field Communications (NFC), tap-and-go card readers, QR codes, cryptocurrencies, and blockchain.
4 Better security methods such as two- and three-factor authentication.
5 Regulatory changes promoting open banking, open APIs, and the opening of the payment rails.

Banks, credit card companies, and other MSBs are fighting back using all the moves in their playbooks: signing partnerships, creating consortiums, investing in or acquiring start-ups, and even filing lawsuits in an effort to protect their franchises.[7]

Big banks have rolled out mobile banking apps with better payment features, offered free payments (such as debit card payments and e-Transfers) and collaborated to lower the cost of international money transfers and remittances. A group of eight US banks, for example, created the digital payments network Zelle to compete with PayPal's Venmo.

Incumbents have acquired leading fintechs or acquired each other. JPMorgan acquired the payments fintech WePay. The payments processor Fiserv acquired its rival First Data, and FIS acquired its rival WorldPay. The credit card network VISA has been an early-stage investor in Square, Stripe, and Klarna. VISA has partnered with PayPal, Paytm, and PayActiv and tried to acquire the fintech data aggregator Plaid. The list of investments and acquisitions goes on and on.

Now that we know what strategies new entrants and incumbents are following, let's look at some examples of innovative fintech solutions to customer pain points.

ALIPAY: CREATING TRUST IN E-COMMERCE

Not everyone is comfortable transacting online, fearing the items they purchase will not be delivered. And not everyone has access to an electronic form of payment such as a credit card.

China's leading e-commerce company Alibaba faced both problems. Chinese customers lacked trust in online shopping and were hesitant to purchase goods unless they were standing in front of the merchant. China's payment system was underdeveloped, with little penetration of either credit or debit cards. Money transfers were time consuming and expensive, so consumers preferred to pay with cash.

Alibaba needed to create trust in e-commerce and solve the online payments problem in order for Alibaba to grow. Jack Ma's solution was to set up Alipay in 2004 as a payment gateway to serve Alibaba's online marketplaces.[8] Alipay provided consumers with an online account where they could load cash and transfer money with no cost. Basically, Alipay created online payments in China.

To build customer trust, Alipay would hold customer payments in escrow accounts that would be released to merchants only once the goods were delivered. Alipay launched a "Full Compensation" campaign with the slogan "As long as you use Alipay, we will compensate you in the case of account theft." The combination was a success, leading to rapid growth in online sales. Alibaba soon opened its website to third parties, creating a digital marketplace for both online and offline merchants.

Alipay was widely successful. By 2007 it had 50 million users and over 300,000 merchants.[9] In 2008 it had 100 million users, with daily transactions reaching 2 million. In 2010 it had 300 million users. E-commerce has gained acceptance and captured market share, with 74% of internet users shopping online by 2018.

In 2019 Alipay launched a mobile payments app that allowed customers to tap and pay for both online and offline purchases. Mobile payment in China benefited from the widespread use of quick response (QR) codes that could be scanned using the Alipay mobile app, allowing offline purchases. In 2011, 3.5% of all payments used a mobile phone. This figure hit 83% by 2018.[10]

Alipay has dominated the Chinese market for mobile payments, consistently capturing a 50%+ market share. In May 2014 Alipay was spun out of Alibaba into a separate entity named Ant Group. As of mid-2020, Alipay had 1.3 billion users, more than
80 million merchants, and was accepted in 50 countries.

M-PESA: DEMOCRATIZING MONEY TRANSFERS

In many countries, large segments of the population are unbanked, without access
to basic banking and payment services. Kenya was one example until the arrival of
M-PESA, a mobile phone–based money transfer service.[11] M-PESA literally stands
for "mobile money": M stands for mobile and Pesa is the Swahili word for money.
M-PESA was developed in 2005, then launched in March 2007 by Kenya's leading
mobile network operator, Safaricom, in partnership with parent company Vodafone
and the UK Department for International Development.

M-PESA allows customers to deposit money into an account stored on their cell
phone using a network of local Safaricom agents. This money can then be used to
make payments, to top up airtime on their phone, to transfer money to other M-PESA
customers, or to shop and pay merchants using text messaging. Users can withdraw
money through a network of ATMs and receive money sent from abroad. It is available 24 hours a day, 365 days a year, and is backed by security measures to protect
the funds. In short, M-PESA provides unbanked customers with a safe, secure, and
low-cost means to send, receive, and store money using a mobile phone.

By year-end 2022, M-PESA had 52 million customers in Kenya and six other countries: the Democratic Republic of Congo, Egypt, Ghana, Lesotho, Mozambique, and
Tanzania.[12] The penetration rate in Kenya was 90% of all mobile phone users. It processed 19 billion transactions and had a network of more than 600,000 agents. Customers
could send and receive money globally due to many partnerships, including PayPal and
Western Union. M-PESA had expanded to offer a savings account, loans, and overdraft.

M-PESA is regulated by the Central Bank of Kenya and operates under a special
license with conditions that are more relaxed compared to banks. Customer funds are
held safely in a trust account. Customers who lose their phone or SIM card are also
protected by a set of password-protected digital accounts held centrally by Vodafone.

WISE: LOWER FOREIGN EXCHANGE COSTS

Exchanging currencies is a frustrating and costly experience for individuals. Banks
and currency exchanges routinely charge 3% or more, even though the true cost for
them to transact is much lower. Worse still, this fee is usually hidden behind misleading statements such as "zero commission," "0% fee," or "best rates."

Wise (formerly TransferWise) launched its money transfer service in January 2011 to address this pain point. The original use-case was to enable P2P FX transfers at mid-market exchange rates.[13] The Estonian co-founders, Kristo Käärmann and Taavet Hinrikus, were frustrated about the high fees charged by banks to exchange currencies. They both lived in London, UK. One worked for Skype in Estonia and so was paid in euros. The other was paid in British pounds but had a mortgage denominated in euros back in Estonia. They devised a simple scheme where each month they would top up each other's bank accounts in the desired currency (British pounds and euros, respectively) using that day's mid-market rate. Both got the currency they needed, and neither paid any hidden bank charges.

The duo set up Wise to provide this FX service to people with international lives like themselves. The Wise online portal matched buyers and sellers of currencies, converting FX at mid-market rates for a small flat fee that is transparent and disclosed upfront. The money is transferred over the traditional payment rails from one bank account to another. It originally took up to two days to be received, depending on the country and the method of transfer.

In 2021 the company was rebranded as Wise ahead of a direct listing on the London Stock Exchange that valued the company at $11 billion.[14] The front page read "Money Without Borders." Wise disclosed it had 10 million users globally and processed £54 billion in payments. It generated profits of £30.9 million on revenues of £421 million, a net margin of 7.3%.

The prospectus reported that Wise was on average up to eight times cheaper than leading UK high street banks. Over 38% of transfers were delivered instantly and about 83% in less than a day. Wise customers can send money in 56 currencies to more than 80 countries. Wise has expanded from its consumer-focused FX roots to offer bank accounts with debit cards to individuals and small businesses in 10 countries through partnerships with local banks and challenger banks. It has partnerships with VISA and MasterCard. It also white-labels its FX service to banks and businesses.

WORLDREMIT: CHEAPER INTERNATIONAL REMITTANCES

A remittance is a money transfer sent from abroad, often by a foreign worker to support a family member or friend back home. The World Bank expected global remittance flows to reach $630 billion in 2022, driven by record flows to Ukraine following the Russian invasion.[15] Unfortunately, the cost to send remittances averages 6.5% of the amount and can be 10% or more. It may take days or weeks to arrive. This is a significant burden on individuals with low incomes.

WorldRemit was set up in 2010 by a former employee at the United Nations Development Programme to provide lower-cost remittance services to migrant communities around the world.[16] WorldRemit helped 2 million users make a mobile-to-mobile transfer on its network in 2020. Money can be sent from 50 countries and received in over 130 countries, with over 90% of transfers available in minutes. It may take longer to receive, however, depending on the recipient's country and choice of how to receive the funds. WorldRemit is regulated by the UK Financial Conduct Authority, and users who send money must verify their identity and the source of funds to comply with AML legislation.

WorldRemit is 100% cashless. Money is sent from a WorldRemit account on the sender's mobile phone to a recipient's mobile phone. The recipient can then choose to deposit the money in a bank account, pick up cash, deposit mobile money in a digital wallet, or top up airtime on a mobile phone. The money is transferred through major mobile money services globally, including M-PESA, MTN, and bKash.

The transfer can be tracked, with both the sender and the recipient notified when the transfer is initiated and received. The transfer fees vary depending on where the money is sent, but the fee for most countries is $3.99, with a currency conversion rate of only 1%.

When comparing sending US$1,000 using Western Union versus WorldRemit, one reviewer found that the recipient would receive EUR 888 using Western Union in six days and EUR 920 using WorldRemit in three days – a savings of 3.5% (EUR 32) and half the time.[17]

THE OCTOPUS CARD: A CASHLESS MEANS OF PAYMENT

Many large cities have different transportation options that each require different forms of payment: buses, streetcars, subways, ferries, and tunnels. In Hong Kong, these services can be accessed with the Octopus card – a contactless, stored-value card that provides a simple, safe, and secure way to pay.[18]

Octopus was introduced by MTR Corporation in 1997. MTR operates Hong Kong's mass transit railway system. It collaborated with the independent bus companies and ferries to develop a single payment solution for Hong Kong residents. By loading funds onto an Octopus card, customers can pay for fares using tap-and-go on any form of public transportation.

In 2000 Octopus got a boost when the Hong Kong central bank granted a deposit-taking license to Octopus Holdings, opening the door for the Octopus card to be used for non-transit-related purchases. Then in 2004 the Hong Kong government installed new parking meters that accepted the Octopus card.

The Octopus card has become a cashless means of payment accepted by 140,000 Hong Kong merchants including restaurants, supermarkets, vending machines, convenience stores, taxi rides, and many other retail businesses.[19] The card is used by 98% of Hong Kong residents, with 33 million cards in circulation, when Hong Kong's population is 7.5 million. Octopus processes 15 million transactions each day.

Octopus has expanded its product to include a mobile app for online shopping, a credit card co-branded with MasterCard and Union Pay, and a linked account with Huawei Pay and Samsung Pay. Users can collect reward points, set up automatic top-ups with bank partners, and track spending in the app.

THE RISE OF INSURTECH

The global insurance industry is a vast profit pool facing disruption from a class of fintechs called insurtechs. The size of the insurance industry is measured by the dollar value of insurance premiums paid by customers, called gross written premiums. The consultancy McKinsey & Company estimates that gross written premiums globally was US$5.7 trillion in 2020.[20]

Figure 9.3 shows that premiums have grown by around 4% per year since 2010, but growth has slowed in recent years. The most promising opportunities are in emerging markets such as Asia Pacific, Latin America, and Africa.

An insurance policy is a document detailing the terms and conditions of a contract between the insurance company and the customer. The insurance company that stands behind the policy is underwriting it. They price the risk of a payout and

Figure 9.3. Gross Written Premiums in the Global Insurance Industry

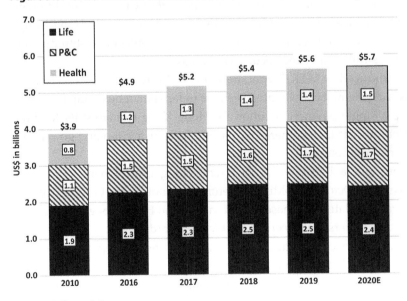

Source: McKinsey & Company.

calculate the price for coverage. The customer makes a one-time or regular payment, called the premium, which is the main source of revenues for insurance companies. The main expense are claims. A claim is when a customer seeks to collect money under an insurance policy after suffering a loss. When a claim is paid out to a customer, we call it settlement.

Insurance can be broken down into three major product sectors: life insurance, representing 42% of gross written premiums in 2020; property and casualty (P&C) insurance at 31%; and health insurance at 27%. Life insurance pays a lump sum to beneficiaries in case of disability or premature death of the insured individual. Health insurance covers expenses associated with medical treatment, drugs, and checkups. Property insurance covers damage to buildings due to fire, theft, or weather. Casualty insurance covers everything else such as auto, theft, and liability insurance.

The insurance industry has two B2B sectors that do not generate premiums but are major profit pools: distribution and management of policies and the reinsurance market. The distribution and management of insurance products is a major business, with insurance brokers selling and servicing policies written by the big insurance companies. Chances are you bought your car or travel insurance from one of these distributors. The reinsurance business is where insurance companies transfer some of their risk to other parties. Effectively, reinsurance allows an insurance company to buy insurance to protect against claims on their policies.

The characteristics of the insurance industry have created many customer pain points. Historically, insurance has featured crude pricing, inefficient paper-based onboarding and claims processing, expensive distribution networks, and a general lack of service. Insurance policies are priced based on the average from large cross-sections of customers, with little to no customization or personalization. This leads to insurance products that are generic and commoditized, with little to distinguish policies written by major insurers. If there is not enough data to price the risk accurately or demand for a niche type of coverage, insurance is not available.

On top of these features, the insurance industry is complex and highly regulated, and it requires economies of scale to be profitable. It becomes more economical for an insurer to underwrite a risk when policies are sold to a large group of customers, because the premiums from the policies that do not pay out subsidize the claims from a minority of policies. The nature of insurance underwriting does not lend itself to a P2P model, as it presents concentrations of risks that rely on scale and portfolio diversification to be managed effectively.

In summary, policies were generic, service was poor, claims processing was slow, and the prices charged to consumers were high. Complexity, regulation, and scale created barriers to entry, protecting the incumbents. These factors have created an industry ripe for disruption by technology.

Digital Transformation by Insurtechs

Insurtechs are exploiting mobile apps, cloud computing, biometrics, sensors, data science, and AI to disrupt this industry. These fintechs are exploiting big data to create customized and personalized products. They are developing new products that were not economic under the cost-heavy incumbent business models. They are creating new distribution channels using mobile apps and the internet. They are automating business processes, especially claims management, to provide a cheaper, faster, more convenient experience for customers.

Fintech disruption and investment in insurtech start-ups was slow post-2010, lagging the large investments and innovation in other lines of business. Then, starting in 2015, insurtech took off, becoming one of the hottest and fastest-growing fintech areas. Insurtechs raised close to $50 billion between 2018 and 2022, with $17.8 billion raised in the year 2021 alone. CB Insights was tracking 44 insurtech unicorns globally in 2022 with private market valuations of greater than $1 billion.[21] Some unicorns have gone public, with 20 US IPOs by insurtechs in 2020. While only a handful of insurtechs have gone public since 2020, exits via mergers and acquisitions have skyrocketed. And unlike other fintech segments, early-stage funding continues to dominate in insurtech.

These impressive figures hide a bigger story of creative destruction. While a few insurtechs are raising massive amounts of capital and growing rapidly, many smaller ones are shutting down. The consultancy Towers Wilson Watson followed a sample of 760 insurtechs that had raised capital and were a going concern at the start of 2019 and found that one-quarter had shut their doors by year-end. And the reason is not what you think. The report explains,

> Invariably these insurtechs end commercial activity for a myriad of reasons – and in many cases it is not because of bad business ideas, or bad tech, but simply a lack of market appetite or issues with personnel.[22]

Figure 9.4 shows the first-year performance of four insurtech IPOs, which all listed on a US exchange in 2020. Two of the IPOs, by Lemonade and Duck Creek, rose post-IPO to deliver a total return of 55% and 13%, respectively. But two of the IPOs, by GoHealth and Root, sank with a first-year total return of −48% and −88%, respectively. This mixed performance illustrates how the business model is crucial for determining success.

The Insurance Value Chain

The insurance industry favors scale. A few large incumbents dominate each market segment. Similarly, the B2B market for insurers is concentrated. Technology by itself

Figure 9.4. Insurtech Performance First Year Post-IPO

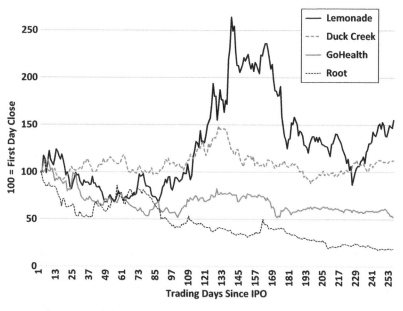

Source: Refinitiv.

does not provide a sustainable competitive advantage because it can be replicated, licensed, or acquired. The report by Towers Wilson Watson concludes that the industry simply does not need hundreds of insurtechs that essentially do the same thing but do it worse than their peers.

Figure 9.5 shows the value chain for underwriting insurance policies, broken down into two customer-facing processes and two back-office processes.

On the customer-facing end, product design and pricing describe the process of creating an insurance product to protect against a given risk and determining what premiums to charge. This step relies on historical data and statistical models to determine a price that will allow the insurer to earn a profit over time while paying out claims on some percentage of the policies. Once a product is created, it is sold to customers. The industry calls this process quote, bind, and issue. A customer meets an insurance agent, receives a quote, and purchases the policy, and the agent puts coverage in place.

On the back-office end, administration covers everything to do with records management. The insurer must keep track of the details of the policy, the customer, and their beneficiaries. The back office looks after billing and tracking changes over time. Claims and settlement are what happens when a customer wants to collect on the

Figure 9.5. The Insurance Value Chain

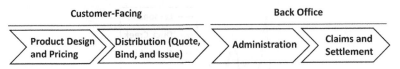

policy. The insurance company conducts an investigation and evaluates the damage, contracts with third parties to carry out any repairs, and disburses cash to the policy holder. Claims is where the insurance rubber hits the road. A customer wants to be looked after when a bad event occurs and it is time to collect on a policy.

Customer-Facing Insurtechs

Many insurtechs are using technology to customize existing insurance products or to develop innovative products that target niche markets or unmet customer needs. Greater personalization is made policy by analyzing large datasets collected by sensors, biometrics, smart devices, and the internet-of-things (IoT). Customer insights are then extracted using machine learning.

Let's take the example of customized auto insurance. Rather than pricing based on broad categories such as age and gender, the insurtech Root uses data collected from sensors in your smartphone to evaluate your driving behavior and customize the cost of your car insurance.[23] The Root mobile app measures acceleration and braking, speed of turns, average speed and driving times, and route consistency. It determines who is a safe driver and who isn't and only offers insurance to the safer drivers. The reason is simple: Because 30% of drivers cause nearly 45% of all accident costs, Root doesn't think good drivers should have to pay for other people's bad driving, so they do not insure bad drivers. This choice allows Root to offer lower-cost insurance to good drivers.

Insurtechs are selling and distributing policies directly to end-customers using online marketplaces and mobile apps. Examples of digital-only insurance companies are ZhongAn (health, accident, liability, bond, credit, auto, and lifestyle), Oscar (health), Clover (health), and Lemonade (homeowner and renter insurance).

Let's look at Lemonade, one of the most high-profile customer-facing insurtechs. Founded in New York in 2015, Lemonade started off selling insurance to renters and homeowners, before expanding into car, pet, and term life insurance. Powered by AI and behavioral economics, Lemonade set out to replace brokers and bureaucracy with bots and machine learning, aiming for zero paperwork and instant everything. By the time of its IPO in 2020, it had 730,000 customers, of which 70% were under the age of 35.[24]

The IPO prospectus described the business in glowing terms:

> Lemonade is rebuilding insurance from the ground up on a digital substrate and an innovative business model. By leveraging technology, data, artificial intelligence, contemporary design, and behavioral economics, we believe we are making insurance more delightful, more affordable, more precise, and more socially impactful. To that end, we have built a vertically integrated company with wholly-owned insurance carriers in the United States and Europe, and the full technology stack to power them.
>
> A two-minute chat with our bot, AI Maya, is all it takes to get covered with renters or homeowners' insurance, and we expect to offer a similar experience for other insurance products over time. Claims are filed by chatting to another bot, AI Jim, who pays claims in as little as three seconds. This breezy experience belies the extraordinary technology that enables it: a state-of-the-art platform that spans marketing to underwriting, customer care to claims processing, finance to regulation. Our architecture melds artificial intelligence with humankind and learns from the prodigious data it generates to become ever better at delighting customers and quantifying risk.

Further reading in this prospectus leads to this disclosure about the risks from investing:

> We have not been profitable since our inception in 2015. ... We expect to make significant investments to further develop and expand our business. In particular, we expect to continue to expend substantial financial and other resources on marketing and advertising as part of our strategy to increase our user base. ... We expect that our net loss will increase in the near term as we continue to make such investments to grow our business. Despite these investments, we may not succeed in increasing our revenue on the timeline that we expect or in an amount sufficient to lower our net loss and ultimately become profitable.

Insurtechs Targeting Emerging Risks

Insurtechs are leveraging technology to develop new products that target emerging risks in the modern economy, such as climate-related risk and cybersecurity risk. Again, underwriting new risks is possible by applying machine learning to big datasets. Examples are the Climate Corporation (weather monitoring and simulation), Traffk (big data and AI for insurance underwriting and distribution), and Cyence (cyber risk modeling).

Cyber-attacks represent one of the largest business risks globally, costing the insurance industry more than $1 trillion each year. A cyber-attack is an attempt by hackers to steal sensitive data or to damage a computer network. P&C insurance companies have been working hard to develop products to insure against cyber-attacks, but they lacked the extensive claims history and modeling capabilities to accurately price and underwrite these complex risks.

To meet this challenge, Cyence was founded in 2014 in Silicon Valley by Arvind Parthasarathi and George Ng, data scientists who had been working on AI solutions for financial service firms. While cybersecurity risks and practices were receiving a lot of attention, they saw a gap in the market for quantifying the financial impact of cybersecurity risks for insurance companies. Their value proposition was to combine cybersecurity, data science, and economics with internet-scale data collection, adaptive machine learning, and insurance risk modeling.

In 2016 Cyence raised $40 million in its first and only Series A offering. The team of data scientists, modelers, and insurance experts developed a subscription-based data listening and risk analytics solution based on machine learning. In late 2017 Cyence was acquired for $275 million by Guidewire, a B2B software provider for the P&C insurance industry.

Insurtechs Automating the Back Office

Insurtechs are developing software to help insurance companies improve their businesses. These insurtechs offer outsourcing for key functions such as marketing, underwriting, policy administration, billing, claims management, and employee benefits administration. Examples are Zenefits (cloud-based human resources), Gusto (online payroll, human resources, and employee benefits), and Namely (cloud-based human resources and employee benefits).

Insurtechs are automating many processes to reduce costs while also improving the customer experience. They respond to customers more quickly using chatbots, text messages, and streaming video. They are speeding up the process of customer onboarding, insurance applications, and claims using automation and smart contracts. They are optimizing pricing and underwriting algorithms and improving risk management of insurance portfolios using data science and machine learning. They are lowering the cost and increasing the efficiency of back-office processes using blockchain and distributed ledger technologies.

A key use-case is claims management. Insurtechs are using AI and machine learning to automate the processing of insurance claims and communications with customers. Consumers can capture and share data that is then analyzed using machine learning. Examples are Shift Technology (fraud detection), Clara

Analytics (AI-enabled workers' compensation), and Snapsheet (auto claims by photo).

Snapsheet is a self-serve mobile app that allows a customer to submit a claim for damage to their car using photos. The customer uploads photos to the app that are analyzed using computer vision, with the customer receiving a cost estimate of the repairs in 2.7 hours on average. While this front-end use of AI and digitization gets the most media attention, the real value-added is the automation of the back-office process, with 90% of auto claims handled electronically within 30 days. Most insurance companies take weeks to months to process claims using complex systems, physical interactions with customers, and a large back-office staff. Using technology, Snapsheet is faster and cheaper, addressing a major customer pain point.

Snapsheet was founded in 2011 by Brad Weisberg, a serial entrepreneur who experienced the pain customers face after being involved in an auto accident. He pivoted his initial start-up idea from focusing on auto body and repair shops to streamlining the auto insurance claims process. In 2013 he raised $10 million in a Series B round backed by the venture capital arm of the United Services Automobile Association. Snapsheet built a cloud-based claims management software that leverages digital images and automation. By early 2021 Snapsheet had raised $100 million over six funding rounds. It has more than 100 corporate partners, including many of the largest insurance carriers, insurance brokers, insurtechs, and sharing economy technology start-ups.

CASE STUDY: ZHONGAN, CHINA'S ONLINE-ONLY INSURANCE COMPANY

ZhongAn Online P&C Insurance ("ZhongAn") is China's largest online-only insurance company. It was launched in October 2013 as China's first online insurer. In September 2017 it went public on the Hong Kong Stock Exchange at HKD 59.70 (ticker: 6060.HK).[25] Following this initial public offering, its largest shareholders were Alibaba (16%), Tencent (12%), and China's largest insurance company, Ping An (12%).

ZhongAn develops and offers innovative insurance products and solutions to customers through scenario-based settings. It classifies its insurance products under "ecosystems": lifestyle consumption, travel, consumer finance, health, auto, and other. In each ecosystem, ZhongAn has partners that white-label ZhongAn's insurance products to their customers.

ZhongAn grew rapidly by partnering with leading Chinese e-commerce platforms (such as Alibaba) and online travel agencies (such as Ctrip) and has now signed more than 200 other partners (such as Didi Chuxing, Xiaomi, Ant Financial, and Bestpay). Using data on customer transactions from these partners, ZhongAn uses AI to develop and optimize new products that address unmet customer needs. For example, it pioneered shipping return insurance for e-commerce purchases, phone screen crack coverage for mobile phones, and real-time travel delay and cancelation insurance for air travel.

ZhongAn has leveraged technology to develop a competitive advantage in insurance underwriting, specifically AI and machine learning. The company operates its core insurance business entirely on its proprietary cloud-based platform Wujieshan. The company applies machine learning to the large and expanding customer data originating from its own platform and the platforms of third-party data providers. ZhongAn's product lines are capital-light in nature as it operates entirely on a cloud-based system, providing security and scale in processing the large amounts of customer data. At the time of its IPO, more than half of ZhongAn's 1,700 employees were engineers and technicians.

Table 9.3 shows ZhongAn's financial statements for the last three years, showing how it has struggled. Revenues have increased, driven higher by gross written premiums. But operating expenses have risen as well, partly due to rising claims. With operating expenses higher than total revenues in 2022, ZhongAn suffered a large loss in 2022, following modest profits in 2020 and 2021. ZhongAn was forced to take on debt in 2020, with liabilities continuing to increase to 69% of assets in 2022.

Table 9.3. ZhongAn Financial Statements

	2020	2021	2022	2020	2021	2022
INCOME STATEMENT	RMB (millions)			% of Revenues		
Gross premiums written	16,709	20,480	24,005	90	93	103
Total revenue	18,493	21,940	23,352	1	3	−7
Less: Operating expenses	18,347	21,111	25,368	99	96	109
Less: Income taxes	−108	72	−383	−1	0	−2
Net income	254	757	−1,633	1	3	−7
BALANCE SHEET	RMB (millions)			% of Total Assets		
Assets	45,673	51,772	54,557	100	100	100
Liabilities	28,280	32,642	37,531	62	63	69
Equity	17,393	19,130	17,026	38	37	31

Source: ZhongAn IPO Annual Reports.

Not surprisingly, Figure 9.6 shows ZhongAn's share price has underperformed the Hong Kong's Hang Seng stock market index. While ZhongAn's price shot up by more than 40% following the IPO, it had fallen 70% by year-end 2022 versus −15% for the Hong Kong market.

Figure 9.6. ZhongAn Share Price vs. Hang Seng Index

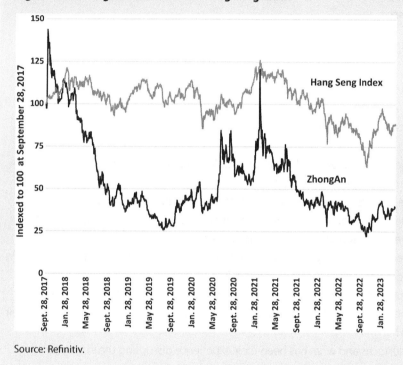

Source: Refinitiv.

Key Terms

anti-money laundering (AML)
bid-ask spread
credit card network
cyber-attack
foreign exchange (FX) transaction
gross written premiums

health insurance
insurance claim
insurtech
interchange fee
issuing (customer) bank
large value transfer system (LVTS)

life insurance
merchant (acquiring) bank
method of payment
money service business (MSB)
money transfer
payment
payment gateway
payment processor

payment rails
point-of-sale (POS) machine
property and casualty (P&C) insurance
quote, bind, and issue
real-time gross settlement (RTGS)
reinsurance
remittance

QUESTIONS FOR DISCUSSION

1 What are some of the pain points facing customers in the payments, money transfer, and foreign exchange businesses?
2 How important are payments for banks and what are the different sources of revenue?
3 What are the payment rails and what is the difference between the large value transfer system and the system for small payments?
4 Who are the players in the payments ecosystem and what roles do they play?
5 What are the sources of revenue for payment and money transfer companies? Which revenues are fee-based and which are risk-based?
6 What has been the strategy for new entrants into payments and how did they benefit from technological and regulatory changes?
7 What are examples of pain points in payments and the fintechs that solved them?
8 What are the different segments of the insurance market and how can we assess their relative size?
9 What are insurtechs and what has been their experience disrupting the insurance industry?
10 What are some examples of pain points solved by different insurtechs in customer-facing and back-office businesses?

ADDITIONAL READING

Bech, Morten Linnemann, and Jenny Hancock, "Innovations in Payments," *BIS Quarterly Review* (March 2020): 21–36, https://www.bis.org/publ/qtrpdf/r_qt2003f.htm.
McKinsey & Company, "The 2021 McKinsey Global Payments Report," October 2021, https://www.mckinsey.com/industries/financial-services/our-insights/the-2021-mckinsey-global-payments-report.

McKinsey & Company, "Creating Value, Finding Focus: Global Insurance Report 2022," February 15, 2022, https://www.mckinsey.com/industries/financial-services/our-insights/creating-value-finding-focus-global-insurance-report-2022.

Tompkins, Michael, and Ariel Olivares, "Clearing and Settlement Systems from around the World: A Qualitative Analysis," *Bank of Canada Staff Discussion Paper* 2016-14, June 2016, https://www.bankofcanada.ca/2016/06/staff-discussion-paper-2016-14/.

Willis Towers Watson, "Q3 2021 Quarterly InsurTech Briefing," October 2021, https://www.willistowerswatson.com/-/media/WTW/Insights/2021/10/quarterly-insurtech-briefing-q3-2021.pdf.

10

Digital Banking and the Response of Incumbents

SUMMARY

- Fintechs are targeting customer pain points in managing their day-to-day banking and personal finances, delivering a superior customer experience that is easier, cheaper, faster, and more convenient.
- This disruption has been enabled by technological advancements and the loss of trust post–Global Financial Crisis, propelled by open banking legislation globally.
- Fintech app developers are unbundling financial services and solving specific use-cases, selling directly to end-customers (B2C) or partnering with incumbents (B2B).
- Challenger banks began by unbundling but are now rebundling financial products and services with transparent fees, quicker service, and more personalized products.
- Financial marketplaces use application programming interfaces (APIs) to build an online platform offering third-party financial products and services to consumers.
- Financial incumbents have responded with a range of strategies based on incumbents' capabilities and scale, including building in-house, setting up innovation labs, forming strategic partnerships, licensing software, buying equity or acquiring companies, and targeting fintechs as customers.

The previous chapter examined how fintechs are disrupting payments and insurance using a variety of innovative product offerings and business models.

This chapter examines the strategies of three categories of fintechs in banking and personal finance: fintech app developers, challenger banks, and financial marketplaces. It then looks at the various strategies used by incumbents to respond to this disruptive threat.

THE NEW WORLD OF DIGITAL BANKING

Just as with other part of the financial system, fintechs are disrupting day-to-day banking and personal finance. Technological change has lowered the barriers to entry, increasing competition from within and outside the industry. Attracted by high profit margins and the many dissatisfied customers, fintechs are challenging the incumbents and transforming the customer experience.

These fintechs are following the disruption playbook outlined in Chapter 2: Target underserved customers at the bottom end of the market with a cheaper product that is good enough and establish a foothold to move mainstream. Or identify a gap that is not being served by incumbents and build a new market.

As we discussed in Chapter 1, the fintech label hides tremendous variation in both the scale and ambition of these digital challengers. They range in size from small, entrepreneurial start-ups with a handful of employees to larger, digital-only banks, to massive technology companies with global reach and billions of customers (bigtech and techfins).

Some challengers may be looking to disrupt and replace incumbents, but others want to partner with them and sell to their customers. While some fintech founders are new to financial services, others are insiders that are using technology to attack the profit pools of the incumbent banks, insurance companies, and asset managers.

Similar to the other business lines that we have examined, fintechs in banking and personal finance are solving the pain points faced by individuals and small businesses when managing their finances. The fintech value proposition is to deliver a superior customer experience that is easier, cheaper, faster, and more convenient. Even entrepreneurial start-ups with few resources are challenging larger, better-funded incumbents by leveraging technologies such as the internet, mobile phones, APIs, cloud computing, and AI. These tools allow them to rapidly and inexpensively launch mobile financial apps that provide a better user experience at a lower cost than the products and services offered by incumbents.

In this chapter, we start by looking at the strategies and business models of three distinct categories of fintechs: fintech app developers, challenger banks, and financial marketplaces. As a preview of the coming discussion, Table 10.1 highlights key features of these three types of fintechs:

- Fintech app developers are one-sided businesses that earn revenues from fees, subscriptions, advertising, and licensing of mobile apps. They are centralized and function as agents that provide software used by other financial intermediaries.
- Challenger banks are one-sided businesses that earn revenues from lending and fees and commissions from banking and money transfer businesses.

Table 10.1. Categories of Fintechs in Digital Banking and Personal Finance

	Business Model	Centralized or Decentralized?	Agent or Principal?	Monetization Strategy	Fintech Paradigm
Fintech app developer	One-sided business	Centralized	Agent	Fees, advertising	Traditional
Challenger bank	One-sided business	Centralized	Principal	Fees, commissions	Traditional
Financial marketplace	Multi-sided platform	Centralized	Agent	Fees, commissions, advertising	Transformational

- Financial marketplaces are multi-sided platforms that earn fees, commissions, and advertising revenues from the sale of financial products and services on their platforms.

We will wrap up this chapter by examining the response of incumbents, whether it is to build in-house, license, or partner with or acquire new entrants.

Pain Points in Banking and Personal Finance

People everywhere feel uncomfortable with or stressed out by banking and finance. Banks are seen as monolithic, conservative gatekeepers who control access to the financial system, earning high profits by overcharging consumers and businesses for everyday products and services. Customers may feel intimidated or anxious when meeting a bank representative.

Individuals, particularly minority and lower income groups, may struggle to access credit, be underserved, or – worse still – be shut out from the financial system. This lack of access exists in even the wealthiest economies. In 2019 an estimated 7 million US households were "unbanked," meaning no one in the household had a checking or savings account at a bank or credit union.[1]

It's not hard to find anecdotal evidence about how consumers feel about this area of their lives. Surveys routinely find most people struggle with their finances and their ability to repay debt.[2] Here's a typical headline: "70% of Americans Are Feeling Financially Stressed, New CNBC Survey Finds."[3] This 2023 survey found that fewer than half of US adults said they have an emergency fund, and more women than men admit feeling financially stressed.

A 2022 survey conducted by the UK Mental Health Foundation found 10% of UK adults were feeling hopeless about financial circumstances, more than one-third were feeling anxious, and almost 3 in 10 were feeling stressed.[4]

The COVID-19 pandemic made matters worse, destroying jobs and wealth overnight. At the onset of this crisis, two-thirds of Americans were not financially healthy, with little financial cushion.[5] A Canadian survey found that over half of the people surveyed were within $200 of not being able to cover their bills and debt payments.[6] Many individuals were struggling to save, pay for debt, or plan for the future in ways that would allow them to be resilient over time.

And then there is this thing called a credit score. This number, put together by credit agencies like Equifax and Transunion, measures the default risk you represent to lenders.[7] Your credit score is not only used by lenders and credit card companies who wonder about your ability to repay. It is also used by mobile phone and internet providers, auto dealers, insurance companies, property owners, and potentially employers.[8] Most consumers are not aware they are being graded against other people based on their risk to creditors. Do you know your credit score?

Global Financial Crisis Opens the Door

These pain points in managing personal finances represent a giant market opportunity for fintechs. But new entrants into banking face two major hurdles: regulation and trust.

Banking is a highly regulated industry. Banks and other financial intermediaries have to meet capital and liquidity requirements, and they must submit to monitoring of their operations by regulators and supervisors. Satisfying these regulations is costly and time consuming and requires deep expertise and resources.

Why are banks so heavily regulated? As we saw in Chapter 2, banks and other financial intermediaries provide valuable services to the economy, channeling savings to productive investments and providing credit and liquidity to help households and businesses manage their finances. Banks provide maturity transformation and risk sharing.

But banking is a commodity business that features low profitability. Banks offer undifferentiated goods with many substitutes, leading to high competition. Bank profit margins are below 2% on average. As we saw in Chapter 4, banks are only able to generate high returns for shareholders by using leverage, with their businesses featuring high amounts of debt (in the form of deposits and borrowing). And high leverage brings high risk of failure. This explains why bank supervisors restrict who can operate a bank, set minimum capital requirements, and enforce stringent regulations designed to limit how much risk a bank can take.

Trust in banking is built up slowly over time but can evaporate quickly. For decades, banks have invested in their brands and built relationships, attracting large customer bases and building relationships with end-customers. But the 2008–2009 Global Financial Crisis was a turning point that lowered both hurdles, opening the door for fintechs and non-financial new entrants alike.

The 2008–2009 Global Financial Crisis exposed the weaknesses in bank risk management and destroyed the trust in many of the largest incumbents in countries around the world. It opened the door to fintechs and unleashed a wave of innovation from inside and outside the industry.

Banking and currency crises occur around every five to seven years somewhere around the world. But the Global Financial Crisis was unique. It brought down the strong with the weak, infected a range of financial intermediaries (banks, money managers, insurance companies, government-sponsored entities), and spread like a contagious virus around the world. Worse still, it damaged the real economy, causing a coordinated global recession. To save their economies, politicians were forced to bail out banks using taxpayers' money.

These bank bailouts and the global recession caused a loud, intense backlash against these incumbents. Angry voters pushed politicians to pass comprehensive new banking regulations designed to make the financial sector safer and more stable by ring-fencing banking activities and reducing their leverage and profitability. Politicians also looked for ways to increase competition to increase the resilience of the financial system while lowering the costs of banking for consumers. Many countries adopted policies to encourage new entrants, introducing legislation requiring banks to share customer data (known as open banking) and easing or ignoring regulatory requirements for fintech start-ups.

Most importantly, the Global Financial Crisis tarnished or destroyed the public's trust in banks and other incumbents. A 2012 survey by *The Guardian* newspaper announced that trust in banking had hit a five-year low, with 71% of people surveyed indicating that they did not think banks have learned their lesson from the financial crisis.[9] The trust that banks had built up slowly over centuries was destroyed in a matter of months.

This loss of trust was greatest among younger generations. A 2016 survey found that 71% of millennials would rather visit the dentist than listen to their banks, while 73% would rather manage their financial services needs through Google, Amazon, Apple, PayPal, or Square.[10] Not surprisingly, millennials have been the earliest adopters of fintech applications.

The Global Financial Crisis had an unexpected benefit. It unleashed a wave of innovation from inside and outside the industry. Many disgruntled industry insiders left their former employers to launch entrepreneurial fintech start-ups. They saw an opportunity to disrupt financial services while the incumbents were weak and unhappy customers were willing to try new financial providers. These former bankers understood where the industry profit pools were located and set about draining them. These fintechs drew inspiration from innovations in consumer-product, social media, design, and e-commerce companies.

Open Banking Fuels Disruption

The loss of trust and new policies designed to encourage new entrants opened the door to fintechs in banking and financial services. But a final hurdle remains: access to banking data. Technology companies are fueled by data. And banks have been jealously guarding customer data, refusing to share it with fintechs. That's why new open banking regulations are so important for fintechs. Let's see why.

Remember the expression, "Data is the new oil," coined by British mathematician Clive Humbly? Back in 2006, Humbly was explaining the importance of big data to a British grocery store.[11] But he might as well have been talking to banks or their fintech competitors.

Customers have pain points and unmet needs. To identify these needs and develop a solution, a fintech needs data. But customer banking data is hoarded by the banks, who collect it when a customer account is opened and every time a transaction is made. This data belongs to the customer, but it is jealously guarded by the bank that holds it. These banks understand the strategic value of data.

Many people like you are willing to share their banking data with a fintech that can help solve your financial problems. You might share data with your accountant, your financial planner, or some other professional. Until recently, if you wanted a more comprehensive picture of your finances, you had two choices. You could download the data onto your computer and try to make sense of it yourself. Or you could share it with a software company like Intuit or Yodlee that has a software app to organize it.

The traditional way for a consumer to share their banking data with these fintechs is called screen scraping. Screen scraping uses software to convert screenshots into data that can be analyzed and read by a software package.

But here's the catch. Given that banks have been unwilling to share your data securely, customers using screen scraping must share their online banking details and password with the fintech. In most countries, this violates your bank user agreement, exposing you to the risk of loss. It also creates a security risk for the fintech who harvests and holds your data.

In written testimony to the US Senate, the CEO of a large US bank stated it bluntly:

> [M]any data aggregators that power third party financial technology applications continue to rely on credential-based, "screen scraping" methodologies to gather consumer financial information from financial institutions, including banks. By requiring consumers to share their bank credentials (e.g., online banking log-in ID and password), these data aggregators create significant risk to consumers' financial health, including the potential for account takeover, unauthorized payment transactions, and identity theft.[12]

Despite being a direct violation of bank user agreements, more than 4 million Canadians have used screen scraping to get their data out of their banks.[13] Why? Because frustrated consumers need help to manage their personal finances! And the incumbents won't help them.

An application programming interface (API) is a safer, faster way to share data. An API is software that allows two computers to exchange data over a network. The API takes a request from one computer, delivers it to a connected computer, and returns with the requested information.

APIs have been used for decades to transfer data inside banks, or between banks and trusted partners. Banks run closed and private APIs behind their security firewall to share data between branches located in different parts of the world. Banks use an open (or external) API to share data with other banks or with partners such as the VISA or MasterCard credit card networks. These open APIs are coded using agreed standards, data formats, and security arrangements.

Many countries are introducing open banking regulations, motivated by a desire to increase competition and help consumers. Open banking legislation came into force in 2018 in the UK and European Union, with many countries around the world following their lead. Open banking gives customers control over their banking and transaction data, allowing them to share it with third parties. The regulation forces a bank to comply with a customer's request to share this data. The bank is required to set up a secure, open API with the third party that has received customer authorization. This authorization can be revoked by the customer at any time, with the third party required to return or destroy the data.

We will see that open banking and APIs are supporting disruptors to develop fintech apps, create digital-only challenger banks, and launch financial marketplaces. These innovations are transforming how customers manage their banking and finances.

Some academic research suggests open banking may be a double-edged sword. Open banking is found to promote competition when it helps level the playing field in screening borrowers between incumbents and fintech lenders; however, if it provides fintechs with monopoly power, it can also hinder competition and leave all borrowers worse off.[14]

FINTECH APP DEVELOPERS

Personal finance software has been around for more than 30 years, led by pioneers such as Intuit (founded 1983), Yodlee (founded 1999, acquired by Envestnet 2015), and Mint (founded 2006, acquired by Intuit 2009). This dedicated software ran on desktop computers. The first banking apps for mobile phones appeared shortly after

Table 10.2. Most Downloaded Free Financial Apps, April 2023

Apple iPhone	Google Android
Square Cash App	Square Cash App
Intuit TurboTax	PayPal
PayPal	Intuit TurboTax
Venmo	Venmo
Zelle	Zelle
Capital One Mobile	Google Wallet
Credit Karma	Chime Mobile Banking
Chase Mobile: Bank & Invest	Capital One Mobile
Chime Mobile Banking	Google Pay: Save and Pay
Bank of America Mobile Banking	Credit Karma

Source: Apple App Store, AppBrain.

the 2007 release of the iPhone and Google's Android operating system. Hundreds of mobile finance apps soon began to appear, created to help customers manage their everyday personal finances. Table 10.2 lists the most downloaded free finance apps from the Apple and Google app stores.

There are fintech apps to track spending, schedule bill payments, create budgets, encourage savings, access credit, or manage loyalty points, along with many other day-to-day financial needs. There are apps to see your credit score with tips on how to improve it. There are apps that aggregate multiple accounts to generate a holistic view of a customer's finances. And there are apps designed to increase financial literacy and educate young and old consumers about managing their finances.

The value proposition of a fintech app developer is to provide an innovative, inexpensive solution that solves a specific customer pain point. To be successful, the app needs to feature simple onboarding, an intuitive user experience, strong security, and a personalized (customized) experience. Big data analytics can be used to anticipate user needs, define and target customer segments, and build deeper relationships with every user. Incorporating gamification can boost engagement. While earlier software relied on screen scraping, the latest finance apps use APIs and machine learning to securely access and analyze customer data electronically.

Single-product fintech apps may be sold directly to the end-customer (B2C), through an app store or financial marketplace, or licensed to bank partners (B2B), who integrate them in their mobile app. For the B2C channel, the app may be free to install but then charge a one-time fee. It may rely on in-app purchases or require a regular subscription. Or it may be a freemium model, where a basic version is available free for download, but a premium version with more features requires a one-time fee or subscription.

Unbundling and Rebundling Strategy

Taking a step back, we would say that these fintechs are following an unbundling strategy. Unbundling involves identifying a specific, profitable bank product and offering a better version to customers at a lower cost. For example, a fintech may offer customers a prepaid credit card but not any other products, such as bank accounts, loans, or other services. The fintech can attack incumbents at the point where they are weakest, without trying to compete based on a range of financial services.

From the point of view of an entrepreneurial start-up, unbundling and focusing narrowly makes sense. A typical start-up has a small team with limited funding and capacity. It makes sense to launch a minimum viable product and focus on building monthly recurring revenue to attract investors and raise the funding required to scale and grow the business. We talked about funding and growth stages in Chapter 3.

The fintech can offer the same product for less by minimizing product development and overhead costs. Unbundling avoids the cross-subsidies that reduce bank profitability. Banking, like grocery stores, has some products that are loss leaders to attract customers initially. These loss leaders are subsidized by more profitable products that a customer may sign up for later. The bank offers a full menu of products and services and looks at the profitability of the portfolio, not the individual items.

A bank savings account, for example, is a loss leader with high administrative costs, high regulatory costs, and low profitability. A savings account is usually required to attract a customer, who may then sign up for a credit card that is very profitable. By ignoring the loss-leader savings account, a fintech can offer the credit card more cheaply than the bank and still earn a high profit due to the lower expenses.

This strategy of unbundling financial services and focusing only on what customers want has allowed successful fintechs to establish a foothold with a group of early adopters, particularly millennials.

Once the foothold is established, the fintech can pursue a strategy called rebundling. To grow its revenue streams, it diversifies and adds complementary products and services. This portfolio of products helps engage and retain customers, making them "sticky." It also allows the fintech to attract other customers who see the value and are convinced to switch.

Unbundling and rebundling fit into Christensen's theory of disruptive innovation discussed in Chapter 2. Successful fintechs start by offering customers a cheaper product with fewer features that is good enough. The disruptor uses this product to establish a foothold at the low end of the market, then improves its quality and features to move up-market by appealing to an incumbents' mainstream customers. Table 10.3 shows examples of three fintechs that have pursued this unbundling and rebundling strategy.

Table 10.3. Fintechs Unbundling and Rebundling Financial Products

Fintech	Unbundled Product	Rebundled Products
Credit Karma (acquired by Intuit 2020)	Credit scores and reports	Credit cards, personal loans, auto loans, auto insurance, tax preparation, identity monitoring, mortgages
Revolut	Digital wallet	Bank account, debit card, payments, early salary, on-demand pay, rewards, donations, crypto, stock trading, commodities, international transfers, currency exchange, travel bookings
SoFi	Student loan	Personal loan, bank account, credit card, crypto, stock trading, mortgage, insurance (home, auto, life), small business loans, budgeting, credit score
Wealthsimple	Robo-advisor	Cash app (cash card, payments, money transfer), crypto, stock trading, tax preparation

Source: Company websites.

Fintechs Pivoting from B2C to B2B

Many fintechs have found it extremely difficult to grow and scale a consumer-facing (B2C) business. The costs to acquire new customers and build brand recognition are very high, estimated at $500 to $1,000 in advertising per customer. While millennials and later Gen Z have been early adopters, older or less tech-savvy customers have not been, continuing to view incumbents as more trustworthy.

For this reason, many fintechs in the banking and personal finance space have pivoted from a B2C to a B2B business model. While this may seem like a sell-out, the strategic rationale is compelling. Incumbent banks have large customer bases, deep pockets, and regulatory expertise. They are more hierarchical and therefore less innovative, held back by legacy information technology (IT) systems and culture. In other words, they are the perfect customers for fintechs. This realization has dawned on both founders and their venture capital investors, who want to see a path to a successful exit to their investment.

Most fintechs that sell a mobile app through the B2B channel adopt a software-as-a-service (SaaS) monetization strategy. They license the app to a bank and potentially to its rivals. The bank negotiates a monthly licensing fee that may depend on the number of users, the amount of traffic, the level of features, or some other criteria. The terms of the licensing agreement are not disclosed because it may be a source of competitive advantage for a bank.

Let's look at how two fintechs, Sensibill and Moven, have built successful businesses by partnering with banks to offer innovative products to the bank's customers.

Founded in Toronto in 2013, Sensibill has developed a mobile app for managing receipts.[15] Sensibill raised CA$2 million in seed funding in 2015 before launching the next year. Sensibill licensed its app to four Canadian banks who integrated it into the banks' mobile apps. Sensibill expanded to the US in 2017 and the UK in 2018. To use Sensibill's app, a customer takes a picture of a paper receipt or forwards an electronic receipt from a restaurant, store, or other merchant. The app processes the image, converting the text to digital format using optical character recognition (OCR) software. A machine learning algorithm uses a data library to extract up to 150 pieces of data, which are analyzed and stored.

The receipt can be tagged as a personal or business expense and automatically assigned to a specific category. The user can search and filter receipts, match receipts against credit card records, and submit receipts for reimbursement. Data can be exported to create expense reports, share with tax software, or create budgets. Receipts associated with a product warranty or specific return period are stored, with reminders set automatically as the date approaches.

We say that Sensibill's receipt management app is "white-labeled" to its bank partners. Sensibill's app is integrated into the bank's mobile app, but the bank's customer does not see any mention of Sensibill. We call this arrangement *white label* because the Sensibill logo and brand are replaced by the bank's logo and brand. Sensibill continues to run and maintain the app in the background, collecting a monthly licensing fee from the bank. Sensibill benefits from gaining access to a large customer base and stable recurring revenues that are attractive to its shareholders (and potential future investors). The bank benefits by providing their customers with an innovative solution without having to develop it in-house.

Some fintechs have evolved from white-labeling a sole product to providing a full suite of projects to their bank partners. Take the example of Moven, which was founded in the US in 2010. Moven created a mobile app that allows bank customers to better manage their personal finances.[16] Moven's value added was that its app was built using insights from behavioral economics, backed by AI software. The Moven app aggregates data across a customer's bank cards and credit cards, providing real-time spending insights while highlighting suboptimal decisions. The tagline was "make smarter decisions and increase savings." TD Bank integrated Moven's app into its own, calling this feature "TD MySpend."[17]

By 2022 Moven had rebranded as a financial wellness company, offering a suite of capabilities to bank and non-bank partners.[18] The app continues to provide account aggregation, real-time spending insights, and account services. But the product line has expanded to include access to credit, money transfer, payment options, savings tools, and wish lists. The app promotes financially healthy behaviors by supplying customer insights on spending, saving, and living smarter. Moven argues that this suite allows its B2B partners to acquire, engage, retain, and grow their customer bases.

CHALLENGER BANKS

A challenger bank is also called a digital bank, an online bank, or a neobank. These fintechs are offering the same products and services as bricks-and-mortar banks but are doing it electronically. They offer current and savings accounts, debit and credit cards, personal and business loans, mortgages, investments, and other banking products to individuals and small businesses. The end-to-end digital experience is what sets a challenger bank apart. This electronic-only experience initially appealed to millennials and Gen Z who appreciated the convenience and speed of online banking.

As a new challenger bank customer, you open an account on your mobile phone or online. The process may take less than 10 minutes and a handful of clicks. There is no need to drive to a physical branch, wait in line to meet a bank representative, or fill out multiple paper forms. In fact, no face-to-face meetings are required, although you will be required to upload identification to verify your identity (called know your customer, or KYC).

Once onboarded, your banking experience is 100% digital. The bank is open 24/7 and 365 days per year. The website and mobile app are attractive and easy-to-use, with intuitive dashboards that appeal to digital customers when viewed on mobile phones. Depositing and moving money are quick and easy. The mobile app provides graphical reports, spending statistics, and complementary tools developed by other fintechs. There are blogs, videos, and just-in-time educational resources. Often these apps incorporate gamification to boost engagement and increase retention. Any customer queries not covered in frequently asked questions (FAQs) are escalated by a chatbot to a live chat, a call center, or video chat with a representative.

Growth and Expansion

While challenger banks gained early traction with millennials, they have found it harder to attract banks' mainstream customers, who are older and more cautious and continue to put their trust in established bank brands. The view from incumbents was that digital banking might gain some market share but would never replace physical branches.

Then the COVID-19 pandemic hit. Digital banking and payments exploded. During the early months of the lockdown (between December 2019 and March 2020), time spent on digital banking apps increased by 35% year-over-year in the United States and by as much as 85% in emerging markets.[19] Over the next year, challenger bank app downloads worldwide exceeded 264 million, led by Brazil and Latin America. Challenger banks raised billions in new equity from venture capitalists and strategic partners.

Table 10.4. Leading Challenger Banks

Bank Nationality (Year Founded)	Description
Revolut UK (2015)	Revolut offers payments and banking services, including a pre-paid debit card (MasterCard or VISA), currency exchange, cryptocurrency exchange, P2P payments, and investments. Its mobile app supports spending and automated teller machine (ATM) withdrawals in 120 currencies. It secured a European banking license in 2018 and has applied for UK and US banking licenses. In 2022, it had 15 million customers in the UK, Europe, the US, Australia, Japan, and Singapore. Revolut's mid-2021 funding round valued the digital bank at US$33 billion.
N26 Germany (2013)	N26 launched in 2015, offering free online bank accounts and a MasterCard in Germany and Austria. In 2016, N26 secured a European banking license, giving it all the abilities but also the obligations of a physical bank. In 2019 it became Europe's most valuable fintech following its Series D round with a private valuation of EUR 3 billion. In 2022, N26 had 8 million customers across 24 countries in Europe, the UK, the US, and Brazil. It serves both personal and business customers.
Nubank Brazil (2013)	Nubank launched a no-fee MasterCard in Brazil in 2013, then added a cashback rewards card, a debit card, a personal bank account, payments, personal loans, life insurance, investments, and business accounts. It expanded to Mexico and Colombia. In late 2021, Nubank went public on the NYSE, valuing the digital bank at US$45 billion. At the time of the initial public offering (IPO), it had 48 million customers. By 2022, this total had grown to 75 million worldwide, of which 70 million were in Brazil.
Chime US (2013)	Chime is a fintech company, not a bank. Its banking services are provided by two FDIC-registered partners, the Bancorp Bank and Stride Bank. Its 13 million account holders have access to VISA debit cards or credit cards, free checking accounts with no minimum balance, free overdraft, an automated savings feature, and early wage access. In August 2021 Chime Financial raised $750 million in a Series G funding round that valued the company at $25 billion.

Source: Company websites.

Challenger banks can now be found in every major country, with more than 300 globally, with the fastest growth in Brazil, India, and the United States. These markets are particularly attractive given the larger number of underbanked and unbanked consumers. Table 10.4 profiles four leading challenger banks that together served 111 million customers as of year-end 2022.

The Challenger Bank Playbook

The challenger bank strategy has been to build a foothold with a sole product in their home market, serving both retail and small business customers. From this initial beachhead, challenger banks have grown their product offerings through rebundling, adding products directly or partnering with other fintechs to offer innovative products using APIs. The value proposition is lower cost, transparent fees, a fast digital-only service, and a better customer experience. They earn fees and commissions using a one-sided business model like incumbents.

The New York consultancy CB Insights has been tracking the go-to-market strategies of challenger banks. The European challenger banks began with a streamlined product offering that allowed them to onboard customers to their platforms quickly and have expanded over time to offer different banking products: deposits, loans, mortgages, credit cards, insurance, and cryptocurrencies.

For example, N26 began with a free deposit account with a debit card, with no monthly fee and no minimum balance. The account charged no fee on foreign exchange transactions and included two free ATM withdrawals per month.

The UK challenger bank Revolut followed a different strategy that was quicker, less costly, and less onerous. It registered as a licensed money service business (MSB), which allowed it to offer payment services and money transfers. Revolut initially targeted travelers by offering a digital wallet with a no-fee, prepaid debit card denominated in different currencies. This card allowed travelers to spend money in different countries without the need to have multiple bank accounts or pay foreign exchange fees. It then offered a cryptocurrency wallet and exchange that went viral.

Having established themselves in a home market, many challenger banks are moving into neighboring countries. Germany's N26 is in Europe and has expanded to the UK, the United States, and Brazil. The UK's Revolut has expanded into Europe followed by the United States, Australia, Japan, and Singapore. Brazil's Nubank has expanded into Mexico, Colombia, and Argentina.

Many challenger banks are partnering with other fintechs to grow their product offerings and scale their businesses. By connecting via API to a central platform, challenger banks can offer a full range of financial products and services to their customers. For example, Germany's N26 wants to become a fintech hub and collaborates with fintechs such as Wise on foreign exchange transfers and incumbents such as Allianz for insurance products. Starling Bank launched an API marketplace in 2018 and, by 2022, had partnered with 10 fintechs to provide credit scores, reward points, receipt management, investments, insurance, mortgages, and pension management. Revolut is using fintech partnerships to provide pension management, mortgages, real estate investing, insurance, lines of credit, and wealth management.

Regulation of Challenger Banks

Challenger banks fall into two types: ones with a banking license and ones without. A banking license is required to offer deposits covered by deposit insurance and access to central bank support. A money service business license is required to access electronic fund transfer networks, exchange one currency for another, or process money orders. But many day-to-day banking activities are not regulated, such as providing loans, overdrafts, credit cards, or other forms of credit.

A banking license is granted by the national banking supervisor who verifies the challenger bank's business plan, management team, capital structure, IT systems, risk management practices, and governance. Licensed banks must meet minimum regulatory capital and liquidity requirements, as well as ongoing reporting and supervisory requirements. The process of applying for a full banking license is time-consuming and expensive but opens many business opportunities.

The European challenger banks started by applying for banking licenses, allowing them to operate across the continent under the EU's banking passport system. Revolut began as an MSB and did not receive a banking license until 2018, when it was approved for a European banking license, allowing it to offer bank accounts and brokerage services.[20] Revolut continues to operate without a UK banking license and is waiting for approval of its US banking license.

A challenger bank without a banking license may be restricted in both its operations and its marketing. It can still manage customer relationships and offer unregulated services such as credit cards and loans, but it must partner with a licensed bank to provide the full scope of banking products and services. For example, Germany's N26 has entered the US by partnering with an FDIC-registered bank that white-labels its services to N26.[21] The US's Chime was sanctioned by regulators in 2021 and had to remove the term "bank" from its advertising, as it does not have a US banking license. Its website has the disclaimer "Chime is a financial technology company, not a bank." Chime offers banking services through two regulated banks, the Bancorp Bank and Stride Bank.

CASE STUDY: NUBANK BUILDS LATIN AMERICA'S SIXTH LARGEST BANK

The Brazilian challenger bank Nubank was founded in São Paulo in 2013 by David Vélez, Cristina Junqueira, and Edward Wible. Following a stint at Morgan Stanley, then a Stanford MBA, Vélez worked at the venture capital firm Sequoia Capital developing their Latin American business for several years until that office was shut down.[22] A year later, with $2 million in angel funding, he recruited Junqueira, who had worked at the Brazilian bank Itaú Unibanco S.A. and Boston Consulting Group, and Wible, who had worked at the private equity firm Francisco Partners and Boston Consulting Group. The three founders set about building Brazil's first digital-only bank.

Nubank's mission, as stated on their 2021 IPO prospectus, is to "Fight complexity to empower people in their daily lives." Nubank wants to reinvent financial services for consumers and small businesses to make banking simple and intuitive, convenient, low-cost, empowering, and human. The prospectus explained the core principles of the business:

> We are building our business based on four core principles: (1) a highly curated customer-centric culture that permeates everything we do; (2) the prioritization of human-centric design across all of our mobile apps, products, services, and interactions to create extraordinary customer experiences; (3) the development of advanced proprietary technologies built from the ground up by some of the best talent from around the world; and (4) the utilization and optimization of data science and powerful proprietary models that support every aspect of our business.

Nubank's product lineup covered what it called the "Five Financial Seasons" of a consumer or small business (SME) customer's journey: spending (mobile payments, credit card), saving (personal and business accounts), investing, borrowing, and protecting (insurance). By the time of its IPO, Nubank had more than 5 million customers in Brazil, Colombia, and Mexico.

The IPO prospectus explained Nubank's monetization strategy. Nubank's cost to acquire customers (CAC) was US$5 per customer, of which paid marketing accounted for approximately 20% and the remainder was printing and shipping of cards and credit bureau costs. Nubank tracked monthly average revenue per active customer (ARPAC), which by the IPO averaged $4.9 per customer. Nubank's goal was to increase monthly ARPAC by capturing a greater share of customer wallets by cross-selling additional products.

By tracking different cohorts of customers, Nubank found it was recovering the CAC in less than 12 months on average, with the contribution margin growing over time. Nubank's contribution margin is the sum of revenue from credit card, personal lending, and NuAccount products, less variable expenses (interest and other financial expenses, transactional expenses, and credit loss allowance expenses). This contribution margin was the driver of lifetime value (LTV) of customers. The earliest Nubank cohorts of customers were generating an LTV/CAC ratio of 30x (e.g., $150 LTV for $5 CAC).

By the third quarter of 2022, Nubank was one of the largest and fastest-growing digital financial services platforms worldwide, and the sixth largest financial institution in Latin America by number of active customers. Customer acquisition continued to grow, with Nubank hitting 70 million customers. Nubank reported quarterly revenues of $1.3 billion and a net profit of $7.8 million, breaking even at the holding company level. Monthly ARPAC expanded to $7.9, with the monthly average cost to serve per active customer at $0.80, underscoring Nubank's ability to scale its platform leveraging sustainable cost advantages.

Despite this success, Nubank's share price languished as the company was unprofitable on an annual basis (Table 10.5).

Table 10.5. Nubank Financial Statements, 2020-2022

US$ in millions	2020	2021	2022	2020	2021	2022
INCOME STATEMENT		US$ millions			% of Revenues	
Net interest income	269	679	2,007	43	51	62
Noninterest income	354	651	1,237	57	49	38
Revenues	623	1,330	3,244	100	100	100
Less: Provision for credit losses	169	481	1,405	27	36	43
Less: Other operating expenses	647	1,020	2,148	104	77	66
Less: Income tax	−22	−5	56	−3	0	2
Net income (loss)	−172	−166	−365	−28	−12	−11
BALANCE SHEET					% of Assets	
Cash and securities	6,722	11,787	14,253	66	59	48
Loans and other assets	3,432	8,071	15,663	34	41	52
Total assets	10,154	19,859	29,917	100	100	100
Total liabilities	9,716	15,416	25,026	96	78	84
Total equity	438	4,443	4,891	4	22	16

Figure 10.1 shows that Nubank's shares were down 65% since the IPO versus the Bovespa index, which was up 3% over the same period.

Figure 10.1. Nubank Share Performance vs. Brazil's Bovespa Index

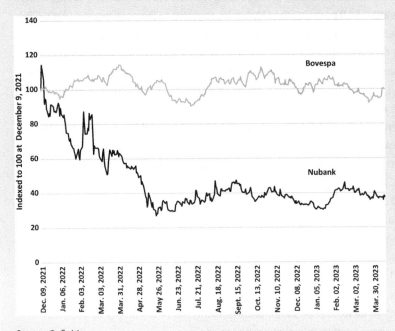

Source: Refinitiv.

FINANCIAL MARKETPLACES

Financial marketplaces are multi-sided businesses that are leveraging the cloud, APIs, and open banking to transform financial services. A financial marketplace connects customers with product offerings from fintechs, incumbents, and other financial service providers. The goal is to build an ecosystem around the online portal by creating network effects.

By bundling third-party products and services, these financial marketplaces offer customers the variety and quality of products and services of a full-service bank without the capital and regulation – banking, payments, cryptocurrencies, investments, and insurance – to appeal to mainstream customers. The financial marketplace charges a fee or commission to the money-side of their platform, namely the third party selling a product or service to a customer. They may also earn advertising revenues like ad-based e-commerce marketplaces (eBay) or social media platforms (Facebook).

Let's look at Germany's Fidor, a digital-only bank launched in 2009. The name Fidor is derived from the Latin word for trust. Fidor is built more like an app store than a traditional bank. It provides core banking services to 120,000 customers directly and provides products and services from fintechs through an API-enabled financial marketplace, called Fidor Market. Through Fidor Market, customers can get loans, crowdfunding, foreign exchange transfers, and cryptocurrencies provided by third-party partners.

Fidor's founder describes the business as an infrastructure platform with a banking license.[23] The website describes Fidor Market as a bank-as-a-marketplace: "This open banking ecosystem brings together the best products right in your customers' hands. It gives them a place to compare and choose the products of your choice, all in a secure and trusted environment."[24] Fidor was acquired by a French banking group in 2016 but by 2019 was independent again.

Not all financial marketplaces started out with a strategy to build a multi-sided platform. Some were launched as one-sided businesses targeting consumers (business-to-consumer [B2C]) but were forced to pivot after struggling to acquire customers and scale their business.

This path describes Canada's Borrowell, which originally launched in 2014 to offer low-cost online loans to individuals with good credit who were carrying expensive credit card debt.[25] Despite partnering with a major Canadian bank to offer loans to its customers, Borrowell struggled to attract customers whose credit profile fit their requirements. Too many lower-rated individuals were applying for a loan, only to be turned down.

Part of the problem was that most consumers were unaware of their credit scores. Borrowell borrowed an idea from Credit Karma in the US and began providing free credit scores to Canadians. Borrowell would only offer an online loan to customers whose credit score was high enough. While this free credit score product attracted hundreds of thousands of Canadians to Borrowell's website, few of these customers were looking for a loan. Instead, they were interested in other financial products that Borrowell was not providing. Borrowell was incurring a cost to provide a free credit score to each visitor but was unable to monetize these customers.

Recognizing an unmet customer need, Borrowell transformed its business to become a financial marketplace selling third-party financial products to Borrowell's customers. With more than 1 million Canadians having accessed their free credit score, Borrowell's platform began selling credit cards, auto loans, mortgages, savings accounts, checking accounts, and insurance from more than 40 financial partners. This financial marketplace has become Borrowell's primary business. As of 2021 Borrowell was raising capital to acquire related businesses and diversify its product offering.

CASE STUDY: CREDIT KARMA'S $7 BILLION MULTI-SIDED PLATFORM

Founded in 2007 in San Francisco by Ken Lin, Credit Karma launched its flagship product in 2008 – a mobile app that gave US consumers free credit scores and credit reports. These scores and reports, created by US credit agencies Equifax and TransUnion, are used by a variety of lenders to evaluate the creditworthiness of individuals. The Credit Karma app was free to download and use. There were no one-time or monthly fees and no paid upgrades. But users had to provide their name, address, and partial social security number to sign up and receive their credit score.

This marketing strategy was a tremendous success. By giving away something for free, Credit Karma attracted 4 million users within four years and became profitable.[26] But rather than sitting on its laurels, Credit Karma expanded its product offering. It added a comparison feature for credit cards, auto loans, mortgages, home equity loans, and student loans. It added spending alerts, bill reminders, and a "my spending" section that shows where a customer's money is going. It also added a free tax preparation product.

In 2014 Credit Karma had 32 million users and was valued at over $1 billion. By 2015 it had 40 million users and was valued at $3.5 billion. The founder talked about an IPO in the next one to two years. In 2016 revenues passed $500 million with more than 70 million users, including about half of all millennials in the US.

The product offering kept expanding. It added a product to help Americans find unclaimed money balances. After a high-profile hack at Equifax, Credit Karma launched a free identity monitoring tool that searched for public breaches of a user's personal data. It created an automotive information center that collected data from the Department of Motor Vehicles, the black book value of a customer's car, and alerts on auto recalls.

By 2018 Credit Karma had 85 million users in the US and Canada and was valued at $4 billion. It acquired a US mortgage lending platform and a UK-based credit reporting service. While the platform suffered with the onset of the COVID-19 pandemic, losing ad revenues and laying off staff, it quickly bounced back. Then, in 2020, Intuit acquired Credit Karma for $7 billion.

So, what is the secret to Credit Karma's success? It built a multi-sided platform and attracted millions of consumers by giving away credit scores, then diversifying its product offering to generate network effects. It then monetized these users by creating a financial marketplace where banks and other financial service providers paid a commission on products sold to its users. By mining data on demographics and credit scores, Credit Karma was able to customize recommendations to each user's needs. It also provided valuable analytics for the companies selling on its platform.

THE RESPONSE FROM INCUMBENTS

In his 2014 "Letter to Shareholders," JPMorgan's CEO Jamie Dimon pointed to the threat from fintechs, writing, "Silicon Valley is coming. There are hundreds of start-ups with a lot of brains and money working on various alternatives to traditional banking."[27] Not surprisingly, JPMorgan has been one of the most active US banks when it comes to investing in, partnering with, and acquiring fintech companies.

JPMorgan can afford this response, given its massive balance sheet and IT budget, thousands of staff, and millions of customers. The same is true of asset management giants like BlackRock and Vanguard, insurance companies like Manulife and Ping An, brokerages such as Charles Schwab, credit card companies like VISA and MasterCard, and investment banks like Goldman Sachs.

But what about the smaller players in banking and financial services? Our tendency is to focus on industry leaders – the apex predators in the financial ecosystem – and not to consider the mass of players who survive in their shadow.

North America and Europe feature tens of thousands of regional banks, community banks, credit unions, agricultural banks, and savings and loans institutions. In the US alone there are over 5,000 regulated deposit-taking institutions.[28] These smaller fish lack the economies of scale and deep pockets to keep up with the whales in the financial system. And they are also vulnerable to agile, innovative fintechs entering the ecosystem armed with cutting-edge technologies and design thinking. How will these smaller players survive?

There is no simple answer. The strategy to respond to fintech disruption depends on a bank's capabilities and scale.

We see bigger players building and launching in-house mobile banking apps, while smaller players are licensing apps from fintechs and providing white-label solutions to their customers. Bigger players are investing in or acquiring fintech start-ups to secure their innovative products, intellectual property, and human capital. Smaller players are partnering and collaborating with them.

Some banks are reinventing their business models. Instead of viewing fintechs as a threat, they see an attractive customer segment. These banks are providing "banking-as-a-service" – an outsourced banking back office that provides identify verification, account administration, risk management, and regulatory compliance and reporting.

During this transformation, the biggest incumbents have natural advantages that protect them. They have competitive moats around their franchises, bolstered by regulations that limit entry into some areas of their business. They have large customer bases, access to funding, financial and regulatory expertise, and the scale and budgets to outspend the fintechs. They may be held back by bureaucratic and hierarchical cultures, legacy IT systems, and expensive regulation and compliance costs. But they are much better off than the small fish.

Table 10.6 summarizes the strategies that incumbents have been following to respond to fintech disruption.

These strategies are not mutually exclusive but provide a menu of options that can be combined to achieve the incumbent's business strategy. We will illustrate these strategies by looking at examples from different incumbents.

Build In-House

The biggest incumbents have chosen to build their own digital banking apps. Among the most downloaded mobile finance apps on the Apple and Google app stores we see JPMorgan and Bank of America in the US; Lloyds and Barclays in the UK; TD and RBC in Canada; and DBS and HSBC in Asia. In only a handful of cases, incumbents have built a digital bank in-house, such as Goldman Sachs.

Table 10.6. Incumbent Strategies to Respond to Fintech Disruption

Response	Description
Build in-house	Develop and launch a mobile banking app or challenger bank
R&D	Set up an innovation lab or incubator to pursue routine or radical innovation
Partner	Sign a joint venture or strategic partnership with fintechs, competitors, or ecosystem stakeholders (venture capitalists, accelerators, universities, research partners)
License	Purchase a subscription to a fintech product or service and provide it to the end-customer, either as a branded or a white-label solution
Invest	Establish a corporate venture capital arm to buy equity stakes in a portfolio of start-ups
Acquire	Purchase a fintech start-up to acquire its technology, patents, and human capital
Target	Target fintechs as a new customer segment by providing banking-as-a-service (BaaS)

An age-old question in financial services is whether to buy or to build a modern technology. Buying a technology may speed time to market if the solution is available, but it will be expensive and may come with little or no ability to customize it. Building in-house may be less expensive and lead to a customized solution, but requires an investment in talent, management time, and other resources with no guarantee of success. The process of innovating in financial services is also complicated because the industry is highly regulated with many security and operational concerns that need to be addressed.

The consultancy Oliver Wyman recommends this strategy, keeping in mind that it is high risk and high return.[29] To be successful, the project must have strategic support from above and dedicated resources to execute it. It relies on agile methods, a cross-functional team, active customer involvement, and rapid prototyping. These principles form the basis for much of agile software development.[30]

In theory, building a fintech app in-house should bring several benefits. The project can accelerate change in a bank by challenging the conventional wisdom. Employees will gain experience building a new business, not just experimenting with new technologies. By running it like a start-up, the incumbent will give the project a more agile operating model. Like a fintech, the project should engage customers to collect feedback on design, develop a rapid prototype, test and refine it, and bring it to market quickly. This agile capability, if successful, can set an example to be leveraged across the whole business. In practice, however, these benefits are hard to realize.

Fortunately, the time-to-market and build costs have decreased dramatically thanks to advances in cloud-based services and technology. The experience of fintech start-ups has shown that it is possible to build and launch a digital banking platform in under 12 months. By leveraging technologies including cloud computing, these platforms can be brought to market at a cost under $5 million.

Set Up an Innovation Lab

One of the most common strategies for incumbents has been to set up an in-house innovation lab, complete with ping pong tables or a bowling alley, located in the company headquarters or at a stand-alone location. These research and development (R&D) facilities pursue routine or radical innovations, such as developing mobile banking apps, software to generate customer insights, or other tools.

A 2019 CB Insights report profiled over 30 fintech innovation labs run by incumbents from all parts of the world.[31] The Spanish bank BBVA was the first bank to launch an innovation lab in 2007, followed by Citigroup in 2011 and the regional Bank OZK in 2012. Dozens of banks around the world set up innovation labs between 2014 to 2017. But there has not been much to show for it.

Some innovation labs are in a unique location, while others are spread across multiple locations and countries. Some are only open to internal staff, while others collaborate with external parties. There are a variety of business models: laboratory, incubator, accelerator, or venture capital arm. Many involve partnerships with customers, existing incubators, suppliers, or local communities. Some develop apps for multiple lines of business, while others focus on a single use-case (e.g., wealth management).

While opening a fintech innovation lab is a great media opportunity, the true value is only realized over time as new apps and supporting technologies are moved from prototype and proof-of-concept phases into production. Too often innovation labs are ribbon-cutting exercises where incumbents engage in innovation theater – putting on a show for external stakeholders but never delivering results. Innovation labs may be seen as "techwashing" – a public display that does not produce results.

Form Strategic Partnerships

Incumbents are responding to the fintech threat by forming joint ventures with other incumbents, partnerships with fintechs, and business relationships with external organizations such as accelerators, venture capitalists (VCs), and universities.

An example of a successful fintech joint venture is Canada's system of electronic money transfers called e-Transfers. Canada's six largest banks dominate the banking and payments system. Being a small number in an open economy, the Canadian banks have a history of working together to solve common problems and head off competition from foreign banks, particularly US banks looking to expand northward. In the 1980s they formed the non-profit Interac Association to set standards for electronic fund transfers and later added debit card and other point-of-sale methods of payments.

While the banks were not facing a direct fintech threat, they agreed to collaborate nonetheless to provide fast, cheap, and secure P2P money transfers. In 2003 they created Interac e-Transfers, which allow customers to send money directly to each other via email (and later via mobile app) without sharing any personal financial information. An e-Transfer can be received by entering a password or deposited automatically at participating Canadian banks, credit unions, and trusts.

Another strategy is to form partnerships with third parties that bring expertise and capacities missing in the incumbent. In 2016 Canada's Scotiabank launched a new digital strategy designed to support the shift to becoming more customer focused. One pillar of this strategy focused on partnerships, explicitly recognizing that the bank did not have the required expertise in-house. Scotiabank signed agreements with three classes of partners: venture capitalists, fintechs, and researchers.

Scotiabank began working with two venture capital firms that specialized in AI and fintech, respectively. The bank signed licensing agreements with fintech start-ups in online lending, payments, personal financial management, blockchain, AI, and digital identity. And it signed research agreements with leading business schools in Canada and the United States and technology accelerators. While it is hard to assess whether these partnerships have been successful or not, they have brought outside expertise into the bank and exposed bank employees to many external innovations and forms of collaboration.

The US banks were facing disruption from Venmo, a mobile payments app launched in 2009 and acquired by PayPal in 2013. Venmo's fast, safe, and cheap money transfers, combined with its social networking features, allowed it to quickly become one of the most widely used apps among millennials. The largest US banks responded with the joint venture Zelle, a competing mobile app. The seven banks – Bank of America, BB&T, Capital One, JPMorgan, PNC Bank, US Bank, Citibank, and Wells Fargo – jointly owned Early Warning Services LLC, a private company formed in the 1990s to share data and reduce deposit losses. Over the next two decades, these banks used this company to tackle shared problems: check validation, fraud detection, and identity risk management.

Faced with disruption by Venmo, they developed and launched Zelle in 2017 to allow their customers to send money instantly through the banks' mobile apps. Zelle is now available to the 100 million customers of the 280 US banks and credit unions on the Zelle network.[32]

License Software

Many incumbents are fintech customers, licensing their software or capabilities through a SaaS model. This is the flip side of a B2B strategy for a fintech mobile app developer. We saw how the fintechs Sensibill and Moven were white-labeling their mobile banking apps to banks in Canada, the US, and the UK.

There are countless examples of banks licensing mobile apps from fintechs. For example, in late 2018, JPMorgan announced an agreement with the fintech data aggregator Plaid. JPMorgan recognized that its customers want to use popular financial apps and wanted to give customers this ability while protecting their financial data. In effect JPMorgan has seen the open-banking writing on the wall and decided to give their customers control over how their data is accessed and used. By connecting Plaid to the bank's secure API, JPMorgan's retail bank allows its customers to share data safely and quickly with the fintech apps supported by Plaid, while protecting their bank username and password.

Founded in San Francisco in 2012, Plaid is the leading data aggregator for financial services. Data aggregators are multi-sided platforms that earn fees for collecting customer data across multiple financial intermediaries to provide a complete picture of a customer's finances. With a customer's permission, Plaid uses APIs to collect data from banks, credit card companies, brokerages, mutual fund companies, fintechs, and many other financial and non-financial businesses. This data is linked and aggregated to create a holistic picture of the customer's activity and needs.

The Plaid co-founders' original plan was to create a personal financial app for consumers. The founders struggled, however, to connect customers' bank accounts. They realized that there was a business need and so pivoted Plaid's core business to build a data aggregator that serves fintechs and incumbents.

Plaid has built a suite of APIs that provide secure access to a customer's accounts for mobile banking and personal finance apps. Plaid describes its business as "the easiest way for users to connect bank accounts to an app." Plaid's APIs verify a user's identity, assets, income, and employment; access detailed transaction history and real-time account balances; authenticate bank accounts for payments; and build a comprehensive view of a customer's accounts and investments.

Plaid has signed more than 10,000 partners, including banks (American Express, Bank of America, Capital One, JPMorgan), payment fintechs (Paysafe, Wise, Venmo), online lenders (LendingClub), robo-advisors (Acorns, Betterment, Robinhood), personal finance apps (Intuit, Wave, Drop), and cryptoexchanges (Coinbase, Gemini). In 2020, VISA made an offer to acquire Plaid for $5.3 billion, but the US Department of Justice blocked the merger on competition grounds. Undeterred, Plaid raised $425 million in a Series D funding round in April 2021, valuing the fintech at $13.4 billion.

Buy Equity in Start-Ups

Many incumbents have become early-stage investors in fintech companies, setting up in-house venture capital funds to screen and invest in fintech start-ups. According to CB Insights, the most active banks making equity investments in fintechs (based on number of deals) are Goldman Sachs, Citigroup, and JPMorgan in North America, and Santander, UBS, and BNP Paribas in Europe.[33] These banks are investing across data analytics, infrastructure, alternative lending, payments and settlement, and capital markets software. In recent years, these incumbent VCs have focused on infrastructure software to respond to new open-banking and privacy regulations.

One example is Canada's Royal Bank of Canada (RBC), which unveiled its VC-investing business called RBC Ventures in mid-2018.[34] The staff of 150 report to the chief strategy officer, who reports to the CEO. Under the slogan "Beyond Banking," RBC Ventures began investing in start-ups that would allow the bank to engage with customers in four areas of their lives other than banking: home, mobility, business, and lifestyle.[35] One of the acquisitions was MoveSnap, a personal moving software for real estate agents that would allow the bank to engage with customers around their homes. RBC wanted to be the first choice for taking out a mortgage, taking out a loan or home equity line of credit, or setting up a new bank account. RBC Ventures has also bought mobile apps specializing in setting up small businesses (Ownr) and helping immigrants to Canada to get settled (Arrive) and a company that helps consumers measure and reduce their carbon footprint (Goodside).

Acquire Fintechs

If an incumbent is not satisfied holding a minority stake in a fintech alongside its rivals and other investors, it can always buy the company. Acquisitions allow the buyer to take control of the company and its intellectual property and potentially retain talented employees.

In October 2017 JPMorgan announced the acquisition of the payments company WePay. While the price was not disclosed, it was believed to be above $220 million, making it JPMorgan's largest fintech acquisition as of that date. Founded in 2008, WePay allows merchants, e-commerce vendors, and online marketplaces to accept different forms of payment. WePay also makes it easy for mobile app developers to integrate payments into their software. This acquisition was part of JPMorgan's digital strategy: to provide customers with the products and services they want, when and how they want. JPMorgan planned to roll out WePay's payment technology to its 4 million small business customers.

But acquisitions of fintechs do not always work out. Take the 2016 acquisition of the challenger bank Fidor by BCPE, France's second largest bank, for EUR 150 million. After only two years, BCPE and Fidor announced plans to separate. Fintech blogger Chris Skinner summed up the BCPE strategy this way: "They absorbed Fidor Bank and did nothing with it. No integration, no development, no plan."[36] Skinner concluded that there was a clash of cultures between an innovative fintech start-up and an old, risk-averse, incumbent bank. The lesson: Banks need to devise a clearer strategy for their fintech acquisitions, instead of holding them at arm's length and occasionally dipping into their technology brain trust for ideas.

Target Fintechs as Customers

Banking is a highly regulated industry with rules around compliance, reporting, and risk management. Many fintechs do not possess this expertise, which is costly and time-consuming to acquire. And the fintech may find it difficult or impossible to get the banking license required to offer deposits.

Some banks see this pain point for fintechs as a market opportunity. Instead of seeing a threat, these banks view fintech as a new and attractive customer segment. They offer a product called banking-as-a-service (BaaS). BaaS allows fintechs to offer banking products and services to their customers, white-labeled through the fintech's mobile app. The fintech looks and acts like a bank to its customers. But the regulatory side of the business is managed by the bank partner, leaving the fintech to focus on what they do best: providing their customers with a wonderful experience using technology.

The BaaS bank is regulated and meets with bank supervisors. They hold customer deposits, underwrite loans, comply with capital and liquidity regulations, and satisfy KYC and AML requirements. Through this partnership, a fintech's customers get access to FDIC-insured deposits and global payments, providing the ability to transfer money cross-border and trade in foreign exchange.

Rather than giants like JPMorgan or RBC, smaller, regional banks have seized this opportunity. These are the banks that lack the scale to compete with the largest banks head-on. These smaller banks also lack the agility and innovation to compete with fintechs. But smaller banks have regulatory expertise and hold a license to run a bank. Smaller banks are also more agile and responsive than large incumbents and can respond quickly to the needs of fintechs, including integrating systems and creating new products.

As a result, a growing number of low-profile regional and community banks are quietly running the plumbing underneath billion-dollar fintechs such as the challenger bank Chime, the cryptoexchange Coinbase, the online lender LendingClub, the trading app Robinhood, and the payment company Square.[37] These banks have names such as the Bancorp Bank, Celtic Bank, Cross River Bank, Evolve Bank & Trust, and Sutton Bank. The leader in this space is WebBank, an FDIC-insured, state-chartered bank headquartered in Utah. Table 10.7 shows a selection of WebBank's 25 fintech customers in 2020.

Table 10.7. WebBank's Fintech Partnerships and Product

Fintech	Product
Avant	Consumer installment loans and MasterCard credit card
CAN Capital	Business loans
Klarna	Consumer revolving credit accounts
LendingClub	Unsecured personal loans, small business loans, auto refinance loans
PayPal	Working capital and business loans
Prosper	Unsecured personal loans
Shopify Capital	Merchant loans
Upgrade	Unsecured personal loans

Source: WebBank.

CASE STUDY: MARCUS BY GOLDMAN SACHS

In October 2016 US investment bank Goldman Sachs attracted headlines when it launched Marcus, a digital bank targeting US retail customers. It was named after Goldman Sachs' founder and set a goal of helping people achieve financial well-being. Marcus initially offered personal loans and savings accounts but expanded to offer deposits, credit cards (co-branded with Apple and General Motors), a robo-advisor for investment and retirement accounts, and a soon-to-be-launched checking account.

The Marcus website explains the value proposition: value (with products designed to help customers meet their financial goals); transparency (about pricing and fees); and simplicity (with no jargon, an intuitive digital experience, and real people available through the contact center). Privacy and security are protected with multi-factor authentication, firewalls, and other safeguards.

Goldman moved from inception to launch of Marcus in 12 months, using existing platforms, open-source software, and external APIs. Marcus has grown through acquisitions: GE Capital's US online deposit business in early 2016, the personal finance app Clarity Money in 2018, and the buy-now-pay-later lender GreenSky in 2021. Marcus expanded into the UK retail banking market in 2021 with plans to add a robo-advisor later.

By Q3 2022 Marcus served more than 15 million customers, with $110 billion in deposits and $19 billion in loans outstanding. The segment information for consumer banking for fiscal year 2021 showed revenues of $2.2 billion, consisting of net interest income on loans, credit cards, and deposits. Expenses were at 84% of revenues in 2021. The consumer banking segment generated a return on average common equity of 4%, far below the 23% earned by the entire investment bank.

Despite this early success, Marcus has disappointed investors, with equity analysts voicing their criticism of the business. Segment results showed that Marcus lost $3 billion from early 2020 to late 2022. In October 2022 Goldman Sachs CEO David Solomon announced the bank was pivoting away from its previous strategy of building a full-scale digital bank after making many missteps with Marcus: product delays, executive turnover, branding confusion, regulatory missteps, and deepening financial losses.[38] Goldman will continue to use Marcus to provide services to its wealth management clients but no longer serve retail clients. Goldman has stopped originating loans and rolled Marcus into its Asset & Wealth Management Business (and no longer discloses consumer banking as a segment). The mediocre performance of Marcus shows that it is not only new entrants who have struggled to be successful in fintech!

Key Terms

banking-as-a-service (BaaS)

business-to-business (B2B)

business-to-consumer (B2C)

challenger bank

credit score

data aggregator

financial marketplace

incumbent

joint venture

neobank

open banking

pain point

rebundling

screen scraping

unbanked

unbundling

white label

QUESTIONS FOR DISCUSSION

1 What is an example of a customer pain point in banking and how does a fintech address this?

2 How did the 2008–2009 Global Financial Crisis lower the barriers to entry for fintechs into banking?

3 What is the value proposition of a fintech app developer and their strategy for building and scaling their business?

4 Why do fintechs want to adopt a B2B model and white-label their mobile apps to incumbents?

5 What is a challenger bank and how is it different from a traditional bricks-and-mortar bank?

6 How are challenger banks doing around the world and who are some leading players?

7 What has been the go-to-market strategy of challenger banks and are they regulated?

8 What is the business model and monetization strategy of a financial marketplace?

9 What are some of the strategies adopted by incumbents in response to fintech new entrants?

10 What is banking-as-a-service (BaaS) and what are the advantages for both the fintech and the bank partner?

ADDITIONAL READING

11FS, "Decoding: Banking as a Service," accessed April 1, 2022, https://info.11fs.com /decoding-banking-as-a-service.

CB Insights, "The Challenger Bank Playbook: How 6 Digital Banking Upstarts Are Taking on Retail Banking," June 3, 2021, https://www.cbinsights.com/research/report/challenger -bank-playbook/.

Senate of Canada, "Open Banking: What It Means for You," June 19, 2019, https:// sencanada.ca/en/info-page/parl-42-1/banc-open-banking/.

Oliver Wyman, "Time to Start Again: The State of the Financial Services Industry 2019," accessed July 30, 2019, https://www.oliverwyman.com/our-expertise/hubs/the-state -of-the-financial-services-industry-2019.html.

11

Techfins and Bigtech in Financial Services

SUMMARY

- While fintechs were initially seen as disrupting financial services, the consensus is that the greatest threat comes from Chinese techfins and North American bigtech companies.
- Alibaba and Tencent have built platform ecosystems that addressed institutional voids in China's economy by providing financial services to underserved or unbanked consumers.
- From a foundation in payments, Alibaba's Ant Group and Tencent expanded to offer money market funds, loans, wealth management, insurance, and banking to their large user bases.
- The North American bigtech companies are following the techfin playbook by moving into select financial services but have failed to move beyond payments.
- Amazon's payments, cash products, and merchant loans support its e-commerce business. It has built internally, learning through trial and error, rather than relying on external partnerships.
- Apple has partnered with incumbents to protect its share of the smartphone market by providing increased functionality on the iPhone and Apple ecosystem.
- Facebook and Google have struggled to move beyond payments; Facebook's cryptocurrency project was canceled, while Google's launch of bank accounts was scrapped.

The previous chapter examined how challenger banks and financial marketplaces are disrupting banking, and the responses of incumbents.

This chapter examines the entry of the Chinese techfins and North American bigtech companies into the financial service industry.

THE MOST DISRUPTIVE FINTECHS?

When the media first started covering the fintech sector, the consensus was that agile, innovative fintechs were set to disrupt the financial sector and were targeting the industry's profit pools. This view was supported by the billions of dollars of venture capital investment that flowed into these entrepreneurial start-ups globally.

A widely read Goldman Sachs analyst report stated: "We see over $4.7 trillion of revenue at the traditional financial services companies at risk for disruption by the new, technology-enabled, entrants. Assuming a 10% profit margin implies a $470 billion total profit pool at risk."[1]

These grim predictions have not materialized. While a handful of fintech companies have established themselves as leaders in their respective businesses, the majority of fintechs are struggling to scale. Entrepreneurs and their venture capital backers have recognized how costly it is to acquire customers and build consumer-facing brands. Meanwhile, regulatory scrutiny has increased, and financial incumbents are responding with their own digital innovations. Many fintechs have pivoted from competing head-to-head with incumbents to licensing or partnering with them.

Bank insiders and industry experts point to a bigger threat coming from outside the industry. The new entrants are global technology companies such as Alibaba, Tencent, Amazon, Apple, Facebook, and Google. These agents of disruption are known as techfins and bigtech.

The term *techfin* was coined by Alibaba's Jack Ma in 2016 to describe Alipay, the payment arm of the Alibaba ecosystem. He reversed the fintech acronym to acknowledge that these companies are technology platforms first and offer financial services second. They began with e-commerce, online shopping, social media, and gaming. But over time they have expanded into financial services to meet the needs of their growing customer bases, starting with payments, then adding money market funds, wealth management, and insurance. They provide these products directly or via third parties.

Bigtech is an apt nickname, as the stock market capitalization of these companies is far bigger than the world's largest financial institutions, including VISA, JPMorgan, MasterCard, and Bank of America from the United States; and state-owned Industrial and Commercial Bank of China (ICBC), China Construction Bank, and Bank of China from China (Figure 11.1).[2]

Figure 11.1. Market Capitalization of Bigtech/Techfin vs. Financial Incumbents

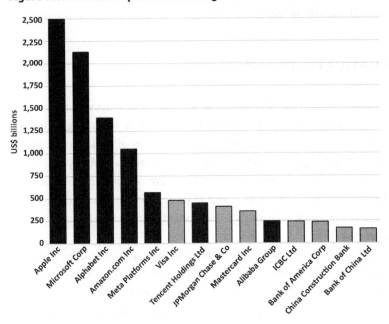

Source: Refinitiv Eikon, December 31, 2022.

The new consensus is that Chinese techfins and North American bigtech companies pose a threat to financial incumbents. But do they really? These technology companies are not looking to replace the banks, because they do not view banks as their competitors. Instead, techfins and fintechs are focused on their customers and want to create a simple, low-cost, and delightful experience. In so doing they are bundling financial services with non-financial products. Their goal is not to displace the banks but to meet the needs of their customers.

Techfins and bigtech are customer-centric. They share this focus with fintechs. But unlike fintechs and other financial intermediaries, techfins and bigtech are not selling financial products and services to customers to make a profit. The goal is to provide financial services to help customers live better lives.

In other words, techfins and bigtech view financial products and services as enablers (or loss leaders) to attract and retain customers on their platform ecosystems. The profits then come from creating network effects and selling non-financial products and services to users and monetizing the other sides of their multi-sided platforms.

This paradigm shift is the reason that financial incumbents should be worried. Banks, insurance companies, and asset managers are product centric. They view

customers as a source of profit. With techfins and bigtech platforms providing a superior user experience and variety of products and services to meet customer needs,
the incumbents risk losing contact with customers and becoming manufacturers of financial products and services. These incumbents are becoming the bakers and farmers whose commodity products are fighting for space on the shelves of the online
marketplaces controlled by Alibaba and Amazon.

The CEO of Canada's largest bank highlighted this risk of disintermediation
in a media interview about the threat from techfins and bigtech: "The massive
fear … is you're beholden to the platform to sell your customer back to you.
That is the fear that [bankers] all have. That they have these massive, powerful
portals that will see consumer intent and initially sell it back to us and take a
disproportionate share of the margin in doing so. Or worst case, meet that need
themselves."[3]

Commentators point out that banks have been under threat of disruption before
but have survived and in fact thrived over time. In this view, banks have the unique
ability to offer safe, liquid deposits that are subsidized by deposit insurance schemes.[4]
This claim may be true now, but it is undermined by the willingness of banks to license this ability to technology companies by partnering with them or selling it as
banking-as-a-service (BaaS). And supervisors may be forced to change the rules, like
the way they allowed investment banks to become chartered banks during the height
of the 2008–2009 Global Financial Crisis.

Critics argue that techfins and bigtech companies are simply monetizing user data
by adding a financial layer to their e-commerce and social networking businesses.[5]
These new entrants have benefited from a permissive regulatory environment. But as
their financial activities have grown, regulatory scrutiny has been increasing. In this
view, the threat of disruption is overstated and – like the predictions about disruption
by fintechs – will fade with time.

These critics are describing the world as it is, not necessarily the world as it may
be. In the coming years, techfins and bigtech may be brought inside the regulatory
perimeter much like efforts to encircle shadow banks. Techfins and bigtech are addressing supervisory concerns by partnering with regulated banks, addressing this
concern in both advanced and emerging market economies.[6]

The key question: I is the threat from these new entrants real or not? Will the
Chinese techfins be able to export their business model abroad? And will North
American bigtech companies succeed in their push into financial services? To answer these questions, we review the history and strategies of techfins and bigtech
as they have moved into financial services. We examine their key competitive
strengths and gauge the threat they pose to financial incumbents over the coming
decade.

CHINESE TECHFINS: ANT GROUP AND TENCENT

Tencent is China's social media and gaming platform, founded in 1998, which operates the WeChat instant messaging app. It added a payment feature in 2005, but it did not really take off until 2014, when the WeChat red envelope campaign went viral following a highly successful launch at Chinese New Year.

How serious is the threat from the techfins? Very serious. Alibaba and Tencent combine the culture of innovation and technical expertise of Silicon Valley start-ups with the customers and scale of Wall Street banks. Both techfins have attracted hundreds of millions of customers. Starting from a beachhead in payments, they have expanded into financial services: deposits, loans, investments, and insurance.

Ultimately, the Chinese techfins want to create a world where customers have access to financial services just like tap water – you turn the tap and water just flows out. The customer does not have to worry about where the water comes from or even who is supplying it. They just know that it is there when they need it.

Interestingly, Alibaba and Tencent did not set out to disrupt financial services. It was never their goal. Instead, they were pushed into it as they sought to overcome problems posed by China's underdeveloped banking system. This journey is illustrated by the creation of Alipay.

Alibaba Creates Mobile Payments

As a pioneer in Chinese e-commerce, Alibaba recognized early on that its online marketplace was being held back by a lack of trust between buyers and sellers.[7] We talked about this problem in Chapter 9 on payments. Customers were hesitant to pay for goods purchased online, fearing merchants would not deliver them.

At the time, China featured an underdeveloped payment system, with little penetration of cards and debit cards.[8] It was time consuming and expensive for consumers to transfer money. Small businesses were held back by a lack of credit, financially constrained and underserved by the local state-run banks. The Chinese financial system and telecommunications infrastructure needed massive investment for China's economy to continue to grow and meet the needs of its citizens.

Alibaba set up Alipay in 2004 to fill these institutional voids. Alipay is an online payment gateway modeled on PayPal (which had begun operation in 1999). Alipay charged no transaction fees and increased trust in e-commerce by holding customer payments in escrow accounts that would be released to merchants once the goods were delivered. This model proved so successful that Alibaba soon opened Alipay to third parties, both online and offline merchants and service providers.

Alipay was very successful and grew exponentially. By late 2008 its internet payments service had 100 million registered users, with daily transactions reaching 2 million. A year later it had doubled to 200 million users with 5 million daily transactions, then tripled to 300 million users by March 2010.

In November 2009 Alipay launched its first mobile payments app. Alipay grew even faster to become the dominant player in third-party mobile payment transactions, processing more than 50% of all mobile transactions within a few short years.

But here's the interesting part. Alipay's rapid growth was made possible by strategic partnerships with the Chinese banks. The banks had the customers and controlled access to the payment rails. Alipay offered these incumbents a fantastic innovation that addressed their customer pain points. Alipay signed partnership agreements starting in 2005 with the 5 major state-owned banks and 15 national banks, as well as the credit card network VISA. Through these partnerships, Alipay made it possible for customers to pay with a credit card or other electronic means of payment, which had not been widely available due to few Chinese customers having either credit or debit cards.

Alipay introduced product innovations to solve customer pain points. Early on Alipay recognized that Chinese consumers were nervous about e-commerce and concerned about theft. So Alipay set up a 24-hour customer service hotline and began offering compensation against account theft.

Alipay developed voice-controlled payments for mobile users and open-sourced its mobile Wireless Application Protocol (WAP) to allow third parties to connect to Alipay's services. Alipay signed partnerships with utility companies that allowed individuals to pay their bills online. They added biometric payments using fingerprint and face recognition.

Alipay launched a digital wallet to facilitate mobile payments. Using the Alipay Wallet, users could store and pay with credit cards, gift cards, and discount coupons and make electronic fund transfers via the internet. The Alipay wallet made it possible to pay offline by scanning ubiquitous quick response (QR) codes. These innovations made it easier for customers to shop online on Alibaba's marketplaces or offline in physical stores.

A similar desire to help its customers led Alibaba to begin offering other financial services. Alipay began with a money market fund (Yu'ebao), then added a wealth management marketplace (Zhao Cai Bao), a small business lending business (Aliloan), a credit scoring business (Zhima Credit or "Sesame" Credit), and digital banking (MYbank).

- **Money market fund (Yu'ebao)**: As e-commerce expanded, Alipay saw users were holding large balances in their Alipay accounts, which did not pay any interest. So, in June 2013, Alipay launched a high-interest money market account called Yu'ebao, which means "spare treasure."[9] Alipay customers could transfer as little as RMB1 into their Yu'ebao account, which paid an annual interest rate of 5% to 6%, double the rate available on a bank deposit. By mid-2017 Yu'ebao had attracted $165 billion, making it the world's largest money market fund (ahead of JPMorgan's US$150 billion government money market fund). Yu'ebao peaked at $250 billion in March 2018, before regulatory pressure led Alipay to impose daily liquidity limits, contributing to a decline in deposits to $168 billion by year-end 2018.

- **Wealth management (Zhao Cai Bao)**: Most Chinese consumers have little financial literacy and no familiarity with investing and financial products. China did not have a wealth management industry; Chinese banks only offered investment advice to high net worth individuals. So, in April 2014, Alipay launched a marketplace for third-party investment products called Zhao Cai Bao, providing an electronic source of wealth management services for regular citizens.
- **Small business lending (Aliloan, renamed Ant Credit)**: Alibaba found that its merchants could not get loans to finance working capital due to a lack of collateral. In 2010 Aliloan began offering unsecured microloans to merchants with the credit limit determined using big data analysis of merchant behavior in the Alibaba ecosystem. At the time of its US initial public offering (IPO) in 2014, Alibaba's prospectus disclosed that it had made US$2.1 billion in microloans to merchants. By year-end 2017, this total had reached $5 billion.
- **Credit scores (Zhima Credit)**: China did not have a comprehensive system of individual credit scores or histories, limiting access to credit for most consumers. Ant Financial, therefore, set up Zhima Credit (Sesame Credit) in 2015, which leveraged big data to provide consumer credit scores based on users' past payment history and their online behavior, including reputation scores on Alipay, Taobao, and Tmall and connections in their social network.
- **Digital banking (MYbank)**: In 2015 Ant Financial launched an online bank, MYbank, with a mission to serve small businesses and farmers in rural locations who had no access to banking. MYbank is a joint venture with a privately owned conglomerate, with Ant Financial holding a 30% stake. Within its first two years, MYbank had provided microloans averaging RMB 30,000 to 5 million small businesses, with a non-performing loan ratio between 2% and 4%.

We need to recognize that Alibaba did not create Alipay as a strategy to grow its revenues. Instead Alipay emerged organically as a solution to the pain points faced by merchants and customers. In fact, Alipay did not receive an official license to operate a money payment business until May 2011, six years after it began operation. As a regulatory condition for receiving this license, Alibaba was required to set up

Alipay as stand-alone company, called Small and Micro Financial Services Company. Alibaba retained a 33% minority stake, with Jack Ma as Alipay's majority shareholder with 46% control.[10]

From Alipay to Ant Group

In May 2014 Alibaba announced plans to list its shares in the US through an IPO. In preparation for this stock exchange listing, Alibaba was restructured to address regulatory restrictions that prevented foreigners from owning a Chinese payment gateway. Alibaba spun off its other financial units (Yu'ebao, Zhao Cai Bao, Ant Credit, and MYbank) in Alipay, creating Ant Financial Services.

Ant Financial's stated mission was to "bring small and beautiful changes to the world." The ant was chosen as its logo, symbolizing the combined efforts of these small but powerful insects to work toward a common goal. This goal: to use technology to enable financial inclusion. Ant Financial would provide access to capital and financial services to young people, small businesses, and poor consumers globally that were underserved or unbanked.[11]

In June 2015 Ant Financial completed a Series A round of financing for an undisclosed amount, then a US$4.5 million Series B round in April 2015, and finally a massive US$14 billion Series C round in June 2018 (led by Singapore's Temasek Holdings and GIC).[12] Ant Financial raised US$3.5 billion in debt in May 2017 to finance expansion and international acquisitions.

Ant Financial expanded to become a full-service financial intermediary. It provided customers with the products and services to manage their financial lives, called "FinLives."[13] In addition to the existing payment, lending, wealth management, and banking services, Ant Financial added other products:[14]

- **Consumer lending**: In 2014 Ant Financial set up two consumer lending businesses, Ant Credit Pay (Hua Bei) and Ant Cash Now. Using Zhima Credit scores, consumers can apply for a loan using the Alipay app in three minutes and get approval in one second with no human intervention.
- **Wealth management**: In August 2015 Ant Financial established Ant Fortune as a comprehensive wealth management platform catering to users with little financial expertise. It charges no fees and provides access to Yu'ebao and Zhao Cai Bao. In 2017 Ant Financial opened a wealth management marketplace, Caifu Hao, allowing third parties to sell wealth management products to its customers.
- **Insurance**: In late 2013 Ant Financial partnered with Chinese insurance company Ping An to launch China's first online insurance company, ZhongAn Online P&C Insurance Company. Ant Financial developed an insurance marketplace called

Table 11.1. Ant Group's Size and Scale

1,000+ million Alipay app annual active users	80+ million Alipay app monthly active merchants
711 million Alipay app monthly active users	729 million Alipay app digital finance annual active users
2,000+ partner financial institutions	200+ countries with online payment services
RMB118 trillion total digital payment volume in mainland China	RMB1.7 /0.4 trillion credit tech consumer / SMB credit balance
RMB4.1 trillion invest tech assets under management	RMB52 billion insurtech insurance premiums and contributions

Source: Ant Group 2020 IPO Prospectus, p. 139.

Ant Insurance Services, where 80+ insurance partners can sell insurance online. Ant Insurance promises a seamless claims process that takes two minutes to file online, with reimbursement in two hours. Ant Financial launched a health insurance plan that provides basic medical coverage with the risks and expenses distributed across all members.[15]

- **Equity crowdfunding**: In 2015 Ant Financial established ANTSDAQ, the first licensed equity crowdfunding platform in China. Entrepreneurs raise capital from high net worth investors who meet minimum wealth and income limits.[16]
- **Global payments**: Alipay has expanded globally, partnering with Paytm in India, Ascend Money in Thailand, Kakao Pay in South Korea, Mynt and GCash in the Philippines, bKash in Bangladesh, Easypaisa in Pakistan, Touch 'n Go in Malaysia, and Dana in Indonesia. Working with GCash, Alipay has launched a blockchain-based cross-border remittance service.
- **Other financial services**: Ant Financial Cloud provides cloud computing services to financial customers. Ant Financial is also investing in AI to detect payment risks such as fraud. Ant Financial has developed proprietary blockchain to handle identity verification, remittances, charitable donations, mutual insurance, and hospital invoices.

Ant Financial is now known as Ant Group.[17] It was set to go public in an IPO at the end of 2020, but the listing was pulled days before launch following intervention from China's central bank. The move followed a speech by Jack Ma where he questioned the state of the Chinese financial system. The Chinese banking regulator struck back, saying that Ant Group was indifferent to the law, circumvented compliance requirements, and engaged in regulatory arbitrage.[18] As of May 2022 the IPO plans remained shelved. Table 11.1 shows Ant Group's size and scale at the end of 2020.

Tencent Follows Alibaba

Tencent was founded in 1998 in Shenzhen, China, by Ma Huateng (known as Pony Ma) and four friends. It launched its first service in 1999 – a free, PC-based instant messaging service for Chinese consumers called QQ. QQ was modeled on the popular and open-source ICQ service, launched in 1996 but not available in China. QQ had a penguin as its logo and attracted 1 million users in its first year.

In 2001 Tencent raised $32 million by selling a 46.5% stake to the South African media company Naspers. This funding allowed Tencent to launch Mobile QQ for smartphones. By adding optional premium services and selling advertising, Tencent became cash-flow positive and profitable by 2001. In 2004 Tencent listed on the Hong Kong Stock Exchange with a market value of US$1 billion. By May 2022 its market capitalization was US$3.7 billion.

With its mission to improve the quality of life through internet value-added services, Tencent began building out its QQ social communication platform by adding games and entertainment. In 2003 Tencent set up the internet site QQ.com, a closed portal that offered a wide range of proprietary features: games, music, videos, news, dating functions, chatrooms, and bulletin boards.

Tencent's profitability increased. It sold advertising and premium user subscriptions, with additional revenues coming from other value-added services. Until 2005 all customer funds were held with Chinese banking partners and payments were processed by established third-party providers China Mobile, China Unicom, and China Netcom.

Following the growth of the user base for its desktop messenger app QQ, Tencent launched a mobile instant messaging app called Weixin in January 2011. When Weixin passed 100 million users in 2012, it was rebranded as WeChat for the international market.[19] It would go on to become the super app that we know today, attracting 1.3 billion monthly active users by year-end 2022.

Key to WeChat's viral success was the addition of a mobile payments feature. Back in 2005, Tencent launched its own proprietary payment service called TenPay in response to the success of Alibaba's Alipay. The uptake of TenPay was slow, however, leading Tencent to try various improvements. In 2013, Tencent doubled down by launching a mobile wallet (WeChat Wallet) together with the payment app Weixin Pay that customers could connect to their bank accounts to load their WeChat accounts. Weixin Pay is known outside China as WeChat Pay.

In late 2014, WeChat Pay went viral following the release of the WeChat Red Envelope service. During the Chinese Lunar New Year, many Chinese people send a cash gift wrapped in a red envelope to relatives and friends. WeChat Red Envelope allowed customers to transfer money digitally using their WeChat wallet.

The service required both parties to have an account and combined a peer-to-peer (P2P) payment service with messaging and some gaming features. More than 40 million WeChat red envelopes were exchanged with an average size of RMB10 (US$1.60). At its peak at midnight on New Year's Eve, 4.8 million users accessed the system.

On the back of this success, WeChat (Weixin) Pay had captured close to a 40% market share of third-party mobile payments by year-end 2018, second only to Alibaba's Alipay. Over the next decade, Alipay and WeChat Pay dominated Chinese mobile payments with a more than 90% market share. By year-end 2022, Tencent reported that WeChat and WeChat (Weixin) Pay had 1.3 billion monthly active users. Tencent's fintech and business services division generated 31% of revenues, primarily commissions from payments and wealth management.

Tencent's strategic goal is to expand its capabilities, broaden its revenue base, and increase its scale by diversifying into financial services. It has built on its successful payments app to offer a money market fund, a challenger bank, and an insurtech.

- **Money market fund**: Imitating Alibaba's Yu'ebao, in 2014 Tencent partnered with a Chinese bank to offer a money market fund called Licaitong, which translates as "wealth management facility."[20]
- **Challenger bank**: In 2014 Tencent established an online bank (WeBank) as a separate entity but retained a 30% stake.[21] WeBank began offering microloans (called Weilidai) through WeChat Pay and QQ digital wallets, then moved into small business loans and auto loans.
- **Insurtech**: In 2017 Tencent launched the WeSure insurtech platform.[22] WeSure has partnered with major domestic insurance companies to enable users to purchase insurance, make inquiries, and file claims through WeChat. WeSure also offers insurance to WeChat Pay's 50 million small-business customers.

Exporting the Techfin Business Model

Have the Chinese techfins been able to replicate their domestic success by moving abroad? The answer is yes and no.

Alibaba and Tencent have expanded in India, Asia, Latin America, and the Caribbean. Many emerging market economies feature the same institutional voids that supported the rapid growth of mobile payments in China. These regions feature large, growing, and younger populations with high penetration of internet and mobile phones. The potential for e-commerce and online financial services that leapfrog the existing financial infrastructure are present. Both techfins have expanded through acquisitions and partnerships with incumbents.

Alibaba and Tencent have had little success expanding in North America and Europe. They have faced competition from bigtech and larger fintechs, as well as opposition from policymakers and regulators.

In 2013, for example, Tencent ran high-profile advertising campaigns in European nations with soccer star Lionel Messi but ultimately withdrew from the market, largely due to the dominance of Facebook and WhatsApp.[23] While Tencent retains a US branch office in California, the US business is focused on video games and entertainment products, not expansion.[24]

In 2018 Ant Group's proposed $1.2 billion acquisition of MoneyGram International was rejected by the US government's Committee on Foreign Investment in the United States over security concerns, despite Jack Ma visiting the US to meet with President Donald Trump a year earlier.[25]

As a result of these setbacks, both Chinese techfins have narrowed their ambitions to serving Chinese citizens traveling overseas and foreigners shopping on Chinese e-commerce sites. By working with local partners, both audiences can pay with Alipay and WeChat Pay using funds in domestic bank accounts.

NORTH AMERICAN BIGTECH: AMAZON, APPLE, FACEBOOK, GOOGLE

When we talk about bigtech, we are referring to the North American–headquartered, global technology companies: Amazon, Apple, Facebook, and Google. The name *bigtech* highlights their main competitive strength: vast multi-sided platform ecosystems, billions of customers, massive datasets on transactions, and billions of customer insights that are mined using artificial intelligence (AI).

The North American bigtech companies are following the techfin playbook: Build a foothold in payments, then expand to offer related financial products and services or to bundle financial products with non-financial transactions.

Amazon was the first to enter financial services when it started offering payment solutions in 2007 to increase sales on its marketplace and capture revenues from interchange fees. Apple, Google, and Facebook have followed with Apple Pay, Google Pay, and Facebook Pay, respectively.

There are some differences in the bigtech strategies. Several bigtech have concentrated on their home market, while others are experimenting with financial capabilities abroad. Some bigtech are partnering with financial incumbents, while others go it alone.

Whatever the strategy, all bigtech companies possess the required ingredients to be successful: massive, loyal customer bases; well-recognized brands; a history of innovation; a focus on customer experience and design; and expertise in the technologies driving fintech innovations.

Let's take a deeper dive on Amazon before touching briefly on examples from the other bigtech brands.

Amazon Builds on Payments

Amazon has been building a foundation in payments for nearly two decades. Amazon has developed a full payments infrastructure that includes credit and debit cards, digital wallets, cash deposits, and biometric payments technology (using its smart speaker Alexa). From this entry point, Amazon has expanded strategically into select financial services that support buyers and sellers on its e-commerce platform. Amazon has added loans for merchants, cash deposits for customers, and product insurance.

CB Insights, a market intelligence company, has been studying Amazon in financial services and concludes the retail giant is not planning to become a conventional bank:

> Amazon isn't building a traditional bank that serves everyone. Instead, Amazon has taken the core components of a modern banking experience and tweaked them to suit Amazon customers (both merchants and consumers). In a sense, Amazon is building a bank for itself – and that may be an even more compelling development than the company launching a deposit-holding bank.[26]

Rumors surfaced in both 2019 and 2021 that Amazon was partnering with major US banks to offer checking accounts and mortgages. But nothing materialized. Amazon is quiet about its ambitions but has reportedly dropped this strategy to avoid regulatory scrutiny.

Let's look at Amazon's three main financial products: payments, merchant loans, and cash accounts.

Amazon Pay launched in 2007, providing a digital wallet for shopping online, both at Amazon and third-party websites. Amazon customers link their account to a debit card or credit card with no additional registration required. Amazon does not share this information with merchants, who only receive the information they need to complete a transaction. There is no additional cost to use Amazon Pay and no interchange fee. As we will see later, Amazon has made many changes and improvements over the years, some of which were successful and some that failed.

In 2011 Amazon Lending began providing loans to merchants who sell on its platform.[27] The goal is to increase sales by helping merchants finance their Amazon inventories. Amazon Lending is by invitation only and restricted to financing inventories with Amazon, with merchants invited to apply based on past sales metrics. Qualifying merchants can borrow a term loan up to one year of $1,000 to $750,000 or access a business line of credit up to $1 million, in partnership with Bank of America and Goldman Sachs.[28] The application is completed online with a response of five days on average. Rates are not disclosed but are reportedly from 7% to 21%.

Amazon Cash launched in 2017. It allows customers to add cash deposits to their Amazon account to shop online. To make this service available to unbanked populations, Amazon partnered with retailers such as CVS and 7-Eleven. Customers can load cash to their Amazon cash account using their mobile phone number or a barcode downloaded from Amazon that is scanned at the checkout. They can also buy an Amazon Gift card that can be used to make online purchases. In May 2018 Amazon Cash partnered with Coinstar to allow customers to deposit spare change at 20,000 kiosks and cash out digitally with the Amazon Cash app.

Amazon has moved methodically into financial services using a strategy of experimentation and learning through trial and error, always with the goal of increasing sales on its online marketplace.

- In 2007 Amazon Pay was introduced, allowing customers to pay using credit and debit cards stored in their Amazon account.
- In 2013 "Login and Pay with Amazon" launched, allowing customers to pay merchants on third-party websites using their Amazon account. This service directly competes with PayPal. It was rolled out in India, then Europe in 2014.
- In 2018 Amazon opened its first Amazon Go grocery store, where consumers shop with no checkout required. Customers scan their Amazon app to gain access to the store, then can "grab and go" without needing a physical checkout to pay for products.
- In 2019 Amazon announced an integration with Worldpay, which serves as a back-end intermediary between banks and credit card companies and is one of the largest payment processors in the world. (Worldpay was acquired by FIS later that year.)
- In 2019 Amazon partnered with Western Union to roll out the PayCode program. Customers can pay with cash when shopping online using a code received at checkout that can be paid in person at a Western Union office.

Along the way, Amazon has demonstrated a willingness to experiment and fail.

- In 2007 Amazon Flexible Payments Service was introduced to allow P2P money transfers using tokenization but was discontinued in 2015.

- In 2008 Amazon released two e-commerce payments solutions, "Amazon Simple Pay" and "Checkout by Amazon." Amazon Simple Pay allowed third-party websites to accept Amazon account information for payment but was discontinued in 2015. Checkout by Amazon was an all-in-one solution that allowed online stores to look and process orders like Amazon, including the one-click option, with the payments managed by Amazon. It was discontinued in 2017 and replaced with "Pay with Amazon."
- In 2011 Amazon acquired TextPayMe, a P2P mobile service that was relaunched as Amazon Webpay in 2011. Webpay failed to gain traction and was shut down in 2014.
- In 2014 Amazon launched a point-of-sale (PoS) card reader for small businesses, Amazon Local Register, which competed directly with Square. It was a failure and shut down a year later.
- In mid-2014 Amazon launched a mobile wallet, only to withdraw it six months later.[29]
- In late 2019 Amazon announced a joint venture with JPMorgan and Berkshire Hathaway to roll out a health care service for its employees called Amazon Care. It disbanded in early 2021 as many of its initiatives failed to take off.

Amazon learns through trial and error and experimentation, spreading bets across several targeted products. It develops and tests new features in select markets over several iterations, before launching them more broadly. It then shuts down projects that fail to gain market traction.

Apple Partners with Incumbents

While Amazon has taken a do-it-yourself strategy in fintech, Apple has pursued partnerships with incumbents and start-ups. Apple's strategy appears to be designed to protect its share of the smartphone market by providing increased functionality on the iPhone and Apple ecosystem. Apple is not trying to disrupt financial services, only to embed banking into its platform ecosystem. Unlike fintechs, however, Apple is not looking to monetize customers using its financial offerings, but instead is using financial apps as loss leaders to keep customers engaged.

Apple Pay is a digital wallet and mobile payment service, just like Alipay, but only runs on iOS devices. The Apple Pay project began in 2013 and launched in the United States in late 2014 with the release of the Apple iPhone 6. Apple Pay supports credit and debit cards from the three major credit card networks – American Express, MasterCard, and VISA – issued by leading banks including Bank of America, Capital One Bank, JPMorgan, Citigroup, and Wells Fargo.[30]

Apple Pay uses Near Field Communication (NFC) technology, tokenization, and biometric security (Touch ID). Cardholders load a debit or credit card into the Apple Pay wallet and can then pay using their iPhone or other Apple device at any retailer that accepts contactless payments. When making a payment, Apple Pay protects the customer's card number and personal data by tokenizing it, using an encrypted digital code at the point of sale. This feature allows Apple Pay users to suspend their account if they lose an Apple device.

Apple has emphasized privacy and protection of customer data. The Apple Pay press release stated,

> Security and privacy are at the core of Apple Pay. When you're using Apple Pay in a store, restaurant, or other merchant, cashiers will no longer see your name, credit card number, or security code, helping to reduce the potential for fraud. ... Apple doesn't collect your purchase history, so we don't know what you bought, where you bought it, or how much you paid for it. And if your iPhone is lost or stolen, you can use Find My iPhone to quickly suspend payments from that device.[31]

Apple Pay does not charge any fees, although customers still pay the interchange associated with an underlying credit or debit card.

Following a successful US launch, Apple Pay rolled out globally through country-specific partnerships such as Australia's eftpos, China's UnionPay, Japan's JCB, and Germany's Girocard. Apple Pay has expanded to allow a variety of payment and stored value cards to be used, such as Hong Kong's Octopus card. Apple continues to expand its payments platform. It is working with US banks to allow users to withdraw cash at ATMs using Apple Pay.

By 2020 Apple Pay had 507 million users globally, 7.5 times more than its 67 million users in 2016.[32] In the United States, Apple pay had a 44% market share of the mobile payment market and a 92% market share of transactions using a mobile wallet. Close to 5,500 banks worldwide offered Apple Pay as a payment method.

In early 2022, for example, Apple acquired the Canadian payments start-up Mobeewave, whose technology turns iPhones into mobile contactless payment terminals.[33] This innovation will allow small businesses to use an iPhone instead of Square's PoS card reader. This technology will also enable P2P payments from one smartphone to another, without the need for a text message or email.

In March 2019 Apple announced the Apple Card, a new credit card issued by MasterCard and backed by Goldman Sachs.[34] What made this announcement significant was the focus on financial well-being and privacy and the elimination of fees. The

Apple Card will help users understand their spending by automatically organizing and totaling purchases into color-coded categories for budgeting and tracking.

The Apple Card mobile app is transparent on the rate of interest and prompts customers to make payments to avoid paying interest. Apple's partner, Goldman Sachs, commits to never sharing or selling data to third parties for marketing and advertising. Finally, Apple Card customers do not pay a fee (no annual, late, international, or over-the-limit fees) and receive 2% cashback on every purchase.

In April 2021 Apple introduced a new Apple Card Family that allows two or more family members who are 13 years or older to share a credit card and earn 3% cashback.[35] Users can merge their credit lines and build their credit together, with the payment history from the Apple Card reported to credit bureaus for each co-owner. Co-owners can track their spending, set spending limits, and develop smart financial habits.

In April 2023 Apple launched its first savings account for Apple Card users with a 4.15% interest rate, backed by Goldman Sachs.[36] With no fees, no minimum deposits, and no minimum balance requirements, users can manage their savings account directly from the Apple Card digital wallet.

Facebook Faces the Regulators

Whether you know it as Facebook or Meta, the social media company has not had much success breaking into financial services. Its efforts to move beyond payments into cryptocurrency failed due to opposition from regulators.

Facebook was slower than its bigtech peers to move into payments. It partnered with PayPal in 2016 to allow users to use PayPal to shop on Facebook Messenger.[37] Then, in late 2017, they expanded the partnership by allowing P2P money transfers over Messenger via PayPal accounts. In 2018 Facebook approached US banks about partnering to provide their services on its platform.[38]

Facebook's efforts bore fruit in November 2019 with the launch of Facebook Pay. It allows users to make payments using Facebook and Instagram and send money using Messenger and WhatsApp. Users link a debit or credit card to their account to get started. There is no fee to send or receive money. Payments are processed in partnership with PayPal, Stripe, and other payment gateways around the world.

If there is no fee, how does Facebook monetize this feature? The answer is advertising revenues. By seeing customer transactions through its app, Facebook can link advertising targeted at users with spending. This conversion link is crucial for convincing businesses to spend more on marketing campaigns on Facebook.

Facebook Pay has rolled out around the globe, with availability varying by country. It has hit some hurdles. For example, it took two years to overcome regulatory hurdles in India, with P2P money transfers over WhatsApp going ahead in 2020.[39]

Similarly, Facebook spent a year convincing regulators in Brazil to allow P2P transfers in 2021, but similar plans to allow consumers to pay merchants stalled in early 2022 after local partners balked at the terms.[40]

Facebook has also faced roadblocks with its cryptocurrency ambitions. In June 2019 Facebook announced plans to launch a stablecoin, Libra, to allow low-cost money transfers and payments globally over Messenger and WhatsApp.[41] Libra would be owned and operated as a Facebook subsidiary. The stablecoin would be backed by fiat currencies and US Treasuries. Transactions would be recorded on an open-source blockchain.

The original group of 28 partners read like a who's who of the digital economy. It included venture capitalists (Andreesen Horowitz, Union Square Ventures), non-governmental organizations (Women's World Banking), crypto companies (Coinbase), credit card networks (MasterCard, VISA), payment providers (PayPal, Stripe), e-commerce marketplaces (eBay, Mercado Pago), telecoms (Vodafone), and ride-sharing companies (Lyft, Uber). Ominously, Libra did not have a single bank partner.

Libra looked like it would give Facebook a foundation to take a leading position in retail financial services, with a stablecoin that would rival fiat currencies. Then it fell apart.

Libra was widely attacked. Regulators in the US and Europe expressed their concern and immediately called for hearings:

> Because Facebook is already in the hands of over a quarter of the world's population, it is imperative that Facebook and its partners immediately cease implementation plans until regulators and [US] Congress have an opportunity to examine these issues and take action.[42]

The Group of Seven nations put together a taskforce to evaluate Libra.[43] Leading partners soon dropped out.[44] PayPal was first in October 2019, followed by MasterCard, VISA, Mercado Pago, Booking Holdings, eBay, and Stripe. Facebook offered to withdraw to secure regulatory approvals. In December 2020 Libra was rebranded as Diem to distance the project from Facebook. But it didn't work, and in January 2022 Diem was shut down, with the code sold to a third party.

Google Struggles with Product-Market Fit

Google has struggled to move into financial services. Google Pay has been relaunched multiple times and has lost ground to Apple Pay for contactless payments and PayPal's Venmo for money transfers. Google's attempts to move into merchant lending and to run a comparison website for mortgages, credit cards, and insurance both shut down within a year. And Google abandoned its bid to offer digital bank accounts. The only consolation: Google's two venture capital arms have profited from being early-stage investors in some of the biggest fintech unicorns.

Google Pay is the search company's answer to Apple Pay. Google Pay is a digital wallet and online payment app that allows contactless payments using Android devices. It has followed a rocky road with many twists and turns. It started in 2011 when Google introduced a digital wallet for online payments. In 2013 Google Wallet was integrated with Google's Gmail to allow users to send money by email. But Google Wallet languished, as consumers were not that interested. In other words, there was no product-market fit.

In 2015 Google released Android Pay, a payments app for Android devices to compete with Apple Pay on iOS smartphones. Android Pay launched in the US and supported MasterCard, VISA, and select bank debit cards. It rolled out internationally starting with the UK, Singapore, and Australia. In 2017 Google launched a payment app in India based on Android Pay, branded as Google Tez. But again, despite these efforts, Android Pay was not as successful as Apple Pay.

With two fintech apps struggling, Google had not achieved its goal of enabling easy, secure payments online and offline using a single account. So it tried again.

In 2018 Google merged Google Wallet and Android Pay into a new product, Google Pay, with a new logo and marketing campaign.[45] (It also rebranded India's Google Tez as Google Pay.) It provided P2P money transfers and payments online and in-store. It allowed payments information saved in a Google account to be used in Chrome for web purchases, in YouTube for renewing subscriptions, in the Android store for app purchases, and at retail outlets with NFC payments.

Google has tried using partnerships with incumbents to grow Google Pay market share. It partnered with Indian banks to offer microloans through Google Pay.[46] In 2020 Google's partner MasterCard made Google Pay available in 10 European countries.

By year-end 2018 Google Pay had attracted 50 million users, ahead of Samsung Pay with 40 million, but far behind Apple Pay (over 150 million).[47] By late 2020 Google Pay had 150 million users in 30 countries. Sounds pretty good, right? Not when you consider that Apple Pay had over 500 million. And while Apple Pay had 92% of transaction volumes among mobile wallet users, Google Pay had only 3%.

In November 2020 Google announced a reboot of Google Pay, along with plans to offer bank accounts in partnership with leading US banks.[48] The app was redesigned to remove the long stack of payment cards and list of transactions, which were replaced with payments organized around conversations like PayPal's Venmo. It included analytics and insights on spending. And it promised to offer a new mobile-first bank account integrated into Google Pay, called Plex accounts, with partners such as Citigroup.

Critics hated it. One website concluded,

> Existing Google Pay users are about to go through a transition reminiscent of the recent move from Google Music to YouTube Music: Google is killing one perfectly

fine service and replacing it with a worse, less functional service. … Basically, everyone is being kicked off the old Google Pay service, and you'll all have to join and reconnect on this new thing.[49]

Users were required to set up a new account as the old app was shutting down. And Google introduced fees for services, whereas the old app was free.

Not surprisingly, the relaunch was unpopular. In October 2021 Google abandoned plans to offer Google Plex accounts, saying it would focus on the business-to-business market for financial services instead of business-to-consumer.[50] As of May 2022 the rating on the Google Play app store was 3.6, with many poor reviews.

If it is any consolation, Google has made money by investing in fintech start-ups. Google's in-house venture capital arm, Google Ventures (GV), has been the most active investor in early-stage fintechs. GV was spun out in 2009 with Google's parent company Alphabet as the sole limited partner. Between 2016 and mid-2021 GV participated in 45 fintech funding rounds.[51] As of early 2021 GV had funded more than 500 companies across all stages and sectors, including Stripe (payments), Lemonade (insurtech), and Ripple Labs (cryptocurrency).[52]

Google also makes investments through CapitalG, a private equity firm founded in 2013, that invests to make a profit. CapitalG has invested in Credit Karma (personal finance), LendingClub (online lender), Stripe (payments), Robinhood (wealth management), and Oscar (insurtech).[53]

COMPETITIVE STRENGTHS OF TECHFINS AND BIGTECH

Let's summarize the three competitive strengths of techfins and bigtech that are particularly important for financial services:

1 Platform ecosystems and network effects
2 Access to customers and brand recognition
3 Big data insights and customer experience

Platform Ecosystems and Network Effects

Bigtech companies are following a platform ecosystem strategy built around a core product that is integrated with other in-house or third-party products through an online portal or mobile app.[54] Alibaba and Amazon's core product is e-commerce. Tencent and Facebook's correct product is social media. Apple's core product is smartphones. And Google's core product is a search engine.

The goal of a platform ecosystem is to attract different categories of users and generate network effects, where adding some customers attracts others to join.[55] As we saw in Chapter 2 when discussing multi-sided business models, same-side network effects occur when an increase in users on one side of the platform attracts even more users on the same side. With cross-side network effects, the growth of users on one side (e.g., customers) attracts more users on the other side (e.g., merchants, advertisers).

Each platform ecosystem seeks to offer a unique combination of core and complementary products and features that makes the platform sticky, leading to loyal, repeat visitors. This stickiness creates a barrier to entry, as users may find it difficult to leave the ecosystem or to multihome on competing platforms.

Once we understand this strategy and business model, it becomes clear that the techfins and bigtech will inevitably offer financial services to their users. To be able to engage in e-commerce or P2P transactions, users need an account and an online method of payment. By adding a payment gateway to the platform, the tech company can monetize users by capturing part of the interchange fee. Customer and merchant accounts on the platform also require cash balances, creating opportunities to cross-sell credit, loans, investments, and insurance products. There are synergies between these financial products and the non-financial products that are sold on these platform ecosystems.

Access to Customers and Brand Recognition

Most financial products are commodities with many close substitutes. For this reason, banks have invested heavily to build bricks-and-mortar branch networks (a tangible asset) and to create a distinctive brand (an intangible asset). The branch network allowed banks to compete for customers based on proximity and convenience. The brand allowed the bank to market a unique value proposition to targeted customer segments.

Both sources of banks' competitive advantage – the branch network and brand – have been eroded in recent years, the former by technologies like the internet and smartphones, and the latter by financial crises and scandals.

Technology has eroded the value of a branch network over decades. During the 1970s to 1980s, we saw automated teller machines (ATMs) and telephone banking removing the need to meet with a teller or visit a branch. During the 1990s and 2000s, the arrival of the internet and online banking made it possible to bank over your computer.

During the past decade, the rollout of faster mobile networks and smartphones put a bank in your pocket, allowing a new generation of customers to bypass physical branches altogether.[56] The number of bank branches in Canada, for example, peaked

Table 11.2. Most Valuable Global Brands 2022

Rank	Brand	Brand Value (US$ billions)
1	Apple	482
2	Microsoft	278
3	Amazon	275
4	Google	252
5	Samsung	88

Source: Interbrand, https://interbrand.com/best-global-brands/.

at 6,400 in 2014; they have declined steadily, dropping to around 5,800 bank branches in 2020.[57] There are close to 70,000 bank machines in Canada, of which one-quarter are bank owned. Meanwhile, 89% of Canadians reported using online banking in 2021, and 65% used mobile app–based banking.[58]

In a digital world, geography and distance are less of a barrier. The most important barriers to entry in financial services have been a bank's brand recognition and the trust associated with it. These intangible assets were heavily damaged in the US and Europe by the 2008–2009 Global Financial Crisis (but not in Canada). Trust in both regions was further damaged by scandals and criminal convictions post-2010 that resulted in billions of dollars of fines paid by banks globally.

The extent of the damage is reflected in Interbrand's annual ranking of the most valuable global brands. In 2006 global financial institutions held 8 of the top 50 most valuable brands, led by Citigroup at #11, American Express at #14, and Merrill Lynch at #21. Technology companies were all lower rated, with Google at #24, Apple at #39, and Amazon at #65.[59] By 2018 these positions had reversed: Apple, Google, and Amazon held the top 3 spots, and only 5 global financial institutions were in the top 50 (led by American Express at #24 and JPMorgan at #26).[60]

Table 11.2 shows the results of the 2022 survey. Bigtech firms are in the top five positions. The first bank to appear is JPMorgan at #24, followed by American Express at #27, Allianz Insurance at #34, VISA at #37, and MasterCard at #41. Goldman Sachs, Citigroup, HSBC, and Morgan Stanley are lagging far behind.

A key metric used to measure the success of techfins and bigtech companies is the size of their user base.[61] Alipay had over 1.3 billion users worldwide in 2020, while Tencent's WeChat Pay had 865 million users. In 2020 it is estimated that Apple iPhone had about 47% of all smartphone users in the United States, Facebook had over 2.5 billion monthly active users, and Google had a market share of close to 90% of searches. Clearly these tech companies have been successful in acquiring customers and developing brand loyalty.

Techfins and bigtech companies have suffered damage to the trust in their brands in recent years. In China, Alibaba and Tencent are accused of collaborating with government authorities to monitor Chinese citizens and suppress free speech.[62] Facebook has been hit by disclosures of security breaches, fake news campaigns, and unauthorized use of customer data by third parties.[63] Numerous episodes have generated critical news coverage, regulatory scrutiny, political inquiries, fines from regulators, and civil lawsuits by privacy advocates.

While these events have mostly focused on the ad-based business models of Facebook and Google, all technology companies that collect customer data have been affected. While these companies have updated and publicized their privacy policies, the damage to customer trust remains.

Big Data Insights and Customer Experience

The media is full of references about how much data is being collected each day on consumer behavior. Data scientists often cite the same statistic: 90% of all data in the world has been collected in the past two years.[64] This data collection has been made possible by the emergence of cloud computing since 2006 and the drop in cost of storage and computing power.

The greater availability of data and computing power has awoken the dormant field of AI and the subfield of machine learning. Machine learning is the science of getting computers to learn and act without being explicitly programmed. We are seeing machine learning in action across all industries: autonomous vehicles, genome mapping, speech recognition, web search, email spam filters, and recommender systems. AI and machine learning are also linchpins for technological improvements in financial services.

The techfin and bigtech platform ecosystems are at the epicenter of this data collection. One of their main competitive strengths is their ability to capture and analyze proprietary data on customer behavior across a range of activities. These platforms are logging each click, key stroke, text message, chat, post, image, and video. These unstructured data sets are being analyzed using AI and machine learning to generate insights on customer behavior.

The techfins have a goal of understanding a customer's needs even before they recognize them. As explained by CEO Daniel Zhang in Alibaba's 2018 investor day, big data and machine learning algorithms allow Alibaba to turn business-to-consumer (B2C) on its head. Instead of Alibaba producing products to sell to customer needs, final customer demand is generating insights that leads Alibaba to create and supply new products (C2B).[65]

The competitive advantage for techfins and bigtech in financial services is not the data itself. It is how this data is used to understand a customer's needs.

CONCLUSION: ASSESSING THE TECHFIN AND BIGTECH THREAT

How serious is the threat from techfins and bigtech for incumbent financial institutions? Will global technology companies make banks, insurance companies, and asset managers obsolete?

The answer is no. The entry of techfins and bigtech into financial services has had mixed success. They may have followed a similar strategy, but the outcomes have been significantly different.

Addressing China's Institutional Voids

The Chinese techfins have modernized parts of China's financial system services but have always worked with domestic banks. Alibaba and Tencent are making progress moving into emerging market economies that exhibit similar institutional voids. But they have not succeeded in breaking into the advanced economies.

The Chinese techfins have succeeded by addressing institutional voids in China's financial system, creating solutions to the pain points faced by Chinese consumers.[66] Alibaba's Ant Group and Tencent have grown organically, offering a range of financial services within the context of a much broader non-financial ecosystem. Their customer-centric approach responded to the unmet needs of users, filling gaps in China's financial system that were holding back their platform businesses.

China's payments infrastructure was antiquated. China did not have a network of credit or debit cards, relying on cash as a primary means of payment. Consumers were forced to use expensive and time-consuming methods to transfer money and make payments. Alipay and WeChat Pay provided digital means of payment and electronic money transfer services that were low cost, secure, and simple to use. They provided cash accounts to facilitate online and offline transactions and created online money market funds so that users could earn a return on their cash deposits.

China's state-owned banking system focused on large companies and government entities. China did not have a system of credit scores or ratings or the history required to create one using traditional metrics. Many small businesses and consumers were financially constrained, with little access to credit. Alibaba and Tencent expanded into providing loans and credit for both consumers looking to make purchases and merchants looking to finance working capital.

China's wealth management industry was undeveloped and focused on high net worth individuals, with little attention to lower-income households. Chinese insurance companies focused on businesses, not consumers, with limited distribution networks and no underwriting history. Alibaba and Tencent set up wealth management and insurance marketplaces that provided these products to users cheaply and conveniently.

At each step of the way, the techfins worked with the incumbent banks. These partnerships gave them access to the payment rails, the banking system, and a range of products from deposits to loans to wealth management to insurance.

Alibaba and Tencent benefited from a combination of features of China's financial system.

China's economy and financial system was underdeveloped and only took off in the 1980s and 1990s. Rapid economic growth created a middle class of Chinese consumers with rising incomes, increasing wealth, and more leisure time. Millennials who were better educated entered the workforce and earned higher salaries. They were more willing to experiment with fintech innovations and to shop and transact online.

China's telecommunications infrastructure was overhauled in the 1990s with the arrival of the internet, personal computers, and mobile phone networks. These tools allowed the techfins to leapfrog into digital banking without the need for expensive branch networks. The techfins also benefited from global technological developments: cloud computing, big data and analytics, AI and machine learning, and QR codes.

China's political and regulatory institutions are centrally controlled. This state apparatus allowed Alibaba and Tencent to enter payments, investments, and banking because the stated missions of both were aligned with government policy. The techfins were promoting economic growth, financial development, and financial inclusion. Meanwhile, China prevented the entry of foreign technology companies such as Amazon, PayPal, Facebook, and Google. The techfins could replicate and innovate on these foreign business models without fear of competition in the Chinese market.

The Future Is Bank-Bigtech Partnerships

The North American bigtech companies have succeeded in building strong footholds in payments. But outside of this niche, they have only made headway in financial services by partnering with incumbents. Otherwise, they have faced regulatory opposition and failed to find product-market fit, causing them to reduce their ambitions.

Amazon offers payments, merchant loans, and a cash account for customers. Apple offers payments and a credit card. Facebook and Google offer only payments. When you put it this way, bigtech firms have not broken out of their initial foothold.

This result is for the best. The entry of bigtech risks creating a new monopoly player in financial services. It may not generate the best outcome for customers, who benefit from a diversity of players competing to meet their needs.

The fear of disruption by bigtech – and fintech more generally – has gotten incumbents to focus on their customers. Banks have been forced to innovate and develop new digital products and services. Competition has raised the level of customer engagement and service in an oligopolistic industry, while putting downward pressure on fees and commissions.

Let's face it. Banks deserve a kick in the pants. They have been too product-centric, viewing customers as a means to an end, namely making money. Customers with different income levels have received unequal levels of service based on their revenue potential. The fact that an estimated 7 million US households are unbanked, without a checking or savings account, is impossible to grasp.[67]

The banks of the future need to be customer-centric, like a fintech. They need to learn from bigtech and follow the customer journey, understanding and anticipating where financial services fit into their lives. No one wakes up each day excited to do their banking. They want to have a rewarding job, buy a home, pay for a child's education, travel, and save for retirement. If they could accomplish these goals without ever speaking to a bank again, many of them would.

Bigtech and fintechs are serving customers by giving them the products they need, when they need them, and at a reasonable price. By focusing on the customer experience, bigtech and fintechs are building customer relationships, making them loyal and sticky. This is the strategy that incumbents need to copy.

The winning combination will be bigtech-bank partnerships that combine their respective strengths. Banks have many customers; access to stable, inexpensive funding; economies of scale and scope; and expertise in risk management and compliance. Bigtech and fintechs have technological expertise, a culture of innovation, design thinking, and a broader perspective on the needs of the customer. Banks can provide bigtech with risk management expertise and regulatory compliance. Bigtech and fintechs can leverage modern technologies, promote innovation, and bring a great customer experience.

In the end, customers will be best served by bigtech-bank partnerships. Ultimately, what is good for the customer is good for the bank, the bigtech, and the fintech partner. Let's hope they figure it out.

Key Terms

bigtech	money market fund
digital wallet	near field communication (NFC)
disintermediation	platform ecosystem
institutional void	techfin
Libra	

QUESTIONS FOR DISCUSSION

1   What is a techfin and why is their name the reverse of fintech?
2   Why did Alibaba create Alipay and how did this business grow over time? How is Alipay related to Ant Financial, later known as Ant Group?
3   How did the instant messaging and gaming company Tencent move into financial services? What was the first financial product that it launched?
4   What is a bigtech and how do they compare in size to the incumbent financial institutions such as banks?
5   What has been Amazon's path into financial services? What financial products does it offer and why?
6   How has Apple found success in embedding financial services into its iOS ecosystem?
7   What was Facebook's Libra project and what happened to it?
8   What was the experience of Google with its payment product? How did it evolve over time?
9   What are the three competitive strengths of the techfins and bigtech in financial services?
10   How serious is the threat from techfins and bigtech for incumbent financial institutions? Will banks, insurance companies, and asset managers become obsolete?

ADDITIONAL READING

Evans, David S., and Richard Schmalensee, *Matchmakers: The New Economics of Multisided Platforms* (Boston: Harvard Business Review Press, 2016).

Financial Stability Board, "Bigtech in Finance: Market Developments and Potential Financial Stability Implications," December 19, 2019, https://www.fsb.org/2019/12/bigtech-in-finance-market-developments-and-potential-financial-stability-implications/.

Frost, Jon, Leonardo Gambacorta, Yi Huang, Hyun Song Shin, and Pablo Zbinden, "Bigtech and the Changing Structure of Financial Intermediation," *BIS Working Papers* No. 779, April 2019.

Stulz, René M., "FinTech, BigTech, and the Future of Banks," *Journal of Applied Corporate Finance* 31, no. 4 (2019): 86–97.

Notes

Preface

1 Laurent Ormans, "50 Journals Used in FT Research Rank," *Financial Times*, September 12, 2016, https://www.ft.com/content/3405a512-5cbb-11e1-8f1f-00144feabdc0.

1. Foundations of Fintech

1 KPMG, "Pulse of Fintech," accessed December 15, 2021, https://home.kpmg/xx/en /home/industries/financial-services/pulse-of-fintech.html.
2 KPMG, "Fintech," accessed December 15, 2021, https://home.kpmg/ca/en/home /industries/financial-services/fintech.html.
3 Thomas Philippon, "The Fintech Opportunity," NBER Working Paper 22476, August 2016, https://www.nber.org/papers/w22476.
4 Klaus Schwab, "The Fourth Industrial Revolution: What It Means, How to Respond," World Economic Forum, January 14, 2016, https://www.weforum.org/agenda/2016/01 /the-fourth-industrial-revolution-what-it-means-and-how-to-respond/.
5 D.W. Arner, J. Barberis, and R.P. Buckley, "Fintech and Regtech in a Nutshell, and the Future in a Sandbox," CFA Institute Research Foundation, July 2017, https://www .cfainstitute.org/en/research/foundation/2017/fintech-and-regtech-in-a-nutshell-and -the-future-in-a-sandbox.
6 Ivana Križanović, "Cell Phone History: From the First Phone to Today's Smartphone Wonders," August 4, 2020, https://versus.com/en/news/cell-phone-history.
7 CERN, "Where the Web Was Born," accessed December 15, 2021, https://home.cern /science/computing/where-web-was-born.
8 Thomas Kuhn, *The Structure of Scientific Revolutions* (Chicago: University of Chicago Press, 1962).
9 Wealthsimple, "Grow Your Money," accessed April 18, 2023, https://www.wealthsimple .com/.

10 Funding Circle, "Simple, Hassle-Free Business Finance," accessed April 18, 2023, https://www.fundingcircle.com/.

11 Revolut, "One App, All Things Money," accessed April 18, 2023, https://www.revolut.com/.

12 Wise, "Money for Here, There and Everywhere," accessed April 18, 2023, https://wise.com/.

13 Barbara Oakley and Terrence Sejnowski, "Learning How to Learn: Powerful Mental Tools to Help You Master Tough Subjects," Coursera, accessed December 15, 2021, https://www.coursera.org/learn/learning-how-to-learn.

14 SoFi, "About Us," accessed December 15, 2021, https://www.sofi.com/our-story/.

15 Xavier Vives, Thierry Foucault, Laura Veldkamp, and Darrell Duffie (eds.), *Barcelona 4: Technology and Finance* (London: CEPR Press, 2022), https://cepr.org/publications/books-and-reports/barcelona-4-technology-and-finance.

16 Suzanne Bearne, "The £1.3bn Finance Firm That Was Conceived in a Pub," *BBC News*, October 22, 2018, https://www.bbc.com/news/business-45900404.

17 Joe Camberato, "2019 Small Business Failure Rate: Startup Statistics by Industry," National Business Capital and Services, January 24, 2020, https://www.nationalbusinesscapital.com/2019-small-business-failure-rate-startup-statistics-industry/.

18 Goldman Sachs, "Marcus by Goldman Sachs Leverages Technology and Legacy of Financial Expertise in Dynamic Consumer Finance Platform," accessed December 15, 2021, https://www.goldmansachs.com/our-firm/history/moments/2016-marcus.html.

19 Saeed Azhar and Niket Nishant, "Goldman Sachs Platform Solutions Business Lost $3 Billion in Nearly Three Years," *Reuters*, January 13, 2023, https://www.reuters.com/business/finance/goldman-sachs-reports-12-bln-loss-platform-solutions-unit-2023-01-13/.

20 Alex Holt and Mark Gibson, "Technology Innovation Hubs," KMPG, accessed November 25, 2022, https://www.kpmg.us/content/dam/global/pdfs/2021/tech-innovation-hubs-2021.pdf.

21 MaRS, "Fintech," accessed November 25, 2022, https://www.marsdd.com/our-sectors/fintech/.

22 The World Bank, "Financial Inclusion," accessed November 25, 2022, https://www.worldbank.org/en/topic/financialinclusion.

23 Board of Governors of the Federal Reserve System, "Report on the Economic Well-Being of US Households in 2018: May 2019," accessed December 15, 2021, https://www.federalreserve.gov/publications/2019-economic-well-being-of-us-households-in-2018-banking-and-credit.htm.

24 Sharmista Appaya, "On Fintech and Financial Inclusion," October 26, 2021, World Bank Blogs, https://blogs.worldbank.org/psd/fintech-and-financial-inclusion.

25 Charles Arthur, "Tech Giants May Be Huge, But Nothing Matches Big Data," *Guardian*, August 23, 2013, https://www.theguardian.com/technology/2013/aug/23/tech-giants-data.

26 Bernard Marr, "How Much Data Do We Create Every Day? The Mind-Blowing Stats Everyone Should Read," *Forbes*, May 21, 2018, https://www.forbes.com/sites/bernardmarr/2018/05/21/how-much-data-do-we-create-every-day-the-mind-blowing-stats-everyone-should-read/.

27 Xorbin.com, "SHA-256 Hash Calculator," accessed November 25, 2022, https://xorbin .com/tools/sha256-hash-calculator.

28 Ethereum, "A Next-Generation Smart Contract and Decentralized Application Platform," accessed June 28, 2019, https://github.com/ethereum/wiki/wiki/White-Paper.

29 To see examples of dapps built on Ethereum, see: State of the DApps, "Explore Decentralized Applications," accessed November 25, 2022, https://www.stateofthedapps.com/.

2. Fintech Economics, Strategies, and Business Models

1 Klaus Schwab, "The Fourth Industrial Revolution: What It Means, How to Respond," World Economic Forum, January 14, 2016, https://www.weforum.org/agenda/2016/01 /the-fourth-industrial-revolution-what-it-means-and-how-to-respond/.

2 Jarrad Harford, Mark Humphery-Jenner, and Ronan Powell, "The Sources of Value Destruction in Acquisitions by Entrenched Managers," *Journal of Financial Economics* 106, no. 2 (2012): 247–261.

3 Thomas Philippon, "The Fintech Opportunity," NBER Working Paper 22476, August 2016, http://www.nber.org/papers/w22476.

4 Patrick Bolton, Xavier Freixas, Leonardo Gambacorta, and Paolo Emilio Mistrulli, "Relationship and Transaction Lending in a Crisis," *Review of Financial Studies* 29, no. 10 (2016): 2643–2676.

5 Arnoud W.A. Boot and Lev Ratnovski, "Banking and Trading," *Review of Finance* 20, no. 6 (2016): 2219–2246.

6 Heath P. Terry, Debra Schwartz, and Tina Sun, "The Future of Finance Part 3 – The Socialization of Finance," Goldman Sachs Equity Research, March 13, 2015.

7 Clayton M. Christensen, *The Innovator's Dilemma: When New Technologies Cause Great Firms to Fail* (Cambridge, MA: Harvard University Press, 1997).

8 Clayton M. Christensen, Michael Raynor, and Rory McDonald, "What Is Disruptive Innovation?" *Harvard Business Review* (December 2015): 44–53.

9 Clayton M. Christensen and Karen Dillon, "Disruption 2020: An Interview with Clayton M. Christensen," *Sloan Management Review* (Spring 2020): 21–26.

10 I wish to thank Andrew Sarta for making this distinction clear to me.

11 Gary P. Pisano, "You Need an Innovation Strategy," *Harvard Business Review* (June 2015): 44–54.

12 A bank's trading operations are typically divided into two parts: (i) the equity trading floor and (ii) the fixed income, currencies, and commodities trading floor (known as FICC). Both equity and FICC will also trade in derivatives, which are securities with a value based on (or derived from) some underlying security (such as an equity option) or asset (such as a gold futures contract).

13 David S. Evans and Richard Schmalensee, *Matchmakers: The New Economics of Multisided Platforms* (Boston: Harvard Business Review Press, 2016).

14 Borrowell, "Start with Your Free Credit Report," accessed November 28, 2022, https:// borrowell.com/.

15 Jean-Charles Rochet and Jean Tirole, "Platform Competition in Two-Sided Markets," *Journal of the European Economics Association* 1, no. 4 (2003): 990–1029. See also Tom Eisenmann, Geoffrey G. Parker, and Marshall W. Van Alstyne, "Strategies for Two-Sided

Markets," *Harvard Business Review* (October 2006); Andrei Hagiu, "Strategic Decisions for Multisided Platforms," *MIT Sloan Management Review* 55, no. 2 (Winter 2014): 71–80; Marc Rysman, "The Economics of Two-Sided Markets," *Journal of Economic Perspectives* 23, no. 3 (2009): 125–143.

16 Angus Dawson, Martin Hirt, and Jay Scanlan, "The Economic Essentials of Digital Strategy" *McKinsey Quarterly*, March 15, 2016, https://www.mckinsey.com/business -functions/strategy-and-corporate-finance/our-insights/the-economic-essentials -of-digital-strategy.

17 Revolut, "Credit Cards," accessed December 2, 2022, https://www.revolut.com/en-LT /credit-cards/.

3. Funding of Early-Stage Fintech Companies

1 InBIA, "Numbers of Entrepreneurship Centers (by Type) in US," accessed December 15, 2021, https://inbia.org/services/resources/.

2 Andy Rachleff, "How to Know If You've Got Product Market Fit," Floodgate, December 2, 2019, https://greatness.floodgate.com/episodes/andy-rachleff -on-how-to-know-if-youve-got-product-market-fit-XxGvX8DH/transcript.

3 Angel Capital Association, *The American Angel Study*, November 2017, https://www .theamericanangel.org/access-full-report.

4 Angel Capital Association, *The American Angel Study*.

5 Angel Capital Association, *The American Angel Study*.

6 Y Combinator, "What Happens at YC," accessed December 16, 2022, https://www .ycombinator.com/about.

7 Techstars, "Inside a Techstars Accelerator," accessed December 16, 2022, https://www .techstars.com/accelerator-hub.

8 Mike Katchen, "How Wealthsimple Raised $2-Million in Two Weeks," *Globe and Mail*, August 11, 2015, https://www.theglobeandmail.com/report-on-business/small -business/sb-money/how-wealthsimple-raised-2-million-in-two-weeks /article25882942/.

9 Slideshare, "Wealthsimple," accessed December 16, 2022, https://www.slideshare.net /wealthsimple.

10 Stripe, "Stripe Has Raised a New Round of Funding to Accelerate Momentum in Europe and Reinforce Enterprise Leadership," March 14, 2021, https://stripe.com/en-ca /newsroom/news/stripe-series-h.

11 CB Insights, "Here Are the Top 5 Most Active Fintech VC Investors," August 12, 2020, https://www.cbinsights.com/research/fintech-venture-capital-most-active/.

12 Sequoia Capital, "Remembering Don Valentine," October 24, 2019, https://www .sequoiacap.com/article/remembering-don-valentine/.

13 Crunchbase, "Sequoia Capital," accessed December 17, 2022, https://www.crunchbase .com/organization/sequoia-capital/recent_investments.

14 Paul Graham, "How to Convince Investors," Y Combinator, August 2013, http:// paulgraham.com/convince.html.

15 BCG, "Global Assets Management 2022 – 20th Edition," May 2022, https://web-assets. bcg.com/ba/c8/5b65e9d643abac4fa8e6820e86f4/bcg-global-asset-management-2022 -from-tailwinds-to-turbulence-may-2022-r.pdf.

16 Wise, "The Wise Story," accessed December 15, 2021, https://wise.com/us/about/our-story.

17 Neil Alexander, "The Next Chapter of Nutmeg's Journey," Nutmeg, June 17, 2021, https://www.nutmeg.com/nutmegonomics/the-next-chapter-of-nutmegs-journey/; Tink, "VISA Signs Agreement to Acquire Tink," June 24, 2021, https://tink.com/press/visa-acquires-tink/.

18 These examples are adapted from Carolynn Levy, "Safe Financing Documents," Y Combinator, accessed December 15, 2021, https://www.ycombinator.com/documents/.

4. Valuation of Fintech Companies

1 Angel Resource Institute, "William Payne," accessed December 15, 2021, https://angelresourceinstitute.org/about-us/team.php?person=11&name=WilliamPayne.

2 William H. Payne, *The Definitive Guide to Raising Money from Angels* (Bill Payne, 2011).

3 Berkus.com, "Official Site for Dave Berkus," accessed December 15, 2021, https://www.berkus.com/.

4 Dave Berkus, "After 20 Years: Updating the Berkus Method of Valuation," Angel Capital Association, November 16, 2016, https://www.angelcapitalassociation.org/blog/after-20-years-updating-the-berkus-method-of-valuation/.

5 Bill Payne, "Valuations 101: The Risk Factor Summation Method," Gust.com, November 15, 2011, https://gust.com/blog/valuations-101-the-risk-factor-summation-method/.

6 Cathie Wood, "Disruptive Innovation and Profitability," ARK Invest, December 1, 2022, https://ark-funds.com/articles/commentary/disruptive-innovation-and-profitability/.

7 The Nasdaq-100 is a market capitalization-weighted stock market index made up of equity securities issued by 100 of the largest non-financial companies listed on the Nasdaq stock exchange. See Nasdaq, "Nasdaq-100 Index," accessed December 18, 2022, https://www.nasdaq.com/solutions/nasdaq-100.

8 For non-financial companies, investors typically define ROE as net income divided by shareholders' equity, where shareholders' equity = common equity + preferred shares + non-controlling interest.

5. Bitcoin, Blockchain, and Cryptocurrencies

1 Satoshi Nakamoto, "Bitcoin: A Peer-to-Peer Electronic Cash System," Bitcoin.org, October 31, 2008, https://bitcoin.org/bitcoin.pdf.

2 Bitcoin Wiki, "Genesis Block," accessed June 26, 2019, https://en.Bitcoin.it/wiki/Genesis_block.

3 Satoshi Nakamoto, "Re: BitDNS and Generalizing Bitcoin," December 10, 2010, https://bitcointalk.org/index.php?topic=1790.msg28959#msg28959.

4 Bitcoin.org, "Choose Your Bitcoin Wallet," accessed January 31, 2022, https://bitcoin.org/en/choose-your-wallet.

5 CoinMarketCap, "Today's Cryptocurrency Prices by Market Cap," accessed December 26, 2022, https://coinmarketcap.com/.

6 The Ethereum whitepaper available on GitHub provides the history of Bitcoin and earlier attempts to create digital money. See: Ethereum, "A Next-Generation Smart Contract and Decentralized Application Platform," GitHub, accessed June 28, 2019, https://github.com/ethereum/wiki/wiki/White-Paper.

7 *Bitcoin Magazine*, "Is Bitcoin Anonymous?" August 17, 2020, https://bitcoinmagazine
.com/guides/bitcoin-anonymous.

8 Programmers prefer to display the 256-hash in hexadecimal format, which is a base-16 numbering system consisting of the numbers 0 to 9 and the lowercase characters "a" to "f." A bit is represented by 4 hexadecimal digits, so a 256-bit hash can be shown using 64 hexadecimal digits.

9 Aaron van Wirdum, "Why Some Changes to Bitcoin Require Consensus: Bitcoin's 4 Layers," *Bitcoin Magazine*, February 26, 2016, https://bitcoinmagazine.com/articles /why-some-changes-to-bitcoin-require-consensus-bitcoin-s-layers-1456512578.

10 The current energy consumption can be viewed on: Digiconomist, "The Bitcoin Energy Consumption Index," accessed December 20, 2022, https://digiconomist.net /bitcoin-energy-consumption/.

11 Ethereum, "The Merge," accessed December 20, 2022, https://ethereum.org/en /upgrades/merge/.

12 Alfred Lehar and Christine A. Parlour, "Miner Collusion and the Bitcoin Protocol," SSRN, March 22, 2020, https://ssrn.com/abstract=3559894.

13 CoinMarketCap, "Today's Cryptocurrency Prices by MarketCap," accessed December 31, 2021, https://CoinMarketCap.com/.

14 The Bitcoin code is available to download at Github, "bitcoin," accessed December 31, 2021, https://github.com/Bitcoin/Bitcoin.

15 Vitalik Buterin, "Launching the Ether Sale," July 22, 2014, https://blog.ethereum .org/2014/07/22/launching-the-ether-sale/.

16 Binance Research, "The Evolution of Stablecoins," May 15, 2019, https://research .binance.com/en/analysis/stablecoins-evolution.

17 Bitcoin Forum, "I AM HODLING," accessed December 31, 2021, https://bitcointalk.org /index.php?topic=375643.msg4022997#msg4022997.

18 CoinMarketCap, "Today's Cryptocurrency Prices by Market Cap," accessed December 31, 2021, https://CoinMarketCap.com/.

19 CME Group, "Bitcoin Futures Frequently Asked Questions," accessed January 25, 2022, https://www.cmegroup.com/education/bitcoin/cme-bitcoin-futures-frequently -asked-questions.html.

20 *Venture Beat*, "Breakout Gaming Announces New Coin and Gaming Destination," September 14, 2014, https://venturebeat.com/2014/09/16/breakout-gaming -announces-new-coin-and-gaming-destination/.

21 CoinDesk, "ICO Tracker," accessed June 29, 2019, https://www.coindesk.com /ico-tracker.

22 Block.one, "Eosio Strategic Vision," Eosio, accessed June 29, 2019, https://eos.io /strategic-vision/.

23 Daniel Palmer, "Messaging Giant Telegram's ICO Token Is at Last Going on (Limited) Public Sale," CoinDesk, June 11, 2019, https://www.coindesk.com/messaging -giant-telegrams-ico-token-is-at-last-going-on-public-sale.

24 Jed McCaleb, "Bitcoin without Mining," Bitcoin Forum, May 27, 2011, https://bitcointalk .org/index.php?topic=10193.0.

25 Crunchbase, "Ripple," accessed June 29, 2019, https://www.crunchbase.com /organization/ripple-labs.

26 Lizette Chapman, "Something Ventured: Cashing in on Bitcoin," *DowJones Newswire*, April 17, 2013.

27 XRP Ledger, "Provide a Better Alternative to Bitcoin," accessed April 25, 2022, https://xrpl.org/history.html.

28 Chloe Cornish and Martin Arnold, "Bitcoin Rival's Rise Unnerves Banking Sector," *Financial Times*, January 18, 2018, https://www.ft.com/content/f739f48e-f62a-11e7-8715-e94187b3017e.

29 "XRP," CoinMarketCap, "XRP," accessed April 15, 2023, https://CoinMarketCap.com/currencies/xrp/.

30 Sean Foley, Johnathan R. Karlsen, and Talis J. Putniņš, "Sex, Drugs, and Bitcoin: How Much Illegal Activity Is Financed through Cryptocurrencies?" *Review of Financial Studies* 32, no. 5 (2019): 1798–1853.

31 Trezor, "Addresses & Transaction History," accessed December 31, 2021, https://wiki.trezor.io/Address.

32 Trezor, "Compare Trezors," accessed December 31, 2021, https://wiki.trezor.io/Trezor.

33 CoinMarketCap, "Today's Cryptocurrency Prices by Market Cap."

34 CME Group, "CME Bitcoin Futures Frequently Asked Questions."

35 Binance, "Binance 2018 Recap," December 30, 2018, https://www.binance.com/en/blog/286445971261435904/Binance-2018-Recap.

36 Ledger SAS, "A Brief History of Crypto Exchanges Hacks," accessed June 27, 2019, https://discover.ledger.com/hackstimeline/.

37 SEC, "Report of Investigation Pursuant to Section 21(a) of the Securities Exchange Act of 1934: The DAO," July 25, 2017, http://www.sec.gov/litigation/investreport/34-81207.pdf.

38 Hester M. Peirce, "How We Howey," SEC, May 9, 2019, https://www.sec.gov/news/speech/peirce-how-we-howey-050919.

39 Ana Alexandre, "New Study Says 80 Percent of ICOs Conducted in 2017 Were Scams," Cointelegraph, July 13, 2018, https://cointelegraph.com/news/new-study-says-80-percent-of-icos-conducted-in-2017-were-scams.

40 SEC, "Investor Bulletin: Initial Coin Offerings," July 25, 2017, https://www.sec.gov/oiea/investor-alerts-and-bulletins/ib_coinofferings.

41 BTC.com, "Bitcoin Explorer," accessed January 25, 2022, https://btc.com/btc.

42 Markus K. Brunnermeier and Dirk Niepelt, "On the Equivalence of Private and Public Money," *Journal of Monetary Economics* 106 (2019): 27–41.

43 For an excellent summary, see: Chapter 2 in Vives, Xavier, Thierry Foucault, Laura Veldkamp, and Darrell Duffie (eds.), *Barcelona 4: Technology and Finance* (London: CEPR Press, 2022), https://cepr.org/publications/books-and-reports/barcelona-4-technology-and-finance. For an overview of the central bank research, take a look at the publications and reports on the BIS Innovation Hub at: https://www.bis.org/about/bisih/about.htm?m=3099.

44 Edward Helmore and Agencies, "Sam Bankman-Fried Headed to US after Extradition from Bahamas," *Guardian*, December 21, 2022, https://www.theguardian.com/business/2022/dec/21/sam-bankman-fried-agrees-to-extradition.

45 Kenneth P. Vogel and Ken Bensinger, "US Scrutinizes Political Donations by Sam Bankman-Fried and Allies," *New York Times*, December 17, 2022, https://www.nytimes.com/2022/12/17/us/politics/sam-bankman-fried-political-donations-doj.html.

46 Ian Allison, "Divisions in Sam Bankman-Fried's Crypto Empire Blur on His Trading Titan Alameda's Balance Sheet," CoinDesk, November 2, 2022, https://www.coindesk.com /business/2022/11/02/divisions-in-sam-bankman-frieds-crypto-empire-blur-on-his -trading-titan-alamedas-balance-sheet/.

47 Nikhilesh De and Cheyenne Ligon, "Lawyers Detail the 'Abrupt and Difficult' Collapse of FTX in First Bankruptcy Hearing," CoinDesk, November 22, 2022, https://www .coindesk.com/policy/2022/11/22/lawyers-detail-the-abrupt-and-difficult -collapse-of-FTX-in-first-bankruptcy-hearing/.

48 Rainer Böhme, Nicolas Christin, Benjamin Edelman, and Tyler Moore, "Bitcoin: Economics, Technology, and Governance," *Journal of Economic Perspectives* 29, no. 2 (2015): 213–238.

49 Foley, Karlsen, and Putniņš, "Sex, Drugs, and Bitcoin."

50 Igor Makarov and Antoinette Schoar, "Blockchain Analysis of the Bitcoin Market," Working Paper No. 29396, National Bureau of Economic Research (October 2021), https://www.nber.org/system/files/working_papers/w29396/w29396.pdf.

51 Neil Gandal, J.T. Hamrick, Tyler Moore, and Tali Oberman, "Price Manipulation in the Bitcoin Ecosystem," *Journal of Monetary Economics* 95 (2018): 86–96.

52 Nikhil Malik, Manmohan Aseri, Param Vir Singh, and Kannan Srinivasan, "Why Bitcoin Will Fail to Scale?" *Management Science* 68, no. 10 (2022): 7323–7349.

53 Nick Arnosti and S. Matthew Weinberg, "Bitcoin: A Natural Oligopoly," *Management Science* 68, no. 7 (2022): 4755–4771.

54 Franz J. Hinzen, Kose John, and Fahad Saleh, "Bitcoin's Limited Adoption Problem," *Journal of Financial Economics* 144, no. 2 (2022): 347–369.

55 Emiliano S. Pagnotta, "Decentralizing Money: Bitcoin Prices and Blockchain Security," *Review of Financial Studies* 35, no. 2 (2022): 866–907.

56 Noelle Acheson, "What Is SegWit?" CoinDesk, February 22, 2018, https://www.coindesk .com/learn/what-is-segwit/.

57 Bruno Biais, Christophe Bisiere, Matthieu Bouvard, Catherine Casamatta, and Albert J. Menkveld, "Equilibrium Bitcoin Pricing," *Journal of Finance* 78, no. 2 (2023): 967–1014.

58 Linda Schilling and Harald Uhlig, "Some Simple Bitcoin Economics," *Journal of Monetary Economics* 106 (2019): 16–26.

59 David Easley, Maureen O'Hara, and Soumya Basu, "From Mining to Markets: The Evolution of Bitcoin Transaction Fees," *Journal of Financial Economics* 134, no. 1 (2019): 91–109; Gur Huberman, Jacob D. Leshno, and Ciamac Moallemi, "An Economist's Perspective on the Bitcoin Payment System," *AEA Papers & Proceedings* 109 (2019): 93–96.

60 Pankaj K. Jain, Thomas H. McInish, and Jonathan L. Miller, "Insights from Bitcoin Trading," *Financial Management* 48, no. 4 (2019): 1031–1048.

61 Igor Makarov and Antoinette Schoar, "Price Discovery in Cryptocurrency Markets," *AEA Papers & Proceedings* 109 (2019): 97–99.

62 Jonathan Chiu and Thorsten V. Koeppl, "Blockchain-Based Settlement for Asset Trading," *Review of Financial Studies* 32 (2019): 1716–1753; Sinan Krückeberg and Peter Scholz, "Decentralized Efficiency? Arbitrage in Bitcoin Markets," *Financial Analysts Journal* 76, no. 3 (2020): 135–152.

63 Yukun Liu and Aleh Tsyvinski, "Risks and Returns of Cryptocurrency," *Review of Financial Studies* 34, no. 6 (2021): 2689–2727.

64 Yukun Liu, Aleh Tsyvinski, and Xi Wu, "Common Risk Factors in Cryptocurrency," *Journal of Finance* 77, no. 2 (2022): 1133–1177.

65 Daniel Cahill, Dirk G. Baur, Zhangxin Liu, and Joey W. Yang, "I Am a Blockchain Too: How Does the Market Respond to Companies' Interest in Blockchain?" *Journal of Banking and Finance* 113 (2020): 105740; Stephanie F. Cheng, Gus De Franco, Haibo Jiang, and Pengkai Lin, "Riding the Blockchain Mania: Public Firms' Speculative 8-K Disclosures," *Management Science* 65, no. 12 (2019): 5901–5913.

6. Ethereum and Decentralized Finance

1   LEGO, "LEGOLAND Billund Resort," accessed April 25, 2022, https://www.legoland .dk/en/.

2   *Bitcoin Magazine*, "Vitalik Buterin," accessed April 25, 2022, https://bitcoinmagazine .com/authors/vitalik-buterin.

3   Vitalik Buterin, "Ethereum Whitepaper: A Next-Generation Smart Contract and Decentralized Application Platform," Ethereum, accessed April 25, 2022, https:// ethereum.org/en/whitepaper/.

4   Vitalik Buterin, "Ethereum: A Next-Generation Cryptocurrency and Decentralized Application Platform," *Bitcoin Magazine*, January 23, 2014, https://bitcoinmagazine.com /business/ethereum-next-generation-cryptocurrency-decentralized-application -platform-1390528211.

5   Vitalik Buterin, "Ethereum: Now Going Public," Ethereum, January 23, 2014, https:// blog.ethereum.org/2014/01/23/ethereum-now-going-public.

6   Vitalik Buterin, "Ethereum: A Next-Generation Cryptocurrency."

7   Adriana Hamacher, "Who Are Ethereum's Co-founders and Where Are They Now?" Decrypt, July 28, 2020, https://decrypt.co/36641/who-are-ethereums-co-founders -and-where-are-they-now.

8   CoinMarketCap, "Ethereum," accessed April 25, 2022, https://coinmarketcap.com /currencies/ethereum/.

9   Vitalik Buterin, "Launching the Ether Sale," Ethereum, July 22, 2014, https://blog .ethereum.org/2014/07/22/launching-the-ether-sale/.

10 CoinMarketCap, "Ethereum."

11 The difficulty bomb was a planned exponential increase in the proof-of-work (PoW) difficulty setting designed to motivate the transition to proof-of-stake (PoS), reducing the chances of a fork. The difficulty bomb was deprecated with the transition to PoS.

12 Anil Donmez and Alexander Karaivanov, "Transaction Fee Economics in the Ethereum Blockchain," *Economic Inquiry* 60 (2022): 265–292.

13 Vitalik Buterin, "Slasher: A Punitive Proof-of-Stake Algorithm," Ethereum, January 15, 2014, https://blog.ethereum.org/2014/01/15/slasher-a-punitive-proof-of-stake-algorithm.

14 Ethereum, "Proof-of-Stake (POS)," accessed April 25, 2022, https://ethereum.org/en /developers/docs/consensus-mechanisms/pos/.

15 Coinbase, "How to Avoid Getting Slashed," January 25, 2022https://www.coinbase.com /cloud/discover/solutions/dont-get-slashed.

16 Ethereum, "The Merge," accessed December 20, 2022, https://ethereum.org/en/upgrades /merge/.

17 Vitalik Buterin, "DAOs, DACs, DAs and More: An Incomplete Terminology Guide," Ethereum, May 6, 2014, https://blog.ethereum.org/2014/05/06/daos-dacs-das-and-more-an-incomplete-terminology-guide/.

18 Solidity, "Solidity," accessed April 25, 2022, https://docs.soliditylang.org/en/v0.8.13/.

19 Ethereum, "Smart Contract Languages," accessed December 20, 2022, https://ethereum.org/en/developers/docs/smart-contracts/languages/.

20 Ethereum, "Introduction to Dapps," accessed December 20, 2022, https://ethereum.org/en/developers/docs/dapps/.

21 David Johnston, Sam Onat Yilmaz, Jeremy Kandah, Nikos Bentenitis, Farzad Hashemi, Ron Gross, Shawn Wilkinson, and Steven Mason, "The General Theory of Decentralized Applications, Dapps," GitHub, accessed April 25, 2022, https://github.com/DavidJohnstonCEO/Decentralizedapplications.

22 State of the Dapps, "Crypto Kitties," accessed April 25, 2022, https://www.stateofthedapps.com/dapps/cryptokitties.

23 Alyssa Hertig, "Loveable Digital Kittens Are Clogging Ethereum's Blockchain," CoinDesk, December 4, 2017, https://www.coindesk.com/markets/2017/12/04/loveable-digital-kittens-are-clogging-ethereums-blockchain/.

24 Jason Farago, "Beeple Has Won. Here's What We've Lost," *New York Times*, March 12, 2021, https://www.nytimes.com/2021/03/12/arts/design/beeple-nonfungible-nft-review.html.

25 CoinMarketCap, "Top Collectibles & NFTs Tokens by Market Capitalization," accessed April 18, 2023, https://coinmarketcap.com/view/collectibles-nfts/.

26 Statista, "Value of Sales Involving a Non-fungible Token (NFT) in Gaming, Art, Sports and Other Segments from 2018 to 2021," accessed April 18, 2023, https://www.statista.com/statistics/1221400/nft-sales-revenue-by-segment/.

27 Vitalik Buterin, "DAOs, DACs, DAs and More: An Incomplete Terminology Guide," Ethereum, May 6, 2014, https://blog.ethereum.org/2014/05/06/daos-dacs-das-and-more-an-incomplete-terminology-guide/.

28 David Siegel, "Understanding the DAO Attack," CoinDesk, June 25, 2016, https://www.coindesk.com/understanding-dao-hack-journalists.

29 Vitalik Buterin, "Critical Update Re: DAO Vulnerability," Ethereum, June 17, 2016, https://blog.ethereum.org/2016/06/17/critical-update-re-dao-vulnerability/.

30 Nikhilesh De, "Tether Lawyer Admits Stablecoin Now 74% Backed by Cash and Equivalents," CoinDesk, April 30, 2019, https://www.coindesk.com/markets/2019/04/30/tether-lawyer-admits-stablecoin-now-74-backed-by-cash-and-equivalents/.

31 Letitia James, "Attorney General James Ends Virtual Currency Trading Platform Bitfinex's Illegal Activities in New York," New York State Attorney General, February 23, 2021, https://ag.ny.gov/press-release/2021/attorney-general-james-ends-virtual-currency-trading-platform-bitfinexs-illegal.

32 *Forbes*, "What Really Happened to LUNA Crypto?" September 20, 2022, https://www.forbes.com/sites/qai/2022/09/20/what-really-happened-to-luna-crypto/.

33 Lin William Cong, Ye Li, and Neng Wang, "Tokenomics: Dynamic Adoption and Valuation," *Review of Financial Studies* 34, no. 3 (2021): 1105–1155.

34 Katya Malinova and Andreas Park, "Tokenomics: When Tokens Beat Equity," SSRN, November 18, 2018, https://ssrn.com/abstract=3286825; Jiri Chod and Evgeny Lyandres,

"A Theory of ICOs: Diversification, Agency, and Information Asymmetry," *Management Science* 67, no. 10 (2021): 5969–5989.

35 Richard Holden and Anup Malani, "An Examination of Velocity and Initial Coin Offerings," *Management Science* 68, no. 12 (2022): 9026–9041.

36 Lin William Cong, Ye Li, and Neng Wang, "Token-Based Platform Finance," *Journal of Financial Economics* 144, no. 3 (2022): 972–991.

37 Cong, Li, and Wang, "Token-Based Platform Finance"; Michael Sockin and Wei Xiong, "Decentralization through Tokenization," *Journal of Finance* 78, no. 1 (2023): 247–299; Jiri Chod, Nikolaos Trichakis, and S. Alex Yang, "Platform Tokenization: Financing, Governance, and Moral Hazard," *Management Science* 68, no. 9 (2022): 6411–6433.

38 For a clear introductory video to DeFi, see: Finematics, "What Is DEFI? Decentralized Finance Explained (Ethereum, MakerDAO, Compound, Uniswap, Kyber)," YouTube, July 2, 2020, https://youtu.be/k9HYC0EJU6E.

39 Ethereum, "Decentralized Finance (DeFi)," accessed April 25, 2022, https://ethereum .org/en/defi/.

40 Curve, "Curve," accessed April 25, 2022, https://curve.fi/. To read the whitepaper, visit: https://classic.curve.fi/files/crypto-pools-paper.pdf (accessed April 15, 2023).

41 DefiLlama, "About Us," accessed April 25, 2022, https://defillama.com/about; Raynor de Best, "Decentralized Finance (DeFi) – Statistics & Facts," Statista, March 31, 2022, https:// www-statista-com.ezproxy.library.uvic.ca/topics/8444/decentralized-finance-defi/.

42 DefiLlama, "Total Value Locked All Chains," accessed December 27, 2022, https:// defillama.com/chains.

43 Campbell Harvey, Ashwin Ramachandran, and Joey Santoro, *DeFi and the Future of Finance* (Hoboken, NJ: John Wiley & Sons, 2021).

44 Cryptopedia, "Yield Farming: Advanced DeFi for Maximizing Crypto Earnings," January 31, 2022, https://www.gemini.com/cryptopedia/what-is-yield-farming -crypto-defi-liquidity-mining.

45 Abracadabra, "Abracadabra.money," accessed April 25, 2022, https://abracadabra .money/.

46 R3, "About Us," accessed December 31, 2022, https://www.r3.com/company/.

47 Clearing is the process of transmitting, reconciling, and confirming transactions prior to settlement. Settlement is the process whereby securities are delivered in simultaneous exchange for payment of money.

48 Santander InnoVentures, "The Fintech 2.0 Paper: Rebooting Financial Services," June 15, 2015, http://santanderinnoventures.com/wp-content/uploads/2015/06/The-Fintech-2 -0-Paper.pdf.

49 R3, "Digital Finance Is Powered by Corda," accessed December 31, 2022, https://www .r3.com/products/corda/.

7. Alternative Finance, Online Lending, and Crowdfunding

1 The terms *portal* and *platform* are often used interchangeably but have slightly different meanings. A *portal* is a digital marketplace (multi-sided business) where individuals, small businesses, or social causes go to raise funding. A *platform* describes the technology or infrastructure on which the marketplace is built.

2 Heath P. Terry, Debra Schwartz, and Tina Sun, "The Future of Finance Part 3 – The Socialization of Finance," Goldman Sachs Equity Research, March 13, 2015.

3 Credit may go to the Boston musician and computer programmer Brian Camelio, who launched ArtistShare in 2003 to allow musicians to raise donations from fans to produce digital recordings. David M. Freedman and Matthew R. Nutting, "A Brief History of Crowdfunding," November 5, 2015, https://www.freedman-chicago.com/ec4i/History-of-Crowdfunding.pdf.

4 Crunchbase, "United States Crowdfunding Companies," accessed April 1, 2022, https://www.crunchbase.com/search/organization.companies/field/hubs/org_num/united-states-crowdfunding-companies.

5 Tetyana Balyuk, "FinTech Lending and Bank Credit Access for Consumers," *Management Science* 69, no. 1 (2023): 555–575.

6 Marco Di Maggio and Vincent Yao, "Fintech Borrowers: Lax Screening or Cream-Skimming?" *Review of Financial Studies* 34, no. 10 (2021): 4565–4618.

7 Boris Vallée and Yao Zeng, "Marketplace Lending: A New Banking Paradigm?" *Review of Financial Studies* 32, no. 5 (2019): 1939–1982.

8 Christophe Croux, Julapa Jagtiani, Tarunsai Korivi, and Milos Vulanovic, "Important Factors Determining Fintech Loan Default: Evidence from a LendingClub Consumer Platform," *Journal of Economic Behavior & Organization* 173 (2020): 270–296; Gregor Dorfleitner, Christopher Priberny, Stephanie Schuster, Johannes Stoiber, Martina Weber, Ivan de Castro, and Julia Kammler, "Description-Text Related Soft Information in Peer-to-Peer Lending: Evidence from Two Leading European Platforms," *Journal of Banking and Finance* 64 (2016): 169–187; Julapa Jagtiani and Catharine Lemieux, "The Roles of Alternative Data and Machine Learning in Fintech Lending: Evidence from the LendingClub Consumer Platform," *Financial Management* 48, no. 4 (2019): 1009–1029.

9 Julapa Jagtiani and Catharine Lemieux, "Do Fintech Lenders Penetrate Areas That Are Underserved by Traditional Banks?" *Journal of Economics and Business* 100 (2018): 43–54.

10 Di Maggio and Yao, "Fintech Borrowers."

11 Dorfleitner et al., "Description-Text Related Soft Information in Peer-to-Peer Lending."

12 Croux et al., "Important Factors Determining Fintech Loan Default."

13 Di Maggio and Yao, "Fintech Borrowers."

14 Ninghua Du, Lingfang Li, Tian Lu, and Xianghua Lu, "Prosocial Compliance in P2P Lending: A Natural Field Experiment," *Management Science* 66, no. 1 (2020): 315–333.

15 Helen Bollaert, Florencio Lopez-de-Silanes, and Armin Schwienbacher, "Fintech and Access to Finance," *Journal of Corporate Finance* 68 (2021): 101941.

16 Douglas J. Cumming, Gaël Leboeuf, and Armin Schwienbacher, "Crowdfunding Models: Keep-It-All vs. All-or-Nothing," *Financial Management* 49, no. 2 (2020): 331–360.

17 Vincenzo Butticè, Francesca Di Pietro, and Francesca Tenca, "Is Equity Crowdfunding Always Good? Deal Structure and the Attraction of Venture Capital Investors," *Journal of Corporate Finance* 65 (2020): 101773.

18 Douglas J. Cumming, Sofia A. Johan, and Yelin Zhang, "The Role of Due Diligence in Crowdfunding Platforms," *Journal of Banking and Finance* 108 (2019): 105661.

19 Sofia Johan and Yelin Zhang, "Quality Revealing versus Overstating in Equity Crowdfunding," *Journal of Corporate Finance* 65 (2020): 101741.

20 Hisham Farag and Sofia Johan, "How Alternative Finance Informs Central Themes in Corporate Finance," *Journal of Corporate Finance* 67 (2021): 101879.
21 Gerrit K.C. Ahlers, Douglas Cumming, Christina Günther, and Denis Schweizer, "Signaling in Equity Crowdfunding," *Entrepreneurship Theory and Practice* 39, no. 4 (2015): 955–980.
22 Bollaert et al., "Fintech and Access to Finance."
23 Philipp B. Cornelius and Bilal Gokpinar, "The Role of Customer Investor Involvement in Crowdfunding Success," *Management Science* 66, no. 1 (2020): 452–472.
24 Joshua M. Madsen and Jeff L. McMullin, "Economic Consequences of Risk Disclosures: Evidence from Crowdfunding," *Accounting Review* 95, no. 4 (2020): 331–363.
25 Kickstarter, "How to Launch a Product on Kickstarter, Part 3: Building Your Community," accessed July 11, 2019, https://www.kickstarter.com/articles/how-to-launch-a-product-on-kickstarter-building-your-community.
26 Cambridge Centre for Alternative Finance, "The Global Alternative Finance Market Benchmarking Report," University of Cambridge, April 2020.
27 Qing He and Xiaoyang Li, "The Failure of Chinese Peer-to-Peer Lending Platforms: Finance and Politics," *Journal of Corporate Finance* 66 (2021): 101852.
28 Cambridge Centre for Alternative Finance, "The 2nd Global Alternative Finance Market Benchmarking Report," University of Cambridge, June 2021.
29 Cambridge Centre for Alternative Finance, "CCAF Publications," University of Cambridge, accessed April 15, 2023, https://www.jbs.cam.ac.uk/faculty-research/centres/alternative-finance/publications/.
30 Committee on the Global Financial System and the Financial Stability Board, "FinTech Credit: Market Structure, Business Models and Financial Stability Implications," BIS, May 22, 2017, https://www.bis.org/publ/cgfs_fsb1.htm.
31 LendingClub, "Member Payment Dependent Notes," August 22, 2014, https://www.lendingclub.com/fileDownload.action?file=Clean_As_Filed_20140822.pdf&type=docs.
32 FINRA, "Funding Portals We Regulate," accessed March 20, 2020, https://www.finra.org/about/funding-portals-we-regulate.
33 OCC, "OCC Conditionally Approves SoFi Bank, National Association," January 18, 2022, https://www.occ.treas.gov/news-issuances/news-releases/2022/nr-occ-2022-4.html.
34 Federal Reserve Bank of New York, "Small Business Credit Survey," accessed July 21, 2019, https://www.newyorkfed.org/smallbusiness/small-business-credit-survey-2018.
35 This misalignment of incentives and risk is the originate-to-distribute problem that was behind the 2007 subprime mortgage crisis that led to the 2008–2009 Global Financial Crisis.
36 Farag and Johan, "How Alternative Finance Informs."
37 Jiefei Liu, "The Dramatic Rise and Fall of Online P2P Lending in China," TechCrunch, August 1, 2018, https://techcrunch.com/2018/08/01/the-dramatic-rise-and-fall-of-online-p2p-lending-in-china/.
38 Bloomberg News, "How China's Peer-to-Peer Lending Crash Is Destroying Lives," October 2, 2018, https://www.bloomberg.com/news/articles/2018-10-02/peer-to-peer-lending-crash-in-china-leads-to-suicide-and-protest.
39 *Economist*, "Ponzis to Punters," February 6, 2016, https://www.economist.com/china/2016/02/06/ponzis-to-punters.
40 Cambridge Centre for Alternative Finance, "The 3rd Asia Pacific Region Alternative Finance Industry Report," University of Cambridge, November 2018.

41 Jagtiani and Lemieux, "Do Fintech Lenders Penetrate Areas?"

42 Pankaj Kumar Maskara, Emre Kuvvet, and Gengxuan Chen, "The Role of P2P Platforms in Enhancing Financial Inclusion in the United States: An Analysis of Peer-to-Peer Lending across the Rural–Urban Divide," *Financial Management* 50, no. 3 (2021): 747–774.

43 Christoph Bertsch, Isaiah Hull, Yingjie Qi, and Xin Zhang, "Bank Misconduct and Online Lending," *Journal of Banking and Finance* 116 (2020): 105822.

44 Manasa Gopal and Philipp Schnabl, "The Rise of Finance Companies and FinTech Lenders in Small Business Lending," SSRN, May 13, 2020, https://ssrn.com/abstract=3600068.

45 Christine A. Parlour, Uday Rajan, and Haoxiang Zhu, "When FinTech Competes for Payment Flows," *Review of Financial Studies* 35, no. 11 (2022): 49855024.

46 Gopal and Schnabl, "The Rise of Finance Companies and FinTech Lenders."

47 Isil Erel and Jack Liebersohn, "Can FinTech Reduce Disparities in Access to Finance? Evidence from the Paycheck Protection Program," *Journal of Financial Economics* 146, no. 1 (2022): 90-118.

48 Greg Buchak, Gregor Matvos, Tomasz Piskorski, and Amit Seru, "Fintech, Regulatory Arbitrage, and the Rise of Shadow Banks," *Journal of Financial Economics* 130, no. 3 (2018): 453–483; Tetyana Balyuk, "FinTech Lending and Bank Credit Access for Consumers," *Management Science* 69, no. 1 (2023): 555–575.

49 Huan Tang, "Peer-to-Peer Lenders versus Banks: Substitutes or Complements?" *Review of Financial Studies* 32, no. 5 (2019): 1900–1938.

50 Marco Di Maggio and Vincent Yao, "Fintech Borrowers."

51 Buchak et al., "Fintech, Regulatory Arbitrage"; Andreas Fuster, Matthew Plosser, Philipp Schnabl, and James Vickery, "The Role of Technology in Mortgage Lending," *Review of Financial Studies* 32, no. 5 (2019): 1854–1899.

52 Fuster et al., "The Role of Technology in Mortgage Lending."

53 John M. Griffin, Samuel Kruger, and Prateek Mahajan, "Did FinTech Lenders Facilitate PPP Fraud?" *Journal of Finance* (forthcoming).

54 Giulio Cornelli, Jon Frost, Leonardo Gambacorta, P. Raghavendra Rau, Robert Wardrop, and Tania Ziegler, "Fintech and Big Tech Credit: A New Database," BIS Working Paper No. 887, September 25, 2020.

55 Tao Chen, Yi Huang, Chen Lin, and Zixia Sheng, "Finance and Firm Volatility: Evidence from Small Business Lending in China," *Management Science* 68, no. 3 (2022): 2226–2249.

56 Hadar Gafni, Dan Marom, Alicia Robb, and Orly Sade, "Gender Dynamics in Crowdfunding (Kickstarter): Evidence on Entrepreneurs, Backers, and Taste-Based Discrimination," *Review of Finance* 25, no. 2 (2021): 235–274.

57 Sofia Bapna and Martin Ganco, "Gender Gaps in Equity Crowdfunding: Evidence from a Randomized Field Experiment," *Management Science* 67, no. 5 (2021): 2679–2710.

58 Yang Duan, Tien-Shih Hsieh, Ray R. Wang, and Zhihong Wang, "Entrepreneurs' Facial Trustworthiness, Gender, and Crowdfunding Success," *Journal of Corporate Finance* 64 (2020): 101693.

59 Peter Younkin and Venkat Kuppuswamy, "The Colorblind Crowd? Founder Race and Performance in Crowdfunding," *Management Science* 64, no. 7 (2018): 3269–3287.

60 Robert Bartlett, Adair Morse, Richard Stanton, and Nancy Wallace, "Consumer-Lending Discrimination in the FinTech Era," *Journal of Financial Economics* 143, no. 1 (2022): 30–56.

61 Nathaniel Popper, "SoFi, an Online Lender, Is Looking for a Relationship," *New York Times*, October 19, 2016, https://www.nytimes.com/2016/10/20/business/dealbook/sofi-an-online-lender-is-looking-for-a-relationship.html.

8. Robo-advisors and Digital Wealth Management

1 Backend Benchmarking, "The Robo Report Fourth Quarter 2021," https://www.backendbenchmarking.com/the-robo-report/.

2 Heredia Lubasha, Simon Bartletta, Joe Carrubba, Dean Frankle, Chris McIntyre, Edoardo Palmisani, Anastasios Panagiotou, Neil Pardasani, Kedra Newsom Reeves, Thomas Schulte, and Ben Sheridan, "Global Asset Management 2021 – The $100 Trillion Machine," BCG, July 2021, https://web-assets.bcg.com/79/bf/d1d361854084a9624a0cbce3bf07/bcg-global-asset-management-2021-jul-2021.pdf.

3 To read about each of these fascinating finance luminaries, see: Andrew W. Lo and Stephen R. Foerster, *In Pursuit of the Perfect Portfolio* (Princeton, NJ: Princeton University Press, 2021).

4 Vanguard, "Facts and Figures," accessed April 1, 2022, https://corporate.vanguard.com/content/corporatesite/us/en/corp/who-we-are/sets-us-apart/facts-and-figures.html.

5 Morningstar, "Unveiling the Truth: The Semiannual Morningstar's Active/Passive Barometer Report," February 2022, https://www.morningstar.com/lp/active-passive-barometer.

6 Investment Company Institute, "2021 Investment Company Fact Book," May 2021 https://www.ici.org/system/files/2021-05/2021_factbook.pdf.

7 ETFGI, "ETFGI Reports Global ETFs Industry."

8 Jon Stein, "The History of Betterment: Changing an Industry," Betterment, July 20, 2016, https://www.betterment.com/resources/the-history-of-betterment.

9 Wealthsimple, "Management Expense Ratio (MER) Fees for Managed Accounts," accessed April 1, 2022, https://help.wealthsimple.com/hc/en-ca/articles/360056584334-Wealthsimple-Invest-management-expense-ratio-MER-fees.

10 Clayton M. Christensen, Michael Raynor, and Rory McDonald, "What Is Disruptive Innovation?" *Harvard Business Review* (December 2015): 44–53.

11 Alessandra Malito, "Vanguard Officially Launches Its Robo Adviser, Drops Minimum Investment to $50,000," *Investment News*, May 11, 2015, https://www.investmentnews.com/vanguard-officially-launches-its-robo-adviser-drops-minimum-investment-to-50000-62263.

12 SigFig, "About Us," accessed April 1, 2022, https://sigfig.com/home/company/about-us.

13 Kate Beioley, "Robo-advice Revolution Comes at a Cost," *Financial Times*, November 21, 2017, https://www.ft.com/content/4488fdd0-cde9-11e7-b781-794ce08b24dc.

14 Wealthsimple, "Wealthsimple for Advisors," accessed June 21, 2019, https://www.wealthsimple.com/en-ca/advisors.

15 Frank Hodge, Kim Mendoza, and Rochan Sinha, "The Effect of Humanizing Robo-advisors on Investor Judgments," *Contemporary Accounting Research* 38, no. 1 (2021): 770–792; Agostino Capponi, Sveinn Ólafsson, and Thaleia Zariphopoulou, "Personalized Robo-advising: Enhancing Investment through Client Interaction," *Management Science* 68, no. 4 (2022): 2485–2512.

16 Francesco D'Acunto, Nagpurnanand Prabhala, and Alberto G Rossi, "The Promises and Pitfalls of Robo-advising," *Review of Financial Studies* 32, no. 5 (2019): 1983–2020.

17 Statista, "Robo-advisors – Worldwide," accessed April 1, 2022, https://www.statista.com/outlook/dmo/fintech/digital-investment/robo-advisors/worldwide?currency=usd.

18 Chuck Grace and Andrew Sarta, "Next-Generation Financial Advice: Reimagining Wealth Management in the Age of Technology," in *The Technological Revolution in Financial Services: How Banks and Fintech Customers Win Together*, eds. Michael R. King and Richard W. Nesbitt (Toronto: University of Toronto Press, 2020).

19 Ernst & Young, "The Evolution of Robo-advisors and Advisor 2.0 Model," accessed June 21, 2019, https://www.ey.com/Publication/vwLUAssets/ey-the-evolution-of-robo-advisors-and-advisor-2-model/$FILE/ey-the-evolution-of-robo-advisors-and-advisor-2-model.pdf.

20 Fidelity Investments, "Fidelity Finds Number of Tech-Savvy eAdvisors Has Grown to 40 Percent; eAdvisors Outperforming Tech-Indifferent Peers," Business Wire, June 20, 2017, https://www.businesswire.com/news/home/20170620005279/en/Fidelity-Finds-Number-of-Tech-Savvy-eAdvisors-Has-Grown-to-40-Percent-eAdvisors-Outperforming-Tech-Indifferent-Peers.

21 Nest Wealth, "About Us," accessed April 1, 2022, https://nestwealth.com/about.

22 BlackRock, "Aladdin Wealth," accessed April 1, 2022, https://www.BlackRock.com/aladdin/products/aladdin-wealth.

23 See: Global Sustainable Investment, "Global Sustainable Investment Review 2020," August 2021, http://www.gsi-alliance.org/wp-content/uploads/2021/08/GSIR-20201.pdf.

24 BlackRock, "2020 Global Sustainable Investing Survey," accessed April 1, 2022, https://www.blackrock.com/uk/about-us/blackrock-sustainability-survey.

25 Clim8 Invest, "Making Money Work for You and the Climate," accessed April 1, 2022, https://clim8invest.com/why-us/.

26 Halah Touryalai, "Forget $10 Trades, Meet Robinhood: New Brokerage Targets Millennials with Little Cash," *Forbes*, February 26, 2014, https://www.forbes.com/sites/halahtouryalai/2014/02/26/forget-10-trades-meet-robinhood-new-brokerage-targets-millennials-with-little-cash/.

27 Michael Carney, "Robinhood Gets $3M to Take from Wall St. and Give to Main St. with Its Mobile-First, Zero-Commission Brokerage," Pando, December 18, 2013.

28 Jeff Kauflin, Antoine Gara, and Sergei Klebnikov, "The Inside Story of Robinhood's Billionaire Founders, Option Kid Cowboys and the Wall Street Sharks That Feed on Them," *Forbes*, August 19, 2020, https://www.forbes.com/sites/jeffkauflin/2020/08/19/the-inside-story-of-robinhoods-billionaire-founders-option-kid-cowboys-and-the-wall-street-sharks-that-feed-on-them/.

29 Nathaniel Popper, Michael J. de la Merced, and David McCabe, "Robinhood, Under the Gun, Raises $2.4 Billion," *New York Times*, February 1, 2021, https://www.nytimes.com/live/2021/02/01/business/us-economy-coronavirus#robinhood-needed-3-billion-to-cover-risky-trades-its-chief-told-elon-musk.

30 Erin Griffith, "Robinhood's Shares Fall 8.4% in Public Trading Debut," *New York Times*, July 29, 2021, https://www.nytimes.com/2021/07/29/technology/robinhood-stock.html.

31 Brad M. Barber, Xing Huang, Terrance Odean, and Christopher Schwarz, "Attention-Induced Trading and Returns: Evidence from Robinhood Users," *Journal of Finance* 77, no. 6 (2022): 3141–3190.

9. Payments and Insurtech

1 The World Bank, "Remittance Prices Worldwide," no. 24 (December 2017), https://remittanceprices.worldbank.org/sites/default/files/rpw_report_december2017.pdf.

2 For the United States, see: Federal Reserve, "The 2016 Federal Reserve Payments Study," July 28, 2017, https://www.federalreserve.gov/paymentsystems/2017-june-recent-developments.htm. For Canada, see: Bank of Canada, "2017 Methods-of-Payment Survey Report," December 2018, https://www.bankofcanada.ca/2018/12/staff-discussion-paper-2018-17/.

3 McKinsey & Company, "The 2021 McKinsey Global Payments Report," October 2021, https://www.mckinsey.com/industries/financial-services/our-insights/the-2021-mckinsey-global-payments-report.

4 JPMorgan Chase, "Investor Day 2018," February 27, 2018, https://www.jpmorganchase.com/ir/events.

5 A merchant bank may be called the acquiring bank, the merchant acquirer, the merchant service provider (MSP), or the merchant account provider.

6 Fiona Lau, "Paytm Seals India's Largest IPO," IFR News, November 11, 2021 (reported on Refinitiv Eikon).

7 Lalita Clozel, "'Fintech Charter' Has No Early Takers as Lawsuit Looms," *Wall Street Journal*, September 12, 2018, https://www.wsj.com/articles/fintech-charter-has-no-early-takers-as-lawsuit-looms-1536764426.

8 Alipay, "Alipay," accessed June 24, 2019, https://intl.alipay.com/.

9 Ant Group, "Our History," accessed April 1, 2022, https://www.antgroup.com/en.

10 Statista, "Digital Payments in China," accessed April 1, 2022, https://www.statista.com/topics/1211/digital-payments-in-china/.

11 Safaricom, "M-PESA," accessed June 24, 2019, https://www.safaricom.co.ke/personal/m-pesa.

12 Vodafone Group, "2022 Annual Report," accessed April 1, 2023, https://investors.vodafone.com/reports-information/results-reports-presentations.

13 Wise, "Our Story," accessed April 1, 2022, https://wise.com/ca/about/our-story.

14 Wise, "Prospectus," July 2021, https://wise.com/owners/.

15 World Bank, "Remittances to Reach $630 billion in 2022 with Record Flows into Ukraine," May 11, 2022, https://www.worldbank.org/en/news/press-release/2022/05/11/remittances-to-reach-630-billion-in-2022-with-record-flows-into-ukraine.

16 World Remit, "How It Works," accessed June 24, 2019, https://www.worldremit.com/en/how-it-works.

17 Gabi Byrnes, "Western Union vs. WorldRemit," Finder, March 15, 2019, https://www.finder.com/western-union-vs-worldremit.

18 Octopus Holdings, "About Octopus Card," accessed April 1, 2022, https://www.octopus.com.hk/en/consumer/octopus-cards/about/index.html.

19 Octopus Holdings, "Statistics at a Glance," accessed April 1, 2022, https://www.octopus.com.hk/en/business/index.html.

20 McKinsey & Company, "Creating Value, Finding Focus: Global Insurance Report 2022," February 15, 2022, https://www.mckinsey.com/industries/financial-services/our-insights/creating-value-finding-focus-global-insurance-report-2022.

21 CB Insights, "State of Fintech 2022 Report," January 18, 2023, https://www.cbinsights.com/research/report/fintech-trends-2022.

22 Willis Towers Watson, "Quarterly InsurTech Briefing Q4 2017," January 2018, https://www.willistowerswatson.com/en-CA/insights/2018/01/quarterly-insurtech-briefing-q4-2017.

23 Root, "The App That Rewards Good Drivers," accessed April 1, 2022, https://www.joinroot.com/.

24 Lemonade, "Prospectus Filed Pursuant to Rule 424(b)(4)," July 2, 2020, https://investor.lemonade.com/financials/sec-filings/sec-filings-details/default.aspx?FilingId=14253775.

25 ZhongAn Online P&C Insurance, "Global Offering," September 18, 2017, http://www.hkexnews.hk/listedco/listconews/SEHK/2017/0918/LTN20170918023.pdf.

10. Digital Banking and the Response of Incumbents

1 FDIC, "Key Findings from *How America Banks: Household Use of Banking and Financial Services* – 2019 FDIC Survey," accessed April 1, 2022, https://www.fdic.gov/analysis/household-survey/index.html.

2 Angus Reid Institute, "Personal Finances & Poverty in Canada," accessed April 1, 2022, https://angusreid.org/personal-finances-poverty-in-canada/; MNP, "Canadians' Confidence in Personal Finances, Debt Repayment Abilities Reaches Lowest Level Ever Recorded," accessed April 1, 2022, https://mnpdebt.ca/en/resources/mnp-consumer-debt-index.

3 Stephanie Dhue and Sharon Epperson, "70% of Americans Are Feeling Financially Stressed, New CNBC Survey Finds," CNBC, April 11, 2023, https://www.cnbc.com/2023/04/11/70percent-of-americans-feel-financially-stressed-new-cnbc-survey-finds.html.

4 UK Mental Health Foundation, "Stress, Anxiety and Hopelessness over Personal Finances Widespread across UK – New Mental Health Survey," November 17, 2022, https://www.mentalhealth.org.uk/about-us/news/stress-anxiety-and-hopelessness-over-personal-finances-widespread-across-uk-new-mental-health-survey.

5 Financial Health Network, "US Financial Health Pulse: 2020 Trends Report," Moven, October 13, 2020, https://moven.com/research/.

6 MNP, "Over Half (53%) of Canadians within $200 of Not Being Able to Cover Their Bills and Debt Payments, Up 10 Points Since December Reaching a Five-Year High," GlobeNewswire, April 8, 2021, https://www.globenewswire.com/news-release/2021/04/08/2206577/0/en/Over-Half-53-of-Canadians-Within-200-of-Not-Being-Able-to-Cover-Their-Bills-and-Debt-Payments-Up-10-Points-Since-December-Reaching-a-Five-Year-High.html.

7 Refresh Financial, "Credit in Canada," accessed April 1, 2022, https://refreshfinancial.ca/wp-content/themes/refresh/images/bankruptcy/pdf-guide/CreditInCanada_guide.pdf.

8 Government of Canada, "Why Your Credit Score Is Important," accessed April 1, 2022, https://www.canada.ca/en/financial-consumer-agency/services/financial-toolkit/credit/credit-5/3.html.

9 Press Association, "Financial Crisis Five Years On: Trust in Banking Hits New Low," *Guardian*, August 9, 2012, https://www.theguardian.com/business/2012/aug/09/financial-crisis-anniversary-trust-in-banks.

10 Johnny Ayers, "How Banks Can Tackle Millennial Skepticism," TechCrunch, November 2, 2016, https://techcrunch.com/2016/11/02/how-banks-can-tackle-millennial-skepticism/.

11 Charles Arthur, "Tech Giants May Be Huge, But Nothing Matches Big Data," *Guardian*, August 23, 2013, https://www.theguardian.com/technology/2013/aug/23/tech-giants-data.

12 William S. Demchak, "Committee on Banking, Housing, and Urban Affairs, US Senate – Written Statement of William S. Demchak, Chairman, President and CEO, The PNC Financial Services Group, Inc.," September 22, 2022, https://www.banking.senate.gov/imo/media/doc/Demchak%20Testimony%209-22-22.pdf.

13 Senate of Canada, "Open Banking: What It Means for You," June 19, 2019, https://sencanada.ca/en/info-page/parl-42-1/banc-open-banking/.

14 Zhiguo He, Jing Huang, and Jidong Zhou, "Open Banking: Credit Market Competition when Borrowers Own the Data," *Journal of Financial Economics* 147, no. 2 (2023): 449–474.

15 Sensibill, "Get Sensibill," accessed July 27, 2019, https://www.getsensibill.com/.

16 Sarah Perez, "Moven Takes Its Mobile Banking App out of Beta" TechCrunch, March 7, 2014, https://techcrunch.com/2014/03/07/moven-takes-its-mobile-banking-app-out-of-beta/.

17 TD Bank Group, "TD and Moven Announce Exclusive Canadian Agreement," Newswire, December 2, 2014, https://www.newswire.ca/news-releases/td-and-moven-announce-exclusive-canadian-agreement-516595721.html.

18 Moven, "About Moven," accessed April 1, 2022, https://moven.com/who-we-are/.

19 John Koetsier, "Banking on Mobile up 35%–85% Thanks to Coronavirus (After 1 Trillion App Opens in 2019)," April 15, 2020, *Forbes*, https://www.forbes.com/sites/johnkoetsier/2020/04/15/report-35-85-fintech-growth-on-mobile-thanks-to-coronavirus-after-1-trillion-app-opens-in-2019/.

20 Chad West, "We Got a Banking Licence," Revolut, December 13, 2018, https://blog.revolut.com/we-got-a-banking-licence/.

21 Romain Dillet, "N26 Launches Its Challenger Bank in the US," TechCrunch, July 11, 2019, https://techcrunch.com/2019/07/11/n26-launches-its-challenger-bank-in-the-u-s/.

22 Jeff Kauflin and Maria Abreu, "How David Vélez Built the World's Most Valuable Digital Bank and Became a Billionaire," April 7, 2021, *Forbes*, https://www.forbes.com/sites/jeffkauflin/2021/04/07/fintech-billionaire-david-velez-nubank-brazil-digital-bank/.

23 Oscar Williams-Grut, "A German Challenger Bank That Works Like an App-Store Just Got Acquired – Here's Why," *Business Insider*, July 29, 2016, https://www.businessinsider.com/fidor-bank-acquired-group-bpce-matthias-kroner-interview-2016-7?r=UK.

24 Fidor, "Fidor Market: A Marketplace for All Financial Needs," accessed July 27, 2019, https://www.fidor.com/solutions/bank-as-a-marketplace.

25 Borrowell, "Who We Are," accessed July 27, 2019, https://borrowell.com/who-is-borrowell.

26 Sarah Perez, "Credit Karma Launches Free Credit Monitoring, Enrolls 100,000 Users in a Day," TechCrunch, January 4, 2012, https://techcrunch.com/2012/01/04/credit-karma-launches-free-credit-monitoring-enrolls-100000-users-in-a-day/.

27 Jamie Dimon, "2014 Annual Report: Letter to Shareholders," JPMorgan Chase & Co., April 8, 2015, https://www.jpmorganchase.com/corporate/annual-report/2014/ar-solid-strategy.htm.

28 Federal Deposit Insurance Corporation, "Statistics at a Glance," March 31, 2019, https://www.fdic.gov/bank/statistical/stats/2019mar/industry.pdf.

29 Oliver Wyman, "Time to Start Again: The State of Financial Services 2019," accessed July 30, 2019, https://www.oliverwyman.com/our-expertise/hubs/the-state-of-the-financial-services-industry-2019.html.

30 See: Kent Beck, Mike Beedle, Arie van Bennekum, Alistair Cockburn, Ward Cunningham, Martin Fowler, James Grenning, Jim Highsmith, Andrew Hunt, Ron Jeffries, Jon Kern, Brian Marick, Robert C. Martin, Steve Mellor, Ken Schwaber, Jeff Sutherland, and Dave Thomas, "Manifesto for Agile Software Development," https://agilemanifesto.org/.

31 CB Insights, "37 Corporate Innovation Labs in Finance," May 15, 2019, https://www.cbinsights.com/research/report/finance-corporate-innovation-labs/.

32 Zelle, "Get Started," accessed July 29, 2019, https://www.zellepay.com/participating-banks-and-credit-unions.

33 CB Insights, "Where the Top 3 US Banks Are Betting on the Future of Fin Services," April 21, 2021, https://www.cbinsights.com/research/goldman-citi-jpm-fintech-investments; CB Insights, "Fintech Funding Trends in Europe," September 14, 2021, https://www.cbinsights.com/research/report/fintech-trends-europe-q2-2021/.

34 RBC Ventures, "About Us," accessed July 29, 2019, https://www.rbcventures.ca/.

35 RBC, "RBC Investor Day 2018," accessed July 29, 2019, http://www.rbc.com/dms/enterprise/investorday/.

36 Chris Skinner, "Clash of Clans … Or New Bank versus Old Bank (Fidor, BPCE)," The Finanser, November 2, 2018, https://thefinanser.com/2018/11/clash-clans-new-bank-versus-old-bank-fidor-bpce.html/.

37 Kate Rooney, "Small Banks You've Never Heard of Are Quietly Enabling the Tech Takeover of the Financial Industry," CNBC, February 15, 2019, https://www.cnbc.com/2019/02/15/small-banks-youve-never-heard-of-quietly-power-the-booming-fintech-industry--.html.

38 Hugh Son, "Rarely Humbled Goldman Sachs Concedes Missteps in Plan to Take on Megabanks in Retail Finance," CNBC, October 18, 2022, https://www.cnbc.com/2022/10/18/goldman-sachs-pivot-from-marcus-shows-that-disrupting-retail-banking-is-hard.html.

11. Techfins and Bigtech in Financial Services

1 Heath P. Terry, Debra Schwartz, and Tina Sun, "The Future of Finance Part 3 – The Socialization of Finance," Goldman Sachs Equity Research, March 13, 2015.

2 Agustín Carstens, "Big Tech in Finance and New Challenges for Public Policy," Keynote Address at the FT Banking Summit, London, December 4, 2018, https://www.bis.org/speeches/sp181205.htm.

3 Martin Arnold, "Royal Bank of Canada Warns on Big Tech Threat to Banking," Financial Times, June 13, 2018, https://www.ft.com/content/e70c827c-6f13-11e8-92d3-6c13e5c92914.

4 René M. Stulz, "FinTech, BigTech, and the Future of Banks," Journal of Applied Corporate Finance 31, no. 4 (2019): 86–97.

5 Dirk A. Zetzsche, Ross P. Buckley, Douglas W. Arner, and Janos Nathan Barberis, "From FinTech to TechFin: The Regulatory Challenges of Data-Driven Finance," European Banking Institute Working Paper Series 2017 – No. 6, SSRN, April 28, 2017, https://ssrn.com/abstract=2959925.

6 Financial Stability Board, "BigTech in Finance: Market Developments and Potential Financial Stability Implications," December 9, 2019, https://www.fsb.org/2019/12/bigtech-in-finance-market-developments-and-potential-financial-stability-implications/; Financial Stability Board, "BigTech Firms in Finance in Emerging Market and Developing Economies," October 12, 2020, https://www.fsb.org/2020/10/bigtech-firms-in-finance-in-emerging-market-and-developing-economies/.

7 Rainny Shuyan Xie, Siew-Kien Sia, and Boon Siong Neo, "Fintech and Finance Transformation: The Rise of Ant Financial," ABCC at Nanyang Technical University, August 25, 2017.

8 Martin Chorzempa, "How China Leapfrogged ahead of the United States in the Fintech Race," Peterson Institute for International Economics, April 26, 2018, https://www.piie.com/blogs/china-economic-watch/how-china-leapfrogged-ahead-united-states-fintech-race.

9 The Yu'ebao money market fund is managed by Tianhong Asset Management, which is 51% owned by Ant Financial.

10 In June 2010 the People's Bank of China issued new regulations that required non-bank payment companies to obtain a license to operate in China. Chinese payment companies could not be foreign owned, which meant that Alibaba had to divest due to the minority stake held by Yahoo! and Softbank.

11 Zen Soo, "TechFin: Jack Ma Coins Term to Set Alipay's Goal to Give Emerging Markets Access to Capital," *South China Morning Post*, December 2, 2016. See also: Chris Skinner, "The Difference between FinTech and TechFin," The Finanser, June 22, 2018, https://thefinanser.com/2018/06/difference-fintech-techfin.html/.

12 Crunchbase, "Ant Financial," accessed June 21, 2019, https://www.crunchbase.com/organization/ant-financial#section-funding-rounds.

13 Ant Financial, "Ant Group," accessed June 17, 2019, https://www.antfin.com/index.htm?locale=en_US.

14 Alibaba Group, "Investor Day 2018," September 17, 2018, https://www.alibabagroup.com/en/ir/investorday.

15 Shu Zhang, "China's Ant Financial Amasses 50 Million Users, Mostly Low-Income, in New Health Plan," *Reuters*, April 12, 2019, https://www.reuters.com/article/us-china-ant-financial-insurance/chinas-ant-financial-amasses-50-million-users-mostly-low-income-in-new-health-plan-idUSKCN1RO0H5.

16 Tracey Xiang, "Alibaba's Online Equity Crowdfunding Platform ANTSDAQ Launches Beta," TechNode, November 25, 2015, https://technode.com/2015/11/25/alibabas-onilne-equity-crowdfunding-platform-antsdaq-launches-beta/.

17 Ant Group, "Bring Small and Beautiful Changes to the World," accessed May 1, 2022, https://www.antgroup.com/en.

18 Raymond Zhong, "China Orders Ant Group to Revamp Its Business," *New York Times*, https://nyti.ms/3plLLWc.

19 Iris Deng and Celia Chen, "How WeChat Became China's Everyday Mobile App," *South China Morning Post*, August 16, 2018, https://www.scmp.com/tech/article/2159831/how-wechat-became-chinas-everyday-mobile-app.

20 China Daily, "WeChat's 'Licaitong' Attracts 800m Yuan, Challenging Yu'E Bao," January 24, 2014, https://www.chinadaily.com.cn/business/2014-01/24/content_17257238.htm.

21 WeBank, "Better Banking, Better Life," accessed May 1, 2022, https://www.webank.com/#/home.

22 Violet Chung, "Insurance of the Future: An Interview with Ren Huichuan of Tencent," McKinsey & Company, December 16, 2021, https://www.mckinsey.com/industries/financial-services/our-insights/insurance-of-the-future-an-interview-with-ren-huichuan-of-tencent.

23 Steven Millward, "WeChat's Global Expansion Has Been a Disaster," TechInAsia, May 25, 2016, https://www.techinasia.com/wechat-global-expansion-fail.

24 Tencent America, "About Us," accessed May 1, 2022, https://www.tencent.com/en-us/about.html.

25 Greg Roumeliotus, "US Blocks MoneyGram Sale to China's Ant Financial on National Security Concerns," *Reuters*, January 2, 2018, https://www.reuters.com/article/us-moneygram-intl-m-a-ant-financial/u-s-blocks-moneygram-sale-to-chinas-ant-financial-on-national-security-concerns-idUSKBN1ER1R7.

26 CB Insights, "Everything You Need to Know about What Amazon Is Doing in Financial Services," March 15, 2022, https://www.cbinsights.com/reports/CB-Insights_Amazon-In-Financial-Services.pdf.

27 Amazon, "Amazon Lending," accessed May 1, 2022, https://sell.amazon.com/programs/amazon-lending.

28 Eugene Kim, "Amazon Has Partnered with Bank of America for Its Lending Program: Sources," CNBC, February 14, 2018, https://www.cnbc.com/2018/02/14/amazon-and-bank-of-america-partner-for-lending-program-but-growth-has-stalled.html; Ron Shevlin, "Amazon and Goldman Sachs: A Small Business Lending Wake-Up Call for Banks," *Forbes*, June 15, 2020, https://www.forbes.com/sites/ronshevlin/2020/06/15/amazon-and-goldman-sachs-a-small-business-lending-wake-up-call-for-banks/.

29 Steven Musil, "Amazon to Fold Its Mobile-Wallet App Beta on Wednesday," CNET, January 20, 2015, https://www.cnet.com/news/amazon-to-fold-its-mobile-wallet-app-beta-on-wednesday/.

30 Apple, "Apple Announces Apple Pay," September 9, 2014, https://www.apple.com/ca/newsroom/2014/09/09Apple-Announces-Apple-Pay/.

31 Apple, "Apple Announces Apple Pay."

32 Julija A., "10+ Apple Pay Statistics That Show Mobile Payments Are the Future," Fortunly, March 10, 2022, https://fortunly.com/statistics/apple-pay-statistics/.

33 PYMTS, "Apple Makes New Moves to Turn iPhones into Payment Terminals," January 27, 2022, https://www.pymnts.com/apple/2022/apple-iphones-will-soon-serve-as-payment-terminals-in-jolt-to-square/.

34 Apple, "Introducing Apple Card, a New Kind of Credit Card Created by Apple," March 25, 2019, https://www.apple.com/newsroom/2019/03/introducing-apple-card-a-new-kind-of-credit-card-created-by-apple/.

35 Apple, "Apple Card," accessed May 1, 2022, https://www.apple.com/apple-card/family/.

36 Apple, "Apple Card's New High-Yield Savings Account Is Now Available, Offering a 4.15 Percent APY," April 17, 2023, https://www.apple.com/newsroom/2023/04

/apple-cards-new-high-yield-savings-account-is-now-available-offering-a-4-point-15 -percent-apy/.

37 Paayal Zaveri, "Facebook Messenger Users Can Now Send Money to Each Other with PayPal," CNBC, October 20, 2017, https://www.cnbc.com/2017/10/20/facebook -messenger-send-money-with-paypal.html.

38 Emily Glazer, Deepa Seetharaman, and AnnaMaria Andriotis, "Facebook to Banks: Give Us Your Data, We'll Give You Our Users," *Wall Street Journal*, August 6, 2018, https://www .wsj.com/articles/facebook-to-banks-give-us-your-data-well-give-you-our-users-1533564049.

39 Saheli Roy Choudhury, "Users Can Now Send Money through WhatsApp in India's Massive Digital Payments Market," CNBC, November 6, 2020, https://www.cnbc .com/2020/11/06/users-can-now-send-money-through-whatsapp-in-india.html.

40 Michael Pooler and Hannah Murphy, "Meta Suffers Setback with WhatsApp Business Payments in Brazil," *Financial Times*, April 19, 2022, https://www.ft.com/content/6d32bd6e -9278-4eba-a64c-482492520ee0.

41 Hannah Murphy, "What Is Libra, Facebook's New Digital Coin?" *Financial Times*, June 18, 2019, https://www.ft.com/content/c3746b5c-90de-11e9-aea1-2b1d33ac3271.

42 Taylor Telford, "Why Governments around the World Are Afraid of Libra, Facebook's Cryptocurrency," *Washington Post*, July 12, 2019, https://www.washingtonpost.com /business/2019/07/12/why-governments-around-world-are-afraid-libra-facebooks -cryptocurrency/.

43 Daniel Palmer, "G7 Forming Task Force in Response to Facebook's Libra Cryptocurrency," CoinDesk, June 21, 2019, https://www.coindesk.com/markets/2019/06/21 /g7-forming-task-force-in-response-to-facebooks-libra-cryptocurrency/.

44 Nikhilesh De, "Diem's Demise: A Timeline of Libra's Long Road from a Facebook Lab to the Global Stage," CoinDesk, April 22, 2020, https://www.coindesk.com/business/2020/04/22 /libras-long-road-from-a-facebook-lab-to-the-global-stage-a-timeline/.

45 Frederic Lardinois, "Say Goodbye to Android Pay and Hello to Google Pay," TechCrunch, February 20, 2018, https://techcrunch.com/2018/02/20/say-goodbye-to-android -pay-and-hello-to-google-pay/.

46 Jon Russell, "Google Is Supercharging Its Tez Payment Service in India ahead of Global Expansion," TechCrunch, August 28, 2018, https://techcrunch.com/2018/08/28/google -is-supercharging-its-tez-payment-service/.

47 Statista, "Number of Apple Pay, Samsung Pay, and Google Pay Contactless Payment Users in 2018, with a Forecast for 2020," https://www.statista.com/statistics/722213 /user-base-of-leading-digital-wallets-nfc/.

48 Caesar Sengupta, "Google Pay Reimagined: Pay, Save, Manage Expenses and More," Google, November 18, 2020, https://blog.google/products/google-pay/reimagined -pay-save-manage-expenses-and-more/.

49 Ron Amadeo, "The New Google Pay Repeats All the Same Mistakes of Google Allo," ARS Technica, March 7, 2021, https://arstechnica.com/gadgets/2021/03/the-new-google -pay-repeats-all-the-same-mistakes-of-google-allo/.

50 Ron Shevlin, "Google Kills the Google Plex: It Could Have Been a Digital Checking Account Killer App," *Forbes*, October 1, 2021, https://www.forbes.com/sites /ronshevlin/2021/10/01/google-kills-the-google-plex-it-could-have-been-a-digital -checking-account-killer-app/.

51 CB Insights, "The Big Tech in Fintech Report: How Facebook, Apple, Google, & Amazon Are Battling for the $28.2T Market," June 21, 2021, https://www.cbinsights.com/research /report/famga-big-tech-fintech/.

52 GV, "Portfolio," accessed July 2, 2019, https://www.gv.com/.

53 CapitalG, "Focused on Tomorrow," accessed May 1, 2022, https://www.capitalg.com /portfolio/.

54 Marco Ceccagnoli, Chris Forman, Peng Huang, and D.J. Wu, "Cocreation of Value in a Platform Ecosystem! The Case of Enterprise Software," *MIS Quarterly* 36, no. 1 (2012): 263–290; Annabelle Gawer and Michael A. Cusumano, 2014, "Industry Platforms and Ecosystem Innovation," *Journal of Product Innovation Management* 31, no. 3 (2014): 417–433.

55 David S. Evans and Richard Schmalensee, *Matchmakers: The New Economics of Multisided Platforms* (Boston: Harvard Business Review Press, 2016).

56 *Economist*, "Special Report: A Bank in Your Pocket," May 7, 2015, https://www.economist .com/special-report/2015/05/07/the-bank-in-your-pocket.

57 Canadian Bankers Association, "See the Latest Statistics on the Number of Bank Branches in Canada by Province," November 10, 2022, https://cba.ca/bank-branches-in-canada.

58 Canadian Bankers Association, "Focus: How Canadians Bank," March 31, 2022, https:// cba.ca/technology-and-banking.

59 Interbrand, "Most Valuable Brands – 2006," accessed June 11, 2019, https://www .interbrand.com/best-brands/best-global-brands/2006/ranking/.

60 Interbrand, "Most Valuable Brands – 2018," accessed June 11, 2019, https://www .interbrand.com/best-brands/best-global-brands/2018/ranking/.

61 Unless noted, these statistics are provided by the market and consumer data company Statista, accessed June 12, 2019, https://www.statista.com/.

62 For two examples among many articles, see: Anna Mitchell and Larry Diamond, "China's Surveillance State Should Scare Everyone," *Atlantic*, February 2, 2018, https://www .theatlantic.com/international/archive/2018/02/china-surveillance/552203/; Blake Schmidt and Venus Feng, "The Companies behind China's High-Tech Surveillance State," *Bloomberg*, February 21, 2019, https://www.bloomberg.com/news/articles/2019-02-21 /the-companies-behind-china-s-high-tech-surveillance-state.

63 Alyssa Newcomb, "A Timeline of Facebook's Privacy Issues — and Its Responses," NBC News, March 24, 2018, https://www.nbcnews.com/tech/social-media/timeline -facebook-s-privacy-issues-its-responses-n859651.

64 Bernard Marr, "How Much Data Do We Create Every Day? The Mind-Blowing Stats Everyone Should Read," *Forbes*, May 21, 2018, https://www.forbes.com/sites/bernardmarr /2018/05/21/how-much-data-do-we-create-every-day-the-mind-blowing-stats-everyone -should-read/#7887ea8860ba.

65 Alizila Staff, "2018 Investor Day," Hangzhou, China, September 17–18, 2018, https:// www.alizila.com/alibaba-investors-day-2018-live-stream/.

66 Xie et al., "Fintech and Finance Transformation."

67 FDIC, "Key Findings from *How America Banks: Household Use of Banking and Financial Services* – 2019 FDIC Survey," accessed April 1, 2022, https://www.fdic.gov/analysis /household-survey/index.html.

Index

Printed and bound by CPI Group (UK) Ltd, Croydon, CR0 4YY

17/06/2024

14516336-0001